MAKING WE THE PEOPLE

What does it mean to say that it is "We the People" who "ordain and establish" a constitution? Who are those sovereign people, and how can they do so?

Interweaving history and theory, constitutional scholar Chaihark Hahm and political theorist Sung Ho Kim attempt to answer these perennial questions by revisiting the constitutional politics of postwar Japan and Korea. Together, these experiences demonstrate the infeasibility of the conventional assumption that there is a clearly bounded sovereign "people" prior to constitution-making that stands apart from both outside influence and troubled historical legacies. The authors argue that "We the People" only emerges through a deeply transformative politics of constitutional founding and, as such, a democratic constitution and its putative author are mutually constitutive. Highly original and genuinely multidisciplinary, this book will be of interest to democratic theorists, scholars of comparative constitutionalism as well as observers of ongoing constitutional debates in Japan and Korea.

Chaihark Hahm is Professor of Constitutional Law at Yonsei University Law School (Seoul, Korea) and an editorial board member of *I•CON: International Journal of Constitutional Law*. He holds law degrees from Yale, Columbia, and Harvard.

Sung Ho Kim is Professor of Political Science and Director of the Social Science Research Institute at Yonsei University (Seoul, Korea). He is the author of *Max Weber's Politics of Civil Society*, which was also published by Cambridge University Press.

COMPARATIVE CONSTITUTIONAL LAW AND POLICY

Series Editors

Tom Ginsburg, *University of Chicago*
Zachary Elkins, *University of Texas at Austin*
Ran Hirschl, *University of Toronto*

Comparative constitutional law is an intellectually vibrant field that encompasses an increasingly broad array of approaches and methodologies. This series collects analytically innovative and empirically grounded work from scholars of comparative constitutionalism across academic disciplines. Books in the series include theoretically informed studies of single constitutional jurisdictions, comparative studies of constitutional law and institutions, and edited collections of original essays that respond to challenging theoretical and empirical questions in the field.

Volumes in the Series

Comparative Constitutional Design edited by Tom Ginsburg (2012)

Consequential Courts: Judicial Roles in Global Perspective edited by Diana Kapiszewski, Gordon Silverstein, and Robert A. Kagan (2013)

Social and Political Foundations of Constitutions edited by Denis J. Galligan and Mila Versteeg (2013)

Presidential Legislation in India: The Law and Practice of Ordinances by Shubhankar Dam (2014)

Constitutions in Authoritarian Regimes edited by Tom Ginsburg and Alberto Simpser (2014)

Social Difference and Constitutionalism in Pan-Asia edited by Susan H. Williams (2014)

Constitutionalism in Asia in the Early Twenty-First Century edited by Albert Chen (2014)

Constitutions and Religious Freedom by Frank Cross (2015)

Reputation and Judicial Tactics: A Theory of National and International Courts by Shai Dothan (2015)

International Courts and the Performance of International Agreements: A General Theory with Evidence from the European Union by Clifford Carrubba and Matthew Gabel (2015)

Magna Carta and its Modern Legacy edited by Robert Hazell and James Melton (2015)

Unstable Constitutionalism edited by Mark Tushnet and Madhav Khosla (2015)

Radical Deprivation on Trial by Cesar Rodríguez-Garavito and Diana Rodríguez-Franco (2015)

Making We the People

DEMOCRATIC CONSTITUTIONAL FOUNDING IN POSTWAR JAPAN AND SOUTH KOREA

CHAIHARK HAHM and **SUNG HO KIM**

Yonsei University

CAMBRIDGE
UNIVERSITY PRESS

CAMBRIDGE
UNIVERSITY PRESS

32 Avenue of the Americas, New York, NY 10013-2473, USA

Cambridge University Press is part of the University of Cambridge.

It furthers the University's mission by disseminating knowledge in the pursuit of education, learning, and research at the highest international levels of excellence.

www.cambridge.org
Information on this title: www.cambridge.org/9781107018822

First published 2015

A catalog record for this publication is available from the British Library.

Library of Congress Cataloging in Publication Data
Hahm, Chaihark, 1963– author.
Making we the people : democratic constitutional founding in postwar Japan and South Korea / Chaihark Hahm, Yonsei University, Seoul; Sung Ho Kim, Yonsei University, Seoul.
pages cm. – (Comparative constitutional law and policy)
Includes bibliographical references and index.
ISBN 978-1-107-01882-2 (hardback)
1. Constitutional history – Japan. 2. Constitutional history – South Korea.
I. Kim, Sung Ho, 1966– author. II. Title.
KNC527.H358 2015
342.519502′9–dc23 2015020956

ISBN 978-1-107-01882-2 Hardback

Tai Young Hahm (1873–1964) and Rin Suh Kim (1894–1964)

Patriots for the Nation
Pastors to the People
Founders of the Republic

Contents

Acknowledgments

The origins of this book can be traced back to a long, late-evening conversation with the late Il-Young Kim and Chulwoo Lee sometime in 2008. As the topic of our discussion shifted freely from history and culture to politics and law, we at one point asked ourselves who "We the People" – the putative authors of a democratic constitution – really are, especially in a context defined by strong ethnic nationalism. What would be a definition of the people that is both historically accurate and normatively attractive? That evening's question proved to be the beginning of a long journey that has come to a close with the completion of this book.

It was, however, not until we took our sabbatical leaves, both in 2009–2010, that we were able to embark on the project in earnest. Once settled in at the Harvard-Yenching Institute (HYI) and The Hague Institute for the Internationalization of Law (HiiL)/The Netherlands Institute for Advanced Study (NIAS), respectively, we started sharing ideas and drafts across the Atlantic. Upon returning to Seoul, we were ready to engage in serious writing, only to find our efforts hampered by our teaching, administrative, and other responsibilities. We found out the hard way that a sabbatical year is better used to finish a book project rather than to start one. It has thus taken many more years than we had anticipated before our reflections on that evening's question finally coalesced into the book as it stands now. Along this long journey, we have incurred many debts.

We have benefited from various conversations and correspondences with numerous friends and colleagues regarding different versions of the ideas contained in this book. We thank William Alford, Sung-joon Cho, Bruce Cumings, Carter Eckert, David Gerber, Andrew Gordon, Ran Hirschl, Ken Ishida, Jonathan Kang, Chikako Kashiwazaki, the late Il-Young Kim, Keigo Komamura, Chulwoo Lee, Hans Lindahl, Barak Medina, Bert van Roermund, Rogers Smith, Thio Li-ann, Mark Tushnet, Joseph Weiler, and Jiunn-rong Yeh.

We especially would like to note our gratitude to Tom Ginsburg who invited us to contribute to the Cambridge series on Comparative Constitutional Law and Policy, and to Gary Jacobsohn for years of encouragement and friendship. Needless to add, any fault that this book may contain is entirely our own.

At various stages, different parts of this book were presented at conferences, workshops, and public lectures. To list them in chronological order: National University of Singapore, Harvard-Yenching Institute, 2010 Annual Meeting of the Law and Society Association (Chicago), University of Texas at Austin, the Netherlands Institute for Advanced Studies, 2011 Annual Meeting of the Association for Asian Studies (Honolulu), Asan Institute for Policy Studies (Seoul), East Asia Institute (Seoul), Yonsei University, Seoul National University, Korea University, Keio Gijuku University (Tokyo), Chicago-Kent College of Law, the University of Chicago Law School, City University of Hong Kong, and Harvard Law School. We thank all who shared their comments with us at these venues.

The Asan Institute for Policy Studies and its president, Chaibong Hahm, deserve our special gratitude for providing the research grant that was indispensable for the successful completion of this book. Without his support and abiding interest, our ideas would not have seen the light of day. We are also thankful to the Asan Institute for enabling us to organize an international workshop in 2011 around the main theme of our book. This was in fact a follow-up on a previous workshop in 2010, for which we are much obliged to Elizabeth Perry of HYI, Sam Muller and David Raič of HiiL, and Wim Blockmans and Jos Hooghuis of NIAS. In addition, the research and writing of this book were greatly facilitated by the logistical support provided by Jinsoo Han, Misato Ido, Sang Joon Kim, and Seok-choon Lew. The expert assistance of Hee Kyoung You, the law librarian at Yonsei, is much appreciated as well.

We are pleased to acknowledge the input and feedback from all the students who attended our graduate seminars at Yonsei, where we were able to test our ideas and arguments in their early stages. We hope they find resonance of their voices in this final product. Research assistance from our graduate students was invaluable especially during the final stage of book writing. Among them, we thank June Mee Jung, Hyun Kim, Seokwon Kim, Sunghan Kim, Shuto Nakamura, Sun-myung Oh, Yoon Keun Oh, and Sohee Whang.

Our greatest debt, of course, is to our families whose unfailing support and boundless patience made it possible for us to indulge in what must have seemed like a never-ending project. Chaihark is especially grateful to his wife, Jumi, for replenishing his soul on a daily basis. For the same reason and in so many different ways, Sung Ho owes much, simply too much, to his daughter, Minjin.

Introduction

Controversy over Japan's postwar constitution entered a whole new phase on 1 July 2014 when Abe Shinzo's cabinet announced a decision to stretch the penumbra of Article 9's meaning via reinterpretation. Under the new interpretation, Japan may exercise the right to engage in collective self-defensive actions abroad even when its own territory is not under direct attack. The decision signals a drastic departure from the long-standing position of previous governments which had interpreted the "peace provision" to permit individual self-defensive measures only. Judging from the intensity of reactions, the decision may have touched a nerve in Japan's constitutional body politic. For nearly seven decades, constitutional pacifism has been embraced by Japan's general public as the cornerstone of their national civic identity. Abe's decision is being vehemently criticized as a dangerous move that will turn Japan into a country that can wage war again, in direct contravention of Article 9. According to a noted Japanese public intellectual, postwar Japan's pacifist spirit may finally be dying.[1] Japan's national identity formed around its "Peace Constitution" is being contested, to say the least, by this decision announced on the sixtieth anniversary of the establishment of the Self-Defense Forces.

On 5 November 2013, the Park Geun-Hye government of Korea took the unprecedented action of instituting legal proceedings at the Constitutional Court to seek the dissolution of a political party.[2] Claiming that the goals and activities of the far-left United Progressive Party (UPP) are unconstitutional, the Ministry of Justice decided to utilize, for the first time in Korea's constitutional history, the Article 8 procedure for disbanding a political party. The government's case was built on the claim that the party was clandestinely

[1] Norihiro Kato, "Japan's Break with Peace," *New York Times*, 16 July 2014, Opinion Pages.

[2] Sang-Hun Choe, "South Korea: Government Seeks to Ban Leftist Party," *New York Times*, 6 Nov. 2013, A11.

following directives from the communist North Korea. In a rather contentious ruling of 19 December 2014, the Court agreed by holding that UPP's platform and activities were directed at destroying the "democratic basic order" of the constitution.[3] It held that the idea of "progressive democracy" as understood and promoted by the party's leadership had no place in South Korea, whose constitutional identity was described by the Court as "liberal democracy." Reconfirming its previous pronouncements, it made clear that Korea's constitutional order was dedicated to the ideals of popular sovereignty, fundamental rights, multi-party system, and separation of powers. It further held that these principles have been at the core of Korea's civic identity ever since the "Founding Constitution" was written in 1948. In light of previous – and still ongoing – public debates, however, it seems quite likely that this decision, announced on the second anniversary of Park's election to the presidency, will not be the last word on the proper characterization of Korea's constitutional identity.

Almost seven decades after their founding, two of the most prosperous constitutional democracies outside the western world are, evidently, riddled with anxiety and self-doubt about their own civic identities. The decision by the Abe cabinet, and the reactions to it, are showing that there are deep cracks in Japan's pacifist identity under the postwar constitution. Apparently, no less grievous is the uncertainty surrounding Korea's constitutional identity. While everyone pays lip service to the constitutional ideal of "democratic basic order," its precise meaning and how to implement it remain deeply controversial. The people of both Japan and Korea are engaged in a search for their constitutional souls. Yet, it should be noted that such discontent is not merely a reflection of contemporary disagreements. It is actually a manifestation of a deeper restlessness or contention concerning the first democratic constitutions of the two countries adopted in the immediate postwar and postcolonial contexts.

In Japan, for instance, not too far below the surface of the recent controversy lies the persistent allegation that the constitution was somehow illegitimate from the very beginning. According to a popular view, the Peace Constitution was not really authored by "We, the Japanese People" but was rather imposed by overbearing American conquerors on a vanquished and helpless Japan. Abe's supporters applauded his cabinet's reinterpretation as a step toward returning Japan to a "normal state" able to defend itself proactively and shoulder its share of responsibilities on the international stage. In their view, the surprise was not that a new interpretation was adopted but that

3 Const. Ct. 2013 Hun-Da 1 (19 Dec. 2014) (S. Kor.).

it took so long to take place. If constitutional pacifism was never a voluntary choice made by the sovereign people themselves, and if this imposed identity is inviting international criticism that Japan is shirking its responsibility for maintaining world peace, then perhaps it was high time that the constitution was amended, or at least interpreted differently. By contrast, defenders of Article 9 go to great lengths to argue that pacifism is a home-grown identity. For them, it has roots that go back, at least, to the Freedom and People's Rights Movement of the early Meiji era and the Christian and Socialist antiwar movements during Taishō democracy.[4] On this view, Abe's decision is not a rectification of the wrongdoings of foreign imposition but a betrayal of the Japanese people's authentic will to unarmed peace. Article 9 is a symbol of native ideals of democracy and pacifism.

In Korea, too, there is a deeper contestation over the principal ideals of its Founding Constitution of 1948. Of the many arguments made in UPP's defense, for example, one that is worth noting is the claim that the party's platform is in fact no more radical or progressive than the spirit of the Founding Constitution which arguably pursued socioeconomic (read socialistic) as well as political (read liberal) democracy.[5] This argument is interesting and provocative in that it seeks to turn the table on the government. The unmistakable charge is that it is Park's conservative government, rather than the UPP, which is distorting and even subverting the original constitutional identity of Korea. On this view, holding liberal democracy to be the fundamental principle of Korea's constitutional order, as is done by the conservative government, cannot be squared with the goals and principles that guided the making of the Founding Constitution. Of course, the Constitutional Court disagrees. For the conservatives, the Korean republic has always aspired to be a liberal democracy from its inception – even before it was formally established. It was mainly on this ground that the Court previously condemned those armed rebels who resisted the 1948 founding of the republic along liberal democratic lines by advocating a communist-inspired "people's democracy."[6] In the Court's view, Korea's constitutional identity has always been a liberal democracy.

In both countries, apparently, there are disagreements regarding the foundational principles of their postwar/postcolonial constitutions. Especially,

4 E.g., Yamamuro Shin'ichi, *Kenpō Kyūjō no Shisō Suimyaku* [Philosophical Sources of Article 9 of the Constitution] (Tokyo: Asahi Shimbun Publications, 2007).

5 E.g., Han Hong-gu, *T'ŭkkang* [Special Lectures] (Seoul: Hangyoreh Ch'ulp'an, 2009), pp. 174–89.

6 Const. Ct. 2000 Hun-Ma 238 (27 Sept. 2001) (S. Kor.). The case involved a historical evaluation of the so-called 4.3 Incident, which had erupted in the Cheju Island on the eve of the May 10 General Election in opposition to the establishment of the Republic of Korea.

with more scholarly attention given to their historical inspirations and original intentions, it is being revealed that neither Japan's "peace" nor Korea's "democracy" have such firm and unambiguous meanings as is often thought. Such historical discussions about their first democratic constitutions are in turn contributing to the intensity of current political debates regarding government decisions and policies. Contestations over the core constitutional identities of the two countries are obviously caused by different perspectives and partisan interests in the current political context. But, they are also being stoked by different understandings and assessments of the original constitutional orders of Japan and Korea which were established in the wake of defeat and liberation, respectively. The relentless contestation over the constitutional soul of each country is about history as much as it is about politics.

Deeply entrenched as those fault lines are, however, our reflections on the Japanese and Korean constitutional dramas are motivated less by what divides those constitutional interpretations than by what those opposing perspectives seem to have in common. Indeed, underlying such sharp differences in both the political and historical arenas is an interesting set of common assumptions regarding the legitimacy and identity of constitutions. Despite the contestations and disagreements, that is, similar outlooks can be detected across the political and ideological divide in both Japan and Korea. It may even be that the shared assumptions are responsible for the heightened tenor of the controversies about their constitutional souls.

First is the assumption that any external constraint on or interference with the process of constitution-making is illegitimate. A constitution must be the product of the autonomous will of the native people. It is largely for this reason that Korea's Founding Constitution, having been adopted in a democratically elected National Assembly for the first time in the nation's history, is still revered as the republic's historic and legal foundation. Both the proponents of the imposed view of the Peace Constitution and their pacifist detractors in Japan share the same belief in the right of people's self-determination unfettered by foreign interventions. A second common assumption is that the constitution must establish an entirely new civic order and identity. Its legitimacy is compromised to the extent that it fails to reject and obliterate the political order that preceded the founding. Even the ardent supporters of Abe's reinterpretation do not openly deny that the new democratic Japan had to be based on a firm repudiation of prewar militarism through the Peace Constitution. The Founding Constitution is an edifying symbol of Korea to this day because it signaled a radical departure from the colonial subjugation under Japanese imperialism. These two assumptions about the legitimacy of constitutional founding are in turn predicated on a third one about the identity of the collective self that adopts a new constitution. It is presupposed that there exists a constitutional subjectivity which can exercise such autonomy from others and enact such a radical break from the past. The agent which makes the constitution is simply assumed to be the entire nation of Japan or Korea, which in turn is understood as a self-contained, primordial entity that remains constant over time. There might be uncertainties at the fringe as to who belongs to the nation, but it is taken for granted that the identity and boundaries of the nation are firm, natural, and self-evident.

One might easily attribute the prevalence of these three assumptions, or attitudes, to the local peculiarities of the two countries. It is not hard, after all, to imagine that their respective historical experiences of the twentieth century, though in different ways, would have created extreme sensitivity to any external encroachments on their right and ability to chart their own political destinies. Similarly, both countries seem to share, again for different reasons, a desire to efface the past and to build a new future on a clean slate. Moreover, the colonial relationship that existed between Japan and Korea would have easily engendered a heightened and robust sense of ethnic peoplehood in both nations. Yet, from a more theoretical perspective, too, it is not at all surprising that such assumptions are widespread in these two successful constitutional democracies. For precisely the same assumptions undergird the conventional theories of constitutionalism grounded in the idea of popular sovereignty. The idea of a self-sufficient sovereign will unhampered by external forces and the call for the creation of a whole new political universe are almost axiomatic in most understandings of democratic constitutionalism. These two axioms are buttressed by a third. The subject of a modern constitutional order is commonly assumed to be "We the People" whose identity and membership are seldom, if ever, in question. The existence of a self-contained people with firm boundaries that is able to make autonomous and self-directed decisions for the purpose of abrogating the past and initiating a new order seems to be the common creed of the modern democratic constitutional faith.

According to this common creed, in sum, the legitimacy of constitutional founding hinges upon the unfettered agency of "We the People." Virtually all modern constitutions claim some mandate of the people who gave birth to it at some discrete point in time. The constitution is also seen as always vulnerable to amendment, even abrogation, by the same people. As such, modern democratic constitutions are destined to have life only insofar as the people find it faithfully implementing their own will. Even for liberal theorists, who quite often cast the people's collective will as a potential threat to individual rights, it is axiomatic that the people must be seen as the ultimate source of constitutional legitimacy. As regards the constitution, "We the People" is its author and fount of legitimacy as well as its master and chief beneficiary. Presupposing the people as the author of the constitution is not only natural (as a matter of logic) but also necessary (as a matter of normative reasoning).

This way of thinking, so intuitively commonsensical, is at work in a variety of contemporary contexts. It is detectible, for example, in the ongoing controversy over the desirability of creating a "constitution" for Europe. There, the debate is in large measure fueled by an anxiety that such a construct might threaten people's agency and mastery over their respective nation's own fate. It is often argued that, since there is no single European "people," or *demos*, yet, there can be no common constitutional edifice for Europe.[7] A similar apprehension seems to underlie the negative assessments of constitutions, such as that of Iraq, which have allegedly been "imposed" from the outside. The argument is that constitutional imposition is improper, impractical, and unsustainable because the local people were not given an active role in drafting the supreme law of their own land. In order to have a robust sense of ownership, the people, neither coerced nor obstructed, must prevail in the making of their constitution.[8] Yet another context where this view plays a crucial role is the recent discourse in the United States on "popular constitutionalism" and the purported discontents of judicial supremacy. Here, the Supreme Court's claim to be the final arbiter of constitutional meaning is challenged and criticized as a usurpation of power that rightfully belongs to the people. The argument is that, as the author of the constitution, "We the People" should be the ultimate authority in its interpretation as well.[9] In addition to these examples, the recent flurry of post-Cold War constitution-making activities in other parts of the world have also been debated and critiqued on the basis of the same set of assumptions.[10]

[7] For a discussion of this issue, see the various "Comments on the German Constitutional Court's Decision on the Lisbon Treaty," *European Constitutional Law Review*, vol. 5 (2009). For a critical analysis of the "no *demos* thesis," see J. H. H. Weiler, "Does Europe Need a Constitution? Demos, Telos and the German Maastricht Decision," *European Law Journal*, vol. 1 (1995).

[8] See, e.g., Zachary Elkins, Tom Ginsburg, and James Melton, "Baghdad, Tokyo, Kabul...: Constitution Making in Occupied States," *William and Mary Law Review*, vol. 49 (2008); Noah Feldman, "Imposed Constitutionalism," *Connecticut Law Review*, vol. 37 (2005); Simon Chesterman, "Imposed Constitution, Imposed Constitutionalism, and Ownership," *Connecticut Law Review*, vol. 37 (2005).

[9] See, e.g., Larry D. Kramer, *The People Themselves: Popular Constitutionalism and Judicial Review* (New York: Oxford University Press, 2004); Mark V. Tushnet, *Taking the Constitution Away from the Court* (Princeton, NJ: Princeton University Press, 2000).

[10] See, e.g., Ran Hirschl, *Towards Juristocracy: The Origins and Consequences of the New Constitutionalism* (Cambridge, MA: Harvard University Press, 2004); Ulrich Preuss, *Constitutional Revolution: The Link between Constitutionalism and Progress*, trans. Deborah Lucas Schneider (Atlantic Highlands, NJ: Humanities Press, 1995); Andrew Arato, "Dilemmas

It is difficult, however, to erase the impression that these cases are raising difficult questions for the common creed of constitutional theory. Theoretically, one of the more fundamental issues they pose is a deep challenge to the conventional understanding that a democratic constitutional order is predicated on a "constituent moment" in which "We the People" lays down its fundamental decision about its political existence on a *tabula rasa*. It may no longer be warranted to assume an autonomous people with near-omnipotent agency vis-à-vis the political and constitutional universe it creates. "We the People" may not always be free, whenever it wants, to make a new world, a *novus ordo saeclorum*, by merely enacting another constitutional founding. It may be that the relationship between the people and the constitution is not so much that of creation and mastery. As a corollary, it may also be difficult to presuppose the existence of a constituent people whose identity remains constant over time despite the deeply transformative politics entailed in the historic act of constitution-making. We cannot simply assume a "timeless" agent with predetermined form and shape, which engages in constitutional founding with preordained goals and interests.

For political and constitutional theorists, then, the challenge posed by recent developments in the global constitutional landscape is profound. The actual making of real-life constitutions entails a process of negotiation and compromise that is far more complex and convoluted than is presupposed by this conventional dogma. A new constitution must declare and manage a clean break from the status quo ante, while somehow plugging itself back into a different "useable past" in order to reinforce its legitimacy and sustainability. In so doing, a constitution must also attempt to promote, or even create, unity and harmony in a context too often racked by conflict and dissension. Furthermore, these negotiations over the past and diversity are frequently made in the shadow of, or under the auspices of, an "external constituency" of sorts that ranges from foreign consultants to international organizations, and even direct foreign occupation. An act of constitution-making can no longer be understood as a pristine domestic affair in which "We the People" qua unitary and homogeneous constituent agent is "rebooting" their own history. According to this critical perspective, constitution-making might be more fruitfully understood as a process through which a different people comes into being as a consequence of protracted negotiations with previous power configurations, pre-constitutional identities, and even external forces. In other

Arising from the Power to Create Constitutions in Eastern Europe," in Michel Rosenfeld (ed.), *Constitutionalism, Identity, Difference, and Legitimacy: Theoretical Perspectives* (Durham, NC: Duke University Press, 1994).

words, the so-called constituent people cannot be the axiomatic presupposition. It is rather the outcome of intense politics for constitutional founding. The emerging lesson seems to be that "We the People" are formed as they make a constitution, rather than pre-existing or presiding over any putative constituent moment. The challenge, in short, is no less than to rethink the identity of the "sovereign people" and the ideal of "popular sovereignty."

This book represents our attempt at such rethinking, one that is done through an extended meditation on the historical experiences of constitution-making in Japan and Korea. Our purpose is to reexamine in a fresh light the increasingly questionable assumptions about the sovereign people and popular sovereignty. The book will take us back in time to the events leading up to and following the drafting of Japan's Peace Constitution of 1946 and Korea's Founding Constitution of 1948. It will seek to inquire as to whether, and to what extent, the conventional framework can account for the experiences of constitutional founding in postwar Japan and postcolonial Korea. Moreover, it will explore if and how the Japanese and Korean experiences may have universal ramifications by way of enriching our theoretical and conceptual discourse on the mutually constitutive relationship between constitution-making and the formation of "We the People."

We believe that the constitution-making experiences of Japan and Korea are particularly well suited to our purposes for several reasons. First, both countries are examples of "older" states which had to go through a "rebirth" after World War II by adopting a democratic constitution in the name of "We the People." Unlike, say, the United States where political union was largely the product of constitutional founding, both Japan and Korea had existed respectively as identifiable political units long before the advent of modern constitutionalism. Such contexts pose the issue of accounting for "We the People" in more acute terms. While the emergence of the people as a constitutional agent is undoubtedly a recent phenomenon, it is also undeniable that both countries have long traditions of relatively well-defined and established peoplehood. Yet it is equally evident that the people of postwar Japan and postcolonial Korea have begun to identify themselves in radically new ways. This calls into question the assumption that the identity of the people has remained unchanged from time immemorial. The two examples thus focus our attention on the changes brought about in the status and identity of the people by the adoption of democratic constitutions.

Second, Japan and Korea merit a comparative examination because the identity of the two peoples becomes clearer when we consider the extent to which one people figured in the other's process of redefining itself constitutionally. "We the People" in both instances emerged through a process of extricating itself from the other because, as of August 1945, the two peoples had been legally incorporated into one and the same polity called the Japanese Empire since 1910. Postwar constitution-making in the name of the people meant that the people of one country had to be defined in contradistinction to that of the other. To be sure, there were other references and resources which informed the process of constructing the people as a constitutional agent. Yet, the significance of the constitution-making process for each people cannot be fully appreciated without considering the fact that both entailed undoing Japan's 1910 annexation of Korea and demarcating the two peoples again in political and legal terms.

Third, investigating these two instances of constitution-making side-by-side will be fruitful because both were done under the same foreign tutelage. It is common knowledge that the U.S. military occupation, led by General Douglas MacArthur as the Supreme Commander for the Allied Powers, played a pivotal role in the making of Japan's postwar constitution. The constitution of South Korea was also drafted while under the same U.S. occupation authority whose military chain of command went back ultimately to MacArthur in his capacity as the Commander-in-Chief of the United States Armed Forces in the Pacific. More interesting, perhaps, are the different approaches adopted by the U.S. military authorities in the two occupied territories. Defeated Japan was ruled indirectly via the Japanese government left intact after the surrender. By contrast, the United States Army Military Government in Korea took direct control of a nation that was liberated from Japan, decreeing itself to be the sole lawful authority in the territory and outlawing all local political groups claiming to represent the Korean people. Ironically, though, the Japanese constitution was largely a product of direct intervention by MacArthur, whereas the Korean constitution was written by Koreans themselves with less coercive involvement of the occupation authorities. The making of the two constitutions under the same foreign presence thus makes them a particularly suitable subject for comparison.

For these reasons, we believe that a comparative study of constitution-making in Japan and Korea will be meaningful not only in its own right, but also because it is an excellent opportunity and vehicle for rethinking the relationship between the people and the constitution. Our hope is to show, through critical reflections on both theories and historical events, that "We the People" is in a crucial sense "constituted" by the very constitution that is being drafted in its name. Thus, we will start by theoretically examining conventional perspectives on democratic constitution-making and the status of the people in that process. This will be followed by chapters each containing comparative analysis of the politics and history of the actual constitution-making in Japan and Korea.

Thematically, all four chapters of the book revolve around the three dimensions that make up the common creed of the democratic constitutional faith – external others, past legacies, and people's boundaries. Chapter 1 will start with some critical reflections at the level of political theory and comparative constitutional law. Our primary concern in this chapter is to revisit those three assumptions that comprise the conventional model of constitution-making based on popular sovereignty. The goal will be to examine if they could be sustained under closer theoretical scrutiny and in light of historical and contemporary examples of constitution-making in various parts of the world. Although these reflections are by no means meant to be exhaustive, our hope is to suggest some theoretically persuasive, and historically grounded, reasons for questioning the soundness of those assumptions. To that end, we will also explore an alternative way of theorizing the relationship between the constituent people and constitution-making. It will be suggested that constitutional politics of founding is a deeply transformative process in the course of which the sovereign "We the People" emerges through interaction with external influences and negotiation with legacies of the past. In short, the processes of constitution-making and people-making will be postulated as mutually constitutive.

Turning to the Japanese and Korean experiences in constitutional founding, we begin by addressing the question of "overbearing outsiders" in Chapter 2. Our focus will be on what may be the most unique and striking feature of the respective constitutions – Article 9 in Japan's Peace Constitution and the Economy Chapter of Korea's Founding Constitution. It hardly needs to be mentioned that unarmed pacifism as outlined in Japan's Article 9 was an entirely unprecedented constitutional principle in world history. Korea's Economy Chapter was also extraordinary because it prescribed a "socialistic" economic regime for the new nation born under U.S. auspices during the nascent stage of the Cold War. Here, it will be shown that these idiosyncratic features of the two constitutions were shaped under external pressures at various levels. We will revisit not only the original making of these provisions which were crucial in forming the respective countries' new constitutional identity, but also their subsequent adoption and adjustment in the immediate post-drafting stage which brought about significant reorientations in those identities. These processes will be analyzed in terms of intense and convoluted negotiations between the external and the local, which were over-determined by the American presence and the dawning of the Cold War in East Asia.

In Chapter 3, we turn our attention to the question of "unmasterable past."[11] The medium for our reflection will be the formation of the "symbol emperor system" in Japan, and, for Korea, the process of forging a republican identity and early efforts at lustration of the colonial past. Announced at the forefront as Article 1 of the respective constitutions, symbol emperor and democratic republic are expressive of the core of the two countries' constitutional identities. They might be, in that sense, compared to the Guarantee Clause of the United States' constitution. Our primary goal in this chapter is to demonstrate how these seemingly novel identities were inscribed into the constitutions of postwar Japan and postcolonial Korea through complex confrontations and engagements with the legacies of the past. For this purpose, in addition to studying the political history surrounding the making of these constitutional identities, we will also examine the discursive formations of the time by which, even as the immediate past was firmly rejected, various "useable pasts" were newly resuscitated to lend historical and ideological support to the new constitutional identities. Also to be investigated in this chapter is Korea's constitutional mandate of "transitional justice" and its frustration, which made colonial past ultimately unmasterable.

By comparison, Chapter 4 adopts a more institutional approach in addressing the issue of the "shifting boundaries" of both countries' respective peoplehood. We will start by noting the ways in which the prewar "family registration system" both integrated and differentiated the Koreans and the Japanese during the colonial era. It will be seen that this institutional practice continued to play a crucial role in demarcating and separating the two peoples after the war. Using this "sticky" institution as the main focus, we will pay close attention to how negotiations with external conditions and continuation of the institutionalized past coalesced to delineate the new boundaries of peoplehood during the founding era of the two countries. Here in this final chapter, our goal is to show how an identifiable constituent people came into being in postwar Japan and postcolonial Korea not prior to but in the course of constitutional founding. "We the People" of Japan and Korea emerged as they struggled to write their postwar and postcolonial constitutions.

The conventional dogma of constitutional theory informed by the ideal of popular sovereignty cannot fully capture the variegated experiences of

11 The expression comes from Charles Maier, *The Unmasterable Past: History, Holocaust, and the German National Identity* (Cambridge, MA: Harvard University Press, 1997).

constitution-making in Japan and Korea. Its inadequacy is perhaps not surprising given its fixation on pristine collective self-determination, aversion to the status quo ante, and presumption of fixed and stable boundaries of a timeless constituent people. It is our hope that revisiting these historical experiences of Japan and Korea will point the way toward fresh theoretical insights which will help bring the "political theology" of popular sovereignty down to the human scale of constitutional theory.

1

The Unbearable Lightness of the People

CHARISMA AND ITS DISCONTENTS

The basic conceptual template for making sense of democratic constitutional founding seems to have remained surprisingly unchanged since the great revolutions of the eighteenth century. The orthodoxy has it that it is "We the People" who "hold these truths to be self-evident" and "ordain and establish this Constitution" upon those truths. Politically sacrosanct and intuitively appealing, the idea of the people as the foundation of constitutional legitimacy, or simply popular sovereignty, has come to form the core of a latter-day "political theology." Despite recent attempts to question its necessity and even the very coherence of the idea, popular sovereignty still refuses to relent its firm grip on our political and constitutional imagination. In the words of Jean Bethke Elshtain, "[w]e like the sound of the locution: 'the sovereignty of the people'."[1]

This political theology, or what Frank Michelman in our time has called "authority-authorship syndrome,"[2] was given succinct expression by the influential Weimar liberal jurist Erich Kaufmann. "A constitution can do nothing more than create and establish frames in which the people's actual ethical and *charismatic powers* can find expression in a legal order."[3] A noted contemporary American constitutional scholar, Richard Kay, echoes this resignation to the authority-authorship syndrome when he states that "at bottom, such democratic legitimacy [as based on popular sovereignty] depends on nothing

[1] Jean Bethke Elshtain, *Sovereignty: God, State, and Self* (New York: Basic Books, 2008), p. 99.

[2] Frank I. Michelman, "Constitutional Authorship," in Larry Alexander (ed.), *Constitutionalism: Philosophical Foundations* (Cambridge: Cambridge University Press, 1998), p. 67.

[3] Erich Kaufman, "On the Problem of the People's Will," in Arthur J. Jacobson and Bernhard Schlink (eds.), *Weimar: A Jurisprudence of Crisis* (Berkeley: University of California Press, 2000), p. 199 (emphasis added).

but its source and is, in that sense, a species of what Weber called *charismatic legitimacy*."[4] These invocations of charismatic legitimacy as a way of expressing this syndrome are a testimony to the religious underpinnings of popular sovereignty that persist to this day. For, originally, charisma was a religious term used in the Old Testament to describe the extraordinary quality of a prophet in the Judaic tradition who successfully claimed to represent the will of God in this secular world.

At Max Weber's hands, famously, this ancient religious term was resuscitated and secularized to explain sudden ruptures in the ordinary routines in our political, legal, and social life. This charismatic rupture sets in motion the beginning of a new institutional order, to be interrupted yet again by another upsurge of charisma at some future point in time. In this Weberian cycle of eternal recurrence, popular sovereignty is the attribution of charisma and its creative-destructive energy to an indeterminate collective agent called "the people."[5] Relying on neither genealogical nor external authorities, charisma of the revolutionary people generates its own legitimacy from within itself by seeking to destroy the routines of the status quo ante in its entirety. To that extent, every democratic revolution in history was necessarily a "usurpation of power" after which legitimacy had to be created illegitimately or in an improvised act of "bootstrapping."[6] Omnipotent and deeply generative at once, Weber's democratic-revolutionary charisma signifies a purely existential will of the people that may do away with reason, universal morals, and even its own past. When it comes to constitutional founding, it is as though charisma of the revolutionary people can tolerate no constraints from a time before the rupture, nor any impositions from outside their putative realm. With this attribution of semidivine charisma to the people, the phrase "*vox populi vox Dei*," originally a mere rhetorical device, has ironically taken on a literal meaning in this modern, democratic, and allegedly secular age.[7]

4 Richard Kay, "American Constitutionalism," in Alexander (ed.), *Constitutionalism*, p. 25 (emphasis added).

5 Strictly speaking, Weber believed that charisma is an attribute of an individual person. Its collectivized and institutionalized form, however, is variously suggested in his vast oeuvre. For a recent discussion of institutionalized charisma, see Sung Ho Kim, *Max Weber's Politics of Civil Society* (Cambridge: Cambridge University Press, 2007), pp. 84–8.

6 Jon Elster, "Constitutional Bootstrapping in Philadelphia and Paris," in Rosenfeld (ed.), *Constitutionalism, Identity, Difference, and Legitimacy*, pp. 57–83.

7 Carl Schmitt was only slightly exaggerating when he wrote: "All significant concepts of the modern theory of the state are secularized theological concepts not only because of their historical development ... but also because of their systematic structure." Carl Schmitt, *Political Theology: Four Chapters on the Concept of Sovereignty*, trans. George Schwab (Cambridge, MA: MIT Press, 1985), p. 36.

At the level of practical reason, this political theology of popular sovereignty raises thorny questions, especially for many liberal constitutionalists. The crux of their discontent is that *vox populi* does not always or necessarily speak for *vox Dei*. For many liberals, voluntary obedience that any constitution worthy of the name commands from its citizenry is, in the final analysis, by virtue of the "rightness" of the constitutional norms. To contend that majority will, assuming it can be ascertained, may supply the source of such normativity, which is what democratic legitimacy boils down to, is presumptuous at best. Worse still, letting majority will prevail without mitigation can menace individual liberty with a new and even more dangerous form of oppression, namely the "tyranny of majority." In this well-entrenched liberal fear since Tocqueville and Mill, fact does not make validity, and nor does popular consent (alone) create constitutional legitimacy. Even democratic constitutions created by the charismatic authority of the sovereign people need to be underwritten by universal practical reason before their normative validity can be recognized. Thus ensues the liberal-constitutional search for some moral-transcendental *and* democratic-immanent standard by which the sovereign people's constituent power can be normatively bound. Before the countermajoritarian difficulty, there was, and still is, a "majoritarian difficulty" that must be coped with by suitable constitutional reasoning and institutions.

We do not intend, however, to partake in this crowded genre, at least not in any immediate way. Our inquiry is rather predicated on the suspicion that the authority-authorship syndrome is not the only trouble that makes popular sovereignty seem ungrounded in sound practical reason. In point of fact, this sort of liberal obsession tends to overshadow other aspects of popular sovereignty that can be as troubling on both normative and empirical grounds. Frequently unexamined by the liberal-constitutional whistle-blowers, in particular, is the ontology of "We the People" itself. How the constituent people has come into existence, and in what shape, is often taken for granted as a historical accident that defies normative evaluation. Instead, what the constituent people, once formed, may or may not decide normatively is the entry point where the liberal practical reason comes to bear, for the first time, on discussions about constitutional legitimacy. Curbing popular majority may indeed be morally imperative. Yet, this liberal attempt to square will (authorship) with reason (rightness) tends to cloud our perspective on how "the people" itself was forged. In other words, popular sovereignty often exhibits questionable assumptions, or "syndromes," about "We the People," which tend to mystify their constituent power and reinforce the political-theological account of democratic constitutional founding. Our goal is to examine these other syndromes that are entailed in the attribution of charismatic powers to the constituent people.

Briefly, first of these may be called the "autonomy syndrome." Democratic constitution-making tends to presuppose that political self-determination of the people has an intrinsic value, and as such, it should be accorded moral respect and legal recognition that are due autonomy claims in general. As a corollary, this collective autonomy is often conceptualized as a matter of noninterference from unwanted foreign influences. As a result, a new constitution may forfeit its legitimacy if and when its "autochthony" is perceived to be compromised by forces from the outside, however well-meaning or reasonable they may be. The mere presence of, to say nothing of intervention by, any external authority is the most critical blow to the people's sovereignty. The second one might be termed the "*tabula rasa* syndrome." Here, collective self-determination frequently connotes liberation not only from foreign and/or tyrannical rule but also from the past itself, and constitutional founding is understood to involve both the extinction of the past and the creation of a whole new order on a *tabula rasa*. On this view, constitutional legitimacy is gained and lost on the extent to which the immediate past has been effectively exorcised by the sovereign people's determination to start from scratch again with a new constitution as its primary tool.

Finally, most conventional views tend to assume the existence of an immutable constituent people with predetermined identity. The two syndromes just mentioned are in fact dependent on such an assumption. Autonomy syndrome presupposes an isolated self-reliant agent with the power to impose its sovereign will on the political universe. Similarly, *tabula rasa* syndrome presupposes an all-powerful constituent agent that is able to annihilate the preexisting order and replace it with a completely new one. As such, these two syndromes make it hard to analyze, or even recognize, how the putatively constituent people is formed or how its boundaries are determined. A sovereign people must simply be postulated. One consequence of this postulation is that it becomes difficult to understand the process by which the people acquires its distinctive identity or articulates its own boundaries. In other words, turning a blind eye to outsiders in the name of self-determination and to the past in the name of new beginning contributes to a theoretically impoverished view in which a charismatic people with all its semidivine powers is presumed to have existed prior to the constitutional founding. Those who find it problematic to assume such a people may just circumvent the issue by positing, for instance, a "closed society."[8] Such an approach, however, will fail to capture

[8] John Rawls, *Political Liberalism* (New York: Columbia University Press, 1993), p. 12.

the truly momentous aspect of constitutional founding, as it cannot recognize the transformations that take place during that dynamic process. In our view, the identity of a sovereign people is less a constant than a function of the constitution-making process that is necessarily encumbered by external influences and past legacies. The relationship between people-making and constitutional founding is better captured in terms of mutual constitution, and the identity of the people as emerging out of this process of negotiation with external others and past legacies.

By all accounts, constitutional founding based on popular sovereignty is an elusive concept to make sense of. Much ink has been spilt over the household liberal-constitutional paranoia over authority-authorship syndrome, perhaps because "linkage of the Constitution's authority to its authorship is a sitting duck for critique."[9] Often overshadowed by this "sitting duck," however, are these other syndromes that make popular sovereignty so hard to pin down conceptually and to cope with politically. The autonomy syndrome and the *tabula rasa* syndrome obstruct adequate theoretical understanding of the boundary and identity of people as such, which is perhaps why most theories of democratic constitution-making tend to take them for granted. Our goal in this chapter is to foreground and problematize these syndromes at the theoretical level. In the following two sections, we will survey a number of theoretical perspectives on the roles of external others and past legacies to see whether they can justifiably be deemed a part of our theoretical framework for conceptualizing constitutional founding by the sovereign people. We will then, in the following section, reflect on the possibility of understanding the constitution-making process from a perspective that does not presuppose a preexisting semidivine people with a fixed identity.

EXTERNAL OTHERS: "AUTONOMY SYNDROME"

Historically, the great democratic constitutions of the eighteenth century were quite the exception. The more common mode of constitution-making was one in which "We the People" played very little role. Indeed, the notable cases of constitutional founding of the nineteenth century hardly conformed to the example set by the American and French precedents. The Bonapartist constitutions that Poland (1791), Spain (1812), and Norway (1814) adopted in the wake of the French Revolution were often dictated at the tip of the conqueror's bayonets. Following the Congress of Vienna, the legitimist charters of Holland (1815), Bavaria (1818), and Portugal (1826) sought to

[9] Michelman, "Constitutional Authorship," p. 67.

restore absolutist monarchy of the *ancien régime*. So-called bourgeois constitutions pioneered by the Belgian Charter (1831) were based on "dualism" in which the monarch and the popular assembly vied for authority while a constitution was promulgated as a royal gift to the (bourgeois) people. The constitutions of Wilhelmine Germany (1871) and Meiji Japan (1889) are merely the best-known examples of this type of constitution-making. Aside from the possible exception of the Latin American republican experiments during the same period, constitutional founding in history was more an act of imposition – be it from the outside or the upside – than that of an autonomous people's self-determination from below. "You the People" seems to be closer to the historical reality of the nineteenth-century than any purported idea of "We the People."

Of course, the idea of autonomy, or self-determination, eventually came to the fore with the rising tide of nationalist sentiments and class consciousness on a grander, worldwide scale. The interwar period in Europe witnessed an effervescence of constitution-making activities in new "nation-states" carved out of the imperial ruins after World War I. More established countries, whether defeated (as in Weimar Germany) or otherwise (as in New Deal America), also underwent a profound constitutional overhauling in the direction of robust socioeconomic justice. At the conclusion of World War II, these two progressive causes merged into a powerful call for national *and* class liberation among many a postcolonial people who demanded a constitutional edifice befitting their dual liberation.[10] Self-determination of the people became the sine qua non for a successful constitution-making in the postwar, postcolonial world. At long last, it appears that "You the People" of the nineteenth century has given way to "We the People" in the twentieth century.

From a more conceptual standpoint, however, it is still worth asking whether constitutions are really no longer "imposed," now that national self-determination has become the new zeitgeist. Constitution-making involves designing the institutions of a body politic, especially the government apparatuses, while carefully engineering a built-in system of their self-restraint. Structures-provisions may do the work alone (as the Federalists at the Philadelphia Convention believed); it may be reinforced by enumerating extensive rights-provisions (as demanded by the Anti-Federalist proponents of the original Bill of Rights). Either way, democratic constitutional founding is often conceptualized in terms of a political *demos* seeking to erect

[10] See, e.g., Said Amir Arjomand, "Constitutional Development and Political Reconstruction from Nation-Building to New Constitutionalism" in Said Amir Arjomand (ed.), *Constitutionalism and Political Reconstruction* (Leiden: E. J. Brill, 2007), p. 3.

an institutional edifice for its collective self-rule, while spawning a web of sticky encumbrances that would hamper the unmitigated exercise of its own power. Constitution, even a democratic one, is meant to empower *and* disempower the sovereign people at the same time.

Loosely building on the classic Aristotelian account of *akrasia*, the conventional answer to this dilemma postulates democratic constitutional founding in terms of collective "self-binding." A common analogy is "Peter sober" hedging himself against the ill-advised decisions of "Peter drunk" at some future point.[11] Putting cumbersome constraints on the people's will can be justified on democratic grounds only insofar as the constraints can be explained away as "self-imposition." In other words, the element of "imposition" has not been completely effaced from the process of constitution-making even in the era of popular sovereignty. It has been only rethought as self-imposition, or self-binding. It may even be that imposition is an unavoidable feature of all forms of law-giving. If that is so, then most disputations surrounding "imposed constitutions," which seem predicated on an ideal type of non-imposed constitutions, may have been misguided all along.[12]

To be sure, the difference between self-imposed constitutions and those imposed at the hands of an alien power is compelling still. By most accounts, one is made autonomously and therefore legitimate, while the other heteronomously and thus illegitimate. This deficiency of foreign imposition cannot be cured no matter how well intentioned it may be or how eagerly accepted by the locals. This belief goes back to the uniquely modern idea of sovereignty itself. According to Jean Bodin, sovereignty is an attribute (*nota*) of the autonomous and independent legislative power that "can give law to all in general and each in particular." He then immediately adds that the power must be exercised "without the consent of any other, whether greater, equal or below."[13] Although Bodin had in mind the exclusionary power of the prince, the essential characteristics of sovereignty did not undergo any change even

11 See, e.g., Cass Sunstein, *Designing Democracy: What Constitutions Do* (Oxford: Oxford University Press, 2001), p. 241; Stephen Holmes, "Precommitment and the Paradox of Democracy" in Jon Elster and Rune Slagstad (eds.), *Constitutionalism and Democracy* (Cambridge: Cambridge University Press, 1988), p. 195; Charles H. McIlwain, *Constitutionalism: Ancient and Modern* (Ithaca, NY: Cornell University Press, 1947), p. 145.

12 In this regard, Frederick Schauer states: "The model of the indigenous constitution is even rarer than the model of the borrowed or imposed one, and understanding the non-indigeneity of even the most seemingly indigenously created constitutions is an important facet of contemporary constitution-making and contemporary constitutionalism." "On the Migration of Constitutional Ideas," *Connecticut Law Review*, vol. 37 (2005), p. 907.

13 Jean Bodin, *On Sovereignty*, ed. and trans. Julian H. Franklin (Cambridge: Cambridge University Press, 1992), p. 56.

after it was attributed to the people. In order for any power to be deemed fully sovereign, its exercise could not be commanded or interfered with by any external power or authority. It had to be exercised *without the consent of any other*. The rise of popular sovereignty has only reinforced this demand for robust autonomy against foreign others by newly grafting it onto the people's right of self-determination. In other words, external sovereignty, a matter of international law, and internal sovereignty, an issue in domestic politics, have come to form an interlocking whole in the dogma of popular sovereignty.[14]

A Right Not to Be Second-Guessed?

In positing freedom from foreign influence as intrinsic to popular sovereignty, the most fundamental concern of this autonomy syndrome is with *who* is to decide rather than *what* is the best or normatively more attractive choice. In democratic constitution-making, the answer is, of course, "We the People" who has a *prima facie* right to self-determination, in which the exclusion of outsiders is seen to undergird the legitimacy of the constitution thus made. In this normative claim, collective self-determination is often seen as a matter of "right," no different in nature from that of individual liberty, which may be defended on one moral ground or another. According to this "rights talk," indeed, collective autonomy is frequently imagined after the freedom and autonomy of an individual. Just as the sovereign individual self should be accorded full autonomy, so the collective self called the people must be autonomous in order to be deemed truly sovereign. This seemingly self-evident use of "freedom" and "autonomy" in understanding popular sovereignty is not without problems, not least of which is that, even at the level of individual, these concepts are not so incontrovertible as they may seem. The standard debate on negative and positive notions of liberty is a testimony to the difficulty inherent in the concept of liberty itself.

At the outset, one may be struck by the structural similarity of the argument for the exclusion of foreign others in order to secure the people's sovereignty with that for the negative conception of individual liberty. Negative liberty is, in a nutshell, the absence of coercion and/or impediments from others, and as such, is built on an unyielding rejection of moral paternalism.[15] The argument

[14] Hans Lindahl thus criticizes recent theoretical attempts to reject state sovereignty on the democratic ground of popular sovereignty since such decoupling pays insufficient attention to the intertwined nature of the international and domestic dimensions of sovereignty. Hans Lindahl, "Sovereignty and the Institutionalization of Normative Order," *Oxford Journal of Legal Studies*, vol. 21, no. 1 (2001), pp. 178–80.

[15] Isaiah Berlin, "Two Concepts of Liberty," in *Four Essays on Liberty* (Oxford: Oxford University Press, 1969), pp. 122–31.

is less that this thin concept of liberty is singularly useful in identifying or exhausting the ways in which an individual may be said to be free. Its main thrust lies rather in the assertion that, if otherwise or more thickly defined, the concept of liberty loses its coherence. Particularly, its central concern is that including more "positive" elements, such as self-government, in the definition of liberty will introduce the possibility of others claiming to have better knowledge of how to be free. In order to be able to resist such "second-guessing" by others on principled grounds, liberty must be understood in strictly negative terms as liberty *from*.[16] It is not so much a celebration of the isolated individual living only in accordance with her unreflective wants and desires as a warning that external scrutiny, no matter how reasonable or well-intentioned, of those wants and desires cannot be squared with liberty rightly understood. Negative liberty is, then, negative in a double sense. One, because it defines liberty as an absence rather than a positive postulation of certain conditions; and two, because it is motivated by a fear of potential paternalism rather than an aspiration for certain normatively attractive goals.

Seen this way, the affinity between negative liberty and the sovereign people's claim to collective autonomy may appear almost self-evident. For the argument for the people's autonomy is driven by the equally strong concern for resisting external interference as such, so as to secure and protect a pristine sphere of the people's collective freedom for its own sake. Unless the absence of external coercion and interference is ensured, the people cannot be said to be sovereign. This is why Hobbes asserted that the primary attribute of sovereignty, as well as individual liberty, is absolute independence from external command and interference.[17] On this view, the core of both negative liberty of the individual and sovereignty of the people consists in the rejection of interference and second-guessing by external others.

Even without picking bones with this negative conception of liberty per se, however, one should be struck by the thinness of the analogy on which this negative argument for the right of collective self-determination is based. Especially from our perspective, the main problem turns on the recognition that the people cannot be deemed so unitary, coherent, and self-enclosed as the individual self is assumed to be by the advocates of the negative conception of liberty. For sure, negative liberty does not necessarily assume a fully integrated self, either; that is indeed one of the sources of its entrenched fear of paternalistic second-guessing from others. Still compelling, nonetheless,

16 Berlin, "Two Concepts," p. 127.

17 Thomas Hobbes, *Leviathan*, ed. Richard Tuck (Cambridge: Cambridge University Press, 1991), ch. 21.

is the difficulty of ascribing to the first-person plural ("We") the same kind of unity and closure that we tend to presume for the first-person singular ("I") subject of negative liberty.

It is hard to maintain that the first-person plural exists before any collective decision-making takes place, for it is actually the efficaciousness of the collective action that certifies the very existence of a collective agent. And this is no more so than during the process of constitutional founding, because this is when the very unity and boundary of "We the People" are still unsettled. As will be seen, such identity is actually acquired through the action of setting out to make a new constitution. Prior to that, the collective agent who instigates revolutionary political action may be subsumed under the rubric of minorities, dissenters, rebels, or secessionists; what they cannot be called, yet, is "We the People." That is to say, unless their collective action meets with a modicum of success in establishing a new constitutional order, a constituent people has yet to come into being. This could not be more different from the kind of seemingly self-evident and pre-given selfhood presupposed by the negative conception of liberty. In order to speak of absence of coercions and/or impediments, one must assume a coherent pre-given individual self. An individual self may fail to achieve its goal due to external interference. We then may say that the agent's liberty was compromised; we do *not* say that its selfhood per se was questioned. There are unfree selves and inefficacious agents at the individual level, in other words. By contrast, an inefficacious constituent people is as real as the unfulfilled romantic yearning – or worse, a figment of imagination – on the part of a band of frustrated revolutionaries.

This recognition prompts us to revisit negative liberty's rival template for conceptualizing freedom, that is, positive liberty, to see if it might supply a more robust link between individual and collective autonomy. In Isaiah Berlin's classic formulation, positive liberty goes beyond the minimalist demand for non-interference and strives to achieve a higher or richer moral goal. Throughout the history of moral and political philosophy, the goal worthy of such pursuit has been variously known as Kantian autonomy, Hegelian *Sittlichkeit* or even Marxist emancipation of the entire humanity via proletariat revolution. What holds these radically divergent views together under the rubric of positive liberty is the underlying assumption that true freedom consists in active "self-realization," rather than in merely being left alone. The basic concern is that freedom, properly understood, must be more than simply following one's unreflective desires. It must, rather, be the fulfillment of one's authentic goals and genuine wishes, of something that one truly desires and for the right reasons. This means consciously identifying oneself with a universal ideal larger than one's own wants and desires. One of those ideals, for some, is collective self-realization, because the political community to which one belongs is deeply constitutive of one's own selfhood, and the community's freedom, autonomy, and independence are seen as necessary conditions for individual liberty. In other words, on this view of positive liberty, self-realization of the individual is predicated on the self-determination of the collective whole of which the individual is an organic part. One is genuinely free only to the extent that one's political community is free. In contrast to the negative conception, there seems to be a more natural and logical connection between individual and collective autonomy.

As such, the distinguishing feature of the positive conception is the recognition that one can be wrong about one's own desires, or that there is a difference between first-order and second-order desires.[18] This means that the positive conception of liberty entails an image of the individual self that is deeply divided between lower and higher selves.[19] The brute wants of the lower self must be subjected to "strong evaluation," or second-guessing, by the reflexive, higher self. Constitutionally speaking, an application of this ontology of bifurcated selves may be found in the so-called precommitment theory alluded to previously, which was devised to explain and justify constitutional constraints on the will of the people. For it also presumes the constituent people to be divided between higher ("Peter sober") and lower ("Peter drunk") selves, giving the former the right of constitution-making so as to insulate itself from ill-advised decisions of the latter. A constitution's rights-provisions in this view are a primary tool of restraint, even coercive imposition, by which a sovereign constituent people may achieve its true "self-realization" against its future self. By serializing the ontology of the constituent people into the present one and the future other, the precommitment theory seems to have it both ways, that is, explaining the constraining function of a constitution and justifying it on account of collective self-determination (albeit spread over time).

For democratic detractors, however, this liberal affirmation of collective autonomy is not without problems. Simply put, to presume that the future people's departure from the original intention and founding scheme is reflective of some collective moral weakness is a highly questionable form of moral paternalism, since such a departure may well be the result of reasoned disagreements between generations that developed over time. This is especially troubling because what the later generation surrenders via the precommitment

18 Charles Taylor, "What's Wrong with Negative Liberty?" in *Philosophy and the Human Sciences: Philosophical Papers 2* (Cambridge: Cambridge University Press, 1985).

19 Berlin, "Two Concepts," p. 132.

strategy is not just a certain specific course of action, but an overall right of judgment. Jeremy Waldron thus concludes that "[p]recommitment cannot preserve the aura of autonomy (or democracy in the constitutional case)."[20] Unless later generations of the sovereign people can be persuaded to be content with *pouvoir constitué* rather than *pouvoir constituant*, "Peter sober" will only appear as the "dead hand of the past" to "Peter drunk" who is thereby being "coerced to be free." The higher self of yesterday may be as good as a total stranger to tomorrow's lower self.

An even more serious problem with the positive conception is that, once second-guessing is permitted across time, it may be difficult to prevent such paternalism across borders. It may be that the model of positive liberty actually invites and justifies some form of overbearing external influence quite incompatible with conventional notions of popular sovereignty. To see why, it is worth recalling why Berlin rejected, albeit not without sympathies, positive liberty as a reliable and defensible conception of individual freedom. The crux of the matter is again moral paternalism that might justify undue interference in the name of freedom – even if such a practice remains only a dormant possibility. As mentioned, positive liberty likely allows for the possibility of second-guessing by others regarding the validity and authenticity of the decision made by the individual. The application of this to the constituent people actually leads to strange conclusions. For, on this view, popular sovereignty à la positive liberty could not mean letting the people have whatever they wish. The quality of their decision must be open to critical scrutiny by others. It turns out that constitutional founding is an act in which agents other than the people themselves are allowed to second-guess the decision of the putatively sovereign people. In other words, if second-guessing is permissible at the individual level, what makes it impermissible at the level of peoples, nations, and states? Or, on what principled grounds are external powers prohibited, under any circumstances, from interfering with the constitution-making process of any given people?

This obviously is a vexing problem not only for good liberals but also for partisans of popular sovereignty. For whatever theoretical cogency achieved by couching the legitimacy of collective self-determination in terms of positive liberty seems purchased only at the expense of allowing for second-guessing about the normative desirability of the constitution made by "We the People." Respect for collective self-determination that a sovereign people demands from others may be given theoretical justification only in a way that opens the

[20] Jeremy Waldron, "Precommitment and Disagreement," in Alexander (ed.), *Constitutionalism*, p. 281.

backdoor to external interference in the name of "true" self-government or the "real" benefit of the constituent people. In short, neither the precommitment strategy nor positive liberty in general seems able to provide satisfactory grounds for counting total exclusion of outsiders as an intrinsic requirement of popular sovereignty. The idea of positive liberty may appear to strengthen the analogy between individual and collective autonomy, but it falls far short of laying a justificatory ground for the robust right of self-determination understood as strict exclusion of external others.

To summarize, neither negative liberty nor positive liberty seems to provide justification for understanding popular sovereignty as a doctrine that entails the autonomy syndrome. Negative liberty makes it difficult to graft the conditions of individual liberty onto collective autonomy; positive liberty makes collective autonomy vulnerable to second-guessing and interference from external agents. Moreover, many contemporary theorists of liberty readily acknowledge that the stark dichotomy between negative and positive liberty does not hold under close conceptual scrutiny. This recognition, however, may not yet warrant the conclusion that the autonomy syndrome is not justifiable.

A *Republic If You Can Make It*

The idea of "republican liberty" may be considered a third candidate for thinking that popular sovereignty requires strict exclusion of external interferences. It is so because republican liberty remains within the orbit of the negative principle of non-interference, while making a positive link between individual and collective liberties. Proponents of this republican notion of liberty maintain that the central concern of liberty is with how to secure a sphere of non-interference in which an individual is left free to pursue one's goal without coercion or impediment. Going beyond the original formulation of negative liberty, however, republican liberty holds that fortification of a zone of privacy alone cannot deliver on the promise of negative liberty. For, as Berlin admitted, benevolent autocracy may also respect such individual citadels.[21] This obviously is not only counterintuitive but also unacceptable to republican democrats. For them, missing in this version of non-interference principle is an attention to the *conditions* for such fortification. A slave under a liberal master may be deemed free, but only so long as the master remains benevolent, which is no less arbitrary (i.e., beyond the control of the slave) than when the master is despotic. Even negative liberty, properly understood,

[21] Berlin, "Two Concepts," pp. 129–30.

cannot be had unless the root-cause for coercive interference is brought under democratic control. For republican democrats, thus, non-interference can be sustained on a secure basis if and only if the potential for undue domination is structurally regulated. That is, individual freedom defined as non-interference is predicated on a political and social liberty of "non-domination."

Thus becomes clear the analytical link between individual and collective freedom. In order to enjoy their own negative liberty, individuals have every reason to participate in the self-rule of the political community they belong to. Also, securing negative liberty requires defending the collective freedom, that is, preventing the formation and consolidation of political, social, and economic structures of undue domination. One is free only by virtue of living as an active citizen in a free political community called the "republic." Republican liberty apparently makes negative liberty compatible with the collective dimension of positive liberty in an analytically more satisfactory way.[22]

Our concern here is not to scrutinize the internal coherence of the concept of republican liberty. Rather, it is whether republican liberty might provide justification for the claim that constitutional founding by the sovereign people calls for strict exclusion of all external forces. It appears plain that the collective autonomy of the people requires rejecting all interference from the outside. There is no reason why non-domination should be confined to the interior of a republic's borders; not being subject to a foreign power's undue domination is also critical for maintaining the conditions of non-domination within the republic. A robust right of collective self-determination (i.e., non-interference from outsiders) can thus be defended in terms of republican liberty (i.e., non-domination by outsiders), not as a matter of weak analogy but of principle. It appears that, on this republican view, a strong case for collective self-determination can be made without becoming vulnerable to the problems of second-guessing or paternalism. According to Philip Pettit, "the free individual is protected against the domination of others by the undominating *and undominated* state."[23]

Sensible as it may seem, however, this republican proposition raises a difficult question insofar as constitutional founding is concerned. What if, that is, the state in question is hardly undominating toward its citizens? Can such a dominating state still demand to be undominated by others as a matter of right? In order for this individual-cum-collective liberty to make sense, the collectivity

[22] For a most systematic articulation of the republican notion of liberty, see Philip Pettit, *Republicanism: A Theory of Freedom and Government* (Oxford: Oxford University Press, 1997), part 1.

[23] Philip Pettit, "A Republican Law of Peoples," *European Journal of Political Theory*, vol. 9, no. 1 (2010), p. 77 (emphasis added).

has to be of a certain kind, namely, a republic ("undominating state"). For collective autonomy is entitled to respect from the outside only because it is a democratic sphere in which individual members can live free of actual and potential dominations. Put differently, those political communities not organized along republican principles may not deserve to claim the equal extent of non-interference from outsiders because their domestic politics hardly allow for conditions of non-domination. On this view, then, there might even be an argument for foreign "republican" intervention to jumpstart a new republic in cases where the polity at hand seems unable to provide the resources for the task from within. Although "*pro tanto* evil," Pettit thus says, a foreign domination under *some* circumstances may well have "compensating effects."[24] Even if the local conditions allow for the creation of a republic by domestic actors (i.e., for democratic constitutional founding), problems still remain. For, at that stage, there is by definition no republic yet. There is at best a nascent republic in which non-domination still remains but a vague hope or an aspiration. This is obviously problematic because it means that, at the stage of constitutional founding, the polity-under-formation cannot avail itself of the claim for unconditional respect for its domestic affairs by outsiders. When you are not a republic, you cannot demand freedom from external others on grounds of republican liberty. In short, the republican argument for rejecting paternalistic interference from outsiders may not be so watertight as it might seem.

Even if one believes that founding periods are precisely the times when non-interference from external others is most crucially needed, the idea of republican liberty offers little help because no republic is in existence yet. We might call this the "external" version of the familiar conundrum of republican founding discussed by political theorists ever since Rousseau. Briefly stated – founding periods are precisely the times when republican virtue is needed the most among the citizens, but virtuous republican citizens can only be created through the experience of living under republican institutions, which by definition do not exist at the time of the founding.[25] This is commonly understood

[24] In broad strokes, he outlines two such circumstances. One is when "controlling the corporate entity [i.e., a state] may mean promoting the non-domination of such other members [i.e., its citizens suffering from domestic domination]"; two is when "a corporate agent ... serves the interests of some or all of its members but does badly – say, in domination terms – with outsiders [i.e., a republic that is dominating towards international others]." Pettit, "Republican Law of Peoples," pp. 76–7.

[25] According to Rousseau's famous words, "the effect would have to become the cause, the social spirit which is to be the work of the institution would have to preside over the institution itself, and men would have to be prior to laws what they ought to become by means of them." Jean-Jacques Rousseau, *The Social Contract and Other Later Political Writings*, ed. and trans. Victor Gourevitch (Cambridge: Cambridge University Press, 1997), p. 71.

to mean that the citizens do not yet have the requisite aptitude and knowledge needed for establishing a new republic. If we were to bring into view the republic's external relations, it might also be taken to mean that the citizens cannot engage in collective self-determination because conditions do not yet exist for their autonomous deliberation free from external interference. Either way, a republic cannot be founded in a republican way.

Recognizing that there was no republican solution for this conundrum, Rousseau, the quintessential republican, was compelled to invoke a deus ex machina called the "lawgiver." Precisely how this figure resolves this chicken-and-egg paradox need not concern us here. Suffice it to note that the lawgiver's task is "to institute a people" as such by "changing human nature"[26] as well as laying down the legal institutional bedrock for a workable republic. More to the point, what enables all these momentous undertakings is the fact that the lawgiver is a foreigner. This foreignness is what provides the virtue and wisdom the people need but do not have at the founding moment. Rousseau does not assume (as Rawls does) that the people can put on the "veil of ignorance" of their own accord. Impartiality is the most crucial, yet rarest, virtue for making the will of all coincide with the general will, which therefore must be imported from outside and imposed on the people. As Rousseau describes it, the lawgiver is also the embodiment of "sublime reason" and the agent of "an undertaking beyond human force." As such, it is not something that can be incorporated into the institutional framework of the republic established by the lawgiver. It represents a charismatic quality that cannot be made routine. Rousseau apparently realized, however reluctantly, that charisma must be attributed not to the people but to a foreign lawgiver in order to jumpstart a self-governing republic based on popular sovereignty. As much as democratic constitutional founding may appear to be predicated on strong claims of self-determination and freedom from external influences, it cannot be carried out without positing an external (even overbearing) agent. The presence of external others seems not only unavoidable as a matter of history and sociology, but also logically necessary.

For some contemporary theorists of agonistic democracy, this necessity of foreign others is not merely an inconvenient truth to be accepted begrudgingly. For Bonnie Honig, for example, Rousseau's lawgiver is more than a charismatic father-figure who mysteriously, but peacefully, disappears after the founding. The foreign founder actually symbolizes the pole of authority that the people, constituted by the lawgiver, continues to challenge, resist, transgress, and even attempt to obliterate, in an ongoing effort to cleanse the

[26] Rousseau, *Social Contract*, p. 69.

memory of the pervasive violence that inevitably haunts any founding experience.[27] It is a political-psychological device for constantly reminding themselves of the impositional nature of law and institutions laid down during the founding period. As such, the foreignness of the institutions that citizens live under plays a dual function for strong democracy. One is that of compelling citizens to realize that strangeness, foreignness, and radical difference are constitutive parts of who they are as sovereign people. For, had it not been for the mediation of such foreign elements, as symbolized by Rousseau's lawgiver, "We the People" as such would not have come into being. The lesson of the foreign founder lies in deterring the citizenry from calling for unity and homogeneity of the *demos*, which might otherwise arise in the name of popular sovereignty.

The other function is to enable the people to engage in participatory democracy against the reifying effects of those laws and institutions that govern democratic process. The moral of the foreign lawgiver story is to disenchant, rather than enchant, the founding authority, so as to prompt and empower democratic citizens who will continually seek to re-found those laws and institutions by themselves in the hope of effacing the foreignness of their origins. Ironically, the foreign founder has the effect of strengthening, rather than undermining, the democratic virtue of the citizenry. On these radically democratic views, the presence of foreigners in the founding and constitution-making experience is to be not only tolerated as a logical necessity, but also embraced and celebrated as instrumental for sustaining a dynamic democracy of an agonistic kind. Remembrance of the foreign founder is critical for the transfer of charismatic power to the people. Whether celebrated or not, foreign others can hardly be obliterated from constitutional founding.

The Outsider Who Wouldn't Quit

Popular sovereignty is based on the claim for self-determination, which requires a strong rights-claim against external interference. It turns out, however, that such a collective right, justified in terms drawn from individual rights-talk, cannot be sustained. Indeed, it is far from self-evident as to why popular sovereignty or collective self-determination should be expressed in terms of a right (what is just and moral), rather than the good (what is desirable or choice-worthy). Couching it in terms of rights-talk leads to the viewpoint that restrictions of sovereignty are a moral injustice in need of condemnation

[27] Bonnie Honig, *Democracy and the Foreigner* (Princeton, NJ: Princeton University Press, 2001), pp. 15–40.

and rectification. Yet, giving prudential concessions to claims of collective self-determination under certain circumstances is not the same as granting an unassailable right of autonomy across the board.[28] To say the least, the claim that constitutional founding based on popular sovereignty requires an a priori rejection of all external forces seems unwarranted. Outsiders may even be an ineradicable presence in all constitutional founding.

Evidently, this is not just an idle matter of conceptual conundrum or theoretical irony. Perhaps Tokyo and Baghdad were not the exceptions after all, but only the more extreme and conspicuous cases of this presence of external others. High-sounding proclamations of the supreme power of the people to forge its own destiny are rarely subjected to careful scrutiny of what it precisely means to be self-sufficient or to reject all agency other than one's own. The story of the American founding is a case in point. For, often neglected in discussions of the making of the American constitution is the presence of external forces. True, there may not have been any foreign founder. Seldom remembered, however, is the fact that the greater part of the Declaration of Independence consists of a long inventory of King George III's "injuries and usurpations" against the people of the thirteen colonies. The presence of these "external" reasons is what provided the motivation and justification for the historic act of founding. It was the foil without which no new republic could have been established. This points to the conceptual impossibility of imagining constituent power in splendid isolation from all external influence. As is well known, the convention in Philadelphia was convened in no small measure in reaction to crises arising from external circumstances, including military establishment, regulations of foreign commerce, and treaty enforcement.[29] The full significance of the drafting of the Constitution of the United States cannot be properly understood without considering the influence of external factors on its contents and orientation.

This suggests that the exercise of constituent power is concerned with not only decisions regarding internal or domestic political life, but also, perhaps more fundamentally, the redrawing of the very line that separates one polity from another. In cases where a new polity is being created via independence,

[28] See, e.g., Ronald Beiner, *Liberalism, Nationalism, Citizenship: Essays on the Problems of Political Community* (Vancouver: University of British Columbia Press, 2003), pp. 155–61. Even the contemporary proponents of national self-determination never fail to qualify their right-based claims by an extensive enumeration of stringent qualifications under which few such claims will likely be sanctioned in practice. See, e.g., Daniel Philpott, "In Defense of Self Determination," *Ethics*, vol. 105, no. 2 (1995); Avishai Margalit and Joseph Raz, "National Self-Determination," *Journal of Philosophy*, vol. 87, no. 9 (1990).

[29] See, e.g., Frederick W. Marks III, *Independence on Trial: Foreign Affairs and the Making of the Constitution* (Baton Rouge: Louisiana State University Press, 1973).

this involves recasting what had been a domestic relationship into a foreign one between two separate polities. The American Declaration of Independence thus begins by proclaiming that the colonists are about to "dissolve the political bands which [had] connected them with another." Viewed from the perspective of the people's agency, this means that constitutional founding can only proceed by blurring the previous demarcation between the internal and the external. As will be seen, founding periods are times when the boundary of "We the People" undergoes redefinition, sometimes quite radically. They are also times when calls for absolute autonomy, understood as a categorical rejection of all external others, are made most vehemently, precisely because the boundary lines that define the people is unsettled. A good example might be the idea of "constitutional autochthony." The term conveys the sense of a strong resolve to look inward for ideas and institutions to be enshrined in the constitution. But, it was in fact prompted by a process crucially concerned with the outside. At least as used among lawyers of the British Commonwealth, it symbolizes the goal to be reached through the intricate and multifarious processes by which the former colonies of the British Empire severed their constitutional ties with the Westminster Parliament.[30] The metropolitan legislature (and the crown) had to be reconfigured as a foreign "other" before the postcolonial subjects could acquire a home-grown constitution "sprung from their own soil." What we are calling autonomy syndrome is in fact a reflection of the historical reality that the constituent people cannot engage in constitutional founding in isolation from the international context defined by numerous external actors. As one international lawyer has observed, "[t]he 'self' does not emanate exclusively from a nation's own history and revolutionary project, but is being reproduced and re-framed in a sequence of communications among a plurality of domestic and global actors."[31] A sovereign people cannot be identified or activated unless and until external agents are brought into full view.

This is even more so in the era of globalization where state boundaries are growing more porous and individuals are increasingly subject to legal norms set by authorities other than their own local legislatures. Indeed,

[30] Kenneth C. Wheare, *The Constitutional Structure of the Commonwealth* (Oxford: Clarendon Press, 1960), ch. IV. For a recent treatment of the process, see Peter C. Oliver, *The Constitution of Independence: The Development of Constitutional Theory in Australia, Canada, and New Zealand* (Oxford: Oxford University Press, 2005).

[31] Achilles Skordas, "Self-determination of Peoples and Transnational Regimes: a Foundational Principle of Global Governance," in Nicholas Tsagourias (ed.), *Transnational Constitutionalism: International and European Perspectives* (Cambridge: Cambridge University Press, 2007), p. 218.

some argue that the international order based on the distinction between inside and outside is no longer viable. Such developments obviously make it harder to distinguish between those who may rightfully participate in the constitution-making process and those who should stay outside. Projects on nation-building and rule of law assistance are now considered a legitimate part of the foreign aid industry led by a host of developed countries, international organizations, and even private groups. In response to this new global reality, Ulrich Preuss has cautiously proposed that we start entertaining the legitimacy of "international constitutional intervention" on humanitarian grounds.[32] The recent nation-building experiments in post-conflict Kosovo, for instance, have led one observer to conclude that we should "pluralize the unitary concept of constituent power and divorce it from the idea of the 'people'" and recognize the "existence of constituent powers on both sides of an often tentative political divide between the 'inside' and 'outside' of an emergent constitutional order."[33] Another commentator goes even further and asserts that "the idea of foreign powers as contributors to the founding of democracy is not only a theoretical possibility, it is a necessary assumption."[34] Constitution-making has rarely been a pristine domestic affair at least since the mid-twentieth century.[35] External influences are not only common; they are now seen as routine. The issue seems more a question of extent or gradation than of propriety or permissibility. If this is the case, then the presence of external others should perhaps be incorporated as an integral component in our efforts to theorize democratic constitutional founding. It would be misguided to question the legitimacy of a constitution solely on account of the influence of external constituent powers.

PAST LEGACIES: "*TABULA RASA* SYNDROME"

The language of modern constitutional theory is still surprisingly dependent on religious vocabulary and imageries. One prime example is the idea that,

[32] Ulrich K. Preuss, "Perspectives on Post-Conflict Constitutionalism: Reflections on Regime Change through External Constitutionalization," *New York Law School Law Review*, vol. 51 (2006–07), pp. 491–3.

[33] Zoran Oklopcic, "Constitutional (Re)Vision: Sovereign Peoples, New Constituent Powers, and the Formation of Constitutional Orders in the Balkans," *Constellations*, vol. 19, no. 1 (2012), p. 90.

[34] Hans Agné, "Democratic Founding: We the People and the Others," *I•CON: International Journal of Constitutional Law*, vol. 10, no. 3 (2012), p. 3.

[35] Some scholars make use of terms like "internationalized *pouvoir constituant*," although their premise is that this is a very recent phenomenon. See, e.g., Philipp Dann and Zaid Al-Ali, "The Internationalized 'Pouvoir Constituant': Constitution-Making Under External Influence in Iraq, Sudan and East Timor," *Max Planck Yearbook of United Nations Law*, vol. 10 (2006).

when a new constitutional order is founded by the sovereign people, it must be a creation *ex nihilo*. Just as God created the world out of nothing through his sovereign will, so the charismatic sovereign people must create an entirely novel political and legal universe. Just as the absolute monarch had been *legibus solutus*, so the sovereign people should not be bound by any legal norms from the pre-founding era. To be so bound would be to admit that the people are actually not sovereign – whoever made those pre-founding era norms would be the real sovereign. In this political-theological outlook, it seems, nothing from the previous age must be allowed to interfere with the charismatic exercise of this creative-destructive power of the people. Constitutional founding by the sovereign people is seen to entail a firm rejection and repudiation of the authority of the past.

God Is Dead, Long Live the People!

This *tabula rasa* syndrome is quite evident in the standard accounts of constitutional founding. For example, Carl Schmitt writes: "The sovereign decision is an absolute beginning.... It springs out of a normative nothingness and from a concrete disorder."[36] Insisting that the people are the only agent who can make such a foundational decision, he further claims that their act of making a constitution cannot be "judged by prior constitutional laws or those that were valid until then."[37] Since the people's decision "requires no justification via an ethical or juristic norm," it can only be made in a normless vacuum.[38] While this may be an obvious expression of Schmitt's political existentialism,[39] it is also an unmistakable sign that his conceptual model is the theological idea of *creatio ex nihilo*. On this point, Schmitt is widely seen as a successor to Emmanuel Joseph Sieyès, whose ideas about the people's constituent power were influential during the French Revolution. It was Sieyès who famously argued that the right to make a constitution belongs to the people – for him *la nation* – who is the only agent with the power to make a constitution.[40] The

36 Carl Schmitt, *Über die drei Arten des rechtswissenschaftlichen Denkens* (Berlin: Duncker und Humblot, 1993), pp. 23–4, quoted in Andreas Kalyvas, *Democracy and the Politics of the Extraordinary: Max Weber, Carl Schmitt and Hannah Arendt* (Cambridge: Cambridge University Press, 2008), p. 94.

37 Carl Schmitt, *Constitutional Theory*, trans. Jeffrey Seitzer (Durham, NC: Duke University Press, 2008), p. 131.

38 Schmitt, *Constitutional Theory*, p. 136.

39 For example, in his meditation on Schmitt's famous text, Paul Kahn repeatedly emphasizes that "existence precedes essence." *Political Theology: Four New Chapters on the Concept of Sovereignty*, (New York: Columbia University Press, 2011).

40 "If we have no constitution, it must be made, and only the nation has the right to make it." Emmanuel Joseph Sieyès, *What is the Third Estate?* trans. M. Blondel (New York: Praeger, 1963), p. 119.

French abbot made it clear that, vis-à-vis the legal and political universe, the nation now occupies the position of God: "The nation is prior to everything. It is the source of everything. Its will is always legal; indeed it is the law itself." As the constitution is the product of the nation's will, the nation cannot and must not be subject to a constitution, and the "nation is always free to amend its constitution."[41] Further, as the all-powerful creator of its constitution, the people-cum-nation cannot be bound by any pre-existing norm or procedure when it makes a constitution. Just as God would cease to be God if he had to obey some independent law or command, a nation would no longer be a free nation if it were to "subject itself to the shackles of a defined procedure."[42] By relying on nothing else than its own will, the sovereign people makes a new constitution, which has the effect of extinguishing all previous laws.

It is perhaps unsurprising that, as an ordained priest, Sieyès would use theological imagery to express the sovereign people's constituent power. At the same time, he also employed the Enlightenment language of social contract theorists: "We must conceive the nations of the world as being like men living outside society or 'in a state of nature', as it is called."[43] Interestingly, however, invoking the idea of state of nature to posit the agent of constituent power outside real-life historical society actually reinforces the theological analogy of re-conceptualizing the people as a timeless agent. As the bearer of powers that pre-exist any social or political institutions, the people is now thought to reside in a realm above and beyond the ordinary temporal dimension. As Bernard Yack puts it, the people in this image exists in an "eternal presence," uncluttered and unencumbered by historical contingencies; it is a being that "never ages or dies."[44] For these political-theologians, constitutional founding is the political analogue of divine creation of the universe, both taking place outside the normal flow of time.

For Hannah Arendt, too, constitutional founding is predicated on a heroic extraction from the temporal dimension. As such, her theory is also not completely free of the *tabula rasa* syndrome. For sure, she has absolutely no use for the notion of sovereignty or for any semi-divine people residing in an eternal celestial kingdom. Sovereignty, for her, is the very antithesis of political freedom.[45] She commended the American revolutionaries for not having

[41] Sieyès, *What is the Third Estate?*, pp. 126, 134.

[42] Sieyès, *What is the Third Estate?*, p. 127

[43] Sieyès, *What is the Third Estate?*, p. 128.

[44] Bernard Yack, "Popular Sovereignty and Nationalism," *Political Theory*, vol. 29, no. 4 (2001), p. 521.

[45] Hannah Arendt, "What is Freedom," in *Between Past and Future: Eight Exercises in Political Thought* (New York: Penguin Books, 1977), pp. 164–5; Hannah Arendt, *On Revolution* (New York: Viking Press, 1965), p. 152.

repudiated their legal heritage, that is, for having built on received procedures and already-constituted bodies, rather than employing the vocabulary of popular sovereignty.[46] Be that as it may, the theoretical reference point for Arendt's concept of constitutional founding remains the idea of "natality," a radical new beginning, a "new event breaking into the continuous sequence of historical time."[47] The lot of the revolutionary is like someone who "had abolished the sequence of temporality itself," or who had been "thrown out of the temporal order and its continuity."[48] Someone who must enact a new beginning is situated in a "gap of time between past and future."[49] This means that the only resource available to the founders is what they themselves bring to the situation.

Her descriptions of the capacity to create power through "mutual promises" are conspicuously devoid of any reliance on anything inherited from the past. Instead, the people who found a body politic apparently do so in the midst of an existential angst, which, interestingly enough, produces timeless moments of perspicuity and self-empowerment. Even though "frightened by the chartless darkness of the human heart," they are also supremely confident of their own powers, "granted and confirmed by no one," to establish a political community.[50] For it is an enterprise "for which neither the historical nor the legendary truth of their own tradition [can] offer any help or precedent."[51] Since constitutional founding takes place through "action-in-concert" outside time, it cannot be under the constraints of the temporal dimension, nor is it subject to any pre-existing transcendental moral imperatives (e.g., natural law). For Arendt, then, despite her attempts to avoid the deification of the people and to banish all allusions to "will" and "sovereignty" from the discourse on political power, constitutional founding remains a timeless and charismatic event, utterly free of any encumbrance from the past. Notwithstanding crucial differences between Sieyès, Schmitt, and Arendt, these classic accounts of constitutional founding tend to posit the sovereign people as an "all-powerful and ever-living"[52]

46 For an argument that, contrary to Arendt's characterization, the American revolutionaries heavily relied on the concept of sovereignty, see Jason Frank, *Constituent Moments: Enacting the People in Postrevolutionary America* (Durham, NC: Duke University Press, 2010), ch. 1.

47 Arendt, *On Revolution*, p. 206. For a different interpretation of Arendt on this score, see Kalyvas, *Politics of the Extraordinary*, pp. 223–31.

48 Arendt, *On Revolution*, p. 207.

49 Arendt, *Between Past and Future*, p. 13.

50 Arendt, *On Revolution*, pp. 166, 195.

51 Arendt, *On Revolution*, p. 214.

52 Reference is to the opening lines of the Eucharistic Prayer in Roman Catholic liturgy: "Father, all-powerful and ever-living God, we do well always and everywhere to give you thanks."

agent who are able to "create new heavens and a new earth: and the former shall not be remembered, nor come into mind."[53]

Der Mann ohne Eigenschaften: *The People Without Qualities*

One consequence of this pervasive *tabula rasa* syndrome is that the process of making a constitution remains mysterious. It is quite telling that both Schmitt and Arendt employ the term "miracle" to describe the founding.[54] For Schmitt, just as God's creation of the world remains an inscrutable mystery, so the eternal people's making of a constitution cannot be subjected to reasoned analysis or normative evaluation. Like a miracle, which defies the ordinary laws of nature, the exercise of people's constituent power is essentially an unfathomable event. The only way to describe it is to call it a "charismatic" decision. To be sure, Arendt eschews analogizing the capacity of enacting a new beginning to divine powers; indeed, for her, it is a quintessentially human capacity. She nonetheless stresses that this power, or freedom, consists in the ability to bring about "the unforeseeable and unpredictable."[55] While she claims that a new beginning is self-authorizing due to "the interconnected principle of mutual promise and common deliberation,"[56] it is unclear how this principle "makes its appearance in the world."[57] It seems that the appearance of the principle can only be described as a miracle, or an epiphany, that takes place when the people engage in action-in-concert.

It should be clear that the agents of such miraculous powers could not be the real flesh-and-blood people engaged in actual political processes. The eternal people in the state of nature is a generic concept that has no distinct identity. Just as God has no nationality, so the people is in effect a spiritual being that cannot be differentiated according to history or geography. Such a people is more an abstract and colorless source of legitimacy than an actual agent of political action.[58] As a result, the constitution made by such a disembodied and deracinated people could only be a generic constitution at best. It could not be identified as the constitution of a particular political community.

[53] Isaiah 65:17 (King James version)

[54] E.g., Schmitt, *Political Theology*, p. 36; Arendt, *Between Past and Future*, pp. 169–71.

[55] Arendt, *Between Past and Future*, p. 170.

[56] Arendt, *On Revolution*, p. 215.

[57] Arendt, *On Revolution*, p. 214.

[58] Bernard Yack maintains: "The people invoked as the ultimate source of the Swedish state's legitimate authority is no different in character than the people invoked as the source of the legitimate authority of the Chinese or Canadian state. In every case, the people is the same." Yack, "Popular Sovereignty and Nationalism," p. 521.

A constitution created *ex nihilo* cannot be situated in any specific historical context because, by definition, such a creation both transcends and obliterates all temporal and spatial contexts. It is radically free of any particularizing narrative or attributes that might endow it with an identity of its own.

This could not be otherwise, for the people in this dogma are as good as an "unencumbered self," to use a term made famous by Michael Sandel in his critique of procedural liberalism.[59] Like the target of Sandel's criticism, the sovereign people in the state of nature do not have any constitutive goals or attachments that define them, much less any specific ties that bind them together, or any commonly shared memories or traditions. Their only known attribute is their supreme willfulness, or their complete and unrestricted freedom to choose. The problem is that they have no criteria by which to make their choice. For, only a "thickly-constituted self, burdened by the accidents of social and cultural contingency"[60] would be able to make any meaningful choice. According to another proponent of the communitarian critique of liberalism, even the freely choosing subject itself is a product of a certain specific historical and social context. That is why, for Charles Taylor, "there is an absurdity in placing this subject in a state of nature where he could never attain this identity."[61] While these arguments were targeted at the image of the individual self allegedly presupposed by contemporary liberalism, they are equally, if not more, applicable to the idea of a constituent people in the state of nature, or a charismatic sovereign making a foundational decision in a state of exception.[62] As a charismatic agent thrown out of temporal order, it follows, the people also cannot have any "horizon of understanding" against which they might make sense of their own choice. Having no sense of where they are situated, where they have been, or where they should be headed, the people can only make an "existential" decision. Michael Walzer's following

59 Michael J. Sandel, "The Procedural Republic and the Unencumbered Self," *Political Theory*, vol. 12, no. 1 (1984).

60 Michael J. Sandel, *Liberalism and the Limits of Justice* (Cambridge: Cambridge University Press, 1982), p. 93.

61 Charles Taylor, "Atomism" in *Philosophy and the Human Sciences: Philosophical Papers 2*, p. 209.

62 The communitarian critique of liberalism tended to be ambiguous about whether it was targeting an already liberal society composed of "atomistic" selves, or if it was a meant to criticize a theory that was based on such an unrealistic and impoverished conception of the self. Michael Walzer, "The Communitarian Critique of Liberalism," *Political Theory*, vol. 18, no. 1 (1990). By contrast, it should be clear that the invocation of the communitarian argument here is not meant as a criticism of any actual "people" living in the state of nature, as there plainly are none.

summation of Alasdair MacIntyre's derision of the liberal self seems an apposite description of the predicament faced by the unencumbered people:

> We liberals are free to choose, and we have a right to choose, but we have no criteria to govern our choices except our own wayward understanding of our wayward interests and desires. And so our choices lack the qualities of cohesion and consecutiveness. We can hardly remember what we did yesterday; we cannot with any assurance predict what we will do tomorrow. We cannot give a proper account of ourselves. We cannot sit together and tell comprehensible stories, and we recognize ourselves in the stories we read only when these are fragmented narratives, without plots, the literary equivalent of atonal music and nonrepresentational art.[63]

To be sure, constitutional founding is often said to take place during moments of "rupture" (maybe even "rapture") when historical continuity is violently disrupted. Actual drafters of constitutions may feel as though they are suspended in time, between a past that has been obliterated and a future that has yet to be called into being. According to Kim Lane Scheppele, the predicament faced by real-life constitution drafters is indeed quite analogous to the existential angst experienced by the eponymous character of the parable "He" by Franz Kafka. Taking issue with Arendt's characterization of "He" as a supremely self-assured character able to impose his judgment on an epic battle between forces of the past and the future, Scheppele argues that a proper reading of the whole text reveals a much less heroic figure. "He" is actually:

> someone who feels completely unprepared for what the present demands, someone for whom freedom is both alluring and frightening … [s]omeone who alternatively does not know who he is or what he wants, and someone who nonetheless struggles against the forces that buffet him.[64]

Scheppele then goes on to argue that this ambivalence and uncertainty plaguing Kafka's "He" is also the predicament shared by constitution drafters. "The last thing most of them feel is that they are in control of events, clear-headed about what has to be done, and sure that they are right."[65] It would appear that they have no choice but to make an existential decision, unsure of who they are or what they are deciding. Perhaps, the constituent people truly are suspended in time – "between past and future."

[63] Walzer, "Communitarian Critique of Liberalism," p. 9.

[64] Kim Lane Scheppele, "A Constitution Between Past and Future," *William and Mary Law Review*, vol. 49 (2008), p. 1393.

[65] Scheppele, "Constitution Between Past and Future," p. 1397.

Scheppele, however, also makes it clear that real-life agents of constitution-making should not be imagined as an unencumbered self dwelling in an eternal present. Her aim is actually to show that constitution-making is invariably conditioned by the past, and that constitution drafters "react most of all to what they take to be the crucial histories of their own countries."[66] A good constitution is one that is made with a keen awareness of the past. She cites the examples of the American, French, and German constitutions, all of which were made by people who, driven by the sense of their own inadequacy, turned to history for guidance and grounding. It turns out that the analogy between constitution drafters and "He" is a thin one. Unlike "He," and unlike Arendt's founders, who have no past or identity, the makers of a constitution not only are "thickly constituted" by their historical context, but also actively seek historical knowledge to carry out their task. The constituent people might be afflicted with Kafkaesque angst during the founding moment. But it can never be a timeless and nameless persona with no history or identity, or *ein Mann ohne Eigenschaften*.

In sum, analogizing the exercise of the sovereign people's constituent power on either God's creation of the world *ex nihilo* or decision-making by an existential agent is not only unrealistic but unhelpful. It fails to provide any guidance on how the actual people are to go about the historic and historical project of constitutional founding. It also provides no basis on which to ground the identity of the people or of the constitution that it makes. Therefore, it makes little sense to conceive of constitution-making as an event that suspends the normal flow of time, in which the pre-existing world is forever extinguished and a new universe created. The legitimacy of constitutional founding does not depend on the complete annihilation of the past by a "timeless" people.

Many Lives of the Past

In practice as well as in theory, it is absurd to posit such a timeless people who obliterates the pre-constitutional past. The question of the past during constitutional founding is not about its presence or absence, but about the kind of relationship that must be established toward it. The past never goes away; it is simply retold. This suggests that constitutional founding, to be properly carried out, must be a new beginning in which not everything from the past is extinguished even as the people seeks to repudiate its pre-constitutional past. It may be that the presence of the past in the constitution and into the

[66] Scheppele, "Constitution Between Past and Future," p. 1380.

post-founding period is not just unavoidable; it may even be requisite for the sustainability and legitimacy of the founding. Constitutional founding must proceed on the basis of recognition that the past is ultimately inextinguishable.[67] More importantly, it must seek to establish a proper stance toward the past and somehow incorporate that stance into the constitution. If this is the case, "then the crucial question to ask about constitutions is how they incorporate the past."[68]

A philosophical answer to this question has been suggested by Michel Rosenfeld who, drawing on Hegel and Lacan, describes this incorporation of the past as a three-stage dialectical process that culminates in the formation of a distinct narrative about constitutional identity. First is "pure negation," which involves the total rejection and repudiation of all that went before. Constitutional identity is secured through denial of everything "found within the relevant spatiotemporal framework." Second stage comes with the recognition that constitutional identity cannot be constructed in a vacuum, which leads to the search for a positive identity from among the identities that had been discarded in the first stage. This necessarily involves selective incorporation of pre-constitutional identities, by "draw[ing] upon the history, traditions, and cultural patrimony of the relevant polity." The final stage is "the negation of the negation," attained when those pre-constitutional identities are selected, combined, organized, and deployed into a coherent whole by subjecting them to "the normative constraints prescribed by constitutionalism."[69] This is when the people – or, the "constitutional subject," according to Rosenfeld – realize that their identity grounded in the constitution is one that they have constructed themselves rather than being shaped by outside forces beyond their control.

Of these three stages, it should be obvious that this last stage will probably take place over an extended period of time. Forging a coherent narrative into which elements from the pre-constitutional past are incorporated is a task not likely to be over with the promulgation of a new constitutional text. The process of formulating a constitutional identity will probably continue as long as the polity is in existence. By contrast, the first stage consisting of "pure negativity" has to be confined to an instant. It is but the conceptual point of departure for the process of negotiating the

67 "It is an illusion to think that personal identity can be abstracted from the larger historical narrative of which it is a part, and so too with constitutions." Gary J. Jacobsohn, *Constitutional Identity* (Cambridge, MA: Harvard University Press, 2010), p. 93.

68 Scheppele, "Constitution Between Past and Future," p. 1389.

69 Michel Rosenfeld, *The Identity of the Constitutional Subject: Selfhood, Citizenship, Culture, and Community* (New York: Routledge, 2010), pp. 46–9.

various pre-constitutional legacies of the past. Having repudiated the past once and for all, the constituent people must start the more nuanced and more difficult task of Rosenfeld's second stage of establishing a proper relationship toward elements selectively incorporated from the past. This is the most crucial stage when a new identity, however tentative, is articulated and encoded in the constitution, which then becomes the basis for later generations' reinterpretations and contestations. This is when the pre-constitutional past is disaggregated and its various elements are put back together into a new coherent narrative about the people's identity. A better and more refined understanding of this stage is, therefore, important for appreciating the modalities by which the past can be brought to bear on constitutional founding.

In order to elucidate Rosenfeld's second stage, we might seek some assistance from recent discussions regarding "transitional justice." For, during transitional periods, the problem of how to deal with the past tends to take center stage in political and legal discussions. In such a context, constitution-making tends to be "backward looking, proceeding from a critique of where past (or other) institutions and principles went badly wrong and taking such critiques as the negative building block of a new constitutional order."[70] Constitutional founding will be colored by and rooted in the people's attempt "to counter the abuses of power that enabled the past regime's evil."[71] Most often, the emphasis is on some form of punishment, or "lustration," of those responsible for injustice under predecessor regimes. According to Jon Elster, issues of lustration have accompanied constitutional transitions ever since ancient Athens.[72] More recently, places like South Africa adopted an innovative approach to transforming the legacies of past injustice with its "amnesty in exchange for truth" formula.[73] Regardless of the specific approach, most cases of constitutional founding include what Ruti Teitel refers to as a "critical" attitude toward the past.

[70] Scheppele, "Aspirational and Aversive Constitutionalism," p. 300.

[71] Ruti Teitel, *Transitional Justice* (Oxford: Oxford University Press, 2000), p. 202.

[72] Jon Elster, *Closing the Books: Transitional Justice in Historical Perspective* (Cambridge: Cambridge University Press, 2004).

[73] After proclaiming that "there is a need for understanding but not for vengeance, a need for reparation but not for retaliation, a need for *ubuntu* but not for victimization," the last clause of South Africa's Interim Constitution of 1993 provided: "In order to advance such reconciliation and reconstruction, amnesty shall be granted in respect of acts, omissions and offences associated with political objectives and committed in the course of the conflicts of the past." For more on that country's post-apartheid constitution-making process, see Heinz Klug, *Constituting Democracy: Law, Globalism and South Africa's Political Reconstruction* (Cambridge: Cambridge University Press, 2000).

Yet, as Teitel points out, constitutions may also be "residual" in the sense of preserving continuity with the past and even containing "features held over from the predecessor constitutional regime."[74] This is often seen as a regrettable but perhaps unavoidable feature of interim measures designed to effectuate a negotiated, piecemeal transition from authoritarian rule. From the perspective of conventional political theology, maintaining legal continuity will no doubt be seen to contradict the very idea of constitutional founding. Yet, it may be that most successful instances of constitution-making contain residual elements. As a matter of sociology, a certain minimum level of social capital needs to have been preserved from the pre-constitutional past so as to sustain a quorum of mutual trust that can underwrite negotiations and compromises necessary for constitution-making. Some sort of functioning administrative apparatus and police power are needed to facilitate the bargaining process by enhancing the enforceability and predictability of the promises exchanged. For some, maintaining legal continuity is actually integral to the success of constitutional founding. Drawing on the experiences of Spain, Eastern Europe, and South Africa, Andrew Arato argues that new constitutional orders can be successfully established without a break in legal continuity. On this view, the more important break or rupture consists in the demise of the legitimacy of the old regime and the construction of a new basis of legitimacy for the new order.[75] As long as a genuinely new order based on new sources of legitimacy is created, maintenance of legal continuity is not a problem. Indeed, for Arato, a piecemeal approach that preserves legal continuity is to be preferred because it allows for a regulated form of constitution-making without which the people are likely thrown back into the state of nature.[76]

In contrast to both critical and residual approaches, which seem to share a negative attitude toward the past, what Teitel calls "restorative" is based on a more positive evaluation of the past. This refers to cases where a new order is founded and legitimated as a "return to the pre-predecessor constitutional order."[77] As in post-communist Eastern European and Baltic states, constitution-makers may consciously opt to return, at least rhetorically, to an

[74] Teitel, *Transitional Justice*, p. 198.

[75] Andrew Arato, *Constitution Making under Occupation* (New York: Columbia University Press, 2009), pp. 5–7. He compares this to the conventional notion of revolution, which is defined by breaks in both legitimacy and legality. An example of legal discontinuity coupled with continuity in legitimacy, by contrast, may be found in the case of the Philadelphia Convention of 1787 that drafted the U.S. Constitution to replace the Articles of Confederation of 1781.

[76] Arato, *Constitution Making under Occupation*, pp. 80–4. For him, more important than maintaining legal continuity is securing "state continuity" because a new founding cannot take place unless there is a state. Ibid. pp. 53–7, 261–3.

[77] Teitel, *Transitional Justice*, p. 197.

older and more "authentic" order that existed prior to the discredited order of the immediate past. Of course, as Elster points out, politicians may adopt a restorative attitude for less than honorable reasons.[78] Nevertheless, restoration offers the benefit of avoiding the tensions that accompany efforts to launch a completely new constitutional order: "To the extent that such transitional constitutions are restorative, there are seemingly no constitutional beginnings, only returns."[79] This desire to return to an original constitution as a way of legitimizing a new one is of course an age-old trope that goes back to the Roman period.[80] The idea is that authority of the constitution will be secured only if it can be seen as a restoration or reestablishment.[81]

This suggests a more general point about the past as a source of legitimation in constitutional founding. Constitution-making often requires summoning a "useable past" that can sustain the new constitution and the identity of its people.[82] This may take the form of invocations of valiant struggles to (re) gain independence or a proud reference to particular cultural or linguistic traditions. It may be something more abstract and general as the "republican tradition" or even "rule of law." They are often culled from the more distant past, held up as more "authentic," and asked to stand in judgment of the more immediate past that needs to be rejected. In other words, while some parts of the past needs to be effaced, others must be re-inscribed into

78 "It seems that sometimes the pre-Communist constitution is invoked in defence of an idea that has no good substantive justification; sometimes it serves as a convenient focal point among a plethora of possible arrangements; and sometimes it is harnessed to a genuine need to assert the continuity of the nation's life and the parenthetical character of the Communist regime." Jon Elster, "Constitution-making in Eastern Europe: Rebuilding the Boat in the Open Sea," *Public Administration*, vol. 11, nos. 1/2 (1993), p. 193.

79 Teitel, *Transitional Justice*, p. 206.

80 Arendt, *On Revolution*, p. 198–9.

81 On this view, "even the foundation of Rome was not understood as an absolutely new beginning." It would rather be understood as "the resurgence of Troy and the re-establishment of some city-state that had existed before." Arendt, *On Revolution*, p. 211. Arendt also notes that this link between founding and restoration was underscored by Machiavelli, who essentially elided the two concepts. Successful renovation of a republic was possible only if it amounted to a whole new founding. By the same token, in order for a republic to endure over time, it had to engage in periodic renovations that returned the polity to its founding principles. From this, one might also infer that the establishment of a completely new order must take the form of a return to an earlier – perhaps even counterfactual – founding. Niccolo Machiavelli, *Discourses on Livy*, trans. Harvey Mansfield and Nathan Tarcov (Chicago: University of Chicago Press, 1996), pp. 28–30; 209–12.

82 Vicki Jackson suggests that this may be a universal phenomenon: "Without a linkage to some imagined past, constitutions could not do the work of helping to constitute a particular community." Vicki C. Jackson, "What's in a Name?: Reflections on Timing, Naming, and Constitution-making," *William and Mary Law Review*, vol. 49 (2008), p. 1280.

the new constitutional order. The balance of how these tasks are carried out will be related to the different outlooks or orientations that are embodied in the constitution.[83] Of course, neither the past to be effaced nor the past to be re-inscribed is an unmediated datum of fact. They are necessarily products of selective memory and willful amnesia. As such, they sometimes require heroic efforts to reinterpret the past so as to create a narrative that can inspire the people and legitimate the constitution. Such reconstructions are the result of a selective reading of the past that may even involve the construction of a new narrative out of whole cloth. As Rosenfeld wrote, "to establish a viable constitutional self-identity, the real must be supplemented by the ideal, or, to put it in another way, facts must be enriched by *counterfactual imagination*."[84] Events will be re-interpreted, heroes and villains re-evaluated, and traditions (re-)invented. They will be invoked to legitimate the new constitutional order. These will in turn constitute parts of the new identity of the people, which is encoded in the constitution at founding.

In sum, constitutional founding entails various modes of relating to the past. Most constitutions include more than one attitude toward the past. It would thus be a mistake to conclude that any trace of past legacies in the constitution undermines the legitimacy or the sustainability of the founding. The fact that the status quo ante has not been extinguished in its entirety should not be a cause for questioning the efficacy and legitimacy of constitutional founding. The past does not constitute an illegitimate constraint on the people's constituent power.

PEOPLE'S BOUNDARIES: "WE THE PEOPLE" UNBOUNDED

In this section, we take our previous reflections about the two syndromes to bear on the crucial question of the identity of the constituent people. By asking "Who are the people?" we intend to focus on the issue of "Who belongs to the people?" In other words, we will be asking "How is the membership boundary of the people drawn?" Particularly, what are the roles of external

83 An example might be what Gary Jacobsohn has described as the distinction between "militant" and "acquiescent" forms of constitutionalism. If the constituent people regard "effacement" as the more urgent task, the general orientation of the constitution will likely be toward active suppression and/or transformation of the past's influence on the present, resulting in a relatively more militant orientation. By contrast, if "re-inscription" is seen as more important, then the constitution will be weighted toward the restoration and preservation of selected past inheritance, leading to a more acquiescent outlook. Jacobsohn, *Constitutional Identity*, pp. 213–70.

84 Michel Rosenfeld, "The Identity of the Constitutional Subject," *Cardozo Law Review*, vol. 16 (1995), p. 1064 (emphasis in the original).

others and past legacies in the delineation of that boundary? As diverse as they are in thematic and analytical inclinations, all the theoretical literature we have visited so far seems to share the assumption that the constituent people walk into the constituent moment in an already identifiable, unmistakably delineated, and fully formed shape. Questions regarding the ontology and genealogy of the constituent people per se are typically bracketed out and relegated to the realm of a conceptual and/or historical a priori. A clearly bounded collective self called "the people" is simply taken for granted as the starting point of discussion and not put under careful scrutiny.

We believe that it is incumbent on any theory of constitutional founding to cast a suspicious eye onto the assumption that the sovereign people with a clearly legible boundary exists prior to the constituent moment. This is important not only because, as a factual matter, such a people cannot be assumed. It will also yield an impoverished theory because such an assumption will likely lead us to overlook the deeply "constitutive" aspect of constitutional founding. The constituent people, in and of itself, cannot be assumed to be the Archimedean point from which legitimacy of the new constitutional order may be evaluated. Rather, "the people," particularly its identity and boundary, must be foregrounded as a primary field of analysis, meriting both theoretical and historical investigations.

Free to Choose Who We Are?

Who ought to be included in the constituent people, and how should its boundary be drawn? We might expect some assistance from discussions by democratic theorists on the so-called boundary problem. This genre is broadly about deciding who ought to be included in the *demos* or the constituency when democratic decisions are made. The first answer to be taken off the table is a simple majoritarian rule. Joseph Schumpeter famously concluded that, since there is no objective criteria by which to set the boundary of a *demos*, we must "leave it to every *populus* to define [it]self."[85] If we follow Schumpeter, we will likely end up in a normatively unattractive position where the majority may abuse minority groups by legitimately expelling them from within the boundary of the people. Rejecting this crude majoritarian solution, contemporary democratic theories have attempted to articulate a normatively objective criterion, which usually comes in two shapes. One argues that all those individuals whose interests are "relevantly affected" by a decision ought to

85 Joseph Schumpeter, *Capitalism, Socialism, and Democracy* (New York: Harper & Bros., 1950), p. 245.

have an influence over its making. The other suggests that the boundary of the people should be expanded to include all those who will be coerced by its decisions.[86] Intuitively sensible, these formulae seem to provide some promise for deciding on the boundary of the people in a democratically acceptable manner.

When it comes to constitutional founding, however, we believe that these standard democratic answers do not provide satisfactory answers to the boundary problem. Both principles of affected interests and coercion may be deployed effectively for pushing an already established boundary of the people in a more inclusive direction, but they can hardly explain how the boundary was initially determined the way it was. For those two principles walk right into the trap of "infinite regress" that has haunted so many attempts to make sense of democratic constitutional founding. It might be thought that the democratic way to determine whose interest will be affected or coerced by a given decision is to put it to a vote. Yet, that only raises the further question of who is eligible to participate in that prior vote. Clearly, it cannot be answered through another vote, for this move only sets off an infinite logical regression from which no procedural escape is possible. Frederick Whelan, one of the main interlocutors in this genre, had it about right when he concluded that, in delineating the boundaries of a sovereign people at the constituent moment, these principles are as good as attempts "to bypass the crucial question and to propose what is a logical as well as procedural impossibility."[87] This kind of infinite regress has to be stopped somewhere, and, for many democratic theorists in the boundary problem genre, the only escape seems to be to assume the existing boundary of the people as much as they seek to criticize and deconstruct it on normative grounds.

Also favoring consent and choice as the normative ground for deciding on the people's boundaries is the common liberal sympathy for what is called "civic nation." While it comes in a variety of forms, perhaps the most ambitious is what is known as "constitutional patriotism." For, unlike its classical republican predecessor, constitutional patriotism seeks to ground patriotic attachments and an abiding sense of belonging to one's political community solely in abstract principles of reason rather than in such contingent

86 David Miller, "Democracy's Domain," *Philosophy and Public Affairs*, vol. 37, no. 3 (2009), pp. 213–24.

87 Frederick Whelan, "Prologue: Democratic Theory and the Boundary Problem," in J. Roland Pennock and John W. Chapman (eds.), *Nomos XXV: Liberal Democracy* (New York: New York University Press, 1983), p. 19. For a recent critical survey of this genre, see Sarah Song, "The boundary problem in democratic theory: why the demos should be bounded by the state," *International Theory*, vol. 4, issue 1 (2012).

and particularistic features as affects and sentiments.[88] Insofar as the people's boundaries are concerned, however, the difference is a question of more or less. For both liberals and democrats have it in common that, in the final analysis, political membership and the boundary of the people can and ought to be determined on the basis of the individual's voluntary choice. Whether it be grounded in abstract reason or affects and sentiments, individual consent remains the most crucial foundation.

Jürgen Habermas suggests, for instance, that certain universal normative principles as contained in a constitution should make the central pole of civic identity around which the peoplehood is formed. The people, in this account, is held to consist of those individuals who are rationally persuaded by the constitutional principles and have agreed to abide by them in organizing their political lives together. Further, Habermas the Kantian believes that it is the formal and procedural principles, such as symmetrical rights and mutual respect, which may elicit rational consent in an "ideal speech situation." It is precisely those procedural principles that underwrite and sustain a public sphere of rational communication, and the constitution which thus arises from this collective deliberation cannot but be the institutionalization of those principles into a set of positive law. In his own words, a constitution worthy of patriotic allegiance contains "in nuce" those principles that obtain in what Rawls would call an "original position."[89] At least on a theoretical plane, it may be taken as a promising solution to the conundrum of infinite regress since liberal rights thus understood are constitutive, rather than constrictive, of the sovereign constituent people. At the same time, more importantly for us, it becomes easier to conceptualize how the constituent people's boundaries are determined; it is formed by those individuals who gave consent to these procedural principles for collective deliberation. In short, the people and the constitution are mutually constitutive in Habermas's co-originality thesis.

Analytically satisfactory and normatively attractive as it may seem, however, Habermas's constitutional patriotism begs many questions once applied to the real world of constitution-making. For one, even if we concede that unified Germany is built around the universal liberal principles encoded in the *Grundgesetz*, yet to be explained is the brute fact that East Germany became a liberal democracy (of sorts) not by merging with, say, Czechoslovakia, but with West Germany. Conceptually speaking, in other words, even the free

[88] Patchen Markell, "Making Affect Safe for Democracy?: On 'Constitutional Patriotism,'" *Political Theory*, vol. 28, no. 1 (2000).

[89] Jürgen Habermas, *Between Facts and Norms: A Contribution to a Discourse Theory of Law and Democracy*, trans. William Rehg (Cambridge, MA: MIT Press, 1996), p. 453.

and mutual communication in the so-called ideal speech situation cannot but rely on a shared language, even cultural heritage and historical memories, all of which are pre-constitutional artifacts. It is essentially for the same reason that Dieter Grimm criticized Habermas's support for constitutionalizing the European Union.[90] According to this well-known criticism, Habermas's attempt to articulate and establish the mutually constitutive relationship between constitution-making and people-formation falls short because he is unable to dispense with a common language as a medium of communication – a commodity not yet available in Europe even after decades of integration. In other words, Habermas's linguistic turn to discourse theory of law and democracy has made it even more difficult to discard the conceptual dependence on some kind of pre-constitutional and pre-political foundations such as shared language or culture.[91] Habermas's best efforts seemed to succeed in expelling the assumption of a pre-constitutionally bounded people, only to bring it back in through the backdoor.

In sum, neither the democratic nor the liberal efforts to ground constitutional founding in choice and consent seem able to free themselves completely from positing a pre-constitutionally formed boundary of the people. When it comes to the question of constitutional founding, the democratic theories of the boundary are vulnerable to the conundrum of infinite regress. While Habermas's liberal thesis of co-originality may have avoided the logical trap, its crucial reliance on his discourse theory makes it hard to dispense with presupposing a pre-constitutional people bound by a common language. Either at conceptual or historical level, these voluntarist accounts of the people's boundary-setting seem compelled to posit some kind of constituent people existing prior to constitution-making.

Making People Out of Necessity

These shortcomings in the liberal and democratic theories about the people's boundaries often lead to the conclusion that boundary-setting is ultimately a matter of "blood and soil." For example, nationalists since the Romantic era tend to valorize a historically given cultural *ethnos* and equate it with the political *demos*. This is why popular sovereignty is so often identified with national

90 Dieter Grimm, "Does Europe Need a Constitution?" *European Law Journal*, vol. 1, no. 3 (1995).

91 This is what causes him to make such valiant efforts to affirm the existence of a civil society at the European level, despite the absence of a common language shared by all. See Jürgen Habermas, "Comments on Dieter Grimm's 'Does Europe Need a Constitution?'" *European Law Journal*, vol. 1, no. 3 (1995).

self-determination, and "We the People" with an ethnic group. Given the difficulty of pinning down the constituent people via consent and choice, flight is taken from norms and principles to the realm of what nationalists regard as brute facts of history. Yet, the call of history can never be a matter of recognizing incontrovertible and irresistible facts; histories are interpretive constructs and products of negotiation. Failure to appreciate this insight often results in that fateful substitution of the political *demos* by the cultural *ethnos*. Undeniably, this two-way process, that is, nationalization of political community and politicization of national community,[92] has been responsible for a long and well-documented list of human tragedies and unspeakable atrocities in modern times.

Yack explains this conflation by making a distinction between "the people's two bodies."[93] As with the monarchical idea of "the king's two bodies," which posited an abstract and everlasting "kingship" alongside the physical and mortal king, the principle of popular sovereignty has created an abstract and even "mysterious" being called "the people" which is superimposed on the real historical people. A uniquely modern invention, this imagined people is evidently unbounded and unbindable in and of itself. Its premodern counterparts such as *plebs* or *demos* could clearly be identified in terms of their class membership or political citizenship. By contrast, the modern people is a generic category that goes beyond all such parochial distinctions and claims to encompass everyone. This is indeed the source of their legitimacy according the doctrine of popular sovereignty that postulates a generic people that is self-sufficient and timeless. Since it is self-sufficient, the people is seen to be an agent in no need of relationship with others, and because it stands out of time, the people has no particular history that could differentiate it from others. A being that has neither relationship nor history cannot have a particular boundary.

Yack points out that this creates a paradox for understanding the people's boundaries. Although the modern doctrine of popular sovereignty asks us to imagine an unbounded people that pre-exists the establishment of the state, the only way in which we can identify a people is by reference to the territorial boundary of a given state. In other words, "it is shared subjection to a particular state's authority that distinguishes one people from another."[94] The state is supposed to be a creation of the people, who can dissolve it at

92 Bernard Yack, *Nationalism and the Moral Psychology of Community* (Chicago: University of Chicago Press, 2012), pp. 145–53.

93 Yack, *Nationalism and the Moral Psychology of Community*, pp. 101–02. For a more classical statement, see Edmund S. Morgan, *Inventing the People: The Rise of Popular Sovereignty in England and America* (New York: W. W. Norton & Co., 1988), ch. 4.

94 Yack, *Nationalism and the Moral Psychology of Community*, p. 105.

will, but the people is a set of individuals residing within the territory of a particular state more or less permanently. The people is held to come before the state, and yet it is the territorial state that defines the human boundary of the people.

Solving this paradox as such is not our immediate concern.[95] More important is its implication for conceptualizing the relationship between constituent people and constitution-making. For, if boundaries of the people can be ascertained only after the establishment of a territorial state, then the people might be constituted by the constitution as much as they author it. The people is not a pre-given entity that remains constant throughout history, much less a demiurge that stands outside history to make and remake constitutions at will. Making a constitution has the effect of calling a people into existence, whose political and legal identity is grounded in that very constitution. As Sheldon Wolin noted, "a constitution not only constitutes a structure of power and authority, it constitutes a people in a certain way. It proposes a distinctive identity and envisions a form of politicalness for individuals in their new collective capacity."[96] To be sure, recognition of this aspect of founding is nothing new. It was Hobbes who asserted, in an oft-quoted passage: "For it is the unity of the representer, not the unity of the represented, that maketh the person one."[97] He clearly perceived that it is only with the creation of the "artificial person" in whom the people vests sovereign powers, that the multitude is transformed into a people. According to Joseph Weiler, the phenomenon may be as old as the announcement of God's law by Moses to the Jewish people, through which "a bunch of pre-Torah slaves" were constituted into a free people though their acceptance of the covenant.[98] In relation to the American founding, Jacques Derrida has famously remarked: "The signature invents the signer."[99] Even Sieyès, in his less theologically inspired moments, seems to have conceded that the people can be identified only by referring to the constitutional order that they purportedly establish: "What is a nation? A body of associates living under common laws and represented by the same legislative assembly."[100]

[95] For those further interested in the so-called paradox of people and territory, see Paulina Ochoa Espejo, "People, Territory, and Legitimacy in Democratic States," *American Journal of Political Science*, vol. 58, no.2 (2014), pp. 472–3.

[96] Sheldon S. Wolin, *The Presence of the Past: Essays on the State and the Constitution* (Baltimore: Johns Hopkins University Press), p. 9.

[97] Hobbes, *Leviathan*, ch. 16.

[98] J. H. H. Weiler, *The Constitution of Europe: 'Do the New Clothes Have an Emperor?' and Other Essays on European Integration* (Cambridge: Cambridge University Press, 1999), pp. 5–6.

[99] Jacques Derrida, "Declarations of Independence," *New Political Science*, vol. 15 (1986), p. 10.

[100] Sieyès, *What is the Third Estate?*, p. 58.

Yet, it was perhaps Hans Kelsen who not only recognized this relationship between the people and its constitution but also took it to its logical extreme. He wrote: "the people – from whom the constitution claims its origin – comes to legal existence first through the constitution. It can therefore be only in a political, not in a juristic sense, that the people is the source of the constitution."[101] This is of course understandable given his "pure theory of law" according to which no exercise of "will" could ever give rise to a valid legal norm. If the people are deemed the originator of the constitution, that could only be in the rhetorical sense, as a political assertion rather than as a statement of legal science. For Kelsen, the people is at most a placeholder for the agent to whom legal norms, including the constitution, might be attributed – even that, only retroactively.[102] Although he recognizes the need for a democracy to posit the people as a unity, he states that such a unity is ultimately "an ethical-political *postulate*," which can only be secured through "the unity of the state's legal order."[103] Indeed, the only cognizance that may be given to the people within the Kelsenian system is as an element of the state (which for him is identical with the legal order), rather than as any purported creator of the legal order. The term "people" refers to "the personal sphere of validity of the national legal order," the same way that "territory" refers to the spatial sphere of the legal order.[104] That is why, "in a juristic sense," the people becomes intelligible through the constitution only after the establishment of a legal order.

Despite his insight that the people are constituted by the constitution, it would appear that Kelsen went too far. It may indeed be that the identity of the people can only be known retrospectively, but his views seem to end up eliminating the people entirely from the constitutional order, thereby rendering superfluous any notion of agency, popular or otherwise. As pointed out by Hans Lindahl, Kelsen's idea of attribution ultimately plays no role in his system, because the validity of a constitutional order in the end does not depend on any agency to which it might be attributed.[105] Rather, as is well known, for him the source of a constitution's validity lies in the postulation

[101] Hans Kelsen, *General Theory of Law and State*, trans. Anders Wedberg (New York: Russell & Russell, 1945), p. 261.

[102] Hans Kelsen, *The Pure Theory of Law*, trans. Max Knight (Berkeley: University of California Press, 1967), p. 291–2.

[103] Hans Kelsen, "On the Essence and Value of Democracy," in Jacobson and Schlink (eds.), *Weimar: Jurisprudence of Crisis*, p. 90 (emphasis in the original).

[104] Kelsen, *General Theory of Law and State*, p. 233.

[105] Hans Lindahl, "Constituent Power and Reflexive Identity," in Martin Loughlin and Neil Walker (eds.), *The Paradox of Constitutionalism: Constituent Power and Constitutional Form* (Oxford: Oxford University Press, 2007), pp. 10–12.

of *Grundnorm*, a logical-psychological presupposition that must be accepted if the normative validity of legal systems is to be secured through norms only. The constitution might be attributable to the people as a matter of political rhetoric, but the people has no role in grounding the constitution's validity or identity. In his desire to purify legal science of the contaminating influence of politics and to reject political-theological conceptions of an eternal people, Kelsen has constructed a pure system of norms in which the people have become superfluous. As a result, despite Kelsen's support for social democracy during the Weimar period, "the people" of his legal theory remains strangely passive, impotent, and utterly lacking in agency. In the hands of Kelsen and his legal positivist ilk in Weimar Germany, the people was made out of logical necessity, but no virtue was made out of it. It might not be too harsh an historical judgment to hold this utter disempowerment of the people in legal positivism accountable for its eventual capitulation to National Socialism.[106]

Theoretically, too, this is problematic because most conceptions of democratic self-government require an image of the people that has some sort of agency. However the boundaries of the "self" might be drawn, some notion of a self that is able to take action seems almost axiomatic. Take away that agency, or the idea of an active people, and it would be very difficult to explain or justify democratic self-government. Especially in relation to the constitution, the people must be somehow seen as the active agent, if not its author. The conventional way of empowering such a democratic agent is of course to posit a people with pre-given interests, identities, and boundaries, as was done by the political-theological conceptions and even some social contract theories that assumed the existence of a people in the state of nature. We have already seen, however, that constitutional founding cannot be conceived of on such assumptions. Instead, what we need is a perspective that can properly account for the fact that the people's boundaries are determined through the process of constitutional founding, while avoiding Kelsen's extreme position of denying their agency *in toto*. Put differently, it seems that we must be able to reject the viewpoint that posits a pre-constitutional people with pre-given boundaries and fully formed

106 See Sung Ho Kim, "A Constitutional Politics of the Extraordinary: Carl Schmitt, Hans Kelsen, and the 1932 Crisis of the Weimar Constitutional Order," *Korean Political Science Review*, vol. 41, no. 2 (2007); David Dyzenhaus, *Legality and Legitimacy: Carl Schmitt, Hans Kelsen, and Herman Heller in Weimar* (Oxford: Oxford University Press, 1999); Peter C. Caldwell, *Popular Sovereignty and the Crisis of German Constitutional Law: The Theory and Practice of Weimar Constitutionalism* (Durham, NC: Duke University Press, 1997).

identity, while affirming the active role of the people in constituting themselves as agents of democratic self-government.

Facio ergo sum: *We the People Make Therefore We Are the People*

Without purporting to provide a full-blown answer to this line of query, we only note here that some pointers might be taken from theories of individual self-constitution as moral agents. The suggestion is that, rather than imagine the people's identity independently of their agency as actors, it might be better to regard the two as fused with each other, such that their identity emerges through, and only insofar as, they take action. We take our cue from philosopher Christine Korsgaard who claims that an agent becomes who she is by engaging in action. Or, more precisely, the agent constitutes herself as a unified actor by the very action that she engages in.

> It is as the possessor of personal or practical identity that you are the author of your actions, and responsible for them. And yet at the same time it is in choosing your actions that you create that identity. What this means is that you constitute yourself as the author of your actions in the very act of choosing them.[107]

An agent's decision to act and her constitution of her own identity are not two different things. To take a certain action is to constitute oneself as the author of that action, which means that one's identity materializes and becomes known through that very action. To analogize this observation to constitutional founding, we might say that a people constitutes itself as the author of the constitution in the very act of making that constitution. This also appears to be the import of Hans Lindahl's rather esoteric statement that the people's "self-constitution begins as the constitution *of* a political unity through a legal order, not as the constitution of a legal order *by* a political unity."[108] The identity of the people, therefore, is not given prior to the action of deciding to be the author of the constitution. As Korsgaard points out, "there is no *you* prior to your choices and action, because your identity is in a quite literal way *constituted* by your choices and actions."[109] The identity of the constituent people is constituted by the choices and actions that go into the activity of exercising their constituent power. Depending on what kind of constitution it makes, the people may create different identities for itself.

[107] Christine M. Korsgaard, *Self-Constitution: Agency, Identity, and Integrity* (Oxford: Oxford University Press, 2009), p. 20.

[108] Lindahl, "Constituent Power and Reflexive Identity," p. 22 (emphasis in the original).

[109] Korsgaard, *Self-Constitution*, p. 19 (emphasis in the original).

On this view, we need not imagine a people with a fully formed identity prior to constitutional founding. At the same time, however, that does not require the elimination of the people as the active agent of constitutional founding. Indeed, to put it crudely, Korsgaard's central argument is that the function of human action is to constitute the agency and identity of the actor. Her starting point is the presupposition that human beings are "*condemned* to choice and action."[110] For Korsgaard, we are, essentially, what we do. Her recognition that "there is no *you* prior to your choices and action" does not lead her to conclude that there is no agent or self who could engage in the activity of constituting oneself. On the contrary, it highlights the fact that to take action is to engage in the project of self-constitution.

If this assertion seems paradoxical, her response is that it is only because of "an artificial freezing of the observer's mental frame."[111] The tendency to think that there must be an agent with fully formed identity prior to its engagement in any action arises because we mistakenly think of human agents as static entities. For Korsgaard, human beings are living things whose identity cannot be apprehended at any given "moment." To be an agent is "not a state, but rather an activity." It is therefore ludicrous to think that the identity of a person can be known at a particular point in time. To imagine a person as a static entity requires a "freezing" of our perspective, which will only provide us with an image of the person no longer engaged in any action. That, however, will be a dead person, and not a living agent. For, "to be a person, or a rational agent, is just to be engaged in the activity of constantly making yourself into a person."[112] That is why for Korsgaard the seeming paradox that you are an acting/self-constituting agent even though there is no you prior to action is not a paradox at all. Since being an agent is an activity, and since activity takes place on a temporal plane, the self-constitution of an agent "is not a state that we achieve and from which action then issues."[113]

The implication of this line of thinking for constitutional founding is, first, that the people do not first constitute themselves as an agent with clearly defined boundaries and then engage in the action of making a constitution. Rather, self-constitution as an agent and the making of a constitution are one and the same activity. The term "constitution-making" becomes a double entendre. On the one hand, it refers to the people's activity of drawing up a document called the constitution. On the other, it also refers to the process

110 Korsgaard, *Self-Constitution*, p. 1 (emphasis in the original).
111 Korsgaard, *Self-Constitution*, p. 36.
112 Korsgaard, *Self-Constitution*, p. 42.
113 Korsgaard, *Self-Constitution*, p. 44.

of constituting the identity and boundaries of the people, of determining its own "constitution." In this regard, Korsgaard would probably agree with Stephen Holmes's view that the rules contained in the constitution, rather than constraining the people's will, actually make possible the formation of that will. "No popular will worth taking seriously has a mystical preexistence; it is always the product of constitutional restraints."[114] When referring to the distinction between constitutive rules (e.g., "bishops move diagonally") and regulative rules (e.g., "no smoking"), Holmes seems quite emphatic that the constitutional framework is a form of constitutive rule that makes it possible to form any kind of will at all. "When a constituent assembly establishes a decision procedure, rather than restricting a preexisting will, it actually creates a framework in which a nation can, for the first time, have a will."[115] Drafting a constitution involves the self-constitution of the people as an agent.

Further extrapolating on this view, second, we might even derive a normative standard for judging the people's action of constituting themselves as a people via the constitution. According to Korsgaard's framework, self-constitution through action is successful when it results in integrating the different roles and parts of the person into a coherent identity, thereby yielding a unified agent. If an action is "less successful in constituting its agent," then it is a defective action; such an action is "to that extent less of an action."[116] Relying on a kind of teleological argument, she also argues that an action that does not follow certain constitutive principles of action will inevitably produce poor results. Yet, she emphasizes that the activity that yields poor results is not a different activity from the one that produces good results: "It is the same activity, badly done."[117] From the perspective of constitutional founding, a constitution will be less of a constitution if it is not so successful in constituting disparate individuals into a people as a coherent political agent. By the same token, a constitution that is made well is one that is successful in creating the conditions for integration of various individuals, or the multitude, into a unified agent – a people with settled boundaries. In fact, she states that a constitution "makes it possible for a group of citizens – who without the constitution would be a *mere*

[114] Holmes, "Precommitment," p. 234.

[115] Holmes, "Precommitment," p. 238. At other times, however, Holmes seems less than fully committed to this view. When he is discussing the idea of precommitment as a prophylactic tool against the undesirable, but inevitable, eventuality that the people might fall below its own standard of conduct, he assumes that the agent is already there before it sets up the constitution. Peter sober already exists before he becomes Peter drunk. Ulysses is already there with a very clear-cut will ("I want to hear the Sirens' song without going shipwreck and killing all of us") before he asks his crew to bind him to the mast.

[116] Korsgaard, *Self-Constitution*, p. 25.

[117] Korsgaard, *Self-Constitution*, p. 37.

heap of individual people – to function as a single collective agent."[118] If, after making the constitution, individuals continue to fight over whether a certain group of persons belongs to the people, the constitution-making activity will have been poorly performed. If the "constitutive rules" that are supposed to unify the individuals into a single agent do not operate properly, we may reasonably conclude that the founding was "done badly." It would be an instance of defective constitution-making, in both senses of the term.[119]

Particularly, if repression and violence are required to maintain a semblance of people's unity, then that would be a sure sign that the drafting of a constitution did not result in successful self-constitution of the people. For Korsgaard, relying on violence to achieve a sought-after effect would indicate that the action was not taken according to its constitutive principles, which she understands in Kantian terms as universal maxims issuing from practical reason that must be adhered to in order for the agent to be deemed autonomous. On this view, any action that does not follow such constitutive principles of practical reason will fail to constitute the actor as an autonomous and unified agent. This has profound implications for evaluating the legitimacy of constitutional founding. The suggestion is that, in order to count as an action called constitutional founding, it must be done in accordance with universal practical reason. Unless the people act on such principles, they cannot be said to be engaging in constitutional founding, and (which amounts to the same thing) they will not have constituted themselves as a unified people.[120]

Lastly, we might infer that constitutional founding, or the self-constitution of the people, cannot be captured in a moment – unless we were to freeze our mental frame. With regard to the individual agent, Korsgaard suggests that self-constitution requires constant work; it is an "endless activity."[121] For an individual agent, self-constitution is an ongoing task that will continue as long as she lives. For a people, by contrast, constitutional founding is commonly thought to be a one-time event. This may suggest the limits of analogizing the political activity of constitutional founding to the individual activity of

[118] Korsgaard, *Self-Constitution*, p. 142 (emphasis in the original). This statement appears in the context of explaining what she calls the "constitutional model" of the soul, by drawing an analogy, following Plato, between the constitution of a city and that of a person.

[119] Korsgaard, *Self-Constitution*, p. 152: "The deliberative procedures that unify the city into a single agent break down, and the city *as such* cannot act."

[120] In our view, this may provide the building blocks for formulating a theory of constitutional authority that enables us to recognize reliance on universal practical reason as a necessary requirement for truly autonomous self-rule, while avoiding reliance on the brute fact of people's authorship as the ultimate ground for the constitution's authority. Fleshing out the details of such a theory, however, is beyond the scope of this book.

[121] Korsgaard, *Self-Constitution*, p. 41.

self-constitution. Yet, it may also suggest the need to rethink our conceptions about the process of founding. For, if we are to follow the Korsgaardian perspective, a people will be an active agent only insofar as it is engaged in the endless activity of self-constitution via the constitution. While the implications of this point are too profound and numerous to pursue here,[122] it should at least be recognized that even the idea of founding cannot be comprehended as an event contained in an isolated moment in time. To be sure, later generations may arrive at some rough agreement as to when the people first successfully engaged in the action of self-constitution. Yet, even that first action must be understood as a temporally extended category that unfolds over time and cannot be completed in an instant. Self-constitution of a people cannot be consummated by merely drafting of a document called the constitution.[123] Much more is required to engage in successful action by which a people constitutes itself as an integrated agent. As a process of self-constitution, the initial founding action may even take years to be successfully carried out. In order fully to understand the process of founding that gives shape to the people's boundaries, in other words, we need to take a wider perspective that encompasses the variegated negotiations, choices, and decisions that take place before and after the drafting.

Constitutive Constitutional Politics

Evidently, unfreezing our mental frame on the relationship between the constituent people and constitutional founding has to go beyond making philosophical analogies and requires more thorough analytical scrutiny. It is indeed easier expressing than articulating the "reflexive" idea that the people and the constitution are constitutive of each other. Yet, such a paradoxical notion makes much intuitive sense, if one takes note of the historical and contemporary realities of the political process surrounding the making of constitutions.

[122] If the people can be an active agent only by ceaselessly constituting itself, it may be that the people must continually engage in constitution-making even after the founding. This suggests that we might need to relativize the difference between making a constitution and remaking, or amending, it. It might even mean that constitutional interpretation is also a form of self-constitution by the people. Alternatively, the Korsgaardian view might be invoked to justify the claim that, after the founding, the people cannot (or should not) be active in the same sense, or to the same extent, as they were during the original action of self-constitution.

[123] Recent cases have shown that even the drafting process may deliberately be extended. Referring to the different strategies of interim or incremental constitution-making adopted by "transitional" constitutions of such places as South Africa, Hungary, and Poland, Vicki Jackson has suggested that our conceptual framework be expanded to allow for a longer period of time. Jackson, "What's in a Name?," pp. 1291–2.

For, one of the most contested issues in recent real-life cases of constitutional founding involved the question: "Who shall be allowed to participate in the making of the constitution?"

Indeed, one of the lessons from recent cases of so-called post-conflict societies should be the recognition that founding a new constitutional order often goes hand in hand with the process of sorting out *for whom* the constitution will be made, or *in whose name* it will be promulgated. As long as there are continuing fights over whether certain groups are entitled a seat at the drafting table, no constitutional founding will get off the ground. And, as one commentator puts it, "determining who should be involved in constitutional negotiations presupposes a substantive judgment regarding what the boundaries of the relevant political community are."[124] At issue might be an ethnic group, a religious minority, or perhaps members of the former ruling elites who had just been ousted. In what form will the Kurds in Iraq, for example, be recognized as a partner in the historic project of making a new constitution to recreate the Iraqi state? Will ethnic Serbians regard themselves, and be accepted by others, as part of the people of Bosnia-Herzegovina? Who are the relevant Montenegrin people that have the authority to decide whether to become an independent state and draft a new constitution? Will the white minorities continue to be part of the new sovereign peoples of Zimbabwe and post-apartheid South Africa? The point is that constitution-making does not take place with the boundary of "the people" already given and taken for granted. Rather, delineation of the people's boundary is, in an important sense, the result of the constitution-making process. The identity of the people remains rather fluid until after the new constitutional order is established. After the founding, the people can be defined, following Yack, as those individuals within the territory of a certain state who submit themselves to the authority of its constitution. Prior to the founding, by contrast, it is not only difficult to specify the boundary of the people; it is even difficult to know if the people can be said to exist as a self-constituted agent. Once we let go of the political-theological dream of an all-powerful and ever-living people, it is not a paradox at all to say that, in order to ascertain the people's boundary, identity, perhaps even its very existence, we must refer to the constitution.

It bears noting that this is not limited to states that have recently come out from under authoritarian rule. As is well known, many instances of post-colonial founding after World War II, especially in parts of Africa, the

[124] Sujit Choudhry, "Old Imperial Dilemmas and the New Nation-Building: Constitutive Constitutional Politics in Multinational Polities," *Connecticut Law Review*, vol. 37 (2005), p. 944.

Middle East, and the Indian subcontinent, involved creating new boundary lines where none had existed before. A similar situation obtained in Southeast Asia where the process of granting and gaining independence was accompanied by quite artificial line-drawing motivated by political and economic calculations. Further, this phenomenon of having to sort out the people's boundary during the process of founding is not necessarily unique to multiethnic or multi-lingual states. To be sure, the problem may be more pronounced in cases where there are more than one "nations" within the state's territory.[125] The issue of the people's boundary, however, may arise even in states commonly deemed to be homogeneous. The founding of the German Reich in 1871 involved a convoluted process of political posturing and even open hostility among the various German-speaking principalities which ended with a boundary being drawn for the "German nation" that excluded a sizeable group of German speakers in Austria.[126] To take an even older example, we might say that the establishment of the French Republic required confronting the question of whether to include members of the First and Second Estates in the new order established by and for *la nation française*. Would they be represented in the constitution made by deputies of the Third Estate? Those more knowledgeable about the history of these countries will surely be able to offer more nuanced accounts of the various processes that went into defining the boundaries of the respective peoples. But the point is that the boundaries are not pre-given and they are the products of historical negotiations that take place during constitutional founding. Sujit Choudhry refers to this as "constitutive constitutional politics," and suggests that it may be conceptually differentiated from "normal" constitutional politics, which deals with the design of governmental institutions and the limits of their powers through individual rights.[127]

This distinction makes a good deal of sense when we consider the actual stages of constitutional politics. At least conceptually, we may discern two distinct stages: one concerns the initial convocation of a constitution-drafting convention, and the other the business of making and drafting the constitutional document itself. To be noted, however, is the fact that typically the

[125] To that extent, we disagree with Choudhry who states that this is a not a problem for states that are not multinational polities. Choudhry, "Old Imperial Dilemmas and the New Nation-Building," p. 937.

[126] True to his political-theological outlook, Carl Schmitt makes the improbable argument that even the founding of the German Reich in 1871 was in fact effected through the exercise of the national will of the antecedent and everlasting German people which had achieved its political unity prior to the founding. Schmitt, *Constitutional Theory*, p. 143.

[127] Choudhry, "Old Imperial Dilemmas and the New Nation-Building," p. 938.

two stages take place almost simultaneously, during which the identity and boundary of the constituent people remain ill-defined. For even if a drafting convention is formally convoked, it will not – indeed cannot – be done in the name of the people, for there is as yet no people as such who could do the convoking. The events of Philadelphia in 1787 and Paris in 1791, for example, show that the drafters could only be summoned by powers other than the sovereign constituent people. It was the Continental Congress and Louis XVI that convened what eventually became the drafting conventions. After being duly constituted, however, the Philadelphia Convention and the Estates-General severed their ties to the convoking authorities and proceeded to reconstitute themselves as representatives of the people via "bootstrapping."[128] A constitution was drafted by the convention and then subsequently attributed to the people, who in effect came into being as a result of that act of attribution and became the author of the constitution only retroactively. This recognition leads us to conclude that even if there were a pre-constitutional community that drew up a constitution, it is difficult to assume that it existed as a democratic people – a political *demos* – defined by their mutual freedom and equality. We might think that constitutional founding is a process in which the people first acquire freedom and equality through their struggle, and then make a constitution to codify and preserve those achievements. Yet, it must be admitted that, prior to the making of the constitution, the status of free and equal citizenship is at most a vague hope and a distant ideal. For such a status can only be realized within a constitutional order. According to Gary Jacobsohn, even after the founding, those ideals of freedom and equality embodied in the constitution are likely to remain a "promissory note," which may be redeemed by later generations through contestation and conflict.[129] At the time of constitutional founding, then, the free and equal people will at best be a potentiality, something that needs to be made real by and through the constitution.

Both as a clearly bounded agent wielding constituent power and as a collective of rights-bearing citizens, "We the People" cannot be said to pre-exist the constitution purportedly authored by them. This does not mean that the people, even at the stage of constitutive constitutional politics, remain merely as passive recipients of their collective identity and political and legal rights. Although not clearly bounded, nor free and equal yet, the people, or some multitude in its semblance, may take active participation in constitutional politics either directly or via their self-appointed representatives. The point,

[128] Elster, "Constitutional Bootstrapping," p. 57.
[129] Jacobsohn, *Constitutional Identity*, pp. 106, 148.

both in theory and practice, is that a new constitution determines the boundaries and identities of the people as much as it is made by the people in the course of constitutional politics. As suggested by Korsgaaard, the meaning of constitution-making is truly a double entendre – it has to encompass the self-constitution of the people as well as the creation of the constitutional universe they will inhabit.

Time, Space, and the People Bounded

What lessons might we draw from these theoretical reflections for investigating how the constituent people's boundary is actually fixed in the course of constitutional founding? First of all, defining the boundaries of the people involves dealing with the call of history, weighing and sorting out the different historical claims for drawing the line here rather than there. In some places, this will be a rather easy task, while in others it will involve adjudicating conflicting claims based on different views of what counts as "relevant" history. That is why a longer view of history is needed. It also bears emphasizing that the key political actors are always heirs to specific institutional and ideational legacies. They may take a variety of attitudes toward those legacies ("critical," "restorative," or "residual"), but they certainly cannot pretend they do not exist. Regarding the process of shaping the boundaries of the people, we should pay particular attention to past concepts, institutions, and ideologies surrounding various notions of membership. These will be the basis and the foil against which a new self-definition of the people will be formed.

The most salient among those legacies will probably be the system of making individuals "legible" to the state – the categories, the matrices, and the classification schemes utilized by the previous regime to govern the populace. Those institutions of population registration may be rejected outright, but they may also be transformed or even reinforced to give shape to the boundaries of the new people. No less important in this regard will be the election law and other procedures for deciding on the specifics of the constitution. The election law for choosing the delegates who will negotiate and draft the actual text will be critical because this will likely have the effect of pre-determining the scope of the people to be represented at the negotiating table and, by extension, the scope and boundary of the people in whose name the constitution will be promulgated. Decisions regarding the manner in which the franchise is distributed; the concrete way in which the ballot is actually cast; whether or not certain groups will be given special representation; whether or not regional identities will be given recognition; whether or not the draft constitution will be subject to review by some designated agency, and if so, how that agency will be structured – these and other questions will have to be resolved before any constitution is set in place. These issues will likely be decided in the process of enacting the election law. As Andrew Arato points out, "the *legal* identity of the sovereign people ... is determined by *prior* electoral and procedural rules that must be given to the 'people' by elites who thereby constitute them as a people capable of action."[130]

This does not mean, however, that the boundary of the people so determined by the election law will necessarily become fixed or enshrined in the constitution. In most cases, the constitution is silent about the boundary of the people.[131] This means rather that, in order to make out the contours of the people as it emerges from the process of self-constitution, we must also look at how the constitution, once promulgated, is then interpreted, implemented, contested, and even transformed. For example, subsequent enactment of key legislations such as nationality law may codify the boundary of the people that was determined during constitutive constitutional politics. But it may also provide the occasion for challenging that boundary. Judicial pronouncements regarding the standard for membership in the newly constituted people may also be of value in this connection. In short, analysis of the delineation of the people's boundaries through constitutional founding must be capacious enough to include the temporally extended nature of the process.

In the same vein, second, we need to expand our spatial perspective. This is because constitutive constitutional politics takes place, by definition, at a juncture where the line distinguishing insiders from outsiders inevitably remains porous. We have already seen that external actors may be a necessary presence during the founding. Theoretically, determining who is to be labeled an external actor is not so self-evident. Thus, we must not assume a narrow viewpoint that focuses only on the existing residents of the given territory. Residents outside the territory may have special connections – ethnic, religious, linguistic, or other – which can translate into claims either for or against their inclusion in the newly constituted people. By contrast, persons residing inside the territory, and hitherto considered part of the people, may find themselves excluded according to a new yardstick which effectively turns them into the "other" against whom the new people defines itself.[132] Sometimes, the

130 Arato, *Constitution Making Under Occupation*, p. 258 (emphasis in the original).

131 The case of Bosnia-Herzegovina seems to be the exception in that its constitution includes a pronouncement that the state is composed of three "constituent peoples," the Bosniaks, the Serbs, and the Croats. Yet, here, too, the specific boundaries (i.e., membership criteria) of those three peoples remain undefined by the constitution. See, generally, Oklopcic, "Constitutional (Re)Vision."

132 What Ulrich Preuss has described as "ethnification of politics" in post-communist Central and Eastern European states might be an example in that ideology was replaced by ethnicity as

territorial boundary of the state itself undergoes quite radical shifts which have obvious ramifications for defining the boundaries of people.

Of course, in some cases, we know exactly whom to label an outsider. Those who brokered the Dayton Agreement that produced the constitution of Bosnia-Herzegovina are outsiders, for example. They had no intention of becoming members of the people of the state they were building. The claim is not that their status as outsiders is unclear. Even if they are and will remain outsiders, however, it is important to bear in mind that such foreign powers can be quite influential in delineating the boundary of the people. Indeed, we know from the recent cases that they can be *the* most important actors during constitutive constitutional politics. The presence of "external constituent power" is no more striking than in cases where a militarily defeated or newly liberated population sets out to reconstruct the nation via new constitution-making under the tutelage of foreign occupying authorities. Through so-called constitutional imposition, the occupying authority oftentimes enmeshes itself in the process not only of instituting a new constitutional framework but also carving out a new people. Such a project will be met with varying degrees of success, for sure; it may be "done badly" due to lack of local knowledge or outright incompetence on the part of the outsiders. But the presence of external influence in the local people's boundary-setting cannot simply be avoided as a matter of empirical theory or opposed a priori on some moral grounds.

There is yet another sense in which our spatial perspective should be broadened. Aside from the foreign diplomats, negotiators, experts, and observers on the ground actively involved in the political process, external influence may come from groups or movements that have no physical presence in the territory. In his article on imposed constitutionalism in Iraq, Noah Feldman discusses what he calls the "human rights left," the "evangelical right," and the "neoconservative democracy exporters," as major sources of the argument for implanting a constitution with equal rights protection for women and with no official role for Islam.[133] The argument was one which the lead negotiator for the occupying forces had to heed, or at least take into consideration when dealing with the locals. In other words, outside actors on the scene are influenced by larger, if amorphous, forces coming from remoter places. While they may

the new criterion for membership. Ulrich K. Preuss, "The Exercise of Constituent Power in Central and Eastern Europe," in Loughlin and Walker (eds.), *The Paradox of Constitutionalism*, p. 211. See also James Johnson, "Inventing Constitutional Traditions: The Poverty of Fatalism," in John Ferejohn, Jack N. Rakove, and Jonathan Riley (eds.), *Constitutional Culture and Democratic Rule* (Cambridge: Cambridge University Press, 2001).

[133] Feldman, "Imposed Constitutionalism," pp. 865–77.

have been formulated without any relation to the country undergoing constitutional founding, they can converge on the scene to shape the geopolitical dynamics of the region, which in turn affects the way in which the boundaries of the people are determined. To be sure, broadening the scope of our view to include dynamics developing in faraway places may entail the danger of infinitely expanding the chain of causality. When done in a principled manner, however, it will help highlight the fact that the interplay between locals and outsiders during constitutive constitutional politics may be crucially shaped by forces beyond both of them. This is why we should not focus simply on the immediate time and place of the drafting.

All in all, the foregoing theoretical reflections lead us to believe that constitution-making and people-formation are mutually constitutive. No constituent people pre-exists a constitution, at least not in the clear form and unmistakable shape that the conventional dogma of popular sovereignty tends to presume. Nor is the constituent people merely a logical presupposition, an abstraction without meaningful agency and useful only for sustaining a semblance of democracy. We believe that the constituent people come into being as they are doing the constitution-making. In order to examine this process of becoming-by-doing, we believe further that the unyielding presence of external others and the unmasterable pre-constitutional past are not merely nuisances to be theoretically bracketed out or rejected in the name of robust self-determination. They should rather be taken as the primary lens through which this mutually constitutive process is unpacked and accounted for.

POPULAR SOVEREIGNTY, CONSTITUTIONAL FOUNDING, AND PEOPLE-MAKING

The modern doctrine of popular sovereignty demands that the people be the charismatic author of the constitution and the ultimate fount of its legitimacy. It is taken for granted that "We the People" is a supreme and self-sufficient agent with a stable identity that stands above the flow of time. Does this doctrine provide an adequate explanation for understanding constitutional founding? Does it have a comprehensive and coherent standard by which to evaluate the legitimacy of the constitutional order? While much ink has been spilt to answer these questions, relatively few attempts have been made to problematize the very ontology of the people itself. Does it make sense logically as well as normatively to simply assume the existence of such a people?

In our view, the idea of a self-sufficient and timeless people needs to be re-examined. Our suggestion is to conduct such an interrogation along the dimensions of time and space. Is it possible to imagine a space outside the people, and if so, what might be the relationship between the people and those who occupy that external space? Is it possible to place the people in a temporal dimension, and if so, how might its past (and future) impinge on the people's agency and identity?

Our theoretical reflections have shown that the presence of both external others and past legacies during constitutional founding not only is permissible but may even be a logical necessity. Positing a solipsistic people that has no relation to external others or to its own past only hampers our understanding of the complex process through which a constitutional order is founded. It promotes the mistaken view that the legitimacy of a constitutional order is necessarily negated or diminished by even the slightest hint of external forces or pre-constitutional pasts. Rather, it should be recognized that the presence of outsiders is a matter of gradation. It should also be recognized that the presence of the past is intrinsic to constitutional founding and may take different modalities. Otherwise, a democratic constitution-making process cannot be adequately explained nor its legitimacy comprehensively evaluated.

These recognitions are critical for unpacking the ontology of the people itself. For constituent people does not, and cannot, have a pre-existing fully formed identity or boundary prior to constitutive constitutional politics. The people's identity and boundary arise through complex negotiations during the founding process vis-à-vis external forces and past legacies. Yet, that does not mean that the nascent constituent people are sitting passively on the receiving end during this constitutive constitutional politics. The people's identity and boundary become crystallized through its own act of constitution-making. To that extent, the people is a self-constituting agent that constitutes its own identity and draws its own boundary via the process of constitutional founding. Giving due theoretical and historical recognition to this two-way dynamics will enable us to reaffirm sovereign people's democratic agency without necessarily embracing the political theology of popular sovereignty.

2

War and Peace

OVERBEARING OUTSIDERS

The influence of external agents during the process of founding cannot warrant, in and of itself, the conclusion that the constitutional order thus created lacks legitimacy. The very nature, indeed, of that politically fraught event seems to require that outsiders be present in various guises to interact with the locals and even to participate in the making of the constitution. This does not mean merely that constitution-making often has foreign-relations and international-legal dimensions, or that it cannot be understood as an insular domestic event. It means that the distinction itself between the "internal" and the "external," or between domestic and foreign, is (re)defined and clarified through the complex and formative politics of constitutional founding. As a consequence, the identity of the constitutional order, as well as that of the constituent people, cannot be comprehended independently of the influence and input of external agents present during constitutional founding. Too often, a democratic constitution itself bears the mark of such external powers – a "birthmark," as it were, of the constituent people.

It seems to be the case, then, that the identity and legitimacy of a democratic constitution can hardly be accounted for in purely democratic terms, that is, as an autonomous self-determination of "We the People." In order to solve this conundrum, Rousseau famously conjured up a deus ex machina called the "lawgiver." For Rousseau, this conceptual contraption was necessary in part because impartiality could not be expected among people who were not yet republican citizens. Impartiality of viewpoint is crucial in order for individuals to align their partial will and interests with the public reason and common good, that is, to make the aggregate will coincide with the "general will." Left to their own devices, they will be "a blind multitude, which often does not know what it wills because it rarely knows what is good for it."[1] It is for want of reason and will at the founding moment that an all-seeing yet impartial lawgiver had to be imported from abroad as a matter of logic. In Rousseau's republican account, the foreign impact and influences seem to comprise both unavoidable and necessary elements in the constitutional founding of a democratic polity. Such an external agent, further, not only sets up the institutional foundation for local self-rule, but also, in so doing, molds the self-governing people as such. The ideal of republican liberty might even justify foreign imposition to jumpstart a republic.

Logically speaking, to be sure, Rousseau's foreign lawgiver has to make a hasty exit after founding; he or she who "gives the republic its constitution has no place in its constitution."[2] A foreign lawgiver has to be a kind of demiurge in naturalistic deism who creates a self-regulating universe that requires no further intervention, for continuing intervention by the lawgiver is contradictory to the very ideal of self-government. But, in another sense, the foreign demiurge never disappears from the constitutional universe it creates. The foreignness at the constituent moment is preserved in the founding myth over the meaning of which the subsequent generations would struggle. Either for or against the foreign lawgiver, this kind of agonistic politics fuels the post-founding democracy, thereby maintaining a dynamic self-rule by the people. From this perspective, the foreign lawgiver never quits. The constitution imposed by the foreign lawgiver is constantly negotiated over by the people themselves in the course of which a new set of legitimacy and identity slowly emerges. Constitutional identity is never determined once and for all at the constituent moment. Nor can the question of constitutional legitimacy be answered conclusively in terms of whether external forces were "present at the creation."

In the case of postwar Japan and postcolonial Korea, the external forces that influenced the constitutional founding of their respective democracies all had origins in the two global wars of the twentieth century. The constitutions of Japan and Korea were both written during the short span of time between the end of World War II and the commencement of the Cold War. In both wars, the United States was the hegemonic player, and to that extent, constitutional founding in both countries was over-determined by U.S. interests and policy choices in East Asia. Still yet, the difference was also remarkable. Whereas Japan's new constitutional order was initially made with a view to bringing World War II to a full close, Korea's was created primarily in the context of

[1] Rousseau, *Social Contract*, p. 68.
[2] Rousseau, *Social Contract*, p. 69.

gearing up for the emerging Cold War. This meant that for Japan, the birthmark left by external influence would be the provision on renunciation of war and permanent disarmament, namely, Article 9. For Korea, the birthmark would be found in those economic provisions that prepared the country for Cold War competition with communism, namely, Chapter VI and related articles.

These were, for sure, not the result of unilateral intervention on the part of the United States. First of all, external influence comes in many different shapes. It may appear in the form of outright imposition of specific provisions, or it may consist of gentle suggestions or inducements to adopt certain principles. In some cases, understanding these influences requires focusing on the agency of a single person or group. In others, it calls for understanding the more diffuse way in which certain legal foundations and political infrastructure are preset so that they remain sticky during the constitution-making process later. The Japanese case was closer to the former, as the whole process of constitutional revision was initiated and overseen by General Douglas MacArthur in his capacity as Supreme Commander for the Allied Powers (SCAP). The Korean experience was perhaps closer to the latter, as the three-year rule by the United States Army Military Government in Korea (USAMGIK) had already set the basic template for many provisions included in the constitution. The external influence in the Korean case was also diffuse in the sense that the United States was not the only external agent involved. Political competition with the emerging communist regime in the north was another major factor that left a lasting imprint on the constitutional order. To the extent that the legal authorization for making the Korean constitution came from the United Nations (UN), we might even say that the international community had a part in shaping its constitutional order.

Constitutional birthmark, second, is the result of a series of complex interactions and negotiations between external influence and local actors. In response to the many forms of external influence, local actors may take a variety of stances ranging from compliance and cooperation, to objection and opposition, to sabotage and subterfuge. These interactions and negotiations tend to take place over an extended period of time, which is why constitutional founding can rarely be understood by focusing on a particular "moment," such as the drafting of the constitution. Critical as it is, the drafting of specific provisions is merely the first step in constitutional founding. The drafting is often closely followed by events and interpretations that may challenge the relevance and viability of those provisions. The post-drafting stage in which political actors, both local and external, scramble to reach an initial settlement is therefore equally, if not more, important to an informed understanding of constitutional founding.

For both Japan and Korea, the post-drafting challenge came with the outbreak of the Korean War, the first "hot war" of the Cold War era. This turn of events stretched the meaning of the "peace provision" in Japan, especially with the United States explicitly demanding rearmament. In Korea, it put to the test the relevance and viability of the constitution's provisions on the economic order. In both cases, the original constitutional birthmark left by external influence was re-thought, re-characterized, and reinterpreted so as to find a way to adjust the constitutional norm to the new realities that the deepening Cold War had wrought. The adjustment produced a constitutional settlement that would condition the manner and course of subsequent political and economic developments in each country. At the same time, the adjustment between norm and reality meant that the constitutional identities of postwar Japan and postcolonial Korea would continue to be characterized by a discourse on whether or not the constitution's original mandate had been betrayed by later generations and on the supposed need to return to it. The birthmark created through interaction with external agents continues to be the focal point of constitutional identity in both Japan and Korea.

JAPAN'S FAREWELL TO ARMS

As seen in the popular shorthand "Peace Constitution," Article 9 is emblematic of the postwar Japan's constitutional order and its profoundly unsettled nature. Having never been revised despite persistent challenges for nearly seven decades, it has successfully withstood the test of time, providing the most enduring platform for the postwar constitutional identity of Japan.[3] Its Peace Constitution notwithstanding, however, Japan has come to have one of the world's largest militaries, making Article 9 seem all but irrelevant as a living constitutional norm. So contested and yet so enduring, so emblematic and yet so dislodged from reality, Article 9 is a paradigmatic case that most clearly discloses the deeply unsettled nature of postwar Japan's constitutional identity. More to the point, it is in the making of this article that the impact, even "imposition," from outside was most undeniably at work.

Article 9 consists of three prohibitions – no war, no armed forces, and no right of belligerency.[4] Straightforward as these mandates may sound, however,

3 Pacifism entrenched in the Japanese constitution also consists of Article 66 (that cabinet ministers "must be civilians") and parts of the Preamble where a "right to live in peace" is declared.

4 As such, it reads in full: "(1) Aspiring sincerely to an international peace based on justice and order, the Japanese people forever renounce war as a sovereign right of the nation and the threat or use of force as means of settling international disputes. (2) In order to accomplish the aim of the preceding paragraph, land, sea, and air forces, as well as other war potential, will never be maintained. The right of belligerency of the state will not be recognized."

the meaning of "peace" in Article 9 has been debated ever since it went into effect in May 1947. Calling the article simply a "no-war" provision, on account of its first paragraph, conveys neither its novelty nor full gravity. To renounce war "as an instrument of national policy" was already an international legal convention by the time the Kellogg-Briand Pact was signed by Japan along with fifteen other nations in 1928.[5] Following the Pact, the constitutions of Spain (1931), the Philippines (1935), Burma (1947), and Italy (1947) had outlawed war, and so did the newly-minted United Nations Charter (1945). What makes it truly unprecedented was rather its second paragraph prohibiting the establishment and maintenance of armed forces. For it is herein that the sovereign right of self-defense, which even the UN Charter recognizes as a universal right, is proactively forsaken.

What makes it novel, of course, makes it controvertible. Over the years, controversies have revolved around three general issues: scope of the outlawry of war, level of (dis)armament, and the right of collective security or "armed alliance." The Japanese government's original interpretation, as expressed during the ratification process in 1946, was both absolute and categorical on all three accounts. According to this early position, even though the first paragraph does not explicitly renounce the inherent right of self-defense, the second paragraph forsaking any armament and right of belligerency makes it all but impossible to wage any war, either for individual or collective self-defense. After the Self-Defense Forces was created in 1954, in sharp contrast, the Japanese government altered its interpretation to sanction the maintenance of the "minimum necessary force" for self-defensive purposes. Naturally, such a radical departure from the original interpretation was bound to provoke controversies in postwar Japan.[6]

5 In point of fact, the Tokyo War Tribunal hinged in part on "the crime against peace," which meant the violation of the Pact by the Japanese war leaders. Theodore McNelly, *The Origins of Japan's Democratic Constitution* (Lanham, MD: University Press of America, 2000), p. 148.

6 According to this drastic departure from the original interpretation, first, it is the "threat or use of force," but not the "sovereign right of the nation," that is prohibited in the first paragraph. Arguably, this interpretation is supported by the international convention that recognizes such a right established under the Kellogg-Briand Pact (Article 1) and the UN Charter (Article 2, Section 4). For domestic sources, the aforementioned Article 66, Paragraph 2 is also invoked, which may be interpreted as presupposing some kind of military establishment. Second, since the sovereign right of self-defense is not prohibited in the first paragraph, the disarmament clause in the second paragraph means that "minimum necessary force" may be maintained for self-defensive purposes and that the use of such force is different from exercise of the "right of belligerency." In the authoritative interpretation of the Cabinet Legislation Bureau, for sure, the disarmament mandate bars Japan from acquiring "modern war potentials," meaning military capabilities for offensive actions including nuclear weapons. Even so, it merely sets the ceiling for the armament that Japan may have, and the level of armament within this limit

Making this debate even more heated is the relentless allegation that Article 9 was a victors' punitive measure imposed on helpless, vanquished Japan after World War II. That Japan's postwar constitution is still commonly referred to as the "MacArthur Constitution" is indicative of the pervasiveness of this perception in Japanese society. The charge is, in short, that its origin is not based on the democratic self-determination of the Japanese people. Without delving into the emotion-rousing and hair-splitting debates among the Japanese scholars, politicians, and general public, suffice it to note that the meaning of Article 9 was not set in stone to begin with and still remains far from settled. In this light, it is not at all surprising that Article 9 was at the epicenter of tectonic realignments in both international ("San Francisco System") and domestic ("1955 System") politics of postwar Japan. Now that both systems are in disarray following the end of the Cold War, also unsurprising is the latest development in which Article 9, especially its genesis, has emerged again to haunt Japanese democracy. Understanding how it came to emblematize Japan's constitutional identity thus requires revisiting its original legislative process as well as the ironic twists of subsequent events prompted by the onset of the Cold War and Japan's reaction to it.

Bootstrapping Peace: MacArthur as Foreign Lawgiver

Dubbed the "greatest mystery" in Japan's constitution-making process,[7] the origin of Article 9 is still debated. This ongoing controversy is surprising since the accounts given by both Douglas MacArthur and Shidehara Kijurō, then-Prime Minister of occupied Japan, are unambiguous and fairly

is deemed a matter of policy decision. A distinct yet related issue is, third, whether a foreign ally's military presence on Japanese soil is a part of armed forces prohibited under the second paragraph. "Armed alliance" is held constitutional on the ground that foreign military presence is exempt from the prohibition. In this regard, even thornier than the foreign military presence in Japan is the alleged right of "collective" self-defense. That is, whether Japan is permitted, under an armed alliance or as a UN member, to engage in military action that does not immediately concern Japan's security. On this issue, the Japanese government has long maintained that exercising the right of collective self-defense exceeds the "minimum necessary" level for self-defense. In July 2014, however, a controversial cabinet decision reversed this interpretation to permit such a right under certain conditions. See, generally, Shigenori Matsui, *The Constitution of Japan: A Contextual Analysis* (Oxford: Hart Publishing, 2011), pp. 233–56 and Curtis J. Milhaupt, J. Mark Ramseyer, and Mark D. West, *The Japanese Legal System: Cases, Codes, and Commentary* (New York: Foundation Press, 2006), pp. 205–07. For the latest reinterpretation regarding the collective self-defensive right, see "Cabinet Decision on Development of Seamless Security Legislation to Ensure Japan's Survival and Protect Its People, July 1 2014 (Provisional Translation)," available at http://japan.kantei.go.jp/96_abe/decisions/2014/__icsFiles/afieldfile/2014/07/03/anpohosei_eng.pdf.

7 RM286. Kades memoir (1984) Takemae Eiji. RM286.2.SP32.

consistent. According to their account, the idea for constitutionalizing pacifism was first raised by Shidehara and enthusiastically endorsed by MacArthur during their historic meeting on 24 January 1946. In addition to the fresh memory of the war that had just ended in total devastation, so the story goes, Shidehara was inspired by the international legal convention already established in the Kellogg-Briand Pact. Long regarded as a rare dove in imperial Japan, this consummate Anglophile had been a leading advocate for joining the pact, against vehement opposition from the militarists. According to their own testimony, then, Article 9 reflects less a unilateral imposition than a collaboration between the Japanese and occupation authorities.[8] According to Miyazawa Toshiyoshi, a constitutional scholar who was himself intimately involved in the constitution-making process, Article 9 was a "joint venture" (*gassaku*).[9]

This seemingly authoritative account is, however, sharply contested on both sides of the Pacific, prompting some skeptics to go so far as calling it an "after-the-fact fabrication" or even a "barefaced lie."[10] According to this skepticism, Shidehara's suggestion at the fateful meeting was never for a *unilateral* renunciation but a general aspiration for peace.[11] Even the Kellogg-Briand Pact, the alleged source of inspiration for Shidehara, was a far cry from what eventually became Article 9 since the pact only prescribed *mutual* renunciation of war and contained no provision for one-sided disarmament. In fact, the Shidehara cabinet's own constitutional draft of January 1946, submitted to SCAP's General Headquarters (GHQ) on 8 February, provided for a military establishment and did not show any hint of outlawry of war, let alone disarmament. Quite the contrary, when the cabinet was presented on 19 February with the draft constitution handed down by GHQ/SCAP, the majority of the ministers including Shidehara himself vehemently criticized it as unacceptable.[12] Yoshida Shigeru, Shidehara's foreign minister at the time, would later testify that "this [story of Shidehara's initiative] too was something that was added at

[8] Ashibe Nobuyoshi, *Kenpō* [Constitutional Law], 5th ed., rev. Takahashi Kazuyuki (Tokyo: Iwanami Shoten, 2011), p. 55; Nonaka Toshihiko et al., *Kenpō* [Constitutional Law], vol. I, 4th ed. (Tokyo: Yūhikaku, 2006), p. 149.

[9] Miyazawa Toshiyoshi, *Kenpō Kōwa* [Lectures on Constitutional Law] (Tokyo: Iwanami Shoten, 1967), p. 201.

[10] Masumi Junnosuke, *Postwar Politics in Japan, 1945–1955*, trans., Lonny E. Carlile (Berkeley: University of California Press, 1985), p. 63; Kitaoka Shin'ichi, "*Kenpō to Nihon no Seiji*" [Constitution and Japanese Politics], p. 8., available at http://jfn.josuikai.net/josuikai/21f/main53-6.htm.

[11] McNelly, *Origins*, p. 107.

[12] Koseki Shōichi, *Nihonkoku Kenpō no Tanjō* [The Birth of Japan's Constitution] (Tokyo: Iwanami Shoten, 2009), pp. 160–1.

MacArthur's suggestion."[13] The veneer of collaboration was, in other words, as imposed as Article 9 itself was.[14]

As recent scholarship has demonstrated, indeed, it was more likely an imposition. After his cabinet endorsed the GHQ draft on 22 February 1946, Shidehara is reported to have sent off the tearful ministers with the following parting words: "today, we cannot do anything but act from our judgment of the whole situation."[15] Overbearing imposition and resentful capitulation as it was, however, the skeptics' account seems too narrowly focused on the events of the time without giving due attention to the "whole situation" as Shidehara put it. For, if Article 9 was imposed and the Shidehara cabinet could not do anything about it, it was mostly because both SCAP and Japanese leaders wanted to save Hirohito in person as well as the emperor system itself. In fact, this goal was even more important for the Japanese leaders whose overriding preoccupation, despite "unconditional surrender," was "preservation of the national polity" (*kokutai no goji*). From this perspective of the "whole situation," Article 9 may be more properly described as a result of "tacit agreement" (*anmoku no itchi*),[16] if not an outright "joint venture," between the occupation authorities and the Japanese government.

At the time constitutional revision was being pushed in earnest, Hirohito, and the emperor system itself, was in an utterly precarious situation. The Potsdam Declaration had already made it clear that wartime leaders were to be indicted as war criminals (Article 10), and there could be no denying that Hirohito was responsible for the atrocities committed in his name. The Tokyo War Crimes Tribunal was looming large on the horizon; on 12 January

[13] Yoshida's "Statement to the Constitutional Investigation Committee" (18 Dec. 1957) quoted in Masumi, *Postwar Politics*, p. 65. Matsumoto Jōji, too, who as minister of state had been the main author of the cabinet's draft that was summarily rejected by GHQ, is adamant that Article 9 had been forced on them. "The abolition of the Japanese military was MacArthur's idea from the start, and against this we put up considerable resistance. For him to say that he acted because we wished to abolish the military is like putting the cart before the horse, and a serious mistake." RM213. Matsumoto on drafting the Constitution. RM213.SP2.P15.

[14] Arguably, both MacArthur and Shidehara had good political reason to cover up the true nature of their exchange, i.e., imposition. The latter would have wished to protect the legitimacy of the new constitutional draft soon to be promulgated in his cabinet's name. The former would have wished to dodge responsibility for Japanese disarmament which was soon perceived as a policy blunder in the early days of the Cold War. McNelly, *Origins*, pp. 105–28.

[15] RM216. Account of Cabinet meetings (5–6 Mar. 1946) Ashida diary. RM216.1.P19. Cf. Shirasu Jiro, Yoshida's confidant and the cabinet liaison officer seconded to GHQ, who was intimately involved in the constitution-making process, echoed the Japanese sentiments behind this high-political drama: "Thus, the draft Constitution, reeking of defeat, was born. Unable to contain my feelings of rage, I secretly wept." Quoted in Masumi, *Postwar Politics*, p. 66.

[16] The expression comes from Miyazawa's successor at Tokyo University, Kobayashi Naoki in his *Kenpō Daikyūjō* [Constitution Article 9] (Tokyo: Iwanami Shinsho, 1982), p. 35.

1946, Australia had already submitted an indictment list in which Hirohito's name was included. Under these hostile circumstances, saving Hirohito was no easy task even for SCAP, and this all-too-reasonable demand for punitive justice had to be heeded in one form or another. In order to carry through with his policy of shielding and using the emperor for the occupation, then, MacArthur needed to offer a plausible deal that would be acceptable to both the Allies and the Japanese. His answer was to constitutionalize unarmed pacifism as a trade-off for saving Hirohito. To draw from one Japanese constitutional scholar, Article 9 was meant to be a "lightning rod" (*hiraishin*) devised to protect Hirohito and the imperial throne.[17]

The appointment of MacArthur as SCAP, in this context, was truly a godsend for Japan. For, even before setting foot on the Japanese soil, the general had already made up his mind to keep Hirohito on his throne.[18] Practically speaking, saving Hirohito was expected to ensure a more efficient implementation of the occupation policies. Japanese compliance with the occupation was crucial for the United States, which was increasingly pinched between the domestic need for early demobilization of its wartime economy and the continuing occupation of Germany under direct Allied military rule. Under the circumstances, Japan's occupation had to be as low-cost as possible, and the emperor's cooperation seemed to be the key to Japanese compliance.[19] Thus arose the need and decision to save the emperor, which became the cornerstone of occupation policy.

This fateful decision, however, was not based on any clear directives from Washington or elsewhere. In light of the Allied chain of authorities, especially, MacArthur's initiative can only be described as boldly preemptive. Established at the Moscow Conference of Foreign Ministers in late December 1945, the Far Eastern Commission (FEC) was to be the highest

[17] Takahashi Kazuyuki, *Rikkenshugi to Nihonkoku Kenpō* [Constitutionalism and the Constitution of Japan], 3rd ed. (Tokyo: Yūhikaku, 2013), p. 51.

[18] MacArthur was influenced by his longtime confidant and propaganda specialist Brigadier General Bonner F. Fellers who, in a pre-surrender report, had recommended driving a "wedge" between Hirohito and the "Tokyo gangster militarists" so as to portray the former as a figurehead and a moderate inclined toward peace who had been willfully and tragically misled by the latter. Given the Japanese worship of their emperor, Fellers argued, the emperor could even be "made a force for good and peace" if only he could be divorced from the militarists. John W. Dower, *Embracing Defeat: Japan in the Wake of World War II* (New York: Norton, 1999), pp. 280–6. For Fellers' own views, see RM038. On preserving the Emperor (2 Oct. 1945) General Bonner Fellers.

[19] Sayuri Guthrie-Shimizu, "Japan, the United States, and the Cold War, 1945–1960," in Melvin P. Leffler and Odd Arne Westad (eds.), *The Cambridge History of the Cold War, Vol. 1: Origins* (Cambridge: Cambridge University Press, 2010), pp. 247–8.

decision-making body in matters of Japan's political reconstruction, including "fundamental changes in the Japanese constitutional structure."[20] Generally more hostile to the emperor and expected to favor more radical, even punitive, reform measures than SCAP was willing to accept, the thirteen-member FEC, including the Soviet Union, was scheduled to begin operating by 25 February 1946. More importantly, its authority could in theory override that of SCAP, and he knew it all too well.[21] MacArthur himself acknowledged, just days before he ordered the drafting of a constitution, that constitutional reform had been taken out of his hands by the Moscow Agreement. The Japanese government, originally entrusted with the task of constitutional revision, was working under the misguided assumption that only cosmetic changes to the Imperial Constitution were necessary to fulfill the requirements of the Potsdam Declaration. Given that this was very likely to provoke severe punitive responses from the FEC, MacArthur seems to have decided that swift action was called for if the emperor was to be protected and the imperial system preserved.[22] In one way or another, a dramatically new constitution had to be insisted on Japan, and it had to be done before the activation of FEC, while there was still some murkiness regarding the precise locus of authority over constitutional revision. In terms of constituent authority, in short, MacArthur's initiative was a clear example of constitutional "bootstrapping."[23]

[20] "Agreement of Foreign Ministers at Moscow on Establishing Far Easter Commission and Allied Council for Japan (27 Dec. 1945)," Paragraph B, Section 6, in *Political Reorientation of Japan, September 1945 to September 1948: Report of Government Section, Supreme Commander for the Allied Powers*, vol. 2 (Washington, DC: U.S. Government Printing Office, 1949), p. 422 [hereafter *PRJ*].

[21] On 1 February 1946, GHQ submitted a memorandum to MacArthur in response to the latter's query, which explored the legal grounds for his authority on constitutional matters. The memo asserted that SCAP had "the same authority with reference to constitutional reform as [he has] with reference to any other matter of substance in the occupation and control of Japan." MacArthur had sweeping discretionary powers in occupied Japan, in other words, and GHQ confirmed the same over matters of constitutional reform. The memo concluded, however, that SCAP's allegedly "unrestricted authority" was soon to be legally subject to FEC's scrutiny when that body came into operation. MacArthur was clearly aware that he was stretching his authority on constitutional matters. RM140. Authority to proceed with revision (1 Feb. 1946) Whitney to MacArthur. RM140.6.P1. (Paragraph 6).

[22] MacArthur is reported to have said that constitution-making was "probably the single most important accomplishment of the occupation.... I am certain that it would never have been accomplished had the occupation been dependent upon the deliberations of the Far Eastern Commission – with the Soviet power of veto." Quoted in Justin Williams, Sr., *Japan's Political Revolution under MacArthur: A Participant's Account* (Athens: University of Georgia Press, 1979), p. 105.

[23] Elster, "Constitutional Bootstrapping," p. 57.

Vis-à-vis Washington, too, SCAP's decision to write a constitution in early February 1946 may be described as "bootstrapping" because no clear policy directives had been issued regarding the military. To be sure, the Potsdam Declaration did require demilitarization and the dismantling of Japan's war-capabilities, but nowhere did it unambiguously call for a *permanent* renunciation of war.[24] The most important directive from Washington during the early stages of occupation seemed to presuppose Japanese rearmament when it emphasized that the emperor, even if preserved, should be stripped of all power and authority over military matters.[25] Also lacking was a clear policy on the fate of Hirohito or the imperial institution, although the general outlook was not necessarily amenable to their preservation.[26] The same directive in fact seemed to suggest that the Japanese people, free though they were in choosing their ultimate form of government, "should be encouraged to abolish the Emperor institution."[27] Washington's initial position was arguably closer to retaining the military instead of the emperor system.[28] In the absence of either a clear chain of authority or policy directives, MacArthur's preemptive decision to trade the military for the emperor was a clear case of bootstrapping.

Thus intended to insulate the emperor, Article 9 had to be drafted in a way that would convince the international community that the Japanese military would be discarded once and for all. This meant that it had to be couched in the universal terms of international law, but at the same time had to go beyond the conventional ban on war as provided for in the Kellogg-Briand Pact or even the UN Charter. Short of such radical measures, preservation of neither Hirohito nor the emperor system would be agreeable to the international community, particularly to the members of the FEC. Thus, while closely following the language of international law, the final outcome was to constitutionalize unilateral and unconditional disarmament (pace Kellogg-Briand) as well as to forsake even the sovereign right of self-defense (pace UN Charter).

[24] Dale M. Hellegers, *We, the Japanese People: World War II and the Origins of the Japanese Constitution*, vol. 2 (Stanford, CA: Stanford University Press, 2001), p. 505–06.

[25] RM056. Reform of Japanese government (SWNCC 228) (early Jan. 1946) SWNCC.

[26] According to one author, "it took months for the State-War-Navy Coordinating Committee to segregate the different components of the problem, let alone develop specific answers. By the time they finished, MacArthur's extemporization had preempted the issue, and SCAP had replaced SWNCC as the arbiter of policy toward the Throne." Hellegers, *We, the Japanese People*, vol. 1, p. 225.

[27] RM056. SWNCC 228. RM056.P4.D. (Art 4-d).

[28] Itō Narihiko, *Monogatari Nihonkoku Kenpō Daikyūjō: Sensō to Guntai no nai Sekai e* [A Story of Article 9 of the Japanese Constitution: Toward a World without War and Military] (Tokyo: Kage Shobō, 2001), p. 36.

These two unprecedented elements of constitutional pacifism made their first appearance in the so-called MacArthur Notes, a basic guideline for the new constitution written by SCAP himself and given to his staff in the Government Section of GHQ on 3 February 1946. In all, the much-fabled Notes laid down three fundamental principles: retention of the emperor system, renunciation of war, and the abolition of feudal elements in Japanese society. The third principle was not entirely novel, since it was merely a rehashing of the Potsdam Declaration Article 10 (demanding an overall democratization) that was already being implemented in occupied Japan. Not a natural extension of early occupation policies, by contrast, the first and second principles were an outcome of SCAP's bootstrapping and clearly show that the emperor and the military issues were conceived in tandem. Thus, after clearly stipulating in Item 1 that the "emperor is at the head of the state," MacArthur Notes provided in Item 2:

> War as a sovereign right of the nation is abolished. Japan renounces it as an instrumentality for settling its disputes and even for preserving its own security. It relies upon the higher ideals which are now stirring the world for its defense and its protection. No Japanese Army, Navy or Air Force will ever be authorized and no rights of belligerency will ever be conferred upon any Japanese force.

This general principle was made into a constitutional provision by a team of twenty-four military and civilian members assembled in the Government Section under the supervision of Colonel Charles Kades. Initially, the renunciation of war and the prohibition of armed forces were incorporated into the draft constitution as part of its preamble. At the behest of Supreme Commander himself, however, it was moved to the main body of the text as Article 8 of the GHQ draft.[29] It would not do to include it as a mere political declaration; it had to be codified as a legal provision with binding force. Further, given its significance, it was originally positioned at the head of the constitution as Chapter I. In the end, it was made Chapter II so as to place articles on the emperor in Chapter I, out of "deference to the Emperor and his place in the hearts of the Japanese people."[30] Even so, in the words of General Courtney Whitney, SCAP's right-hand man and the powerful Government Section chief, "[t]he renunciation of war should not be buried amongst the enunciation of other principles; rather, it must be stated boldly in order to

[29] Yamamuro, *Kenpō Kyūjō*, pp. 253–4.

[30] RM203. Matsumoto Jōji and Yoshida Shigeru meet with SCAP: GS (22 Feb. 1946) SCAP: GS transcript. RM203.4.SP7.P1.

serve its full purpose."[31] Its "full purpose" was evidently to assure the international community in order to protect the emperor.

In rendering such novel and radical pacifism into a binding legal code, Kades initially relied on the language of the Kellogg-Briand Pact with the recently drafted UN Charter in mind. They were a natural choice of reference. Not only was the Kellogg-Briand Pact the best-known example of legally entrenched pacifism until then, but also the new vision of international security underlying the UN system had been specifically referenced by both MacArthur and Whitney.[32] This emphasis on international laws shows that the intended addressee of the peace provision was as much the international community as the Japanese themselves. For instance, these were the words with which MacArthur would personally explain Article 8 of the GHQ draft to Shidehara during their meeting on 21 February:

> We have cut out all the provisions concerning an army for the following reasons: We think the Japanese government should at this moment think of the opinion of foreign countries instead of opinions at home. If the provisions concerning an army are kept, what will other countries say? They will certainly think that Japan is aiming at rearmament.[33]

By locking international legal norms into a constitutional provision, in other words, Article 9 was to be Japan's "precommitment" to the world that it would never pose a threat to world peace again.[34]

While the contents of the peace provision were spelled out in the universal language of international law, however, they did not coincide exactly with international legal norms on the prohibition of war. Unlike the Kellogg-Briand Pact, which only outlawed "war for the solution of international controversies" (Article 1), Article 9 went beyond that and banned even "the threat or use of

31 These were the words with which Whitney explained the peace provision to the representatives of the Japanese government on 13 February 1946. The statement is followed by the importance of international audience: "General MacArthur feels that this principle will do more to attract the favorable attention of the world than anything else." RM203. Matsumoto and Yoshida meet with SCAP. RM203.4.SP2.P1.

32 SCAP's language in his second item, i.e., "the highest ideas which are now stirring the world," was unmistakably referring to the United Nations. In the same vein, Whitney emphasized at the first Government Section meeting on 4 February 1946 that: "[n]o explicit mention need be made of the United Nations Charter, but the principles of the Charter should be implicit in our thinking as we draft the Constitution." RM143. Whitney commissions GS (4 Feb. 1946) SCAP GS minutes. RM143.1.2.P4.

33 RM200. Shidehara reports to Cabinet on meeting with MacArthur (21 Feb. 1946) Ashida diary. RM200.P1.Q2.P4.

34 Craig Martin, "Binding the Dogs of War: Japan and the Constitutionalizing of JUS AD BELLUM," *University of Pennsylvania Journal of International Law*, vol. 30, no. 1 (2008), p. 296.

force" as a means of settling international disputes. This phrase likely came from the UN Charter, according to which member states must refrain from "the threat or use of force against the territorial integrity or political independence of any state" (Article 2, Section 4). Yet, whereas the Charter pledged only to "refrain from" the threat or use of force, Article 9 declared that it was "forever renounced." In its second paragraph, Article 9 further renounced the maintenance of armed forces and the right of belligerency, thereby making even an individual, not to mention collective, self-defense hardly viable. It bears noting that the right of self-defense was never renounced by the Kellogg-Briand Pact, whereas the UN's new security vision was built on a system of collective self-defense. Clearly, the second paragraph was not meant to replicate existing international legal norms. All in all, whereas the language of the first paragraph was lifted mostly from international treaties governing the use of armed forces, the second paragraph went further to deny Japan even the internationally recognized rights of sovereign nations.[35]

Article 9 was not meant to be a mere summation or recitation of international legal norms. In order to do its job of protecting Hirohito and preserving the imperial institution, it had to go beyond the conventional form of codified pacifism and embody a much more radical and absolute idea. According to Whitney, "[t]he enunciation of this principle should be unusual and dramatic."[36] Nothing less would do to convince the international community and to achieve the ultimate goal that GHQ/SCAP and the Japanese government had in common. Article 9 was born, then, with a troubling irony. For peace was bootstrapped into the new constitution, using the language of international law, in order to absolve the emperor from the "crime against peace," in the parlance of the emerging international legal norm which underwrote the Tokyo Tribunal.[37] Abolition of the military would be the road to the emperor's redemption and Japan's rebirth.

Swallowing Peace: Japanese Government's Acquiescence

If the most emblematic feature of Japan's postwar constitution was the result of imposition at the hands of foreign occupying forces, it must also be understood that it was seen – by both foreigners and locals – as the only viable way to preserve what was considered the essential core of Japan's constitutional identity, namely, the emperor system. In this light, MacArthur's assumption

35 Martin, "Binding the Dogs of War," pp. 296–7.

36 RM203. Matsumoto and Yoshida meet with SCAP. RM203.4.SP7.P1.

37 Kobayashi, *Daikyūjō*, p. 35.

of the role of a foreign lawgiver was "motivated by the perception that the government's ultraconservatism was imperiling the goal the old guard cherished most."[38] In other words, Article 9 was imposed for the purpose of achieving what the Japanese leadership, left to their own devices, was not likely to achieve – that is, saving Hirohito.

On 13 February, Whitney gave the GHQ draft to the representatives from the Shidehara cabinet led by Yoshida Shigeru and Matsumoto Jōji. The Japanese delegation was completely caught by surprise because they had come to the meeting with the expectation that they would be discussing the Matsumoto draft, submitted previously on 8 February. After pronouncing the Matsumoto draft "wholly unacceptable," Whitney explained to his flustered audience in a high-handed manner that the new constitutional draft was the result of MacArthur's sincere desire (and his last-minute effort) to protect the emperor system and to insulate Hirohito himself from mounting demands for abdication and even prosecution.

> As you may or may not know, the Supreme Commander has been unyielding in his defence of your Emperor against increasing pressure from the outside to render him subject to war criminal investigation. He has thus defended the Emperor because he considered that that was the cause of right and justice, and will continue along that course to the extent of his ability. But, gentlemen, the Supreme Commander is not omnipotent. He feels, however, that acceptance of the provisions of this new Constitution would render the Emperor practically unassailable.[39]

He also mentioned in no uncertain terms that accepting the GHQ draft would be the last chance for the entire Japanese "reactionary" establishment to remain in power.[40] This was followed by a brusque precaution that, in case of refusal, SCAP would bypass the government and lay the draft constitution directly before the people. Given that the Imperial Constitution's amendment process did not require a popular referendum, this course of action would have meant that even the faux veneer of legal continuity would be abrogated, thereby making dimmer the prospects for the emperor system and the conservative establishment.

As mentioned, there were strong calls for the prosecution of Hirohito as a war criminal at the time, and the FEC, in which China and the Soviet Union would be major participants, was about to commence work in a few week.

[38] Dower, *Embracing Defeat*, p. 362.
[39] RM191. Transmittal of U.S. model to Japanese Cabinet (13 Feb. 1946) Kades, Rowell, Hussey. RM191.P11.Q1.P2.
[40] RM191. Transmittal. RM191.P11.Q1.P4.

The Japanese government must have divined quickly that, in order to protect the emperor (and themselves), they would have to accept the GHQ constitution including its pacifist principle. After an intense but all too brief deliberation,[41] the Shidehara cabinet endorsed the GHQ draft on 22 February with the prime minister's tearful parting words quoted previously. According to one account, it was "like swallowing boiling water."[42]

Insofar as Article 9 was concerned, Japanese government leaders appear to have been especially embittered and resentful. Japan with no military must have been inconceivable to many for whom Japan had been a divine "military state" (*gunkoku*) until only a few months earlier. If the Japanese leaders were resentful, however, it seems that they were not caught completely off guard. The idea of giving up the military as a price to pay for preserving the imperial institution had in fact been entertained within the government even before the surrender.

Until the very bitter end, Japanese government leaders' foremost concern was to maintain and preserve Japan as an "imperial state" (*kōkoku*) at all costs. When the Allies urged Japan in July 1945 to capitulate by accepting the so-called unconditional surrender as demanded by the Potsdam Declaration, the Japanese government's response was a qualified acceptance on the condition that the emperor's status and prerogatives would not be affected. Japan's attempt was simply ignored by the Allies, which replied through U.S. Secretary of State James F. Byrnes, who merely reiterated the language of the Potsdam Declaration to the effect that the ultimate form of government of Japan would be determined by "the freely expressed will of the Japanese people."[43] Somehow presuming that the condition was accepted,[44] Hirohito's

41 It was not until 19 February that the 3 February meeting was reported to the cabinet. Worse still, the cabinet deliberation proceeded without the GHQ draft in complete Japanese translation.

42 Hellegers, *We, the Japanese People*, vol. 2, p. 534. A constitutional historian in Japan calls this capitulation by the cabinet a "second surrender." Koseki, *Tanjō*, p. 167. In the same vein, a Japanese constitutional scholar has described it as a "February Revolution" comparable to the "August Revolution," i.e., Japan's unconditional surrender. Keigo Komamura, "Legitimacy of the Constitution of Japan Redux: Is an Imposed Constitution Legitimate?," occasional paper presented at the Constitutional Revision Research Project, Reischauer Institute of Japanese Studies, Harvard University, 11 February 2010, p. 18.

43 "Reply by Secretary of State to Japanese Qualified Acceptance (11 Aug. 1945)," in *PRJ*, p. 415.

44 Many interpret Byrnes's reply as a firm rejection of Japan's attempt to attach any conditions to the surrender, for it made the form of government (and the fate of the emperor) ultimately dependent on the will of the people. For the United States, Japan's acceptance of the Potsdam Declaration meant that Japan had tendered its "unconditional surrender" and that the Allies were not bound by any contractual relations with Japan in implementing the intents of the declaration. Hellegers, *We, the Japanese People*, vol. 1, pp. 149–58. By contrast, some scholars claim that the acceptance amounted to an international agreement of sorts (Ashibe, *Kenpō*, pp. 27–8), or that it was a "conditional unconditional surrender" (Lawrence W. Beer and John M. Maki, *From Imperial Myth to Democracy: Japan's Two Constitutions, 1889–2002*

famous surrender broadcast of 15 August concluded with a command that his subjects "enhance the innate glory of the imperial state" that he and his government had just led to utter devastation.

As for the substance of the assurance they sought so desperately, however, there seemed to be little agreement within the Japanese leadership. The ultraconservatives, mostly hailing from the army, were hoping to retain imperial sovereignty as provided in the Imperial Constitution, with the emperor's supreme and exclusive command over the military intact. By contrast, the civilian moderates, such as Foreign Minister Tōgō Shigenori, were prepared to accept the Allied terms as long as the dynastic line was maintained, even at the expense of Hirohito in person and the full imperial prerogatives.[45] Along this line, some even contemplated complete demilitarization as a condition for preserving the imperial institution. Marquis Kido Kōichi, Hirohito's closest confidant and Lord Keeper of the Privy Seal, had prepared a "Draft Plan for Controlling the Crisis Situation" even before the Potsdam Declaration was announced, in which he suggested offering voluntary disarmament in return for "safeguarding the Imperial Household and preserving the national polity."[46] Similarly, the "Essentials of Peace Negotiations" drafted by Prince Konoe Fumimaro, a senior member of the court entourage as well as the ex-premier who had started the Second Sino-Japanese War in 1937, also called for a "complete disarmament for an unspecified period of time" in return for the preservation of the imperial line.[47] Even these two imperial grandees, who would soon be indicted as Class-A war criminals in the Tokyo Tribunal, were fully aware that, in order to save Hirohito, the military might have to go.

Following the surrender, the idea of sacrificing the military became a reality virtually overnight. GHQ's demobilization of the imperial military was undertaken at an extraordinary speed and had already become a fait accompli by mid-October 1945. By the time deliberations for a new constitution began, in other words, there were no armed forces to be reflected in the constitution. In part in anticipation of this post-surrender status quo, Irie Toshio, Director of the First Department of the Cabinet Legislation Bureau, began preparing for constitutional revision. In a report dated 18 September 1945, he drew

(Boulder: University of Colorado Press, 2002), pp. 53–8), or that it was an "unconditional acceptance by the loser of conditions provided by the victor" (Makoto Iokibe, "Diplomacy in Occupied Japan: Japanese Diplomacy in the 1940s" in Makoto Iokibe (ed.), *The Diplomatic History of Postwar Japan*, trans. Robert D. Eldridge (New York: Routledge, 2009), p. 22).

45 Herbert P. Bix, *Hirohito and the Making of Modern Japan* (New York: Harper Collins, 2001), p. 513.

46 Richard B. Frank, *Downfall: The End of the Japanese Empire* (New York: Penguin, 1999), p. 97.

47 Bix, *Hirohito and the Making of Modern Japan*, p. 510.

up a list of articles in the Imperial Constitution "that are believed to require amendments when the military institutions are abolished."[48] While this was a private undertaking, it clearly shows that a high official in the government expected the abolishment of the military to be the main focus of any upcoming constitutional revision. It was not only an isolated elite bureaucrat who was preparing for such an unsavory possibility. Even a Class-A war criminal held at Sugamo Prison at the time is said to have proposed disarmament to government leaders. Shiratori Toshio, ex-ambassador to fascist Italy, apparently made a suggestion to Yoshida Shigeru proposing the emperor's renunciation of war, the people's right to resist military service, and prohibition of using national resources for military purposes as core ideas for the new constitution.[49] In an open forum, too, when the last session of the Imperial Diet met on 26 November 1945, debates on the floor were conducted on the assumption that provisions on the military would have to be excised from the constitution.[50]

When the government finally came around to form its own Constitutional Problems Investigation Committee under the chairmanship of Matsumoto Jōji, the same idea of abolishing the military was again widely discussed. It seems evident that elimination of the military provisions in the Imperial Constitution was given serious consideration.[51] Indeed, the committee appears to have commenced its discussion with the understanding that "those calling for the deletion of the provisions on the command and organization of the military are in the majority."[52] In one of its base texts for revision (*Kenpō Kaiseian*) drafted for internal use, this majority opinion seems to have led to the removal of Articles 11 and 12 of the Imperial Constitution on the emperor's exclusive prerogatives over the army and navy.[53] Up until the very end of its activities, the Committee contemplated not including any provision on the military in its outline for the new constitution – in line with the new status quo and in

48 RM058. Constitution needs reform (18 Sept. 1945) Irie Toshio (Legislation Bureau chief). RM058.1.

49 Yamamuro, *Kenpō Kyūjō*, pp. 275–6. This suggestion was contained in a letter written in English, intended to be read by the American censors. Some even argue that this was the origin of the peace provision.

50 Satō Tatsuo, *Nihonkoku Kenpō Seiritsushi* [The Legislative History of the Constitution of Japan], vol. I (Tokyo: Yūhikaku, 1962), pp. 436, 447.

51 As pointed out by Nomura Junji, one of the three senior advisors to the Matsumoto Committee, such elimination was inevitable because the military had already been abolished in postwar Japan. Satō, *Seiritsushi*, vol. I, p. 263 (First General Meeting held on 27 Oct. 1945).

52 Satō, *Seiritsushi*, vol. I, p. 291 (Second session of the Research Meeting held on 2 Nov. 1945).

53 Satō, *Seiritsushi*, vol. II, p. 551. When another draft (*Kenpō Kaisei Yōkō*) that preserved these provisions with minimal changes was debated in the cabinet on 30 January 1946, various concerns were voiced. The Minister of Justice, for instance, argued for a complete elimination of these provisions on the imperial control of the military. See Koseki, *Tanjō*, pp. 82–8.

order to be the "world's first nonmilitary peaceful country."[54] All in all, many, if not most, government leaders divined that post-defeat Japan would have to demilitarize and that this must be addressed at the level of the constitution.[55]

Against this background, it seems disingenuous to claim that the peace provision in the GHQ draft took the Japanese government by complete surprise. That Chapter I of the constitution (preservation of emperor) was predicated on Chapter II (renunciation of war) was an idea that had been contemplated by the Japanese themselves, too. While the trade-off was clearly imposed on the Japanese government, it was accepted, or at least acquiesced in, with relatively little resistance because the idea was not entirely a novel one. Thus after meeting MacArthur on 21 February, Shidehara is reported to have said: "It was in order to protect and maintain the emperor system that the symbolic emperor and the renunciation of war in the GHQ draft was agreed upon."[56] The following day, his cabinet endorsed accepting the GHQ draft. Both the victor and the vanquished fully, if tacitly, understood what was at stake in this Faustian bargain.[57]

After the government endorsement of the GHQ draft, it was translated into Japanese and then made public on 6 March 1946, with the blessing of both Hirohito and MacArthur, as the government's "Outline of a Draft for a Revised Constitution." A complete version of this would be sent in June to the newly elected Imperial Diet for deliberation. As per the Potsdam Declaration, the new charter for postwar Japan would be decided by "the freely expressed will of the Japanese people." The ratification process shows that the government's reluctant acquiescence was quickly turning into eager acceptance of the "tacit agreement" that was Article 9.

54 Satō, *Seiritsushi*, vol. II, p. 505 (Ninth session of the Research Meeting held on 5 Jan. 1946).

55 To be sure, Matsumoto was not one of them. In contrast to the *Kenpō Kaiseian*, the draft finalized by Matsumoto himself and submitted to GHQ on 8 February (apparently without the official approval of either the cabinet or his own committee) included articles on the emperor's supreme command over armed forces as well as his prerogative to declare war and make peace. For Matsumoto, ironically, these military provisions were preventive measures against the resurgence of militarism. See Satō, *Seiritsushi*, vol. II, pp. 708–09.

56 Handō Kazutoshi, *Shōwashi: Sengohen 1945–1989* (Tokyo: Heibonsha, 2009), pp. 195–6.

57 In a sense, the bargain was a matter of course. The war had been fought against militarism of imperial Japan, and its utter defeat was bound to demand that "Emperor's Military" (*kōgun*) should be broken up somehow. Faced with the prospect that the emperor (*kō*) and his military (*gun*) would no longer be allowed to share the same fate, both SCAP and the Japanese government chose to sacrifice the military and save the emperor. See Hideo Otake, "Two Contrasting Constitutions in the Postwar World: The Making of the Japanese and the West German Constitutions," in Yoichi Higuchi (ed.), *Five Decades of Constitutionalism in Japanese Society* (Tokyo: University of Tokyo Press, 2001), p. 50.

During interpellations in the Imperial Diet, the government vigorously defended a maximal interpretation of Article 9 that closely followed the second item of the MacArthur Notes. In preparation for this, the Cabinet Legislation Bureau drew up a list of mock questions and answers, which specifically addressed whether Article 9 precluded even the right of self-defense. The answer to be given was that while the first paragraph did not deny the right per se, "Japan cannot fight such a [self-defensive] war with other countries, pursuant to paragraph 2."[58] Consistent with this, Kanamori Tokujirō, Matsumoto's successor as minister of state in charge of constitutional revision, made clear in the House of Peers that, even if the first paragraph did not explicitly outlaw defensive war, disarmament in the second paragraph made it practically impossible to engage in any war. In the lower chamber, Kanamori went even further and answered that renunciation of the right of belligerency in the second paragraph was so absolute as to bar the government from claiming such a right in a hypothetical civil war situation, even against a domestic group of rebels or secessionists recognized as belligerent under international law.[59] Prime Minister Yoshida himself also appeared in the diet and suggested that paragraph one renounces defensive war, reminding the lawmakers that imperial Japan's wars of aggression, such as the "Manchurian Incident" and the "War of Greater East Asia," had all been justified in terms of self-defense.[60] Again, these public statements by the political leadership were consistent with the expert opinion prepared by the Cabinet Legislation Bureau: "Adding an exception for a defensive war may leave room for Japan to start an aggressive war under the name of a defensive war. An exception for defensive war was not added in order to realize our pacifism."[61]

For sure, a couple of modifications to Article 9 were made during deliberations in the House of Representatives. They consisted of affixing introductory adverbial clauses to its two paragraphs. The first paragraph would now start with the words: "Aspiring sincerely to an international peace based on justice and order," and the second with: "In order to accomplish the aim of the preceding paragraph." Commonly called the Ashida amendment (after Ashida Hitoshi, the chair of the House of Representatives Committee on the Bill for

58 *Kenpō Kaisei Sōan ni kansuru Sōtei Mondai* [Expected Questions Regarding the Draft Revised Constitution], No. 118–52, quoted in Kenneth Port, *Transcending Law: The Unintended Life of Article 9 of the Japanese Constitution* (Durham, NC: Carolina Academic Press, 2010), p. 46. Also see Koseki, *Tanjō*, p. 291.

59 RM337. House of Representatives: Committee on Revision: ninth meeting (9 July 1946). RM337.PM.SP19.

60 RM319. House of Representatives: plenary (26 June 1946). RM319.PM.SP3.P3.

61 Port, *Transcending Law*, p. 46.

Revision of the Imperial Constitution), this additional verbiage would later become the source of controversy regarding whether Article 9 was intended to ban war for self-defensive purposes. Ashida would later claim in 1951 that the new insertions were intended to prohibit only "aggressive war" and to allow the government to maintain military for the purpose of self-defense.[62] Recent studies, however, have shown that when it was first proposed on 29 July 1946, the amendment was understood as mostly a stylistic embellishment designed to make Article 9 sound more aspirational (and voluntarily adopted) than constraining (and imposed upon). That the added words might be interpreted to narrow the scope of prohibition on armaments was not even noticed by the lawmakers.[63] Rather, they were widely seen as a better way of expressing Japan's own understanding that unconditional renunciation of war and complete disarmament would be the key condition under which it might be allowed to return to the international community with its emperor system intact. Indeed, Ashida himself announced at the time that "both phrases are intended to demonstrate the desire of the Japanese people to contribute to world peace."[64] Article 9 was a kind of international accord, in short, and it was understood as such by both the Japanese government and diet members. Pacifism was fast becoming the cornerstone of postwar Japan's constitutional identity.

Manipulating Peace: "San Francisco System" and the Yoshida Doctrine

To the extent that it was written for the international audience still apprehensive of Japan's militarism, Article 9 was generally meant to master the past rather than incubate the future. Aspirational as it may sound, in other words, the peace provision was not really forward-looking. It was written primarily to deal with the perceived evils of Japan's militarist past.[65] The process by

62 Koseki, *Tanjō*, p. 293.

63 By contrast, it was noticed by the FEC, which was by this time closely monitoring the process of constitutional revision. Ever suspicious of Japan's hidden aspiration for remilitarization, the FEC pointed out that this might allow the government to maintain military forces under the pretext of self-defense. This in turn led to the demand that a new provision (Article 66) be included, which required all cabinet ministers to be civilians. Given that there was to be no military at all, such a provision seemed puzzling and redundant at best, but the Japanese side had no choice but to oblige. Koseki, *Tanjō*, pp. 305–13.

64 RM387. House of Representatives: Subcommittee on Revision: seventh meeting (1 Aug. 1946). RM387.AM.SP153.P1. He would also close the deliberation in the House of Representatives with the proud proclamation that "this is the first time in the world that a Constitution … has provided for the abolition of the whole range of armaments and for the repudiation of all war." RM420. House of Representatives: plenary (24 Aug. 1946). RM420.AM.SP1.P9.

65 Promulgated only two and a half years later in 1949, by contrast, the so-called Basic Law (*Grundgesetz*) of West Germany was written after the Cold War had arrived in Europe. As a result, it was reflective of the Cold War anti-communism and its militant liberalism in

which Article 9 became the focal point of postwar Japan's identity, however, cannot be fully understood without considering the unexpected turn of events that quickly unfolded on the heels of its insertion into the constitution. Even before the constitution went into effect on 3 May 1947, new developments in both regional and global geopolitics would stretch the meaning of Article 9 to its limits, which in turn had the ironic effect of making pacifism further deeply entrenched as an essential part of the Japanese people's identity. In the process, the Japanese government would have to weather another wave of imposition from the outside, which forced them to embrace with increasing eagerness the first round of imposition.

As the Cold War began to make itself felt in East Asia, the United States had to make major adjustments in its policy toward occupied Japan. Especially after "losing China" in 1949, the United States came to regard Japan with unrivaled importance for its containment policy in East Asia. Japan was suddenly upgraded from a defeated enemy in need of redemption to a pivotal partner in the common crusade against communism. Often called the "reverse course" in Japan, this new policy signaled a radical departure from the initial policies of "demilitarization and democratization" in order to make Japan politically stable via socioeconomic rehabilitation. In concrete terms, it meant severe limitations on labor rights, beginning in June 1947, which was accompanied by a massive "red purge" from public life in marked contrast to SCAP's earlier tolerance for communist and socialist organizations. The red purge was in due course followed by the "de-purge" of prewar leaders, including future premiers Hatoyama Ichiro and Kishi Nobusuke, who would push for a wholesale revision of Article 9. The tacit assumptions that had undergirded the imposition and acceptance of Article 9 were fast becoming invalid, and Japan's constitutional pacifism was bound to be understood differently.

The seismic change was first made public in SCAP's press conference on 17 March 1947, even before the new constitution went into effect, in which the end of the "demilitarization and democratization" policy was announced. Although this announcement was made without prior consultation with Washington, its main thrust certainly resonated with the Truman Doctrine, the first salvo of the Cold War, declared only five days earlier. In addition to the reverse course, however, MacArthur also suggested an early termination of the Allied occupation and the conclusion of a peace treaty so as to restore

comparison with which Japan's postwar constitution seemed backward-looking toward the anti-fascist war that had already come to an end. One crucial consequence of this sequential difference was the different attitudes of the two documents toward armed forces; that is, unlike the Japanese counterpart, the Basic Law permitted future rearmament as an option. See Otake, "Two Contrasting Constitutions," p. 59.

Japan's sovereignty. This suggestion was certainly ahead of Washington's schedule, because, at this point in time, it was internally divided over the peace settlement with Japan. A diplomatic need to secure Japan as a friendly anticommunist ally was motivating the State Department to seek early peace and economic rehabilitation, whereas Pentagon was more concerned with retaining military strongholds and even rearming Japan before any peace settlement was reached.[66] No less divided were the Japanese government and the general public since an early restoration of sovereignty, although universally welcome, was likely to bring about a "partial peace treaty" from which the Soviet Union and Communist China would be excluded. The foremost concern was whether to take sides in this emerging global rivalry.

The turning point came in 1950 when the Korean War broke out. The war that took millions of Korean lives was an unexpected blessing for Japan – "a gift of the Gods" in Yoshida's own words.[67] For, in addition to the economic boom triggered by the war, it accelerated the early conclusion of the peace treaty and the Allied occupation. The inclusion of the communist adversaries in the peace settlement having become all but impossible, partial peace appeared to be increasingly inevitable. It was finally agreed upon in Washington that, in return for granting early peace, military bases in Japan would be maintained and Japan's rearmament pursued. From Tokyo's perspective, this meant that early peace settlement could be purchased only by conceding to a certain level of rearmament. In February 1951, such an agreement was reached between Yoshida and U.S. Secretary of State John Foster Dulles. The Korean War was the catalyst that cleared the road to early, albeit partial, peace for Japan.

The San Francisco Peace Treaty of 1951 was the result of this bargain, the terms of which were exceptionally lenient and amenable to Japan's recovery. At the same time, the peace settlement was underwritten by the U.S.-Japan Security Treaty that was signed on the same day, which provided the U.S. forces with a carte blanche right of access to military bases in Japan proper as well as in Okinawa, then under the direct rule of U.S. authorities. According to the Security Treaty, these bases were there not only to protect Japan from outside aggressions, but also to maintain "international peace and security in the Far East" and even to suppress "large scale internal riots and disturbances in Japan" (Article 1). Compelled by the deepening Cold War, in other words, Washington granted early independence to Japan in return for its

66 Kazuya Sakamoto, "Conditions of an Independent State: Japanese Diplomacy in the 1950s," in Iokibe (ed.), *The Diplomatic History of Postwar Japan*, p. 51.

67 John W. Dower, *Empire and Aftermath: Yoshida Shigeru and the Japanese Experience, 1878–1954* (Cambridge, MA: Council on East Asian Studies, Harvard University Press, 1979), p. 316.

semi-permanent security dependence and participation in an anti-communist alliance in Asia. It was a triumph for the U.S. "double containment policy" that sought to keep newly independent Japan under control as well as communism in Asia at bay.[68] It was under the terms of this so-called San Francisco System that Japan's sovereignty was restored.[69]

Insofar as Article 9 was concerned, however, the San Francisco System was not entirely an auspicious event since Washington was putting on more pressure for rearmament. Already at the outbreak of the Korean War in June 1950, in order to compensate for the occupation troops dispatched to Korea, SCAP had ordered the Yoshida cabinet to establish a National Police Reserve (NPR) and augment the Maritime Safety Agency. In line with the Yoshida-Dulles agreement, further, the Security Treaty stipulated Japan's obligation to "increasingly assume responsibility for its own defense" (Preamble), that is, to make military contributions in addition to providing military bases.[70] After San Francisco, NPR was escalated into a National Safety Agency in 1952, comprising 110,000 ground troops plus substantial maritime forces. Washington's first policy statement for post-independent Japan, NSC 125/2 (1952), would go even further and demand some air forces in addition to ten army divisions. The new policy now demanded more than domestic police duties for these paramilitary forces. Article 9 was clearly being stretched to the limit, and Washington knew it, too. Vice President Richard Nixon, visiting Tokyo in 1953, would openly press for rearmament, even stating in public that "it was at the insistence of the United States that Japan was disarmed.... I'm going to admit right here that the United States made a mistake in 1946."[71]

In the face of Washington's unrelenting pressure for rearmament, the conservative Japanese government found itself cornered in an ironic position. For the Yoshida cabinet could not welcome such a pressure despite their apparent

68 Mike M. Michizuki, "US-Japan Security Relations in a New Era," in Chae-Jin Lee (ed.), *The United States and Japan: Changing Relations* (Claremont, CA: Keck Center for International and Strategic Studies, 1992), p. 19.

69 For more on the San Francisco System, see John W. Dower, "Peace and Democracy in Two Systems: External Policy and Internal Conflict," in Andrew Gordon (ed.), *Postwar Japan as History* (Berkeley: University of California Press, 1993).

70 Supporting this mandate was the treaty's blanket declaration in the Preamble that Japan had "a right to enter into collective security arrangements" as well as "an inherent right of individual and collective self-defense" as per the UN Charter. The treaty's Article 5(a-5) makes it further clear that Japan has a sovereign and inherent "right of individual or collective self-defense referred to in Art 51 of the Charter of the United Nations." Gavan McCormack thus goes so far as calling the Security Treaty ("the war system") another and even higher constitution for postwar Japan, which could override Article 9 ("the peace system"). See his *Client State: Japan in the American Embrace* (London and New York: Verso, 2007).

71 McNelly, *Origins*, p. 139.

lack of faith in Article 9.[72] Yoshida and his entourage of elite bureaucrats seem to have concluded as early as 1947 that Japan's security would be entrusted to the United States so that Japan could focus exclusively on economic recovery, a critical decision that would set the subsequent course of development for Japan well into the 1970s.[73] It was evident to the advocates of the so-called Yoshida Doctrine that provision of military bases was a price to pay for Japan's independence and economy, but rearmament was an altogether different issue. A large-scale armament was too expensive a proposition for the war-torn economy of Japan. Washington demanded more than military bases, however, and the Yoshida Doctrine had to move incrementally toward a policy of rearmament. Now the question was not whether but to what extent Japan would be armed.

Thus in order to keep the rearmament as low-cost as possible, Yoshida was compelled to embrace Article 9 firmly. If not out of genuine fidelity, then certainly for calculated reasons of *Realpolitik*, the no-armament mandate of Article 9 was regarded as a crucial cornerstone for the Yoshida Doctrine. While in the thick of heated domestic debates over Japan's new security pact with the United States in 1951, for instance, the wily Yoshida stated in a diet session:

> Rearmament is something that Japan is [*sic*] no position to do right now at all. Moreover, the public is not supportive of it.... While it might seem cunning, for the time being, we should let America [be responsible for Japan's defense]. The Constitution's forbidding a military is a true blessing. If America says anything, we just show the Constitution. Politicians calling for its revision are complete fools.[74]

Indeed, Yoshida's diplomacy played the Article 9 card with great dexterity. He would even covertly cultivate the general public's support for the peace provision to fortify his resistance to the American pressure.[75] Washington had also understood all along that only so much could be done to undo Article

[72] Article 9 was never wholeheartedly welcome in the first place. Shortly after the promulgation in 1946 and even before the reverse course, the Yoshida cabinet was secretly sounding out its idea to rebuild a 100,000-strong army and some air force to test Allied nations' resolve. See Koseki, *Tanjō*, pp. 353–9. In this light, the great enthusiasm with which his cabinet is reported to have welcomed SCAP's order to create NPR in 1950 is not at all surprising. See Miyazawa Kiichi, *Secret Talks Between Tokyo and Washington: The Memoirs of Miyazawa Kiichi, 1949–1954*, trans. Robert D. Eldridge (New York: Lexington Books, 2007), p. 31.

[73] For a full account of the Yoshida Doctrine and its impact on postwar Japan, see Kenneth B. Pyle, *Japan Rising: The Resurgence of Japanese Power and Purpose* (New York: The Century Foundation, 2007), pp. 241–77.

[74] Miyazawa Kiichi, *Memoirs*, p. 76.

[75] Pyle, *Japan Rising*, p. 230.

9, which they had imposed on Japan only a few years before.[76] At last, after protracted diplomatic back-and-forth, the second imposition culminated in the creation of the air, maritime, and ground Self-Defense Forces (SDF) in 1954. This was the final conclusion of the "armed alliance" first ordained in the U.S.-Japan Security Treaty of 1951 – but with the armament level far below Washington's expectation and not in excess of Tokyo's minimum concession.[77] For this final outcome, no less important than Yoshida's skillful diplomacy was the fact that, by this time, Washington's pressure for rearmament was showing signs of abatement. Armistices in Korea (July 1953) and Indochina (July 1954) had drastically reduced military tension in East Asia, inducing Washington to reassess its regional strategy. With respect to Japan, the conclusion was to pursue rearmament in a way that would not impede the political and economic stability of Japan.[78] It was these external circumstances that made possible the longevity of the "Yoshida Doctrine without Yoshida"[79] and the preservation of Article 9 in postwar Japan.

Against the backdrop of the emerging Cold War in East Asia, in sum, Washington's policy reversal and pressure for rearmament were greeted with ironic recalcitrance on the Japanese side. It was ironic because, coerced by SCAP to adopt Article 9 in the first place, the conservative Japanese government was pushed again by Washington and the Cold War exigencies to embrace it firmly. The U.S. pressure was now in the reverse direction, and Japan may have negotiated more successfully than the first time. Even so, in the final analysis, Japanese resistance against the second imposition only ended up further entrenching the first imposition.

Embracing Peace: "1955 System" and the Peaceable People

Article 9 was written and accepted on the assumption that, internationally speaking, its unarmed pacifism entailed permanent neutrality. As an article of faith, indeed, this assumption made sense. As long as the international community remained undivided, alliance would be redundant, and neutrality seemed to be the natural course of action under Article 9.[80] In fact,

76 Guthrie-Shimizu, "Japan, the United States, and the Cold War," p. 256.

77 "In 1954, the Defense Agency was established with responsibility for ground, maritime, and air self-defense forces with a total of 152,000 men – substantially less than half of what the United States had demanded." Pyle, *Japan Rising*, p. 235.

78 The mature statement of this new policy direction was expressed in NSC 5516/1 "US Policy Toward Japan," 9 Apr. 1955, *Foreign Relations of the United States* 1955–1957, vol. XXIII, pt. 1 (Washington, DC: U.S. Government Printing Office, 1991), p. 57 (hereafter *FRUS*).

79 Makoto Iokibe, "Conclusion: What Was Postwar Japanese Diplomacy?" in Iokibe (ed.), *The Diplomatic History of Postwar Japan*, p. 216.

80 Otake, "Two Contrasting Constitutions," p. 53.

"unarmed neutrality" seems to have been closer to the original intention of Article 9's architects. As late as the spring of 1950, shortly before the outbreak of the Korean War, MacArthur still held fast to the view that Article 9 entailed both disarmament (including the withdrawal of U.S. forces) *and* neutrality (provided that the U.S. air forces continue to be stationed in Okinawa with Russia's understanding).[81] So did the conservative ex-premier Shidehara who had acquiesced to Article 9 in 1946. In his understanding, Article 9 implied unarmed neutrality, even if it might turn out to be an open invitation to a foreign invasion (likely from the Soviet Union), which Japan should resist only by means of nonviolent disobedience.[82] Ironically, this interpretation was not so much different from those of the Socialist Party and the liberal-progressive voices within the Japanese cultural and intellectual establishment. For all these interpretations coming from vastly disparate backgrounds, Article 9 unambiguously entailed a policy of unarmed neutrality.

As a matter of policy option, however, the assumption of unarmed neutrality was conceptually naïve from the beginning. For domestic armament and international alliance are two distinct questions that may produce different combinations. After all, even Switzerland, which was initially invoked as a model pacifist state for the postwar reconstruction of Japan, adhered to the principle of "armed neutrality." Conceptually speaking, then, there was no compelling reason why Article 9 could not sanction a policy of alliance so long as Japan remained unarmed. As the Cold War deepened, thus, Yoshida initially pursued "unarmed alliance," while Washington persistently demanded "armed alliance." By contrast, armed neutrality would be pursued by Yoshida's successor and political archrival, Hatoyama Ichiro, who campaigned vigorously for a wholesale scrapping of Article 9. When Article 9 was put to the further test of reality, these conceptual ambiguities would play themselves out under the pressing circumstances of the deepening Cold War.

After the conclusion of the Security Treaty and creation of the Self-Defense Forces, clearly, Article 9 in its original interpretation could no longer go along with "armed alliance" as demanded by the San Francisco System. Thus came an altogether different interpretation of Article 9, which was unveiled by the new Hatoyama cabinet in December 1954. According to this new position, paragraph one did not expressly prohibit force for self-defense, which implied that "war potential" in paragraph two means only armed forces exceeding a minimum level necessary for self-defense. Since the SDF was established within this limit, it did not constitute war potential and therefore was

[81] Masumi, *Postwar Politics*, pp. 189–91.

[82] Masumi, *Postwar Politics*, p. 200.

not prohibited by the constitution. According to this radical departure from the government's original stance during the deliberation process in 1946, in other words, constitutional pacifism did not renounce the inherent sovereign right of self-defensive war, and maintaining "minimum necessary force" for self-defense did not violate Article 9.[83] In the absence of any judicial interpretation to the contrary, the government's new stance has persisted in its essentials to this day. Through the government's creative reinterpretation and judicial passivism, in short, Japan has come to have it both ways – peace and military under Article 9.

Stretching the penumbra of Article 9 was, however, not the only way the Japanese government strove to disarm constitutional pacifism. A wholesale revision of Article 9 was also pushed openly under the premiership of Hatoyama Ichiro. Trying to undo the Yoshida Doctrine, Hatoyama's foreign policy of "armed neutrality" sought to lessen overall dependence on the United States by normalizing relationships with the Soviet Union and China while strengthening diplomatic ties with Southeast Asian and other Third World countries of the non-alliance camp. The ultimate goal was to gain "complete independence" from the United States by revising the unequal terms of the Security Treaty. Clearly, this proposition was untenable, even quixotic, in the absence of Japan's constitutionally recognized military, and Hatoyama's vision of a new Security Treaty was rebuffed for the same reason by Washington in 1955.[84] Even so, this call for a return to the so-called Normal State, fueled by a loathing of the "MacArthur Constitution," culminated in an earnest attempt at wholesale constitutional revision. By 1956, thus, an official Commission on the Constitution (*Kenpō Chōsakai*) of fifty diet members and civilian experts chaired by an eminent scholar of Anglo-American law, Takayanagi Kenzō, was created to investigate the problems of the present constitution and to submit a revised draft. Manifestly, however, no constitutional revision was ever accomplished in postwar Japan. The Takayanagi Commission, after seven years of diligent work, produced a thick scholarly report, but no revision draft was submitted for lack of internal consensus.[85]

[83] Miyazawa Toshiyoshi, *Kenpō Kōwa*, p. 205. It is still debated as to whether this alteration was an instance of government's constitutional trespassing or a legitimate route of constitutional change via administrative interpretation. See Mark Chinen, "Article 9 of the Constitution of Japan and the Use of the Procedural and Substantive Heuristics for Consensus," *Michigan Journal of International Law*, vol. 26 (2005).

[84] Sakamoto, "Conditions of an Independent State," pp. 63–5.

[85] Ray A. Moore and Donald L. Robinson, *Partners for Democracy: Crafting the New Japanese State Under MacArthur* (Oxford: Oxford University Press, 2004), pp. 320–4; John M. Maki, "The Documents of Japan's Commission on the Constitution" in Dan Fenno Henderson (ed.), *The Constitution of Japan: Its First Twenty Years, 1947–1967* (Seattle: University of Washington Press, 1968), p. 279.

This failure was in a sense preordained by the domestic political template that Hatoyama himself had cast into relief, which would prove to be as lasting as the Yoshida Doctrine was in foreign policy. Hatoyama's new political template was created as a result of the grand conservative merger between the Liberal and Democratic Parties in 1955. This "1955 System" set the subsequent course of conservative hegemony in Japanese politics until the Liberal Democratic Party (LDP) rule was finally brought to an end in 1993. Often overlooked in this story of LDP hegemony is, however, the persistent opposition from the Socialist and Communist Parties, which together consistently commanded roughly a quarter to a third of the diet seats so long as the 1955 System lasted.[86] This disproportionate yet enduring balance of power would be first endorsed by the voters in the 1956 general election, in which constitutional revision was the central issue for both LDP and the opposition.[87] Arguably, in other words, the election was a sort of popular referendum on Article 9, and, even though they accepted SDF as a fait accompli, the voters mandated the preservation of Article 9 by continuing to give the opposition sufficient power to veto any attempt to revise or repeal it. Constitutionally speaking, these mutually sustaining rigidities ensured that postwar Japan would have both "legal" armed forces (despite the progressive opposition) and constitutional peace (against the conservative loathing).[88] Article 9 was the major fault line on which the 1955 System was erected and sustained.

Manifestly, then, this system would not have come into being had it not been for Article 9's popularity among the Japanese voters. Despite the absence of a constituent convention or popular referendum, the Peace Constitution garnered stronger support from the war-weary citizens than from their conservative leaders.[89] When it was first made public in 1946, the approval rate

[86] In point of fact, the conservative merger in November 1955 was itself a reaction to the reconciliation between different factions within the Socialist Party who overcame their feuds by recognizing the need to oppose the rearmament and preserve the constitution. Masumi, *Postwar Politics*, p. 312–13.

[87] Koseki Shōichi, *Kenpō Kyūjō wa Naze Seitei saretaka* [Why Was Article 9 of the Constitution Made?] (Tokyo: Iwanami Shoten, 2006), pp. 44–5.

[88] According to Kobayashi Naoki, Japan's foremost academic authority on constitutional law as well as an ardent defender of Article 9, the Self-Defense Forces, which the 1955 System endorsed, can only be described as a "chimera" that is "unconstitutional yet legal." This paradoxical proposition holds that, on the one hand, Article 9 cannot be construed to sanction SDF in view of the original legislative intent as manifested during the ratification process in 1946. The procedural legality by which SDF was created in 1954, on the other hand, cannot be questioned and invalidated in the absence of clear judicial intervention. See Kobayashi, *Daikyūjō*, pp. 149–54.

[89] One scholar conjectures that this strong popular support was precisely the reason the Yoshida cabinet chose not to resort to a popular referendum as both the FEC and SCAP had encouraged. For "it would have rendered a substantial, conservative revision in the future more difficult by

hovered around 70 percent, which did not diminish considerably in the ensuing years.[90] This sustained popular support is attributable to a number of causes. For one, even before Article 9 was drafted, unarmed pacifism had its share of advocates in the immediate post-surrender Japan; some Japanese scholars even claim deeper roots that go back to the Freedom and People's Rights Movement during the Meiji era and beyond.[91] For another, it had to do with the government's concerted efforts, overseen by GHQ, to popularize the new constitution and its pacifist principles to the general public.[92] Although government propaganda waned after 1947, the overwhelming support for Article 9 was sustained in no small measure thanks to various grassroots organizations, from trade unions and women's rights groups to university student organizations, which had been revivified by occupation-era reforms.[93] The electoral outcome in 1956 was indeed good evidence that this enthusiasm for Article 9 did not dwindle among the general public. In all, the sincerity with which the majority of Japanese people embraced Article 9 seems unquestionable.[94]

In view of the enduring support for Article 9, it does not seem entirely fortuitous that national self-identity had also undergone a sudden reversal. In the immediate postwar public discourse, wartime militarist expansionism that had undergirded the ideology of the multiethnic empire of Japan was castigated as an aberration in Japanese history. For instance, a popular "theory of island nation" (*shimaguniron*) postulated that a traditionally mono-ethnic Japanese people had lived from time immemorial a peaceful life of farming and culture in near total isolation from outside world.[95] By the same token, the symbol

removing the claim that the Constitution is an alien, imposed document." Sylvia B. Hamano, "Incomplete Revolution and Not So Alien Transplants: The Japanese Constitution and Human Rights," *University of Pennsylvania Journal of Constitutional Law*, vol. 1 (1998–9), p. 441.

90 See Kobayashi, *Daikyūjō*, pp. 131–41. The only brief exception was during the early years of the Korean War.

91 See Yamamuro, *Kenpō Kyūjō*, chapters 3 and 4.

92 See Koseki, *Tanjō*, pp. 319–41.

93 The most notable was the National Union for Preserving the Constitution launched in January 1955, which comprised of more than 140 unions and civic organizations under the chairmanship of the former socialist premier Katayama Tetsu. For more on various civic movements against the constitutional revision and rearmament, see Mari Yamamoto, *Grassroots Pacifism in Postwar Japan: The Rebirth of a Nation* (New York: Routledge, 2004).

94 Popular enthusiasm for Article 9 would be demonstrated again, this time out on the streets and in massive numbers, during the so-called Security Crisis, or *Anpo Tōsō*, of 1960 which was triggered by the Kishi cabinet's attempt to renew the U.S.-Japan Security Treaty of 1951. Pyle, *Japan Rising*, pp. 237–8.

95 On the prewar origins and postwar reinvention of *shimaguniron*, see Eiji Oguma, *A Genealogy of 'Japanese' Self-Images*, trans. David Askew (Melbourne: Trans Pacific Press, 2002), pp. 175–202, 260–84.

emperor system and unarmed pacifism, two main pillars of the postwar constitution, were touted as befitting this self-perception of the peaceable Japanese people. Peace and culture under a symbol emperor polity had suddenly come to form an interlocking constellation of values that together defined the postwar identity of Japan.

This sudden identity reversal is of course not without problems. It might be criticized as wishful thinking, if not outright cynical manipulation, by which to avoid facing up to the reality of their past.[96] Wartime militarism and the atrocities committed in the name of the emperor could be forgotten. This amnesia in turn allowed the Japanese to focus on their status as "victims" of the war that had ended with the tragedies of Hiroshima and Nagasaki. Such parochial self-victimization (*higaisha ishiki*) also had the effect of leaving little room for recognizing their former victims.[97] These problems notwithstanding, it is undeniable that the Japanese people's embrace of peace was largely responsible for the frustration of the conservative elites' attempt to revise Article 9. According to John Dower, "[i]n the final analysis, the force that ultimately restrained constitutional revision and remilitarization to the extent desired by Washington was not Yoshida, not the ruling conservatives, but the resistance of the Japanese people themselves."[98] Constitutional pacifism came from abroad, for sure, but it took a peaceable people to keep it. The birthmark left by external imposition has become the heart and soul of the people.

KOREA'S TALE OF TWO CITIES

In comparison with the Japanese experience, constitutional founding in Korea appears to lack a foreign lawgiver, a figure comparable to Douglas MacArthur whose dominating presence left a lasting mark on not only the text of the constitution, but also the identity of the people constituted by the constitution. After Japan's surrender, the southern part of the Korean Peninsula, which was

96 As one German scholar has noted, even progressive Japanese historians portrayed their imperial past as an instance of a resistance against Western imperialism in Asia ("Japan as the colonized, not the colonizer"), while the peace movement denounced war only in general terms without highlighting Japan's responsibility for imperial rule and wartime atrocities. Sebastian Conrad, "The Dialectics of Remembrance: Memories of Empire in Cold War Japan," *Comparative Studies in Society and History*, vol. 56, no. 1 (2014), pp. 13–16. An American scholar goes so far as to explain this tendency as an effort "to lend legitimacy and historical roots to the pattern of behavior that they prefer today." Thomas U. Berger, "From Sword to Chrysanthemum: Japan's Culture of Anti-Militarism," *International Security*, vol. 17, no. 4 (1993), p. 145.

97 John Dower wryly observes that "[f]rom the perspectives of Japan's Asian victims, of course, such an appeal [to peace] would seem shockingly parochial." Dower, "Two Systems," p. 10.

98 Dower, *Empire and Aftermath*, p. 434.

to become the Republic of Korea, was occupied by U.S. armed forces under the command of Lieutenant General John R. Hodge. As Commander-in-Chief of U.S. Army Forces in Korea (USAFIK), Hodge was technically under the supervision of MacArthur, who in addition to being SCAP wore another hat as the Commander-in-Chief, Army Forces in the Pacific (CINCAFPAC). Yet MacArthur does not appear to have been involved deeply with the occupation of Korea, while Hodge, although a seasoned field commander who participated in the Philippines and Okinawa campaigns, had neither the skills nor the ambitions of a foreign lawgiver. The 1948 Founding Constitution of the Republic of Korea would be the product of local politicians, rather than a charter imposed on them by the occupying authorities.

The absence of outright imposition, however, does not mean that there were no external forces at work. The USAMGIK set up under Hodge was in fact a full-blown direct government, in contradistinction to the General Headquarters of SCAP in Tokyo which only ruled indirectly through the Japanese government apparatus. Given that the constitution was written after nearly three years of political, social, and economic engineering by USAMGIK (as opposed to six months in the case of Japan), there may have been less of a need for direct imposition.

Yet, the American influence was but one of many external forces at work in the constitutional founding of Korea. One might even say that the drafting of Korea's constitution and the shaping of its constitutional identity involved a plurality of international *pouvoirs constituants*. For one, the legal authorization for convoking the National Assembly to draft a constitution and to establish an independent (South Korean) government came from a resolution of the General Assembly of the United Nations. The constitution of the Republic of Korea owes its existence, as it were, to the intervention of the international community which mandated the creation of a separate regime in the south. More importantly, the Cold War itself was a powerful influence on the constitution-making of South Korea. The fact that the Korean Peninsula was divided in half at the 38th parallel, at the moment of liberation, by the two emerging superpowers made it all but certain that the Cold War would figure prominently in the postcolonial state-formation of Korea. From the South Korean viewpoint, this meant that the establishment of its constitutional order was inescapably colored by the simultaneous emergence of a rival regime in the northern half of the peninsula. North Korea, in other words, acted as yet another important layer of external influence in the making of South Korea's constitutional identity.

The impact of this multi-layered external influence is arguably most discernible in the constitutional provisions regarding South Korea's economic regime. The irony is that the Cold War rivalry led initially to the adoption of a "socialistic" economy for the side that supposedly represented free market capitalism. Competition for regime legitimacy vis-à-vis North Korea compelled the drafters of the Founding Constitution to opt for a system that promised robust socioeconomic rights, state ownership/control of most economic resources and enterprises, and redistribution of farmland. Both USAMGIK and Washington were also behind this choice. With the completion of the land reform and with the pressing need for economic reconstruction after the Korean War, however, the Founding Constitution's framework for the economy was no longer viable. For the United States, which saw the need to rebuild South Korea as an integral part of the regional security regime in East Asia, it was imperative that the country be turned into a capitalist system in both letter and spirit. Washington essentially demanded an amendment of the economic provisions of the constitution, which would be adjusted in 1954 to be more hospitable to free enterprise. One byproduct of this transition was the political restructuring toward augmentation of presidential powers, which would have long-term effects on later development of Korea's democracy. After the first military conflict of the Cold War era, and under the United States' design to restructure the country as a member of the "free world," the initial formation of Korea's constitutional identity that had begun in 1948 finally came to a close.

Idealism Meets Realism: Economy Chapter and Vested Properties

In 1948, shortly after the Founding Constitution was ratified in South Korea, an American political scientist observed that "Chapter Six, entitled 'Economy,' ostensibly makes the Korean Republic a *socialistic* state."[99] This was not without reason. The chapter began with the proclamation in Article 84 that the basic principle of Korea's economic order shall be to realize social justice, meet every citizen's basic demands, and develop an equitable economy. The economic liberty of the individual citizens shall be protected only within the parameters set thereby. In order to realize this general principle,

[99] Paul S. Dull, "South Korean Constitution," *Far Eastern Survey*, vol. 17, no. 7 (Sept. 1948), p. 207 (emphasis added). Similar assessment is also found in the USAMGIK weekly intelligence report of 23 July 1948, just six days after the constitution was promulgated by the National Assembly. In the report, Charles Pergler, Special Legal Consultant to the Military Governor, wrote that the Economy Chapter "exhibits very strong tendencies toward state socialism." See G-2 Weekly Summary for the Period 16 July 1948–23 July 1948, Number 149, p. 8, reprinted in Institute of Asian Culture Studies, Hallym University (ed.), *HQ, USAFIK G-2 Weekly Summary (1948. 1. 31–1948. 11. 26)* (Ch'unch'ŏn: Institute of Asian Culture Studies, 1990), p. 396.

the Economy Chapter also provided for state regulation of foreign trade and government management of most public utilities (Article 87), as well as state ownership of most natural resources (Article 85). According to the testimony of Yu Chin-o, the main author of these articles,[100] the basic idea was to allow free enterprises for small- and medium-sized business and industry, whereas large-scale ones with public character and in danger of monopoly were to be state-owned.[101] But even those private enterprises could be made state-owned or government-managed when necessary for national security or public welfare (Article 88). Aside from the chapter on economy, other provisions also reinforced these "socialistic" features. While the right of property was recognized, the constitution also made it clear that its exercise must "conform to the public welfare" (Article 15). The state had a duty to protect those unable to work due to old age, infirmity, or incapacity (Article 19). In addition to a general provision for labor rights, the constitution gave special protection for the labor of women and children (Article 17). Most unusual perhaps was the provision on so-called workers' right to equal share in the profits of private enterprises (Article 18).

The strikingly socialistic socioeconomic regime mandated in the Founding Constitution may be puzzling since the Republic of Korea was established at the frontline of the Cold War representing the "free world" led by the United States. In September 1945, the United States military had arrived in the southern part of the Korean Peninsula utterly uninformed of the local conditions with no long-term strategic vision save a vague intention to secure the region under its zone of influence. In the north, by contrast, the Soviet army arrived in Pyongyang on 24 August, shortly after Japan's defeat, relatively

[100] In 1945, Yu Chin-o (1906–87) was a professor of law at Bosung College (later Korea University). Having been educated in law at Keijo Imperial University (the only Japanese national university in colonial Korea), he was reputed to be one of the very few Korean scholars who had more than a passing knowledge of public law. During the colonial period, he also enjoyed popular fame as a novelist and literary figure. Upon liberation, diverse political groups across the ideological spectrum approached him in their efforts to prepare their own draft constitutions. Politically, it was the right-wing Korean Democratic Party that he was most closely associated with. After the National Assembly was established in 1948, Yu's draft was officially adopted as one of the two base texts that were used to write the Founding Constitution. As a member of the Constitution Drafting Committee, he also participated in the deliberation process within the assembly. Later, he served as the Minister of Government Legislation in Syngman Rhee's first cabinet. For more on his life and career, see Lee Young-lok, *Yu Chin-o Hŏnpŏp Sasang ŭi Hyŏngsŏng kwa Chŏn'gae* [Formation and Development of Yu Chin-o's Constitutional Thought] (Paju: Han'guk Haksul Chŏngbo, 2006).

[101] *Chehŏn Kukhoe Sokkirok* [Minutes of the Constituent National Assembly], vol. 1 (1948; reprint, Seoul: Yŏgang Ch'ulp'ansa, 1987), Session 1, No. 17 (23 June 1948), p. 213 (hereafter *CNA Minutes*).

better prepared and organized to govern the territory under its occupation. By December 1945, at the Foreign Ministers Conference in Moscow, the United States agreed to a plan of establishing a four-power trusteeship over Korea and to work through a "U.S.-Soviet Joint Commission" to implement the agreement. Full independence would be granted after a period of trusteeship that could last up to five years. The Joint Commission, however, never got off the ground due to disagreements over how to establish a provisional government representing all Korean people across the ideological divide. Even before the Truman Doctrine was announced in March 1947, the Cold War rivalry between the two superpowers was already ratcheting up in Korea. The United States eventually abandoned the Moscow framework, which had been met from the very beginning with steep opposition in the south, and opted for the establishment of a separate South Korean government under the auspices of the United Nations. The final solution to the Korean question was, thus, the 10 May General Election in 1948 that would convene a National Assembly to draft a constitution for the south.[102]

Against this background, it appears even more anomalous that South Korea's constitution mandated such a socialistic economic regime. One of the explanations, most notably provided by Yu Chin-o himself, is the influence of the progressive Weimar Constitution.[103] One might also attribute this, as an American observer did in 1954, to the long monarchical tradition in which all property was assumed to belong to the king.[104] In terms of constitutional ideas, however, a more immediate inspiration came from the constitutional experiences of the Korean Provisional Government (KPG) established by leaders

[102] On the postcolonial division, U.S. and Soviet policies, and the onset of Cold War in the Peninsula, see Lee Wan-bom, *Han'guk Haebang Samnyŏnsa, 1945–1948* [Post-liberation History of Korea, 1945–1948] (Paju: T'aehaksa, 2007); William Stueck, *The Korean War: An International History* (Princeton, NJ: Princeton University Press, 1997); Bruce Cumings, *The Origins of the Korean War*, vols. I & II (Princeton, NJ: Princeton University Press, 1981/1992).

[103] Yu Chin-o, *Shin'go Hŏnpŏp Haeŭi* [Constitutional Law Explained, Revised Edition] (Seoul: Ilchogak, 1959), p. 253. One significant conduit of the Weimar influence to the drafters of the Founding Constitution may have been Ernst Fraenkel, who was an established social-democrat jurist in Weimar Germany and ardent New Dealer after his emigration to the United States. As a high-ranking legal advisor to USAMGIK in Seoul, according to a recent study, Fraenkel sought to implement in southern Korea the unfulfilled political and economic ideals of the Weimar era. Udi Greenberg, *The Weimar Century: German Emigrés and the Ideological Foundations of the Cold War* (Princeton, NJ: Princeton University Press, 2014), pp. 96–106. For a review of the historical influences on the economic provisions of the Korean constitution, see Sung Nak-in, "Taehan Min'guk Kyŏngje Hŏnpŏpsa Sogo" [Reflections on the History of Korea's Economic Constitution], *Sŏul Taehakkyo Pŏphak*, vol. 54, no. 3 (2013).

[104] John W. Connelly, Jr., "Memorandum: Report on Economic Provisions of the Constitution of the Republic of Korea (24 Mar. 1954)," Records of the U.S. Foreign Assistance Agencies 1948–61, Record Group 469, Entry 422, Box 20, U.S. National Archives at College Park, MD, pp. 7–8 (hereafter Connelly, "Report on Economic Provisions").

of the independence movement in China. Although the KPG constitution, first made in 1919 and revised five times thereafter, did not have a separate chapter on the economy, it did have a strong dose of socialistic tendency in its rights provisions. Justified in terms of the "Principle of Three Equalities" (*Samgyunjuŭi*),[105] this was a reflection of the uneasy truce between the right- and left-wing factions within the independence movement, as well as the influence of the Chinese Republican experiments.[106] This KPG legacy left an indelible mark on the socioeconomic regime of numerous official and private draft constitutions between 1945 and 1948. Practically all of these drafts aimed to fuse political and socioeconomic democracy, albeit with different emphases. The so-called Yu Chin-o Draft, the primary base text used by the National Assembly, was no exception.[107] A predominantly idealistic, egalitarian outlook had already become part of Korea's constitutional heritage even before a constitution was officially adopted.

Constitutional provisions, however, are never purely aspirational or transformative. To be relevant and sustainable, a constitution has to accommodate the given realities even as it aspires to transform them via "militant constitutionalism."[108] A constitution as a living norm may be sustained only when the

[105] The "three equalities" meant equality in the areas of politics, economy, and education. They also referred to equality in the relationships between individuals, between nations, and between states. A brainchild of Cho So-ang, arguably the ablest theoretician among the core KPG leadership, this principle was adopted as the official ideology of the KPG and the future independent state of Korea. For example, "Essential Points for Founding a New State" (*Kŏn'guk Kangnyŏng*), one of KPG's constitutional documents also penned by Cho, clearly showed similarly "socialistic" tendencies of state ownership, planned economy and limited property rights. See "Taehan Min'guk Kŏn'guk Kangnyŏng," Chapter III, Part 6, in Chong Jong-sup (ed.), *Han'guk Hŏnpŏpsa Mullyu* [Constitutional Documents of Korea] (Seoul: Pakyoungsa, 2002), pp. 88, 94–5.

[106] Some attribute the writing of a separate chapter on economy to the so-called 5 May Charter (1936) of the Republic of China. For the influence of the republican Chinese constitutional ideas on KPG in general, see Shin Woo-Cheol, *Pigyo Hŏnpŏpsa: Taehan Min'guk Iphŏnjuŭi ŭi Yŏnwŏn* [Comparative Constitutional History: The Origins of Korean Constitutionalism] (Paju: Pŏpmunsa, 2008), pp. 287–394, 431–8.

[107] The Constitution Drafting Committee adopted another base text that is commonly referred to as the Kwŏn Sŭng-yŏl Draft. This text is often attributed to the Code Drafting Commission of the Justice Department of the South Korean Interim Government (Koreanized executive arm of the USAMGIK), although it remains unclear whether it officially represented the commission's view. As for its contents, there were some differences from the Yu Chin-o draft. For instance, the Kwŏn draft put relatively more emphasis on the executive and judicial powers over the legislature. In the final analysis, however, the differences were rather negligible, and it was the Yu draft that was relied on most heavily. For more on the Kwŏn draft, see Kim Su-Yong, *Kŏn'guk kwa Hŏnpŏp* [Founding and the Constitution] (Seoul: Kyŏngin Munhwasa, 2008), pp. 241–51.

[108] Jacobsohn, *Constitutional Identity*, pp. 217, 238–52.

constitutional norm is designed (and interpreted) to cohere with the social reality of the time. Even the constitution of a new nation emerging from out of colonial repression must take heed of existing social realities, especially with regard to economic matters. Chapter VI of Korea's Founding Constitution was also the result of such realism toward the economic status quo of the time.

In the immediate postcolonial context, the most powerful factors shaping the economic order of Korea were the practices and institutions left over from the Japanese "total mobilization" system of the late World War II period. At the time of liberation, 85 percent of *all* assets in Korea, not to mention major industries, enterprises, and financial institutions, were owned by the Japanese government or its nationals. This basic framework was essentially taken over by U.S. authorities when they occupied the southern half of the peninsula in 1945. The so-called enemy properties (*chŏksan*) were summarily confiscated by USAMGIK and became known as "vested properties."[109] They would later be transferred to the new South Korean government after its establishment in 1948. At the time the Founding Constitution was made, in other words, state ownership of economic entities and infrastructure was the norm, and there were few private enterprises to speak of. Given this baseline, it would have been rather strange and impracticable to provide for a robust free market economy in the constitution, a system premised on the initiative of private economic enterprises which were all but nonexistent at the time.[110] Thus, according to Yu Chin-o, the economic regime mandated by the constitution was not controversial at all during National Assembly deliberations because it was commonly perceived to be a rough facsimile of the economic status quo of the time.[111] Since state ownership of economic resources and government management of the economy were the default condition, the drafters of the 1948 constitution did not regard its socioeconomic regime as particularly socialist or interventionist. The provision on redistribution of farmland (Article 86) may be seen as a "transformative" mandate, but even that was generally consistent with the default system of state-centered economy.

[109] USAMGIK Ordinance No. 33 "Vesting Title to Japanese Property within Korea" (6 Dec. 1945), Art. 2.

[110] Hwang Sŭng-hŭm, "Chehŏn Hŏnpŏp Cheyukjang Kyŏngjepyŏn ŭi Hyŏngsŏng Kwajŏng kwa Kŭ Ŭimi" [The Formation Process of The Founding Constitution's Chapter VI on Economy and Its Meaning], *Pŏpsahak Yŏn'gu*, vol. 30 (2004), p. 149.

[111] Yu Chin-o, *Hŏnpŏp Kich'o Hoegorok* [Recollections on the Drafting of the Constitution] (Seoul: Ilchogak, 1980), pp. 39–41. See also Lee Jong Won, *Higashi Ajia Reisen to Kan-Bei-Nichi Kankei* [Cold War in East Asia and the Korea-U.S.-Japan Relations] (Tokyo: University of Tokyo Press, 1996), p. 132.

This economic status quo formed the background for the inclusion of the socialistic clause protecting the workers' right to have a share in the profits of private enterprises (*Iik Kyunjŏmkwŏn*) (Article 18). The National Assembly had been established through the 10 May 1948 general election in which the leftists and even some "centrists" did not participate. For the assembly dominated by right-wing factions, the adoption of such a pro-labor right – practically unheard of anywhere else in the world – might seem remarkable indeed. It is interesting to note, however, that this pro-labor concept was actually inserted at the suggestion of a labor group backed by rightists.[112] The leftists, and the labor unions they supported, had never argued for such a right, because their goal was the complete state ownership and control of all economic resources and institutions.[113] To demand this right was to presuppose the existence of profit-seeking private enterprises. In the ideological terrain of post-liberation Korea, in other words, this right only made sense for those on the right who expected business activities to be conducted mostly by private actors. As Yu Chin-o stated, small- and medium-sized enterprises would be privately owned and managed; only large enterprises that affected the public interest would be state-controlled.

This expectation in turn presupposed that the vested properties confiscated from the Japanese and held at the time by the U.S. occupation authorities would eventually be sold to private citizens. From the perspective of those advocating the right to profit-sharing, these vested properties (especially the business entities) had to be disposed of in a way that could benefit all Koreans equally. Granting this right was a way of ensuring that the workers would also benefit from the disposal of "enemy properties." It was thus not so much an embrace of a leftist idea as a concession to the nationalistic argument that property taken from the Japanese should be used to improve the lot of all Koreans rather than a handful of would-be capitalists. Seen in that light, this pro-labor right could even be endorsed by right-wing politicians.

As soon as the National Assembly was convened on 31 May 1948, a thirty-member "Committee on the Drafting of the Constitution and the Organization Law of the Government" (Drafting Committee) was formed. As it deliberated on the draft constitution to be considered at the plenary session

[112] Hwang Sŭng-hŭm, "Chehŏn Hŏnpŏp sang ŭi Kŭlloja ŭi Iik Kyunjŏmkwŏn ŭi Hŏnpŏphwa Kwajŏng e kwanhan Yŏn'gu" [A Study on the Constitutionalization of Workers' Right to Share Profit in the Founding Constitution], *Kongpŏp Yŏn'gu*, vol. 31, no. 2 (2002), pp. 299, 307–08.

[113] A good example is the 1946 draft constitution submitted by the leftist Democratic National Front (*Minjujuŭi Minjok Chŏnsŏn*) in response to the survey questionnaire prepared by the U.S.-Soviet Joint Commission for the purpose of canvassing the opinions of local political groups. See Hwang, "Iik Kyunjŏmkwŏn," p. 307.

of the National Assembly, many groups and even individuals submitted their own proposals for a new constitution. One such proposal came from the Federation of Workers for the Acceleration of Korean Independence (*Taehan Tongnip Ch'oksŏng Nodong Ch'ongyŏnmaeng*), which called for, among others, the right of workers to participate in the management of private companies as well as the workers' right to have an equal share in the business profits (in addition to their regular wages).[114] The Drafting Committee had apparently debated whether to recognize such rights, but decided to include neither in its final draft. During the plenary sessions, however, proposals were made once again to insert both of them or at least the right to profit-sharing. Thus arose one of the most intense discussions in the National Assembly during the drafting of the Founding Constitution.[115]

According to the opponents of the proposal, recognizing such rights would not only encroach on the entrepreneurs' rights and sap their entrepreneurial spirit, but also be detrimental to the long-term development of Korea's industries. Its proponents, in response, pointed out that there were very few individuals in Korea at the time who might realistically be expected to act as entrepreneurs.[116] They even argued that labor should not be seen as a commodity in a subordinate position to capital, but rather as a form of capital contributed by workers, and that workers therefore should be entitled to participate in the management of the company and to receive an equal share of its profits.[117] In the end, only the right to share in the profits was adopted, but not before another round of heated debate about its proper place within the text of the constitution. One suggestion was to insert additional language in Article 17 of the draft constitution that dealt with the right and duty to work as

114 As its name indicates, this group was closely affiliated with the National Society for the Acceleration of Korean Independence (*Taehan Tongnip Ch'oksŏng Kukminhoe*), a right-wing political group led by Syngman Rhee. The Federation was formed in 1946 as the rightist response to the National Council of Korean Trade Unions (*Chosŏn Nodong Chohap Chŏn'guk P'yŏngŭihoe*). This latter group had been formed in late 1945 as the successor to the more radical labor movements of the colonial period. It would be outlawed in 1947 by USAMGIK.

115 For the debate and overall assessment of this issue, see Cheon Kwang-seok, "Kŏnkuk Hŏnpŏp ŭi Sahoe-Kyŏngje Chilsŏ Kusang" [Visions of Socio-Economic Order Embodied in the Founding Constitution], in Han'guk Mirae Hakhoe (ed.), *Chehŏn kwa Kŏn'guk* (Paju: Nanam, 2010), pp. 231–7.

116 CNA *Minutes*, Session 1, No. 24 (3 July 1948), p. 413 (statement of Assemblyman Chŏn Chin-han). See also Hwang, "Iik Kyunjŏmkwŏn," p. 310.

117 CNA *Minutes*, Session 1, No. 20 (29 June 1948), p. 293 (statement of Assemblyman Kim Yong-jae). See also Shin Yong-Oak, "Chehŏn Hŏnpŏp ŭi Sahoe-Kyŏngje Chilsŏ Kusŏng Inyŏm" [The Founding Constitution's Ideology for Structuring the Socio-Economic Order], *Han'guksa Yŏn'gu*, vol. 144 (2009), p. 21.

well as labor standards. Another was to move it to Chapter VI on the economy on the grounds that the right is actually a means to achieve social justice and a balanced economy. In its final form, it was added to Article 18, which provided for the labor rights to collective bargaining and collective action.

In this connection, another proposal that did not get adopted is noteworthy. During the plenary sessions, it was proposed that an article be included as a Supplemental Rule, which would confirm that all property which had belonged to the Japanese government and nationals was now the property of the state. As mentioned, proper disposition of enemy properties was of paramount importance for the fragile economic order of the new state to be inaugurated. Those advocating the workers' right to share in their company's profits argued that enemy properties belonged to the entire Korean nation, and, as such, must be used to benefit all Koreans. On that point, in fact, there seems to have been little disagreement at the time. Yet, the proposal to insert an explicit provision was defeated on the ground that the matter was not strictly a domestic issue that could be decided unilaterally by Korea. It was an international matter that would be subject to the final manner and shape of the general peace settlement for the Pacific War.[118] Proponents responded that this was all the more reason to include it in the constitution, for it meant that enemy property could potentially be taken away by the Allied nations as part of their war indemnity.[119] The proposal was nevertheless defeated. Arguments for prudence and diplomacy carried the day, and the disposition of enemy property would have to rely on the good intentions of the Allies. The international community was clearly present at the creation of the economic regime of Korea's Founding Constitution.

As for the United States, its government had actually been promising to transfer all vested properties to the new government of Korea.[120] It probably did not care one way or the other if it was stipulated in the constitution. According to an American report in 1954, USAMGIK was instructed "not to interfere with or to participate in any way in the work of the newly established National Assembly."[121] Yet, this did not mean that Americans were completely indifferent to the future economic regime of Korea. In fact, Washington's directive in

[118] Vested property was apparently under the jurisdiction of eleven different foreign nations. *CNA Minutes*, Session 1, No. 26 (6 July 1948), p. 493 (statement of Assemblyman Sŏ Sang-il).

[119] *CNA Minutes*, Session 1, No. 26 (6 July 1948), p. 492–3 (statements of Assemblymen Shin Sŏng-gyun and Yi Sŏk-chu).

[120] Indeed, the original confiscation of enemy property by USAMGIK and its transfer to the South Korean government would be rubber-stamped by the 1952 San Francisco Treaty (Article 4(B)).

[121] Connelly, "Report on Economic Provisions," p. 19.

1947 made it quite clear that USAMGIK should promote a system with substantial government involvement in the economy.

> Such an economy in Korea might well be of the "mixed" type including various arrangements for industrial organization such as public, private and cooperative ownership, and an agriculture based firmly on a large number of small farmer proprietors. You will encourage popular discussion of economic reforms such as redistribution of land ownership or development of credit cooperatives.[122]

Plainly, Washington's preference did not lay with a classic laissez-faire economy. Along this line, the occupation authorities were to introduce various economic reform measures including farmland redistribution and "equitable distribution of needed goods."[123] This economic outlook would be further reinforced by the experience of the USAMGIK itself. After a disastrous attempt at the beginning of occupation to introduce a free market for rice, USAMGIK quickly resorted in January 1946 to rationing and revived the old rice collection system that had been maintained under Japanese rule. A similar attempt to establish a "free commodities market" for tobacco, salt, sugar, and other goods also resulted in chaos and a reversion to tight government control.[124] In May 1946, the occupation authorities issued a comprehensive law on government regulation of economy (Ordinance No. 90 "Economic Controls") which established a National Food Administration and a National Price Administration.[125] USAMGIK was faced with issues that simply could not be left to the market. Again, the economic reality of the time demanded a system that required the government to assume a dominant role.

122 SWNCC 176/29 "Interim Directive to General of the Army Douglas MacArthur, at Tokyo, for Lieutenant General John R. Hodge, at Seoul," 24 July 1947, *FRUS 1947*, vol. VI (1972), p. 726.

123 SWNCC 176/29, p. 725. A draft constitution in 1946, attributed to Emery Woodall who was chief of the USAMGIK Department of Justice, included a right "to earn a livelihood by lawful work." It also prohibited government from "alienat[ing] natural resources of national importance" and "establish[ing] or permit[ting] to exist any private monopoly except in accordance with law." See "Woodall's 'The Constitution of Korea,'" in Korea University Museum (ed.), *Hyŏnmin Yu Chin-o Chehŏn Hŏnpŏp Kwan'gye Charyojip* [Constitutional Documents of Yu Chin-o] (Seoul: Korea University Press, 2009).

124 Yi Tae-gŭn, *Haebanghu-1950 Nyŏndae ŭi Kyŏngje* [The Economy of Post-liberation Era and the 1950s] (Seoul: Samsung Kyŏngje Yŏn'guso, 2002), pp. 72–5.

125 Ordinance No. 90 also set up a National Economic Board whose mission was inter alia to "[c]onduct national economic planning, determining the potentials and goals of production, the character and volume of imports and exports, allocation of producers' materials, plant, machinery, equipment, power, fuel and labor, the distribution and utilization of imported and locally produced commodities, the stabilization of prices and the rationing of consumers' goods, and the collection or control of goods in short supply."

Korean people under occupation were no more hospitable toward free market. In the summer of 1947, when USAMGIK received the directive on "mixed" economy, the Korean Interim Legislative Assembly (KILA) was deliberating on the first public constitutional draft in postcolonial Korea. Putatively the "legislative arm" of USAMGIK, KILA was composed of ninety local political and social leaders, with the mandate of formulating policy and bills, which would become law upon the "concurrence" of the military governor. Whether it had authority to draft a constitution is thus murky at best, but, be that as it may, KILA prepared a draft which included a provision that was proudly described as "national socialist" (*kukka sahoejuŭi*) by one of its drafters without a hint of apology or irony.[126] Article 4 of KILA's Temporary Constitution of Korea (*Chosŏn Imshi Yakhŏn*) declared a fundamental right to equality of livelihood (*Saenghwal Kyundŭngkwŏn*) for all citizens, and then went on to enumerate ten programs under this principle, which included planned economy, land redistribution, nationalization of large industries and mines, as well as workers' rights and social welfare. To be sure, the KILA draft constitution never went into effect due to the military governor's veto, but it was certainly not due to its "national socialist" character. There is no doubt that this socialistic tendency had an influence on the Founding Constitution, as many KILA members were later elected to the National Assembly.

In summary, the economic regime sanctioned by the Founding Constitution was strikingly socialistic for a fledging republic under U.S. tutelage during the initial phase of the Cold War. On the one hand, such constitutional ideas had deep roots that went back to the KPG constitutions. Constitutionalizing them after liberation was also supported by the Korean people's zeal for socioeconomic equality and economic nationalism, which seem to have been condoned by the occupation authorities operating under Washington's directive on economic matters. On the other hand, not to be overlooked is the economic reality at the time where free-market system and private enterprises were virtually nonexistent. The state's tight control over the economy and active intervention in the market was the default condition in the immediate postcolonial Korea. The "socialistic" or "mixed" economy as outlined in the Economy Chapter and other socioeconomic provisions was the culmination of this unique confluence of idealism and realism that appears to have been shared by USAMGIK and the National Assembly.

[126] *Nam Chosŏn Kwado Ippŏp Uiwŏn Sokkirok* [Minutes of the South Korean Interim Legislative Assembly], No. 113, (16 July 1947), p. 11 [Reprinted in *Nam Chosŏn Kwado Ippŏp Uiwŏn Sokkirok*, vol. 3 (Seoul: Sŏnin Munhwasa, 1984), p. 47] (hereafter *KILA Minutes*).

Preemption: Regime Legitimacy and Land Reform

Aside from the prevailing economic realities of the period, however, there was a much more pressing "external" reason for designing the economic regime of the new South Korean state with such socialistic overtones. From the beginning, arguably, the right-wing coalition that formed a hegemonic bloc within the National Assembly suffered from a legitimacy deficit. The fact that domestic left-wing factions had recently been purged from the South Korean political scene called into question its representativeness. The legitimacy problem was due in large part to the perception that the right-wing coalition – especially those belonging to the Korean Democratic Party, which represented the landowning class interests – had prevailed in the general election, despite suspicions of collaboration under colonial rule, thanks to USAMGIK patronage. More importantly, the communist regime emerging north of the 38th parallel was already carrying out extensive socioeconomic reforms under Soviet supervision, whereas such reform, albeit urgently called for, was not making much progress in the south.

In order to compensate for their contested "regime legitimacy," thus, the drafters of the constitution opted for a socioeconomic regime more progressive than would have been warranted by their narrow class interests or political inclinations. Seen in this light, the Economy Chapter and related articles were a means by which to win the hearts of the general populace in the south and to counteract communist infiltration from the north. According to the main proponent of the workers' right to share their company's profits, for instance, this right was needed in order to prevent workers' discontent and disaffection, which might make them vulnerable to communist propaganda. It was envisioned as a tool for protecting the newborn republic in the south from communism. In short, the Cold War competition with North Korea was a major factor behind the constitutionalization of a "mixed" type economy.

Such regime rivalry was largely responsible for the remarkable convergence between the Economy Chapter and the corresponding articles in the North Korean Constitution of 1948.[127] In particular, land reform was a top priority in both North and South Korea, as can be seen from its inscription into the constitutions of both regimes.[128] As in the north, the land issue was the potential

[127] In Chapter I "Fundamental Principles," the North Korean charter provided for state ownership of major enterprises and natural resources (Article 5), farmland redistribution (Article 6), enumerated private property rights (Article 8), and planned economy (Article 10).

[128] South Korea's Article 86 read in full: "Farmland shall be distributed to the tenant farmers; the method of distribution, the limits of ownership, and the contents and limitations of property rights shall be determined by law." In comparison, North Korea's Article 6 provided: "Land owned by Japan and its nationals and by Korean landlords shall be confiscated; tenancy shall forever be abolished."

source of class struggle in the south, where about 3 percent of the population owned two-thirds of all arable land.[129] The uncompensated confiscation of farmland and its free distribution to tenants in the north, implemented under the Soviet military authority as early as March 1946, was bound to aggravate the volatile political situation in the traditionally more agricultural South Korea. Even USAMGIK felt pressed by this turn of events. On 15 March 1946, only ten days after the Soviet-style abolition of tenancy was proclaimed in Pyongyang, the U.S. military governor, Major General Archer L. Lerch, announced a plan to redistribute farmland vested in USAMGIK. Its effectuation, however, would have to wait two more years.

This delay contrasts markedly with the occupation policy adopted by GHQ/SCAP in Japan, where a liberal land reform was hastily undertaken by the Americans at the same time as the new constitution was being drafted. Although some form of agrarian reform had been contemplated by the Japanese government even before the end of the war, it was MacArthur who put it at the top of his reform agenda in October 1945.[130] It was seen as an essential part of dismantling the "feudalistic" foundation of Japanese militarism (Item 3 of the MacArthur Notes) and building up a new socioeconomic infrastructure for postwar democracy. It was also regarded as a preemptive measure against communist infiltration into impoverished rural areas. Even more "socialistic" than South Korea's Article 86, in fact, the original GHQ draft of Japan's postwar constitution contained a provision for virtual state-ownership of all natural resources, including land (Article 28). This was taken out during the process of translating it into Japanese, apparently without the GHQ's objection or even knowledge.[131] Nevertheless, even before the constitution was finalized, the U.S. occupation authorities made sure that land reform would be swiftly carried out.[132] As it were, land reform and constitution-making were

[129] Ronald H. Spector, *In the Ruins of Empire: The Japanese Surrender and the Battle for Postwar Asia* (New York: Random House, 2007), p. 155. According to a State Department report, in 1945, more than 75% of the cultivated acreage was operated under the tenant system, and only about 17% of the farmers owned all the land they cultivated. U.S. Department of State, *Korea 1945 to 1948: A Report on Political Developments and Economic Resources with Selected Documents*, Department of State Publication 3305, Far Eastern Series 28 (Washington, DC: U.S. Government Printing Office, 1948), p. 30.

[130] Ronald P. Dore, *Land Reform in Japan* (London: Oxford University Press, 1959), pp. 131–2.

[131] Matsumoto Jōji proudly recalled in 1954: "I had omitted the provision on my own responsibility, and did not consult anyone about it. Fortunately, all that became of it was the land reform law." See RM213. Matsumoto on drafting the Constitution. RM213.SP2.P48.

[132] Upon strong and repeated urging from the GHQ, the Japanese government made the first Land Reform Act in December 1945, but this was widely criticized by not only the Allies but also the Japanese public for its conservative approach. In the end, the GHQ made a more direct intervention, and the second law was passed through the newly elected diet in October 1946. Dore, *Land Reform in Japan*, pp. 129–37.

two interrelated pillars of early occupation policy in Japan that were pursued in virtual synchrony.

By contrast, neither agenda was as important for the Americans in Seoul. Although not without a vision for some kind of agrarian reform,[133] Washington's initial policy was geared more toward maintaining the status quo, including the Japanese colonial apparatuses and agricultural infrastructures, pending the trusteeship scheme of the Moscow Agreement. But, as mentioned, the mounting rivalry with the Soviet Union and the eventual decision to establish a separate government in the south had changed the scene, and land reform emerged as a pressing political issue especially in view of the UN-sanctioned general election scheduled to take place in March (later postponed to May) 1948. The election was to form a representative body which would draft a new constitution, and the need arose to contain the communists and socialists who boycotted and planned to sabotage the UN solution. Now, further delay in land redistribution risked making rural voters, an absolute majority of the Korean population, more susceptible to the leftist agitation against the general election. In short, it was only in the final stages of the U.S. occupation that both land reform and constitution-making emerged as interrelated agendas in postcolonial Korea.

Initially, USAMGIK had hoped that KILA would enact a land reform law in an expeditious manner. In December 1947, as it prepared for the general election, USAMGIK submitted a bill to KILA, which was designed to redistribute farmlands of Korean landlords as well as the vested lands confiscated from the Japanese government and nationals. As it turned out, however, many KILA members, even those on the left and the center, showed little interest in passing this bill. According to an American observer at that time, the reason was that "[t]he disposal of 1,400,000 farm plots offered such a tremendous opportunity for political patronage that nearly every group, left as well as right, protested the sale"[134] while under the occupation. After KILA adjourned for one last time without passing the bill, USAMGIK decided to take matters into its own hands and did what it could under the pressing circumstances. It established the National Land Administration on 22 March 1948 and promptly proceeded to sell the vested farmlands to tenant

[133] For varying discussions of reform measures, including the well-known "Bunce Report," see Shannon McCune, "Land Redistribution in Korea," *Far Eastern Survey*, vol. 17, no. 2 (28 Jan. 1948), p. 15.

[134] C. Clyde Mitchell, "Land Reform in South Korea," *Pacific Affairs*, vol. 22, no. 2 (June 1949), p. 152. Mitchell served as the head of the agency set up by USAMGIK to administer vested properties. He later received a doctorate from Harvard with a dissertation on labor management and tenancy reform in Korea under USAMGIK.

farmers.[135] By the end of May, USAMKIG succeeded in distributing about 76 percent of the farmland earmarked for sale, more than 15 percent of all the arable land in South Korea, under this scheme.[136]

The immediate outcome was twofold. On the one hand, land reform, albeit partial, seems to have paid off politically, and the rural voters proved to be largely unmoved by the leftists' attempt to sabotage the general election. At the same time, on the other, the reform also worked as a constraint on the right-wing political groups, which would emerge victorious in the election. Even those with close connections to landowning class interests had to run on a campaign platform that included further redistribution of the farmlands owned by Korean landlords as well. The agenda was simply locked in politically, and there was no turning back after the election.[137] The irreversible commitment to further reform was only strengthened during National Assembly deliberations on the constitution. Whereas the original Yu Chin-o draft had stated that farmland shall be distributed to farmers "in principle," that qualifier was dropped in the final version to allow for no exception to the rule.[138] Giving constitutional status to this transient, albeit urgent, policy issue would likely have been inconceivable, had it not been for the early completion of land redistribution in the north and the USAMGIK initiative for similar reform measures in response. In other words, it was these external circumstances and foreign imposition that, to a considerable extent, account for Article 86's place in the Founding Constitution.

South Korea's land reform, however, had one critical difference from its northern counterpart. Unlike in the north, the Founding Constitution mandated "due compensation" for private property expropriated for public purposes (Articles 15 and 89).[139] This meant the lands expropriated for

135 USAMGIK Ordinance No. 173, "Creation of the National Land Administration" and No. 174, "Dissolution of the New Korea Company Limited" (22 Mar. 1948).

136 U.S. Department of State, *Korea 1945 to 1948*, p. 31. The number would rise to more than 85% in August when the Republic of Korea was inaugurated. Mitchell, "Land Reform in South Korea," p. 148.

137 Mitchell was right on target when he concluded that "the two events [Land Reform and General Election] were related: efficient and equitable disposal of the Japanese farms was in some measure responsible for the repudiation of Communism at the polls by Korean farmers whom agents from North Korea as well as in the south had been urging to boycott the election; and the men who sought election to the Legislative Assembly deemed it politic to pledge support of a continued land reform program." Mitchell, "Land Reform in South Korea," p. 144.

138 CNA *Minutes*, Session 1, No. 26 (6 July 1948), p. 479.

139 Article 89 reads: "Art. 15, par. 3 of this Constitution shall be applicable to the cancellation of a license, the expropriation, use or restriction of property as provided in Art. 85 through 88," whereas Article 15, paragraph 3 reads in full: "Expropriation, use or restriction of private property for public purposes shall be accompanied by due compensation in accordance with the provisions of law."

redistribution according to Article 86 had to be compensated for; in point of fact, Article 15 was invoked more often as the constitutional ground for the land reform act during its legislative process.[140] Moreover, expropriated lands would not be freely given to the tenant farmers as they had to pay 30 percent of their annual yields for up to five years. As for the method of compensation, the landlords were issued "land bond" that could be redeemed in installments. This could not be further different from the North Korean policy of "free confiscation, free distribution" (*musang molsu, musang punbae*).

Syngman Rhee, Korea's first president, was clearly aware of the political urgency of this constitutional mandate and its crucial role for bolstering South Korea's regime legitimacy vis-à-vis North Korea.[141] Relatively free from landowning class interests, he was also motivated by political desire to weaken the material basis of his domestic rivals (especially, the Korean Democratic Party) who had entrenched stakes in the economic status quo.[142] Also not to be overlooked is the consistent pressure from Washington, which demanded the Rhee government to continue further redistribution along the line established by USAMGIK's measure and complete the land reform by the harvest season of 1950.[143] In any case, Rhee's new government immediately set out making the Agricultural Land Reform Act and, even before it was officially approved by the National Assembly in June 1949 (revised in March 1950), began to implement it under the leadership of Cho Pong-am, Rhee's Minister of Agriculture with an ex-communist background. According to the government's account, land reform was "completed" by 15 April 1950.[144] This extraordinary haste

140 Kim Sŏng-ho, "Nambukhan ŭi Nongji Kaehyŏk Yŏn'gu" [Land Reform in North and South Korea], in Hong Sŏng-ch'an (ed.), *Nongji Kaehyŏk Yŏn'gu* (Seoul: Yonsei University Press, 2001), p. 262.

141 Rhee's strong commitment to land reform was driven by his belief that such a reform would be necessary to insulate the rural population from communist agitations. It was also anchored in his economic philosophy that independent Korea should be an industrial nation for which purpose transforming agricultural to industrial capital was crucial. See Lew Young Ick, *Kŏn'guk Taet'ongnyŏng Yi Sŭngman: Saengae, Sasang, Opchŏk ŭi Saeroun Chomyŏng* [Founding President Syngman Rhee: A New Look at His Life, Thoughts, and Achievements] (Seoul: Ilchogak, 2013), pp. 190–1.

142 Gregg Brazinsky, *Nation Building in South Korea: Koreans, Americans, and the Making of a Democracy* (Chapel Hill: University of North Carolina Press, 2007), p. 19.

143 E.g., "Memorandum by the Assistant Secretary of State for Far Eastern Affairs (Butterworth) to the Secretary of State (16 Dec. 1949)" in *FRUS* 1949, vol. VII, pt. 2 (1976), pp. 1110–1. According to one interpretation, the persistent pressure from U.S. authorities was driven by their deep suspicion of Rhee's commitment to the land reform program. Jun Sang-in, *Kogae Sugin Sujŏngjuŭi: Han'guk Hyŏndaesa ŭi Yŏksasahoehak* [Revisionism in Decline: Historical Sociology of Modern Korean History] (Seoul: Chŏnt'ong kwa Hyŏndae, 2001), pp. 114–15.

144 The date was given by the Agricultural Ministry to the National Assembly in 1951. Kim Sŏng-ho, "Nambukhan," p. 267. To be precise, official notification of the distributed plots to tenants was

turned out to be highly fortuitous because, by one estimate, up to 80 percent of the farmland would be redistributed by the time the Korean War broke out in June 1950.[145] Both the timeliness and the contents of the reform would have a lasting impact on the subsequent development of South Korea's constitutional identity.

First, thanks in part to its timeliness, later land reforms introduced in the south under communist occupation during the Korean War were not entirely successful despite the North Korean propaganda to the contrary.[146] The small-landowning farmers created overnight by the south's land reform had little reason to welcome yet another measure of redistribution by the communists who, unlike the South Korean government, imposed restrictions on ownership rights and merely granted cultivation privileges.[147] Together with the heavy taxation in kind and violent purges witnessed during the occupation, this wartime experience would spread virulent anticommunism among

done by this date, while legal registration of the new deeds was interrupted by the outbreak of the Korean War in June. Even further delayed was the issuing of "land bonds" to the landlords, which was not completed until 1957. Kim Sŏng-bo, "Ippŏp kwa Silhaenggwajŏng ŭl t'onghae bon Namhan Nongji Kaehyŏk ŭi Sŏngkyŏk" [The Characteristics of Land Reform in South Korea as reflected in the Legislative Process], in Hong Sŏng-ch'an (ed.), *Nongji Kaehyŏk Yŏn'gu*, pp. 156–60.

145 Kim Il-Young, *Kŏn'guk kwa Puguk* [State-Building and Wealth-Building] (Seoul: Saenggak ŭi Namu, 2004), pp. 117–21. Also to be noted is the fact that, in anticipation of land reform, landlords sought to sell their lands preemptively. As a result, for example, farmlands owned by big landlords were reduced by almost 70% by the time land reform began. Hong Sŏng-ch'an, "Nongji Kaehyŏk Chŏnhu ŭi Taejiju Tonghyang" [The Situation of Big Landlords before and after the Land Reform], in Hong Sŏng-ch'an (ed.), *Nongji Kaehyŏk Yŏn'gu*, p. 193. Whether for good or ill, this reaction by the landlords had also contributed to the expeditious completion of land reform in South Korea. In a recent estimate, for instance, 49.2% of all distributed lands were a result of market transaction before the land reform law was implemented. See Yoong-Deok Jeon and Young-Yong Kim, "Land Reform, Income Redistribution, and Agricultural Production in Korea," *Economic Development and Cultural Change*, vol. 48, no. 2 (2000), p. 255.

146 In the first three months of the war, North Korea was in control of 90% of the South Korean territory and 92% of its population. During this brief occupation period, 43.4% of the farmland was confiscated, of which 96.2% was redistributed. The confusion, violence, and discontent among the general peasantry were inevitable. For more on North Korea's land reform in the occupied south and its utter infertility, see Myung-Lim Park, *The Requiem for Peace: A Critical-Constructive Reflection on the Korean War* (Paju: Nanam, 2005), pp. 245–65.

147 Article 10 of the North Korean Land Reform Ordinance (March 1946) strictly prohibited the new land owners from selling or using it as a financial leverage. Coupled with the Tax Ordinance issued shortly thereafter, which imposed 25% taxation in kind on all agricultural yields, the emerging North Korean government had become a de facto landlord, practically turning all peasant population into state sharecroppers rather than property-owning farmers. It was this same measure that was imposed on the occupied South. See Jang Sang-Hwan, "Land Reform and Capitalist Development in Korea," Spring Conference Paper, Institute for Social Sciences, Gyeongsang National University (2005), pp. 12–13.

the South Korean populace for a long time to come. Just as Bonapartism of the Second Empire in France relied on the self-tilling, small peasantry, these small-landowning farmers in postwar Korea would form a conservative voting bloc that Rhee and his political machine could exploit for their authoritarian rule. In a sense, the deeply conservative, anticommunist template of South Korean politics that lasted until as late as the 1980s was already set in place by the class realignment that had been effected by land reform before the war.[148]

Second, although landlords were given compensation, its method hampered their successful transition into a modern industrial capitalist class. The built-in policy bias against a swift and adequate compensation was reinforced by the government's financial cringe and the raging inflation triggered by the war.[149] As a result, by the time of the postwar economic recovery, few members of the previous large-landowning class had sufficient money to take advantage of the government sale of enemy properties intended to jumpstart industrial capitalism. Instead, many of the new industrial capitalists, who became today's *chaebŏl*, would hail from new upstarts with crony political connections to the government.[150] Demise of the landowning class had a beneficial effect, too. South Korean politics and economy would remain remarkably free of a reactionary hegemonic class entrenched in the traditional agricultural interests that, in many other Third World countries, would time and again frustrate the causes of both democracy and development. In this sense, South Korea's dynamic democratization as well as the stunning economic growth in the following decades owes in no small measure to the successful land reform of this era.[151]

By the war's end, the Economy Chapter had largely accomplished its mission in land reform, while many parts of its allegedly "socialistic" principles had increasingly become outdated. The Korean War, which entrenched the Cold War on the peninsula, only strengthened the south's regime legitimacy vis-à-vis the communist north. The constitution had created a nation of small-landowning farmers who would soon be mobilized as an industrial labor army for the new capitalist class that replaced the traditional landlords. Economic rehabilitation and industrial growth were to be the new zeitgeist, spurred in part by the government sale of large vested enterprises in which the former landowning class could rarely partake. The consolidation of the Cold War order worldwide meant that the Economy Chapter would no

[148] Kim Il-Young, *Kŏn'guk*, pp. 172–3.
[149] Jang, "Land Reform," p. 15.
[150] Kim Il-Young, *Kŏn'guk*, pp. 163–8.
[151] Gi-Wook Shin, "Agrarian Conflict and the Origins of Korean Capitalism," *American Journal of Sociology*, vol. 103, no. 5 (1998), pp. 1313–14.

longer be necessary vis-à-vis North Korea, nor would it be relevant for the immediate postwar recovery and the developmental state that soon followed. Ironically, the successful completion of the constitutional mandate of Article 86 produced socioeconomic outcomes – both intended and unintended – that would increasingly undermine the viability of the original Economy Chapter. From this perspective, it was perhaps a matter of course that an adjustment of the constitution's provisions on economy would take place to tone down the socialistic features. Private enterprises and free market economy had to be given more robust constitutional recognition. In this sense, the constitutional amendment that took place in 1954 represents the final step in the process of forming the economic regime identity of postcolonial Korea. A proper understanding of Korea's constitutional founding would therefore be incomplete without an account of this process of revision, in which the United States' role was much more proactive than had been in 1948.

Realignment: Free Enterprise and Regional Integration

For the fledgling South Korean republic, the Korean War, which broke out less than two years after it was launched, had the effect of confirming and solidifying its membership in the "free world." This meant that Korea's constitutional order would have to undergo another reorientation under external influence, even before it had had a chance to be firmly established. Having signed the San Francisco Peace Treaty with Japan in September 1951, in the midst of the war in Korea, the United States sought to "contain" communist forces on the peninsula and to ensure Japan's economic recovery. Preventing the communist takeover of South Korea was critical, in other words, for the success of the San Francisco System, which was as much an economic order as a political-military framework.[152] After the conclusion of hostilities in 1953, Korea's new role in the Cold War order was to be a military bulwark against the communist bloc, while providing raw materials as well as a market for Japanese products. This was a corollary of newly-elected Eisenhower's "New Look" policy, which sought to combine fiscal conservatism (balanced budget via reduction of military expenditure) with internationalism in foreign affairs (continuation of the Truman administration's containment policy). In order to prevent the cooling down of the Japanese economy once the boom caused by the Korean War came to an end, Korea (and Taiwan) had to be integrated into a regional economic order in which Japan would be the "industrial

[152] See, generally, Bruce Cumings, "Japan's Position in the World System," in Andrew Gordon (ed.), *Postwar Japan as History* (Berkeley: University of California Press, 1993).

heartland of the area."[153] This was particularly urgent because Japan's "natural market" in Manchuria and North China was no longer accessible. Also, for Washington's policymakers, given that Korea was likely to fall to the communist side without continued economic assistance from the United States, the only financially viable option was to retain South Korea under the economic influence of a rehabilitated Japan.

This turn of events signified another "reverse course" in Washington's East Asian policy comparable to that in postwar Japan. The original goal of the U.S. occupation of Korea in 1945 had been "[t]o eliminate all vestiges of Japanese control over Korean economic life" and "[t]o foster conditions that will separate Korea from economic dependence upon Japan."[154] Before the Korean War, some of the aid provided by the United States was designed to make Korea's postcolonial economy self-sustaining.[155] Now, Washington's new goal in Korea was to turn it into "a hinterland for Japanese industry and a frontyard of Japanese defense."[156] It essentially consisted of a partial resurrection of the Greater East Asia Co-Prosperity Sphere that had been propagated by the Japanese militarists during World War II. This reverse course obviously had profound ramifications for how South Korea, as a weak member of the free world, was to chart its course in the period following the Korean War. First, South Korea was expected to create a more robust market economy based on free enterprise, which would be more amenable to foreign investment. Second, it was compelled to accept, or at least acquiesce in, the restoration of an economic status subordinate to, and dependent on, Japan. If the first proposition was rather disagreeable to South Korean leadership, which had favored a more state-centered approach to economic recovery, the second was positively abhorrent, for obvious reasons. Both would be hotly debated during the 1954 constitutional amendment that followed on the heels of the armistice agreement that ended the Korean War. At stake was the constitutional identity of Korea as an independent republic with a mixed economy dedicated to the socialistic goal of "meeting every citizen's basic demands."

153 This characterization of Japan comes from a prewar document of the State Department. "Memorandum by the Chief of the Division of Northeast Asian Affairs (Bishop) to the Director of the Office of Far Eastern Affairs (Butterworth)," 17 Dec. 1948, *FRUS 1948*, vol. VI (1974), p. 1340.

154 "Basic Initial Directive to the Commander-in-Chief, U.S. Army Forces, Pacific, for the Administration of Civil Affairs in Those Areas of Korea Occupied by U.S. Force," SWNCC 176/8 in *FRUS 1945*, vol. VI (1969), p. 1082.

155 Tae-Gyun Park, "U.S. Policy Change toward South Korea in the 1940s and the 1950s," *Journal of International and Area Studies*, vol. 7, no. 2 (2000), pp. 94–6.

156 Cumings, *Origins*, vol. II, p. 50. Cumings argues that the idea of reconnecting Korea with Japan goes back to 1947, even before the new republic was established. Ibid., p. 45–61.

By the time the armistice agreement was signed in July 1953, there was already an elaborate institutional framework in place that enabled the United States to oversee the postwar economic recovery of South Korea. The basic groundwork for the U.S. supervision of Korean economic policy had already been laid in 1948, before the war, with the conclusion of two treaties – one on the transfer of the entire, mostly vested, properties of the USAMGIK to the new Korean government and the other on a Marshall Plan-type framework for economic assistance, which imposed a set of tight obligations on Korea's fiscal and monetary policy, foreign exchange, and international trade.[157] In 1952, while hostilities were still continuing, the so-called Meyer Agreement was signed between Korea and the "Unified Command" of the United Nations forces, which had assumed operational control of all war efforts.[158] This agreement established a Combined Economic Board (CEB), consisting of one representative each from the United Nations Command and the Korean government, as a de facto economic czar of Korea. Practically all decisions concerning the economy now had to be cleared with the United States. This institutional framework was the main instrument by which Eisenhower's New Look policy was to be implemented in postwar South Korea.

In April 1953, Eisenhower dispatched Henry J. Tasca, a career diplomat, as the Special Representative for Korean Economic Affairs, whose report stressed the importance of support for Korea in the global war against communism and laid out a three-year plan for recovery and reconstruction. According to the Tasca Report, which was adopted as the basis of the U.S. aid policy toward Korea,[159] economic assistance to Korea had to be increased so as to "[p]rovide an example to the rest of free Asia and the free world generally that resistance to aggression will bring forth effective moral and material assistance from other nations of the free world." It also made it clear that providing aid for Korea was intended to reduce the cost borne by American taxpayers since a stronger Korean economy would "[r]elease U.S. armed forces from present assignment in Korea by substitution with ROK [Republic of Korea] forces." Perhaps most telling is the report's statement that the U.S. assistance program

[157] The agreements were: Initial Financial and Property Settlement (September 1948) and Agreement on Aid between the Republic of Korea and the United States of America (December 1948). For the implication of these arrangements, see Yi Tae-gŭn, *Haebanghu-1950 Nyŏndae ŭi Kyŏngje*, pp. 170–3.

[158] Agreement on Economic Coordination between the Republic of Korea and the Unified Command (24 May 1952).

[159] NSC 156/1 "Strengthening the Korean Economy." For the Tasca report, see David Ekbladh, *The Great American Mission: Modernization and the Construction of an American World Order* (Princeton, NJ: Princeton University Press, 2010), pp. 135–7 and Yi Tae-gŭn, *Haebanghu-1950 Nyŏndae ŭi Kyŏngje*, pp. 283–4.

to Korea should seek to connect the Korean economy with that of Japan and to contribute to the stabilization of the regional economic order. One of the goals of the proposed program was to:

> Provide strong collateral support to the Japanese economy and Japanese economic orientation toward the free world by developing increased trade between Japan and Korea at a time when potential reduction in U.S. military procurement in Japan and continued loss of a large export market in China may tempt Japan to seek additional markets in Communist areas.[160]

These policy ideas were implemented promptly. In August 1953, C. Tyler Wood arrived in Seoul as the Economic Coordinator for the United Nations Command, a new position that had been created in accordance with the recommendations of the Tasca Report. Over the next four months, he engaged in intense negotiations with the Korean government to set up the basic framework for postwar assistance. The result was the so-called Paik-Wood Agreement, signed in December 1953, between Korea's Prime Minister Paik Tu Chin and Wood, which further strengthened and entrenched CEB as the highest decision-making body for administering all economic and military assistance provided by United States as well as other UN agencies.[161]

Of the many issues that arose during negotiations for the Paik-Wood Agreement, the one that triggered the most heated response from the Korean side was probably the United States' demand that Korea spend the aid dollars to procure goods produced in Japan. Proceeds from the sale of aid goods (so-called counterpart funds) were also to be spent on purchasing industrial products from Japan.[162] Around the same time, Washington was openly pressuring Seoul to negotiate an economic treaty with Tokyo, even before establishing formal diplomatic relations, something which Koreans were extremely loath to do. Reestablishing economic ties with Japan was so objectionable to Rhee's government because it would likely reintroduce a vertical division of labor between the former colony and its master. According to this suspicion, Korea's economic policy would be oriented toward maintaining stability rather than growth, while Japan was to provide economic support for the virtual military garrison-state that Korea was meant to be. In the words of the Tasca report, however, Korea's aversion to economic integration with Japan was seen

[160] "The Special Representative for Korean Economic Affairs (Tasca) to the President," *FRUS 1952–1954*, vol. XV, pt. 2 (1984), p. 1247.

[161] Combined Economic Board Agreement for a Program of Economic Reconstruction and Financial Stabilization between the Republic of Korea and the United States of America (14 Dec. 1953). See Yi Tae-gŭn, *Haebanghu-1950 Nyŏndae ŭi Kyŏngje*, pp. 286–7.

[162] Lee Jong Won, *Higashi Ajia Reisen*, pp. 176–83.

merely as "irrational, emotional reactions" that needed to be rooted out.[163] Thus, despite the Korean government's vehement objection,[164] the U.S. economic aid was given mostly in kind, that is, consumer goods and raw materials that would induce financial stability, rather than long-term capital goods which might spur growth and development.[165] Any serious investments toward import-substitution industrialization were discouraged on the grounds that they might further exacerbate the already raging inflation caused by the war.

This reverse course and the new aid policies were bound to put strains on the Economy Chapter in the Founding Constitution. Clearly, an economic regime that inhibited private initiatives was hardly compatible with plans for recovery based on U.S. assistance and foreign investment as suggested by the Tasca Report. In particular, those provisions that mandated state ownership of most economic resources and government control of major economic enterprises were deemed incompatible with such a recovery plan. Immediately after the conclusion of the Paik-Wood Agreement, thus, the Rhee administration submitted, on 23 January 1954, a bill to the National Assembly for amending the Economy Chapter.

The timing of the amendment bill may suffice to demonstrate that it came about as a result of the intense American scrutiny of Korea's economy that culminated in the Paik-Wood Agreement. As its direct cause, some point to the so-called Queeny Report of August 1953, which called attention to the state-ownership provision and other articles of the constitution as a major obstacle to attracting foreign investment and suggested their amendment in the direction of a more private enterprise-centered economy.[166] Others refer

[163] Brazinsky, *Nation Building in South Korea*, p. 34.

[164] For example, in a letter of 29 December 1954 to Eisenhower, Rhee complained:

> We cannot avoid being disturbed when we are told that it is the American policy to secure two dollars of benefit (one for Japan and one for Korea) from every dollar expended. What this means is that our own recovery is slowed, as we are expected to buy more from Japan, and accordingly to use less to build up our own productive facilities. This has an immediate effect of once more placing our economy at the mercy of the Japanese.
>
> *FRUS* 1952–1954, vol. XV, pt. 2 (1984), p. 1940.

[165] On one count, the former category accounted for 81% of all U.S. aid given in the 1950s. Jung-En Woo, *Race to the Swift: State and Finance in Korean Industrialization* (New York: Columbia University Press, 1991), pp. 52–7.

[166] Lee Jong Won, *Higashi Ajia Reisen*, p. 154. Immediately following the conclusion of the armistice agreement, a private group called the American-Korean Foundation, headed by Milton Eisenhower, the president's brother, sent a mission to Korea. Its report, authored by an industrialist named Edgar M. Queeny, made suggestions for measures that might be taken to ensure the effectiveness of the United States aid to Korea. For more on the American-Korean Foundation, see Brazinsky, *Nation Building in South Korea*, p. 43.

to a report of 5 March 1954 from the U.S. Embassy in Seoul to Washington, which described the proposed amendments as reflecting "in part suggestions made by US officials and private individuals," as definitive proof of U.S. intervention.[167] It seems undeniable that American pressure provided a crucial impetus to the amendment of the Economy Chapter, and the entire process was indeed closely scrutinized by Washington. Against this background, it is natural that the Rhee administration's constitutional revision bill resonated strongly, at least in its general outlook, with the reorientation of Washington's aid policies. According to Prime Minister Paik, who had negotiated and signed the Paik-Wood Agreement only a few months earlier, the main reason for submitting the revision bill was that the economic regime mandated in the Founding Constitution was too heavily weighted toward state ownership and public control to be compatible with liberal democracy based on private property and individual economic freedom.[168]

Despite this overall agreement between Washington and Seoul, however, the way in which each side viewed the proposed amendments revealed a vast gap. For Americans, the Korean government's effort to introduce changes to the constitution, while welcome in principle, was ultimately unsatisfactory. The suggested changes fell short of their expectation. Several reports characterized them as cosmetic and even insincere.[169] For Koreans, by contrast, the amendment bill signified a momentous change in the very identity of their constitutional order. It threatened to undermine the most basic principle of their economy enshrined in Article 84, namely, the ideal of realizing social justice through an equitable economy in which everyone's basic needs would be met. In other words, whereas the United States essentially approached the matter from a pragmatic perspective of how best to rebuild the war-torn economy, Korea saw it more as an ideological issue going to the heart of their constitutional identity.

[167] Myung-lim Park, "Constitution, National Agenda, and Presidential Leadership: Focusing on a Comparison between the Articles on Economy in the 'National Founding Constitution' and the 'Post-Korean War Constitution'," *Korean Social Science Review*, vol. 1, no. 1 (2011), p. 285.

[168] *Che 2-dae Kukhoe Sokkirok* [Minutes of the Second National Assembly], Session 18, No. 26 (25 Feb. 1954), pp. 9–10 (hereafter *SNA Minutes*). Referring to the influence of the social-democratic Weimar constitution, Paik also concluded that the desire and need to mitigate the excesses of advanced capitalist economy was inapposite in the case of Korea where the war had pushed an already "backward" economy back to a "primitive" state.

[169] For instance, according to Lee Jong Won, the aforementioned report of the U.S. Embassy in Seoul ends with a conclusion that the proposed revision was merely a "propaganda" meant to conceal the continuation of the state-centered economic practices favored by Rhee. Lee Jong Won, *Higashi Ajia Reisen*, p. 154.

The American approach and evaluation are well-captured in a State Department memo prepared in March 1954, shortly after the Korean government proposed the constitutional amendment. This memo was drafted by John W. Connelly, Jr., who had served as a legal officer in USAMGIK, in response to queries from the UN Economic Coordinator in Seoul regarding the economic provisions of the Korean constitution and the proposed amendments. In Connelly's view, Koreans traditionally lacked "a way of life" that is necessary for sustaining free market economy and private enterprises.[170] The memo thus welcomed, in principle, the proposed change in the constitution whose purpose, according to the government, was "to expand and encourage the individual freedom and initiative of the people in their economic activities, and thus to stimulate a rapid increase in productive capacity and efficient development of the national economy."[171]

On close review of each of the proposed amendments, however, Connelly concluded that they would not likely achieve this professed goal. The proposed revision to Article 85 would eliminate the principle of state ownership of important natural resources, but still provided for government regulation of their "disposal, extraction, exploitation or utilization." While the omission of the state licensing scheme, a potential source of corruption, was an improvement, it did not express any new policy or principle according to Connelly. Regarding Article 87 on state or public management of enterprises with "public character" (e.g., utility companies), the proposed revision would have deleted the language in the original text that specifically enumerated such enterprises. Connelly noted that this would only introduce uncertainties which could be exploited by a "reactionary legislature." Similarly, he found that the proposed amendment to Article 88 regarding expropriation of private enterprises "really adds nothing." The only merit was "psychological" in that it was phrased in the negative (i.e., no taking permitted unless necessary to meet urgent necessities) as compared to the original which assumed an affirmative right of the state to take private enterprises in case of urgent necessities. As for Article 89 prescribing compensation for various expropriations, the proposed amendment added a specific reference to farmlands, while deleting the mandate to compensate for cancellation of licenses. This was deemed "no improvement" since the general requirement for compensation in the existing provision would have covered the taking of farmlands anyway. In sum, Connelly found that there was nothing in the proposed amendments which

170 Connelly, "Report on Economic Provisions," p. 70.
171 Connelly, "Report on Economic Provisions," p. 77.

would "give new encouragement to free enterprise."[172] From the U.S. perspective, the proposed revision simply did not go far enough.[173]

For Koreans, too, the revision was also a source of complaints but for completely opposite reasons. It potentially undermined the integrity of the Economy Chapter and the very identity of the Founding Constitution – it went too far. Thus, when the amendment bill was first introduced to the National Assembly in January 1954, it sparked a debate on the "original meaning" of the Economy Chapter. With the entrenchment of the Cold War, the same economic provisions were now understood in quite radically different ways. Along with the government, supporters of the amendment on the floor increasingly characterized them as making the Founding Constitution a "socialist" document.[174] For instance, they argued that those provisions on state ownership of natural resources and nationalization of private enterprises were creating "anxiety and apprehension" on the part of foreign investors who generally regarded the Korean constitution as socialistic.[175] On this view, the Economy Chapter was a major hindrance to foreign investment, which was indispensable for postwar recovery.

Those opposing the amendments, by contrast, insisted that the original Economy Chapter had nothing to do with socialism or any form of leftist ideology. This understanding was even shared by Connelly, who concluded that the economic provisions were "not the outgrowth of an advanced socialistic philosophy."[176] Their original author, Yu Chin-o, also confirmed, during the constitutional debates in 1954, that they were rather meant to embody a form of "reformed capitalism" designed to address the excesses of free market economy in its purer form.[177] Sure, the constitution did grant the state an important role in regulating and managing the market, but that was intended

[172] Connelly, "Report on Economic Provisions," pp. 77–9.

[173] Disappointed as he was with the proposed amendments, Connelly still recommended that free enterprise be promoted by other means, i.e., via legislative and administrative actions. He pointed to, for example, provisions in the statute on the sale of vested properties which limited eligible buyers to Korean citizens. Connelly suggested that revising such provisions would encourage foreigners to invest in Korea, thereby promoting the spread of free enterprise. Connelly, "Report on Economic Provisions," p. 74.

[174] Shin Yong-Oak, "Chehŏn Hŏnpŏp mit 2ch'a Kaejŏng Hŏnpŏp ŭi Kyŏngjejilsŏ e taehan Insik kwa kŭ Chihyang" [Perceptions of the Economic Order of the Founding Constitution and Its Amendment], *Sahak Yŏn'gu*, vol. 89 (2008), pp. 164–70.

[175] *SNA Minutes*, Session 18, No. 26 (25 Feb. 1954), pp. 10–12 (statement by Minister of Government Legislation Shin T'ae-ik). As seen previously, such perception could be traced back to such American observers as Charles Pergler and Peter Dull who had reported on the Founding Constitution after its adoption in 1948.

[176] Connelly, "Report on Economic Provisions," p. 5.

[177] Shin Yong-Oak, "Kaejŏng Hŏnpŏp ŭi Kyŏngjejilsŏ," pp. 196–8.

to ensure more genuine freedom for private economic actors. Similarly, for those opposed to the amendments in the National Assembly, eliminating such controls over the economy was likely to invite the rise of monopolies, which would in turn feed workers' discontent and result in communist insurrection.[178] Rather than promoting socialism, on this view, the Economy Chapter was the best insurance against the threat of communism or any kind of socialist ideology. In short, the proposed amendments would amount to a retrograde movement toward "pure capitalism" which had been rejected by the original Economy Chapter.

For the detractors, pure capitalism also posed a threat to economic autonomy and independence of the nation. Liberalizing and opening up the economy to induce foreign investment was an anti-nationalist idea, because it would bring about the subjugation and enslavement of Korean people to foreign capitalists. While the economic situation of the late Qing China was mentioned as an example, the more pertinent reference point, one closer to home, was Japan's economic "invasion" of Korea, which had led to the annexation in 1910. Surrendering state control over natural resources, as happened on the eve of colonization, would be an open invitation to the Japanese takeover of Korean economy once again.[179] Rather than bringing in foreign capital, on this view, priority had to be given to nurturing domestic capital for national economic autarky. This kind of nationalistic apprehension was even shared by a supporter of the amendment who also expressed concern over Korea becoming an appendage to the Japanese economy.[180]

Despite fierce disagreement on the floor, however, there was also a widespread underlying consensus. Most members of the National Assembly recognized that some kind of constitutional reorientation in the direction of an open and market-friendly economy had to be made so as to spur the urgently needed economic reconstruction and recovery from the war.[181] The disagreement, in other words, was mostly over the efficacy of the proposed amendments in achieving this widely shared goal. Despite such broad-based consensus in the legislature, however, the government suddenly withdrew its amendment bill in March 1954. The prime minister's explanation was that, given the apparent

178 SNA *Minutes*, Session 18, No. 28 (2 Mar. 1954), pp. 14–15 (statement by Assemblyman Chŏn Chin-han). It was exactly the same logic that was used to advocate workers' right to share in their company's profits.

179 SNA *Minutes*, Session 18, No. 29 (3 Mar. 1954), pp. 17–18 (statement by Assemblyman Chŏng Nam-guk).

180 SNA *Minutes*, Session 18, No. 29 (3 Mar. 1954), p. 10 (statement by Assemblyman Kim Pong-jae).

181 Shin Yong-Oak, "Kaejŏng Hŏnpŏp ŭi Kyŏngjejilsŏ," p. 199.

need for more deliberations, the next National Assembly to be formed in the upcoming general election in May would be a more appropriate venue for the amendment.[182] The government indeed submitted another amendment bill in November 1954 to the newly elected National Assembly – but with a crucial addendum. In addition to the economic provisions, the second bill proposed to make a number of changes to the government structure. The centerpiece of the new amendment bill was in fact the special provision that exempted the incumbent president at the time of the amendment (i.e., Rhee himself) from Article 55 that limited presidents to two consecutive terms in office. Evidently, Rhee's agenda was to seize the externally induced opportunity to revise the constitution in order to strengthen his own powers and to prolong his time in office, perhaps indefinitely.[183] The ensuing political and constitutional crisis is simply too byzantine to be recounted here.[184] Suffice it to note that the Economy Chapter, the original impetus to the constitutional revision, had to take a backseat during this political pandemonium, and its amendment was passed largely unmodified without further ado. The unintended consequence of the American pressure on liberalizing economic provisions was the concomitant changes in the constitutional power regime that enabled Rhee's autocratic rule to last for six more years, until a popular uprising ousted him in 1960.

As to the final outcome of the constitutional amendment in November 1954, the revised Economy Chapter did not differ materially from the government's original bill submitted in January. The principle of state ownership of natural resources was abolished. Expropriation of private enterprises was prohibited unless urgently needed for national defense or citizens' livelihood. One notable difference was the removal of the clause on the public control of enterprises "with public character." In other words, the principle of state management of communication, transportation, and utilities companies was totally

[182] *SNA Minutes*, Session 18, No. 35 (15 Mar. 1954), pp. 4–5.

[183] A suggestion has been made recently that, more than merely seizing the opportunity, the 1954 amendment was an outcome of a tacit trade-off between liberalizing the economic provisions and augmenting the presidential power. According to this interpretation, Americans had to accept the prolongation of Rhee's hold onto power, something they were extremely loath to do, in return for his cooperation with the constitutional revision for a more open and market friendly economy. Further, such a bargain with Washington was made possible thanks to Rhee's adroit political maneuvering against the backdrop of the U.S. aid policies in Korea and East Asian regional strategy at large. See Myung-lim Park, "Constitution, National Agenda, and Presidential Leadership," pp. 293–4.

[184] In a nutshell, the amendments were adopted against strong political opposition on the basis of what many consider an unlawful interpretation of the procedural rules for amending the constitution. Dae-Kyu Yoon, *Law and Political Authority in South Korea* (Boulder, CO: Westview Press, 1990), p. 99.

eliminated from the new Article 87, which now only stipulated government control of foreign trade "as provided by law." Interestingly, the revision left untouched Article 84, which stated the general principle of South Korea's economic order. Thus, despite the changes toward a more market-oriented economy, the constitution still mandated the pursuit of social justice so as to "meet the basic demands of all citizens" by developing a "balanced economy." Apparently, it was the same constitutional commitment that contributed to the preservation of Article 86 on land reform.[185]

In all, the 1954 revision may be deemed a compromise between Washington and Seoul. From the United States' perspective, the elimination of the principle of state management of enterprises with public character might be seen as a further step in the desirable direction. As stated in Connelly's memo, however, the overall result of the revision still fell short of their expectations. For the Koreans, by contrast, the revision came perilously close to undermining their long-held commitment to equitable economy. Even the preservation of the general mandate for socioeconomic justice in Article 84 was seen by many as a hollow victory at best. Yet, if neither side was fully content with the final outcome, the 1954 revision nonetheless completed the initial formation of Korea's constitutional identity. More to the point, it cannot be fully accounted for without understanding the role of external forces. The final outcome of this constitutional realignment – a process that began as soon as the constitution was adopted and came to an end under increased foreign pressure – would set the basic template for the future economic and political developments of Korea. From 1954 onward, South Korea would be a capitalist, market-oriented economy overseen by a powerful, increasingly authoritarian, president.

PRESENT AT THE CREATION

Constitutional founding never takes place in a vacuum. Foreign others are inescapably present in the initial formation of a constitutional order as well as in its subsequent transformations. The subject of a constitutional order is not a pre-given, self-sufficient, autonomous being; it is rather molded and given shape as a result of constitutive constitutional politics in which outsiders play

[185] These two articles left untouched in 1954 would ultimately be changed in the revised constitution of 1962. Land reform having been completed, the article on farmland redistribution would be replaced by a provision banning tenancy (Article 113). The mandate to pursue social justice to meet everyone's basic demands would be preceded by a general proclamation that Korea's economic order is premised on respect for the individual's economic freedom and creativity (Article 111, Section 1).

a significant role. This means that constitutional identity is better understood as the product of an interactive engagement between external forces and local agents. That does not mean, however, that the two sides contribute equally to the creation of constitutional identity. In some cases, external influence may be decisive and even overwhelming, leaving very little room for local initiatives. In others, it may be very subtle and indirect, providing the general backdrop against which the locals take on a more active role. Neither foreign imposition nor local autonomy can fully capture the process of negotiation between the two. Moreover, such an interactive relationship is not fixed once and for all at the "moment" of drafting the constitution itself. This is why it is necessary to look beyond the drafting process to the broader negotiations between external forces and local agents that take place both before and after. A constitutional identity thus emerging out of this initial phase of negotiation with outsiders may be deemed legitimate insofar as it endures over time and provides the framework and language for its own subsequent development. In this sense, foreign others never quit even after founding.

The making of Japan's postwar constitution is commonly seen as a case in which external influence was all but overwhelming. The fact that the text itself was drafted and imposed by the occupation authorities seems to provide conclusive evidence for this view. Indeed, it was foreign pressure that jumpstarted the whole process of drafting a new constitution, while the locals were willfully oblivious to the need for such a measure. However, local agency was not at all absent during the process. Even Article 9, arguably the most "imposed" part of the constitution, was the result of intense negotiations between the Americans and the Japanese. While the story of collaborative authorship may be an exaggeration, there was certainly a "meeting of the minds" regarding its underlying purpose, namely, the protection of Hirohito and the imperial institution. Moreover, the negotiations that continued into the post-drafting phase reveal that the imposed ideal of unarmed pacifism was eagerly embraced by both the government and the general public to form the core of Japan's constitutional identity. Whether to avoid the economic costs entailed in rearmament or to emphasize their own "victimhood," unarmed pacifism has come to be entrenched in postwar Japan's political credo. To be sure, the precise meaning of the peace provision has been substantially altered by a series of so-called interpretive revisions (*kaishaku kaiken*). Even so, Article 9, originally a bequest of the foreign lawgiver, continues to provide a common, if controversial, idiom through which Japanese constitutional identity is articulated, debated, and gradually transformed.

In the case of Korea, it was the locals who clamored for a new constitution, while the external forces remained, for various reasons, disinclined to be involved in such a project. Still, foreign presence is more than palpable in the formation of South Korea's constitutional identity. The three years of tutelage under USAMGIK had set in place many ideas and institutions which were crucial in laying the groundwork for the drafting process. As the Cold War turned "hot" with the outbreak of the Korean War, the United States began to assume a much more assertive role, which resulted in the readjustment of the Economy Chapter of South Korea's constitution. Also, the Cold War rivalry with North Korea loomed large not only in the original drafting of the economic provisions, but also in the first stages of their implementation as well as during the later process of revision. Throughout, local agents advocating indigenous, more "socialistic," ideas regarding economic justice had to engage in complex negotiations with these external forces. The resulting settlement reached in 1954 brought to a close the initial formation of Korean constitutional identity. South Korea's identity as a member of the "free world" would be buttressed by a constitution that mandated an economy based more on free enterprise and market initiatives. At the same time, the call for pursuing social justice through the creation of an equitable national economy continues to be an important part of that identity. South Korea's basic framework and vocabulary for understanding and debating economic justice was, in effect, set by that convoluted process in which the locals negotiated with American pressures while trying to fend off communist threats from North Korea.

3

The Ghost of Empire Past

UNMASTERABLE PASTS

Founding can never be done on a clean slate. The past is not only present at founding, but also the primary material out of which a new constitutional identity is forged. As such, a new constitution embodies various attempts to cope with the pre-constitutional legacies. Sometimes it stands in judgment of the past, while at other times it exalts the past. More importantly, it reinterprets the past and tries to incorporate it into a new narrative about the constitutional identity of the people. In the process, the constitution may even invoke an imaginary past that never was. The constitution therefore is bound to embody in its text certain tensions and perhaps even contradictions. These tensions may be resolved to become integral parts of a coherent constitutional narrative, or they may become so great as to make it impossible for such a narrative to emerge. The choice may ultimately depend on the imagination and storytelling skills of the later generations. Yet, the narrative choices that may be made by later generations are also influenced, to a great extent, by the attitudes toward the past which the framers have incorporated into the constitution. That is why it is crucial to have a proper understanding of the different ways in which the constitution deals with the past, and of the different intra-textual tensions created thereby.

To begin with, there is bound to be a tension between the attempt to negate and reject the past and the efforts to maintain some continuity with the past. At first blush, the former attitude may appear to be more salient in the case of Japan and Korea. The Japanese postwar constitution was primarily an effort to radically transform that nation's government structure, political ideology, and even the people's mindset. Anything having to do with the rabid militarism and emperor worship of the prewar era had to be rejected, and constitutional reform was thought to be a key vehicle for effecting such change.

Similarly, Korea's postcolonial constitution was first and foremost a symbol of that nation's resolve to be free from the subjection and oppression that had characterized the Japanese colonial period. An entirely new chapter in the political history of Korea was to be opened through the establishment of the constitution.

Interestingly, in both Korea and Japan, the founding generation thought it necessary to posit a "revolution" to support and justify such a negative attitude toward the past. In the Japanese case, a counterfactual revolution was required purely as a matter of logic or as a postulate of legal reasoning. As such, a revolution was retroactively posited and made the basis of a cataclysmic rupture that separated the postwar constitutional order from that of the prewar era. In the case of Korea, a revolution was also thought to be necessary in order to assert that a new republic was being built on a constitutional *tabula rasa*. Perhaps less counterfactual than Japan's, the revolution invoked by the Korean drafters was still based on a reading of history that put more store in symbolic meaning than in factual accuracy. Partly due to this "creative" use of the past, in the end, the constitution-making of both countries came to feature a more ambivalent outlook on history than was perhaps intended by their drafters. In Japan, the "August Revolution" ironically enabled the preservation of imperial formalities, while in Korea the "March First Revolution" allowed for the maintenance of continuity with a largely notional republic that existed even during colonial occupation.

This simultaneity of rupture and continuity effected by the so-called revolutions is actually symptomatic of a larger tendency inherent in constitutional negotiations with the past. Despite assertions from different quarters emphasizing a radical break from the status quo ante, the constitutions of both Korea and Japan were also intended, both explicitly and implicitly, to preserve the past. This naturally occasioned troublesome strains, and even anxiety, in the way the constitution was understood and implemented. For example, having been introduced as an "amendment" to the old Imperial Constitution, the new constitution of Japan, grounded in the principle of popular sovereignty, raised questions as to whether the traditional "national polity" (*kokutai*) had been preserved. As for the Korean constitution, even though it mandated lustration of colonial collaborators, it also stipulated the maintenance of continuity with the pre-constitutional legal institutions, which in effect contributed to the (selective) preservation of the colonial past.

With a view to understanding why and how such anxieties were built into the constitutions of postwar Japan and postcolonial Korea, this chapter examines the drafting and implementation of those provisions that were meant to carry out a radical break from the past as well as those that implied preservation of and respect for the past. It will be found that, in the Japanese case, the same articles, namely, the first chapter of the new constitution on the symbol emperor system, included mandates for both rejection and revival of the imperial status quo ante. The process of their implementation ensured that various elements from Japan's imperial past would be a constant presence in the political and discursive practices of the postwar era. In the case of Korea, two articles will be examined: Article 1 mandating the creation of a democratic republic and Article 101 authorizing the retroactive punishment of the so-called national traitors. While both provisions were expressive of a negative judgment on the past, their actual implementation would disclose an entrenched tension between them, which rendered the past ultimately unmasterable. Although in different ways, the constitutions of Japan and Korea both enacted a simultaneous effacement and re-inscription of the past that persists to this day.

THE JAPANESE EMPEROR'S NEW CLOTHES

As with any constitutional founding, the adoption of Japan's postwar constitution featured, and represented in significant ways, the nation's resolve to cope with its past. All the major actors involved in the constitution-making process, "from Douglas MacArthur to the Japan Communist Party," attempted "to identify the elements that have been responsible for the events of Japan's dark years."[1] This collective reckoning with history, however, was not just to dwell on the past for its own sake. The "dark years" had to be scrutinized and criticized, for sure, but the emphasis was more on severing the past from the present so as to make a new beginning – to build an entirely new Japan from scratch.[2] Thus, the 1947 constitution has often been regarded as a symbol of Japan's determination to create a new nation and a new identity by dissociating itself from the past. Writing on the twentieth anniversary of the postwar constitution, for instance, an American expert on the Japanese constitution attributed its endurance to "a general determination to support and maintain a discontinuity" with the "traditional order which has been rejected."[3] By contrast, the distinctive feature of the previous Imperial Constitution was for

1 Carol Gluck, *Japan's Modern Myths: Ideology in the Late Meiji Period* (Princeton, NJ: Princeton University Press, 1985), p. 4.

2 "It was as if history itself had been severed and could start again from scratch." Carol Gluck, "The Idea of Showa," in Carol Gluck and Stephen R. Graubard (eds.), *Showa: The Japan of Hirohito* (New York: W.W. Norton & Co., 1990), p. 3.

3 John M. Maki, "The Japanese Constitutional Style," in Henderson (ed.), *The Constitution of Japan*, p. 15.

him its connection to the blighted past with all its imperial myth and idolatry. This interpretation, of course, accords well with the conventional view that constitutional founding is predicated on a firm rejection of the past in order to herald an entirely new era.

There is no doubt that the rhetoric of making a clean break with the militarist past was dominant during the period when the new constitution was made. It is debatable, still, if the significance of Japan's postwar constitution can be fully captured in such terms alone. For, even as it attempted to create an entirely new polity, the constitution preserved numerous aspects of the past both in intent and effect.[4] The process of its drafting and adoption might in fact be better understood as a series of complex efforts to redefine and re-present the constitutional status quo ante, a past which ultimately remained unmasterable. The new constitution actually ensured that the past would be given a new lease on life by recasting it in new vocabularies and institutions. Furthermore, this process of negotiating the past was made all the more complex because the constitution was adopted under foreign occupation. In some sense, the desire to look to the past may have been a natural part of the way in which a fallen nation sought to salvage whatever was left of its dignity after total defeat. Forced to renounce its identity rooted in militarism and emperor-worship, Japan responded by delving ever deeper into its history to excavate some useable past on which to peg and build its future identity. As John Dower has written, "the Japanese ransacked their national history for precedents pertinent to their 'new' circumstances" with a view to "finding – inventing, if need be – something familiar to hold on to."[5] Perhaps it was a way of making the present more bearable, a way of "enduring the unendurable and suffering the insufferable."[6] Yet, it would be too simplistic to view this merely as a desperate attempt by a defeated nation. Revisiting and revising the past was, indeed, as much a part of the strategy of the occupying authorities. The making of the Japanese postwar constitution is all the more interesting

4 One might also quarrel with the characterization of the Imperial Constitution as a continuation with the past. It is now widely recognized that the whole Meiji state and its constitution were the product of the resolve to create a modern state based on the project of "civilization and enlightenment," as well as a newly crafted ideology of emperor worship. See, e.g., Kazuhiro Takii, *The Meiji Constitution: The Japanese Experience of the West and the Shaping of the Modern State*, trans. David Noble (Tokyo: International House of Japan, 2007); Takashi Fujitani, *Splendid Monarchy: Power and Pageantry in Modern Japan* (Berkeley: University of California Press, 1998).

5 Dower, *Embracing Defeat*, p. 30.

6 With these famous words, Hirohito informed his subjects of his "sacred decision" (*seidan*) to surrender to the Allied Powers. See RM027. Japan surrenders (14 Aug. 1945) Emperor Hirohito: Imperial Rescript.

and revealing because both the victors and the vanquished were very much complicit in this process of preserving and redefining the past, all the while inaugurating a new era in that nation's history.

This convoluted negotiation with the past is nowhere more discernible than in the fact that the principle of popular sovereignty was newly constitutionalized by following the revision process of the old constitution based on imperial sovereignty. That is to say, the new democratic constitution was made in observance of Article 73 of the Imperial Constitution, (i.e., "by Imperial Order"). This unresolved tension, if not outright self-contradiction, pervades the text of the new constitution.[7] Article 1 declares sovereign power to reside with the people in line with the Preamble's first sentence that it is "We, the Japanese People" who "proclaim" and "establish" the new constitution. As John Maki noted, however, "[t]he principle of popular sovereignty was stated in the text of the Constitution simply as a subordinate clause in Article 1" whose main subject was the emperor.[8] In other words, the exact locus of sovereignty remains less than fully articulated in the text. Further, the entire document is prefaced by the Imperial Edict (*jōyu*) from Hirohito who "rejoiced" at the opportunity to "sanction and promulgate" these "amendments to the Imperial Constitution." Thus, according to this edict, the constituent agent that ordains the new national charter may still be interpreted as the emperor, contrary to the sovereignty statement in Article 1 and the Preamble. In short, popular sovereignty was enshrined for the first time in Japanese constitutional history by following the old imperial formalities and procedures, which the new democratic constitution was designed to displace.

Clearly, Japan's postwar constitution was caught between these conflicting claims of the past (the emperor) and the future (the people). The symbol emperor system would be the main venue for the contestation of these claims. In this process, pasts were reinterpreted and newly "discovered," which could be used to garb the old emperor in new clothes.

7 For example, confusion is evident in the first sentence of the Preamble, where the Japanese people are said to be "acting through our duly elected representatives in the National Diet" (*Kokkai*). In truth, it was the Imperial Diet (*Teikoku Gikai*) that passed the new constitution, rather than the National Diet. The latter would not be formed until May 1947, after the constitution went into effect. It is also not entirely accurate to claim that the representatives were "duly elected," since only the members of the lower chamber of the Imperial Diet had been elected by the people. The upper chamber, called the House of Peers (*Kizokuin*), was composed of members of the imperial family and the aristocratic class, as well as imperial appointees.

8 John M. Maki, "The Constitution of Japan: Pacifism, Popular Sovereignty, and Fundamental Human Rights," in Percy R. Luney, Jr. and Kazuyuki Takahashi (eds.), *Japanese Constitutional Law* (Tokyo: University of Tokyo Press, 1993), p. 45.

The People's Emperor between Past and Future

Even if the past proved to be ultimately unmasterable, there was little doubt at the time of defeat that Japan needed to be fundamentally reshaped through the infusion of entirely new principles, outlooks, and values. Particularly for the U.S. occupying forces, there was a broad consensus from very early on that Japan's imperial past had to be negated, clearly and most emphatically. Often labeled "demilitarization and democratization," the initial occupation policy goal was to dismantle the war-making powers of the state and the institutional apparatuses that had allowed militarism to take over. The "dual government" had to be eliminated, which had emerged under the Imperial Constitution and enabled the military to pursue tragic and senseless goals with little political accountability.[9] Beyond institutional reform, further, there was wide agreement on the need to transform the entire political culture of Japan and the allegedly authoritarian mindset of its people. The goal was no less than an "ideological conversion of society."[10] John Dower has noted that many of the occupation reforms were carried out with "messianic fervor."[11]

Probably the best way to gauge the magnitude of the conversion, or discontinuity, sought by the American drafters of the new constitution is by examining Chapter 1 of the new constitution entitled "The Emperor." Compared to its predecessor, there is no doubt that Japan's postwar constitution was intended to reduce the status and power of the emperor. Gone are the incantations of a "line unbroken for ages eternal" (prewar Article 1) or affirmations of the "sacred and inviolable" nature of the emperor (prewar Article 3). No mention is made at all of the emperor being the "head of the state" (*kuni no genshu*) or exercising the "rights of sovereignty" (*tōchiken*) (prewar Article 4). In their place, the new constitution declares that the emperor is "the symbol of the State and of the unity of the people" and that sovereign power (*shuken*) resides with the people (Article 1). It further provides that the emperor is not to have any "powers related to government" (*kokusei ni kansuru kennō*), but may only perform ceremonial "acts in matters of state" (*kokuji ni kansuru kōi*) that are enumerated in the constitution itself (Articles 4 and 7). Moreover, all acts in matters of state are to be performed "on behalf of the people" (Article 7) and require the advice and approval of the cabinet (Article 3). The new

[9] Moore and Robinson, *Partners for Democracy*, pp. 85–6. For a critical understanding of Japan's "dual government" under which the emperor's military was legally separated from his civilian government, see Kenneth W. Colegrove, *Militarism in Japan* (Boston: World Peace Foundation, 1936), pp. 16–27.

[10] Moore and Robinson, *Partners for Democracy*, pp. 9–10.

[11] Dower, *Embracing Defeat*, pp. 73–84.

constitution also made it unmistakably clear that the National Diet shall be the "highest organ of state power" (Article 41). As the new constitution empowers the National Diet to author the Imperial Household Law (Article 2), the emperor is not even allowed to regulate his own household, let alone the entire "family state" that prewar Japan was meant to be under the Imperial Constitution.[12] Whereas the constitution had previously been the emperor's gift to his loyal subjects in both form and content, the symbol emperor was not even expected to play the ceremonial role of promulgating the new constitution, at least, according to the original GHQ draft. Clearly, the symbol emperor is no longer a sovereign ruler.

As seen in the previous chapter, the decision to preserve the imperial institution was largely made by MacArthur himself. Yet, even for the Supreme Commander, the emperor was not to remain a divine ruler with unlimited and unquestioned sovereign powers. Despite his favorable disposition toward the emperor as a person, in other words, MacArthur realized that the imperial institution had to be restructured. This was particularly so given the wartime policy of the United States. To be sure, a clear policy regarding the Japanese emperor was never formulated until the end of the war. Still, it was widely understood that the surrender meant the acceptance of the terms of the Potsdam Declaration, which included the demand that "a peaceful and responsible government" be established "in accordance with the freely expressed will of the Japanese people" (Article 12). It also called for the establishment of "freedom of speech, of religions, and of thought, as well as respect for the fundamental human rights" (Article 10). Insofar as the emperor was concerned, this demand meant that his Meiji status as the head priest of state Shintoism would be denied by strict separation of state and religion. While it may be debatable as to what "acceptance of the Potsdam Declaration" exactly meant, there was no disagreement within the Allied Powers that it must be followed by radical changes in the emperor's status.

When the Japanese government tried, on the eve of the surrender, to attach a condition that "the said declaration does not comprise any demand which prejudices the prerogatives of His Majesty as a Sovereign Ruler,"[13] the Allies'

12 Under the Meiji system, this Imperial Household Law (*Kōshitsu Tenpan*) was not only under the exclusive control of the emperor himself, but also understood to be on an equal footing with the Imperial Constitution itself. Nonaka Toshihiko et al. (eds.), *Chūshaku Kenpō* [Annotated Constitutional Law], vol. I (Tokyo: Yūhikaku, 2000), pp. 159–60; "Toshiyoshi Miyasawa, Kempō," excerpted in Hideo Tanaka (ed.), *The Japanese Legal System: Introductory Cases and Materials* (Tokyo: University of Tokyo Press, 1976), p. 630.

13 These were the words included by the Japanese governments as a "condition" to accepting the Potsdam Declaration. See "Japanese Qualified Acceptance (10 Aug. 1945)," in *Political Reorientation of Japan September 1945 to September 1948: Report of Government Section,*

attitude was thus rather dismissive, if not scornful, as explained in the previous chapter. Without even addressing the proposed condition, the reply from U.S. Secretary of State Byrnes simply affirmed that "[f]rom the moment of surrender the authority of the Emperor and the Japanese government to rule the state shall be subject to the Supreme Commander."[14] Compared to the language of the Potsdam Declaration, which let "the freely expressed will of the Japanese people" decide their political future, this new clarification can be interpreted as having gone even further in the direction of requiring a complete overhaul of the Japanese constitutional system.[15] As mentioned in Chapter 2, the earliest directive given to SCAP indicates that the abolition of the imperial institution, not to mention Hirohito's abdication, was seriously contemplated as a possible, even desirable, course of action. The Japanese people were to be encouraged to consider getting rid of the "feudal and authoritarian" government even if "the effectuation of such changes involve[d] the use of force by the Japanese people or government against persons opposed thereto." MacArthur was instructed to intervene only if such use of force endangered the security of his forces or the accomplishment of occupation objectives. The early occupation policy was meant to support and endorse, if not actively stir up, the Japanese people's desire to abolish their own imperial institution.[16]

The Japanese leaders nevertheless continued to believe, or hope, that the emperor's prerogatives as sovereign ruler had been left untouched by the defeat and surrender. To a great extent, such hope was shared by the emperor himself, whose rescript broadcast on 15 August 1945 to announce the end of hostilities expressed satisfaction at having "been able to safeguard and maintain the national polity (*kokutai*)."[17] In the same vein, most constitutional experts of the time, including Minobe Tatsukichi, Miyazawa Toshiyoshi, and Sasaki Sōichi, all believed initially that surrender did not require substantial changes to the Imperial Constitution's provisions dealing with the powers of the emperor.[18] Against such background, the idea of making the emperor into a symbol was received with a mixture of disbelief and resistance. Matsumoto

Supreme Commander for the Allied Powers (Washington, DC: U.S. Government Printing Office, 1949), p. 414. [hereafter *PRJ*].

14 "Reply by Secretary of State to Japanese Qualified Acceptance," in *PRJ*, p. 415.

15 Hellegers, *We, the Japanese People*, vol. 1, p. 239.

16 "Basic Principles for a New Japanese Constitution, JCS Directive Serial No. 54 (6 July 1946)," in *PRJ*, p. 661.

17 RM027. Japan surrenders (14 Aug. 1945) Emperor Hirohito: Imperial Rescript (translation modified for literal rendering).

18 For a brief overview of Japanese constitutional scholarship on this issue in the immediate post-war period, see Frank O. Miller, *Minobe Tatsukichi: Interpreter of Constitutionalism in Japan* (Berkeley: University of California Press, 1965), ch. 8.

Jōji's reaction upon receiving the original GHQ draft was a combination of rage and disdain, as seen in his dismissive comment that words like "symbol" may belong in the realm of literature, but have no place in a legal document like the constitution.[19] Similarly, on the first day of the diet deliberation, one member of the House of Representatives cynically commented that the language about symbol "makes a fine work of literature or, in a sense a great philosophy," but it is legally vacuous, "a fruitless flower."[20]

The resistance and cynicism of Japan's leadership is symptomatic of their realization that radical change was being sought by the American drafters of the constitution. The transformation of the emperor into a symbol was, indeed, the Archimedean pivot of the revolutionary reforms undertaken by SCAP to jumpstart democracy in postwar Japan. In the new constitution, the emperor was no longer labeled the "head of the state"; the term does not even make a single appearance in the text.[21] Adoption of the symbol emperor system was meant to signal a clear move in the direction of effacing the past. Stripped of any powers relating to government, further, the emperor would be recast – most ironically and almost overnight – into an exemplar of democratic citizenship required for the new Japan. In order to take on this new role and to personify such a radical departure from the prewar era, Hirohito "the manifest deity" had to be demoted to the rank of humanity first. As per the aforementioned Article 10 of the Potsdam Declaration, SCAP had already issued a directive that ordered the disestablishment of state Shintoism as early as in 15 December 1945, in which the Shinto teaching that the emperor and the Japanese people form a superior race by virtue of "ancestry, descent or special origin" was pointedly banned (Item 2-f).[22] In line with this directive and at the urging of the occupation authorities, Hirohito himself made a statement in the form of a New Year's message on 1 January 1946, in which he repudiated the idea of the emperor's divinity as a "false conception." Commonly known as the "Humanity Declaration" (*Ningen Sengen*), this imperial rescript stated that the ties between the emperor and his people "do not depend on mere

[19] RM213. Matsumoto on drafting the Constitution. RM213.SP2.P18.

[20] RM319. House of Representatives: plenary (26 June 1946). RM319.PM.SP5.

[21] During diet interpellations, many lawmakers had asked why the more traditional head of the state (*genshu*) had not been employed as the emperor's appellation. A few members of the House of Peers, including Miyazawa and Sasaki, even submitted a proposal to replace "symbol" with "head of the state." The government responded that the term *genshu* was associated with the image of a state as a human body and, therefore, may promote needless "mysticism." Besides, it would be wiser to avoid giving the impression that the postwar Japan still wished to preserve the emperor as a political ruler. Moore and Robinson, *Partners for Democracy*, pp. 195, 297.

[22] "Disestablishment of State Religion, SCAPIN 448 (15 Dec. 1945)," in *PRJ*, p. 468.

legends and myths," but on "mutual trust and affection." Closely following the words of the directive, further, he rejected as a false conception the fanatical wartime militarist ideology "that the Japanese are superior to other races and destined to rule the world."[23]

These words were quickly followed by action. In late February, as the draft constitution was being discussed in the cabinet, Hirohito commenced, again with the "assistance" of the GHQ, the first of his nationwide tours that sought to tout him as a champion of peace and democracy. Having renounced his divinity, he would appear for the first time as an ordinary human being to the general public. The famous image of a majestic leader on white-horseback decked out in his full military regalia was traded in for that of a soft-spoken "marine biologist" in plain business suit waving his fedora and attempting small talk with commoners. That these tours occasioned painful discomfort for the socially inept emperor and utter bewilderment on the part of the public who had been brainwashed to worship the "manifest deity" from afar is a telling testimony to the radical change being sought by the symbol emperor system.

This new "human" emperor as a makeshift symbol of postwar peace and democracy had to find an appropriate expression in the new constitution. As a term of art, symbol had already been used often to describe the role of the emperor. For example, in his 25 January 1946 communication to Army Chief of Staff Dwight D. Eisenhower, MacArthur himself referred to the emperor as "a symbol which unites all Japanese."[24] Similarly, the former U.S. Ambassador to Japan, Joseph Grew, is also said to have described the emperor as a symbol during the war.[25] Kenneth Colegrove, a political scientist who was assigned to the GHQ as a consultant, is reported to have called the emperor "the symbol of national unity" in 1942.[26] When it came to the actual drafting of the

[23] RM096. Dispelling false conceptions ("*Ningensengen*") (1 Jan. 1946) Emperor Hirohito. For the GHQ, this was a way to combat the pernicious effects of the Emperor Meiji's famous Imperial Rescript on Education of 1890, which had been used by the militarists to propagate such a "false conception," and which was still being recited in schools with utmost reverence. RM098. Origins of Emperor's statement (late 1946; 1965) Harold G. Henderson; R.H. Blyth; Yamanashi Kakunoshin. The education rescript would be officially abolished in June 1948 by an act of the National Diet.

[24] This letter was sent for the purpose of squelching any plans for prosecuting Hirohito. RM054. On trying the Emperor for war crimes (25 Jan. 1946) General MacArthur to General Dwight D. Eisenhower.

[25] Masanori Nakamura, *The Japanese Monarchy: Ambassador Joseph Grew and the Making of the 'Symbol Emperor System,' 1931–1991*, trans. Herbert B. Bix, Jonathan Baker-Bates, and Derek Bowen (Armonk, NY: M. E. Sharpe, 1992).

[26] Hara Hideshige, *Nihonkoku Kenpō Seitei no Keifu: Sensō Shūketsu made* [Genealogy of the Making of Japan's Constitution: Through the End of the War], vol. 1 (Tokyo: Nihon Hyōronsha, 2004), pp. 156–7 (referring to Kenneth Colegrove, "What Shall We Do with the Japanese Emperor?," *Amerasia*, vol. 6, no. 9 (Oct. 1942), pp. 376–81).

constitution, however, it seems to have been Colonel Charles Kades of the GHQ's Government Section who was most instrumental in having symbol inserted in the text. Upon receiving a copy of the MacArthur Notes, he is said to have penciled in "symbol" above the general's "cryptic first sentence," that is, "[e]mperor is at the head of the state."[27] More importantly, Kades seems not to have known about the prewar use of symbol as a description of the emperor; even if he did, he intended to use the term to embody a radical departure from its prewar use. According to John Dower, in choosing that word, the drafters "redefined the emperor in a way never mentioned by the supreme commander."[28]

The GHQ drafters were clearly animated by a liberal, progressive goal of fundamentally transforming the emperor system. For example, the explanatory notes that accompanied the draft constitution stated: "Establish a constitutional monarchy with sovereignty reposing in the people by modifying the Emperor system and making the Emperor the ceremonial head of the state."[29] Similarly, instructions given by General Courtney Whitney, Chief of the Government Section, at the start of drafting process made it clear that "the Emperor's role will be that of a social monarch, merely."[30] When the Section's Steering Committee met to review the first draft produced by various members of the team, the term "reign" was stricken from the text because "in Japanese usage 'reign' carries the connotation of 'govern' as well."[31] According to GHQ legal expert Alfred Oppler's appraisal, too, the draft constitution was "certainly intended to make him, constitutionally, a colorless figurehead lacking even those minimum powers with which usually the heads of

27 Moore and Robinson, *Partners for Democracy*, p. 94. Commentators still continue to disagree over what was meant by this cryptic sentence, or more precisely how it should be translated into Japanese. For many, it is clear that SCAP had intended to keep the emperor as the head of the state, the position he had occupied under the Imperial Constitution. Its translation should be straightforward, and be rendered *genshu*. See Ashibe, *Kenpō*, p. 24 and Nagao Ryūichi, *Shisō toshite no Nihon Kenpōshi* [Japanese Constitutional History as Theory] (Tokyo: Shinzansha, 1997), p. 215. Others take note of the fact that SCAP had written "*at* the head of the state," which suggests that he was not referring to an official position or title, but was using the term figuratively. On this view, MacArthur's first sentence merely means that the emperor occupies the highest status (*saikōi no chii*). See Koseki, *Tanjō*, pp. 116–17. Still others prefer a more neutral and literal rendering which means "head part" (*tōbu*). See Higuchi Yōichi, *Kenpō* [Constitutional Law], 3d. ed. (Tokyo: Sobunsha, 2010), p. 64.

28 Dower, *Embracing Defeat*, p. 367. Kades also confirms that neither he nor the drafting committee inside the Government Section received any directives from MacArthur concerning the use of "symbol" in the new constitution. Nakamura, *The Japanese Monarchy*, pp. 100–02.

29 RM190. Explanatory notes (ca. 13 Feb. 1946) SCAP: GS. RM190.3.A.P1.

30 RM143. Whitney commissions GS (4 Feb. 1946) SCAP: GS minutes. RM143.1.2.P3.

31 RM149. Emperor: discussion of draft (6 Feb. 1946) SCAP: GS, Ellerman notes. RM149.1.P1.

parliamentary governments are vested."[32] As ruefully pointed out by Nanbara Shigeru, member of the House of Peers during diet deliberations and the first president of the postwar University of Tokyo, the "king reigns, but does not govern" in England, but, in postwar Japan, the emperor was not even expected to reign.[33] Upon being briefed by Prime Minister Shidehara about the GHQ draft, Hirohito is reported to have responded, almost in resignation, "I'm all right being a symbol."[34]

Evidently, however, it was not so all right for the Japanese negotiators. The famous marathon translation session of 4–5 March 1946 revealed that the Japanese government had not translated certain phrases or employed Japanese terms with subtle differences in meaning. They refused to recognize that a radical break was necessary or at least tried to soften the blow that would be caused by such recognition. The best-known example of this kind of quiet subterfuge might be the attempt to avoid using "sovereign" to describe the status of the people in both the Preamble and Article 1. The English phrase "sovereign will of the people" in the GHQ draft was translated as *kokumin shikō no sōi*, which means literally, "supreme collective will of the people." The intent was to avoid using the Japanese word for sovereignty, *shuken* – a term traditionally reserved for the emperor – as an attribute of the people.[35] The negotiators from the Government Section did not notice this significant change during the marathon session even as they pored over the Japanese translation. For, when the phrase was translated back into English, it was rendered again "sovereign will of the people." It was finally brought to their attention during diet interpellations, when Japanese lawmakers and journalists pointed out the difference between the English and Japanese texts.[36] Upon

[32] RM210. Comments (handwritten) on first Japanese draft (5 Mar. 1946) Alfred Oppler. RM210.2.P1.

[33] RM436. House of Peers: Special Committee: fourth meeting (4 Sept. 1946). RM436. PM.SP21.P5.

[34] Handō, *Shōwashi: Sengohen*, p. 197. Among Japanese conservatives, Hirohito's acquiescence in becoming a symbol has been called the second "sacred decision" after his first decision to accept the Potsdam Declaration. Ibid.

[35] Nonaka Toshihiko et al., *Kenpō* [Constitutional Law], vol. I, 4th ed. (Tokyo: Yūhikaku, 2006), p. 82. Koseki Shōichi maintains that this avoidance of "sovereign" and its substitution with an unfamiliar sounding "supreme" was Shidehara's idea. Koseki, *Tanjō*, p. 171. According to Satō Tatsuo's account, also cited by Koseki, however, Shidehara changed "popular will" (*min'i*) in Matsumoto's draft translation into "supreme collective will of the Japanese people," which suggests that Shidehara may have been trying to give a rendering closer to the GHQ draft. Satō Tatsuo, *Nihonkoku Kenpō Seiritsushi*, vol. 3, pp. 74–5. Regardless of Shidehara's intent, however, it soon became clear that "supreme" was unacceptable to the GHQ.

[36] RM335. *Minpo* editorial on translation issues in draft Constitution (7 July 1946) Matsumoto Shigeharu.

learning of this discrepancy, Whitney and Kades expressed grave concern to the Supreme Commander that the democratic spirit of the new constitution was being undermined by the conservatives in the government.[37] Kades, in particular, initiated a "completely personal and 'unauthorized'" meeting with the Japanese government officials to clarify the locus of sovereignty and to make sure that the Japanese text closely followed the views of the GHQ.[38] For him, the term sovereignty had to be reserved for the people only. Any attempt to obfuscate this issue, as the Japanese government was doing during the diet interpellations, could not be tolerated. GHQ's belated but just-in-time intervention would put the word *shuken* back into Article 1 of the Japanese text, thereby unequivocally declaring the people as the only sovereign in postwar Japan.

Even during the initial phase of negotiation, what did catch the eyes of the Americans was how the Japanese had glossed over the term "advice and consent" of the cabinet, which was required for any act of the emperor. A heated confrontation ensued between Kades and Matsumoto when the former demanded to know why the Japanese had employed only one word, *hohitsu*, roughly meaning "advice," and neglected to translate "consent." Matsumoto apparently tried to explain that *hohitsu* in Japanese had a broader connotation than "advice" in English, sufficient to convey the meaning of "advice and consent." Kades, however, insisted that another word, namely *kyōsan*, be put in the text as a translation of "consent." Matsumoto countered that *kyōsan* as used in the Imperial Constitution referred to an act of the diet and therefore was unsuitable to use in relation to the cabinet. This confrontation is interesting less for what was so vehemently disputed by the contestants than for what seems to have remained uncontested. The term *hohitsu*, which was evidently acceptable to Kades as the translation of "advice," had the connotation of a subordinate providing assistance to a superior with ultimate decision-making powers. For instance, it had been employed in Article 55 of the Imperial Constitution to define each minister's duty to provide advice to the sovereign monarch. It is unclear whether Kades was aware of such "imperial" undertones of the term, but it seems evident that the Japanese translators had chosen it deliberately to maintain the appearance of the emperor being the sovereign ruler.[39] In this tug of war over the seemingly trivial choice of words, too, the

37 Dower, *Embracing Defeat*, p. 389.

38 RM340. Kades meets with Irie and Satō (10 July 1946) Katō memo for the record. RM340.P5. See also Kyoko Inoue, *MacArthur's Japanese Constitution: A Linguistic and Cultural Study of its Making* (Chicago: University of Chicago Press, 1991), pp. 205–10.

39 In the end, Satō Tatsuo had to come up with another word, *sandō*, as a translation for "consent," which was agreed to by the Americans. As it happened, however, neither *hohitsu* nor

Americans were adamant that, even as the emperor was to be preserved both in person and as an institution, the symbol emperor's power and status had to be fundamentally altered from its previous incarnation.

The negotiation on the symbol emperor system between the occupation authorities and the Japanese government was so intense precisely because it was clearly understood on both sides that it signified a radical departure from the traditional constitutional identity of Japan. For the GHQ, it stood for the end of the prewar government apparatus and the wartime ideology that had underwritten the reckless military expansion and the emperor worship. For the Japanese leaders, it seemed to imply the loss of an entire *Weltanschauung*, which all subjects of the emperor had been taught to internalize and to identify with. No longer a divine ruler, the "symbol" emperor would now maintain his position only at the pleasure of his former subjects and act only at the bidding of their elected representatives. As a mere symbol, in short, he was meant to be a "people's emperor" – an institution in an ancient garb but, in fact, wholly unprecedented in Japan's political history.

A Paper Revolution by Necessity

Today, the novelty of the symbol emperor system is widely recognized by constitutional scholars in Japan. According to Ashibe Nobuyoshi, for instance, it is an entirely different institution from that enshrined in the Imperial Constitution. The two are grounded in different foundations (divine oracle vs. people's will), are of different nature (sacred and inviolable vs. secular and mutable), and have different powers (supreme governing power vs. ceremonial functions).[40] As such, the emperor's status as symbol is not some leftover that remained after stripping the emperor of his sovereignty, but rather a brand new institution created under the postwar constitution by the sovereign people.[41] Some commentators even claim that, at the time the new constitution went into effect, there should have been a declaration of inauguration of Hirohito as the first symbol emperor as well as a resetting of the reign-name calendar to begin at year one.[42] On this view, the new emperor was

sandō would survive. In the Government draft of 17 April 1946, the phrase was changed to *hosa* and *dōi*. Then, in the draft sent to the Imperial Diet in June, it was altered again to *jogen* and *shōnin*, which was adopted as the official text. Meanwhile, the English version was also changed to "advice and approval." In both languages, it was made clear that the emperor no longer occupied a position superior to the cabinet. Nonaka et al. (eds.), *Chūshaku Kenpō*, vol. I, pp. 191–2; Inoue, *MacArthur's Japanese Constitution*, pp. 165–73.

40 Ashibe, *Kenpō*, pp. 44–5.

41 Takahashi, *Rikkenshugi to Nihonkoku Kenpō*, p. 44.

42 Nonaka et al. (eds.), *Chūshaku Kenpō*, vol. I, p. 117.

to symbolize a constitutional ground-zero as well as "the unity of the people" (Article 1).

Despite – or because of – such apparent novelty, most Japanese political leaders during the negotiation process were reluctant, to say the least, to accept or even recognize a forthright transition to popular sovereignty. Among the newly formed political parties, only the Communist Party was unequivocal in advocating the complete abolition of the emperor system.[43] Even the Socialist Party was circumspect in promoting popular sovereignty. Its proposal for a new constitution pointedly stated that the "[e]mperor system shall be retained" and that "sovereignty shall reside in the State (a corporation which includes the Emperor)."[44] Yet, even if they chose to retain the emperor system, most political groups at the time also recognized that the new constitution would have to include at least some gesture of moving toward a government of more circumscribed imperial powers. For example, even the conservative Liberal Party's outline for constitutional revision, published on 23 January 1946, demanded that the emperor's prerogatives be abolished regarding "emergency ordinances, enforcement ordinances, official institutions, supreme command, martial law, etc."[45] Many of the conservative political elites realized that, in redesigning the emperor system, some kind of discontinuity from the past had to be effected constitutionally – the question was to what extent.

In this regard, more vocal than these political parties in arguing for the circumscription of imperial powers were the general public and some civic groups. As is well known, when the Matsumoto draft was made public by the *Mainichi Daily* in its famous "scoop," it was roundly criticized as "cosmetic, tokenistic, reactionary, and completely out of touch with the temper and needs of the time."[46] The public apparently understood what their leaders did not – that Japan's postwar democracy could only tolerate an emperor with ceremonial functions at most. This is most clearly seen in the private draft constitution prepared by a civilian group called the Constitution Research

[43] Miyazawa Toshiyoshi, "Nihonkoku Kenpō Seitan no Hōri" [Legal Theory of the Birth of Japan's Constitution] in *Kenpō no Genri* (Tokyo: Iwanami Shoten, 1967) (originally published 1955), p. 376; Koseki, *Tanjō*, pp. 59–68. See also RM095. Communist's 7 points outline (30 Dec. 1946) Akahata.

[44] RM122. Socialist Party proposes revisions (23 Feb. 1946) Socialist Party. Another source at the time translated the idea as "people's confederation including the Emperor." RM123. Socialist proposals (press summary) (23 and 24 Feb. 1946) Kyōdō news service. More literally, it might be rendered, "national cooperative body including the Emperor" (*tennō o fukumu kokumin kyōdōtai*). Similar ideas would turn out to be the basis of very conservative moves to deny the radical nature of the change introduced by the new constitution.

[45] RM106. Praise for Liberal proposals (23 Jan. 1946) *Mainichi shinbun*.

[46] Dower, *Embracing Defeat*, p. 359.

Association (*Kenpō Kenkyūkai*). Its leadership included Takano Iwasaburō, Morito Tatsuo, and Suzuki Yasuzō, most of whom had left, or been purged from, academia during the war to pursue socialism and join labor movements.[47] Completed and delivered to the occupation authorities at the end of December 1945, more than a month before the Matsumoto draft, the association's draft was one of the earliest to be prepared by either the Japanese or the American side. After declaring in its very first article that sovereignty resides in the people, it went on to provide that the "[e]mperor shall not administer the country" (Article 2) and that he "shall, by the delegation of the people, deal with rituals" (Article 3).[48] Historians have placed much emphasis on this draft constitution because it was carefully analyzed and well-received by the GHQ before it began preparing for its own draft. In a memorandum of 11 January 1946, Lieutenant Colonel Milo Rowell of the Government Section, another member of the GHQ's drafting committee, praised parts of it as "democratic and acceptable."[49] It has been suggested that the association's draft was the true origin of the symbol emperor system adopted by the new constitution.[50] Pinpointing the originator of the idea is less important than appreciating the fact that calls for turning the emperor into a symbol came also from many Japanese intellectuals who regarded such transformation as crucial for ushering in democracy. For them, the emperor's constitutional status as a symbol was an emblem of the fundamental break that had to be made in the nation's political history.

This sense of radical rupture was expressed most clearly in the views of those who acknowledged that Japan's *kokutai*, or "national polity," had been fundamentally changed with the adoption of symbol emperor system. A good example was Sasaki Sōichi, an eminent constitutional scholar from the University of Kyoto, who, as a leader of Konoe Fumimaro's team in the Office of the Lord Keeper of the Privy Seal, had prepared a predominantly conservative draft constitution that contained no single revision regarding imperial prerogatives.[51] This reputedly liberal constitutionalist in prewar Japan charged that

47 Koseki, *Tanjō*, pp. 38–45.

48 RM094. Proposals of Kempō Kenkyūkai (27 Dec. 1945) Takano Iwasaburō and others.

49 RM102. Critique of Kempō Kenkyūkai proposals (11 Jan. 1946) Milo Rowell, SCAP: GS.

50 McNelly, *Origins*, pp. 98–100. Others point to an obscure article written in November 1945 by a socialist intellectual named Katō Kanjū, in which he advocated that the emperor become a "symbol of the nation's harmony" and a "ritualistic and ceremonial entity." The suggestion is that, since Katō is likely to have influenced the debate within the Socialist Party, which had originally planned to announce a draft with only ceremonial functions for the emperor, Katō and the Socialist Party's use of the term "symbol" not only preceded but also influenced the GHQ draft. Koseki, *Tanjō*, pp. 61–62.

51 Koseki, *Tanjō*, p. 33.

the new constitution as proposed by the government would fundamentally transform the national polity of Japan.[52] More importantly, he criticized the new constitution for abolishing the imperial institution (*tennōseido*), which he defined as the combination of two elements: that the emperor alone holds in his hands the rights of sovereignty and that the emperor occupies his position solely by virtue of his descent. Retaining the position of emperor in name only, while stripping it of its essential elements or defining features, was as good as demolishing the imperial institution as such. Besides, he believed that change of Japan's *kokutai* had not been a part of the conditions for surrender. Only a few minor amendments reducing the emperor's prerogatives and bolstering the cabinet's responsibility would suffice to comply with the Potsdam Declaration. What was in fact demanded by the declaration was that the ultimate form of government be decided by the Japanese people, and Sasaki was convinced that all Japanese (except for the communists) were in "agree[ment] in holding that there is no need to change the *kokutai*."[53] In short, symbol emperor system was objectionable for him because it represented an unwarranted departure from, and repudiation of, the very essence of Japan's constitutional identity.

Sasaki's constitutional interpretation that underscores rupture was shared by Miyazawa Toshiyoshi, a professor at the University of Tokyo and the dean of postwar Japan's constitutional scholarship. For Miyazawa, too, the adoption of popular sovereignty as the new fundamental principle of the postwar constitution made it no longer plausible to maintain that *kokutai* had been preserved. Since sovereignty was a matter of who has the final authority to decide on the state's basic form of existence, and, since *kokutai* meant that this authority lay with the "sacred and inviolable" emperor, it was beyond doubt that *kokutai* as such had changed. If the term simply meant the existence of the emperor, it might be possible to affirm that *kokutai* remained unchanged. Clearly, however, that was not how the term had been understood and practiced under the Imperial Constitution. It had been inextricably linked to the idea that the emperor was the sovereign ruler who derived his authority from divine descent.[54] In the new constitution's symbol emperor system, such political theology had no place. For Miyazawa, then, it was more accurate to conclude that, more than being changed, *kokutai* had been obliterated.[55] As a member

[52] David A. Titus, "The Making of the 'Symbol Emperor System' in Postwar Japan," *Modern Asian Studies*, vol. 14, no. 4 (1980), p. 542.

[53] RM426. House of Peers plenary (28 Aug. 1946). RM426.PM.SP12.P27.

[54] Miyazawa Toshiyoshi, "Nihonkoku Kenpō Seitan no Hōri," pp. 385–6.

[55] Miyazawa Toshiyoshi, *Kenpō Kōwa*, pp. 103–05. See also Titus, "Symbol Emperor System," p. 541.

of the House of Peers during diet deliberations on the new constitution, thus, he argued in favor of being upfront about this brute fact so as to ensure "the correct understanding of the drastic reform that Japan is now undertaking," which he described as a "political rebirth as has never been effected since [Japan's] foundation."[56] Unlike Sasaki, who was critical of the changes being instituted by the new constitution, Miyazawa appears to have been more acquiescent of the proposed reform. Yet, for him, too, there was no doubt that adopting the symbol emperor system signified a complete rejection and repudiation of the past.

Miyazawa went on to articulate this sense of rupture in Japan's constitutional order through his "August Revolution" theory, which is widely accepted today by Japanese constitutional scholars.[57] Simply put, the idea is that Japan's acceptance of the Potsdam Declaration in August 1945 constituted a revolution, at least in the legal sense. Under the Imperial Constitution, deciding on "the ultimate form of government" through "the freely expressed will of the Japanese people" would have been a legal impossibility. The adoption of popular sovereignty would not have been permitted, even if the emperor himself had willed it. This is because, according to Miyazawa, the source of the emperor's authority lay with the gods, in that his position derived from the so-called descent of the Sun-Goddess (*tensonkōrin*). The Imperial Constitution was essentially a theocratic document based on the principle of "oracle sovereignty" (*shinchoku shuken*).[58] There was no way that this principle could legally be replaced by popular sovereignty pursuant to the normal procedures of amendment. Such a transition could only be made through an extra-legal event that shattered the very foundation of the Meiji legal universe – a revolution. Miyazawa argued that Japan's defeat and surrender in the war represented just such an event.

As such, the alleged revolution did not take place with the promulgation of the new constitution in November 1946. It happened almost fifteen months earlier in August 1945 when the Japanese government decided to surrender. Miyazawa holds that it was at the moment of acceptance of the Potsdam Declaration that popular sovereignty had replaced imperial sovereignty as the basic principle of Japan's constitution. For accepting the "freely expressed will of the Japanese people" as the basis of government authority signified a

[56] RM421. House of Peers: plenary (26 Aug. 1946). RM421.PM.SP7.P4. In the same vein, Nanbara Shigeru remarked: "This is a change that we have never before experienced in our history since our State was founded by the Emperor Jimmu." RM436. House of Peers: Special Committee: fourth meeting (4 Sept. 1946). RM436.PM.SP23.P6.

[57] See, e.g., Ashibe, *Kenpō*, p. 30; Nonaka et al. (eds.), *Chūshaku Kenpō*, vol. I, p. 53.

[58] Miyazawa Toshiyoshi, "Nihonkoku Kenpō Seitan no Hōri," p. 380.

fundamental alteration in the ultimate principle of constitutional legitimacy. As a result, even though the text of the Imperial Constitution remained intact, all provisions contained therein that were contrary to the new principle of popular sovereignty must be deemed to have lost their validity.[59] Indeed, for Miyazawa, the emperor's Humanity Declaration of January 1946 was intelligible only on the premise that sovereignty had already been transferred by a revolution from the emperor to the people in August 1945.[60] He even suggests that the process of obtaining the emperor's sanction and the House of Peers' approval in adopting the new constitution may have been an unnecessary and superfluous formality, since such acts no longer had any legal meaning under the new principle of popular sovereignty.[61] As a matter of legal interpretation, in short, the new constitution was a culmination not only of total defeat externally imposed upon, but also of domestic revolution instigated by Japan's unconditional surrender. *Kokutai* had been obliterated, the symbol emperor system was an entirely novel invention, and the utter discontinuity from Japan's constitutional past had to be accepted as a post-revolutionary fait accompli.

If such a rupture was the true meaning of the new constitution, the manner in which it was adopted could not but be highly problematic. That is, relying on the amendment procedures of the Imperial Constitution to usher in such a revolutionary change seemed untenable. When appointed to the House of Peers, for instance, Sasaki was severely critical of not only the substance of the proposed new constitution, but also the entire way in which the proposal was made.[62] He pointed out, as did so many diet members, the difficulty of introducing a constitution made by "We, the Japanese People" by invoking Article 73 of the Imperial Constitution. The irony, even logical paradox, was that an extraordinary change was being introduced to Japan's constitutional order via an ordinary legal process as prescribed in the old constitution, which was

59 Minobe Tatsukichi made the same argument in April 1946 as a member of the Privy Council when it deliberated on the government draft prior to sending it to the Imperial Diet. Chronologically, this precedes the publication of his student Miyazawa's article on the August Revolution in May 1946. It is possible that Miyazawa was elaborating on an idea that his mentor had suggested. Most commentators, however, attribute the idea to Miyazawa. Some even imply that Minobe was citing Miyazawa's idea. Moore and Robinson, *Partners for Democracy*, p. 167. Worth noting here is the fact that the conclusion that Minobe drew from this postulate of revolution was rather contrary to that of Miyazawa. Arguing that procedure for constitutional revision is now "in an unsettled state," Minobe apparently called for a constitution "drafted by a committee really elected by the people, rather than drafted by the Government." RM287. Privy Council: first meeting (22 Apr. 1946). RM287.PM.SP34.

60 Miyazawa Toshiyoshi, "Nihonkoku Kenpō Seitan no Hōri," p. 386.

61 Miyazawa Toshiyoshi, "Nihonkoku Kenpō Seitan no Hōri," p. 389.

62 RM426. House of Peers: plenary (28 Aug. 1946). RM426.PM.SP12.

being negated and supplanted by its alleged "amendment." For Miyazawa, too, this was an impossible legal position to defend because the prevailing theory had it that there were limits to amendments that could be made following the procedures prescribed in the old constitution. The inviolable principle of imperial sovereignty was one of the most important of such limits. Any revision that altered this foundational principle would undermine the very identity of the constitution, resulting in a legal contradiction – or constitutional "suicide" as Miyazawa called it.[63]

It was indeed to explain away this very conundrum that Miyazawa felt compelled to conjure up a paper revolution. And Miyazawa's conclusion is that it is not a conundrum after all. Since popular sovereignty had already become embodied in the Imperial Constitution through the revolutionary act of surrender, using its amendment procedures to manifestly announce this new source of legitimacy did not pose a problem. For no new principle that exceeded the limits inherent in constitutional revision was being introduced through the amendment process. Following the procedures laid down in Article 73 of the Imperial Constitution was thus a matter of course. Even attaching the emperor's Proclamation Edict at the head of the new constitution was not a problem because the position of the emperor himself was no longer based on divine ancestry. Ironically enough, that also meant that it was not problematic to follow the provisions of the old constitution – as long as one understood that they were not constitutionally meaningful. During the interim period until a new constitution is adopted, acts that have no constitutional effect could still be performed according to the old constitution. For example, the consent of neither the House of Peers nor the Privy Council was required since both institutions were premised on the principle of imperial sovereignty being superseded by the new constitution. Under the August Revolution theory, still, adhering to such formalities could be interpreted as a choice made by the sovereign people. By enabling such legal fictions, in effect, Miyazawa's theory ensured that the imperial constitutional order would be accorded the utmost respect even as it was being rejected. In sum, it has the ironic effect of proclaiming legal discontinuity, all the while affirming the façade of legal continuity so as to minimize any foreseeable chaos that might be caused by the rupture.[64] In a curious way, the prewar institutions and practices are negated and sustained at the same time. As much as the August Revolution theory posited a radical rupture, then, it may also be interpreted as making allowance for legal continuity.

63 Miyazawa Toshiyoshi, "Nihonkoku Kenpō Seitan no Hōri," pp. 382, 388.
64 Nonaka et al., *Kenpō*, vol. I, p. 62.

The King Who Would Be People

This ambivalence inherent in Miyazawa's theory between revolutionary rupture and preservation of status quo ante was actually a prevalent feature of the whole project of adopting the postwar constitution. It could not but be so because the new constitution was intended to preserve the past as much as it was designed to reform and reshape Japanese society. Revolutionary changes often have to be wrought in a way that maintains some link with traditions and practices of the past. It was only more so in the immediate postwar Japan. As it were, new democratic principles were to be poured into the old imperial wineskin. And that meant a certain respect was required for that old skin so as not to burst it.

In point of fact, this outlook was implicit in the directive given by the Allied Powers. One might even say that it was already prefigured in Article 10 of the Potsdam Declaration, which states: "The Japanese government shall remove all obstacles to the *revival* and strengthening of democratic tendencies among the Japanese people" (emphasis added). The clear implication is that the creation of a new Japan may involve a measure of returning to its past.[65] This need to have the new constitution linked to, and draw from, certain principles and precedents in the nation's history became clearer with the famous MacArthur Notes. As seen, its very first item stipulated that the imperial institution shall be preserved, while the third item mandated the abolition of the feudal system. The imperial formalities, no matter how empty they may have become, and post-surrender reforms, no matter how limited they would prove to be, had to inhabit the same constitutional ground somehow. To that end, the Supreme Commander called for ensuring the maintenance of "complete legal continuity" in the process of introducing the new constitution.[66] This call was even echoed by the Far Eastern Commission, which had been known to be more hostile toward the emperor.[67] This was the reason behind the decision to adopt a whole new constitution through the amendment procedure specified in the Imperial Constitution. The old imperial wineskin had to be preserved.

Like Miyazawa, however, the occupying authorities were aware of the difficulty involved in adhering to this fiction of legal continuity. Could the existing constitution founded on the principle of imperial or "oracle" sovereignty really

65 Precisely what those past "democratic tendencies" were and where they might be found, however, was never spelled out in the declaration. Many took it as a reference to the so-called Taishō Democracy of the 1920s, before the militarists took over the government.

66 "General MacArthur's Statement on Submission of Draft Constitution to Diet (21 June 1946)," in *PRJ*, p. 660.

67 "Principles Governing the Machinery for the Adoption of a New Japanese Constitution, JCS Directive Serial No. 47 (May 23, 1946)," in *PRJ*, p. 659.

be transformed into a democratic charter by merely following its amendment provisions? To study this matter, the GHQ commissioned Alfred Oppler, a German-trained jurist who had joined the Government Section around the time the GHQ draft was handed over to the Japanese cabinet.[68] In a memorandum of 25 August 1946 to General Whitney, Oppler presented his answers to the legal question of whether an amendment could be proposed that aimed at fundamentally altering the basic principles of the Imperial Constitution. In other words, were there any legal limits to amending the old charter? His conclusion, after surveying the various interpretations, including the authoritative commentary by its main author, Itō Hirobumi, was that, since the emperor was an all-powerful sovereign who alone was authorized to initiate constitutional revisions, there could be no limitations on the extent of changes instituted by an amendment. Finding that neither the Preamble nor Article 73 of the Imperial Constitution contained any limitation regarding the scope and content of amendments, Oppler concluded that its framers apparently "did not go so far as to consider their constitutional pattern as designed for eternity." Besides, the drafters' "respect for and subservient devotion to the Emperor would not have allowed them to limit his initiative power."[69] He agreed that the transition of sovereignty from the emperor to the people signified a change in the "national polity." Such a change, however, did not constitute a break in legal continuity. For Oppler, legal continuity was purely a formal matter, which could be maintained as long as the abrogation of the old constitution and the enactment of a new one took place simultaneously, "both acts being accomplished by the same instrument."

For both the occupation and the Japanese authorities, in sum, using the amendment procedure of the Imperial Constitution to adopt an entirely new charter posed no insurmountable problem. For Miyazawa, because the revolution in August had already introduced popular sovereignty as the constitution's basic principle, the revision was merely a matter of codifying the new post-revolutionary status quo. For Oppler, the sovereign emperor was free to alter the fundamental principles of his own polity and, as such, amending the constitution to adopt popular sovereignty was well within his prerogative. On either view, adoption of the new constitution by following Article 73 of the old constitution preserved legal continuity while abandoning imperial sovereignty and transitioning to a democratic constitutional order. The postwar

[68] Alfred C. Oppler, *Legal Reform in Occupied Japan: A Participant Looks Back* (Princeton, NJ: Princeton University Press, 1976), pp. 17–21.

[69] "Memorandum for the Chief, Government Section: Powers of the Diet with Regard to Constitutional Amendments under the Meiji Constitution (25 Aug. 1946)," in *PRJ*, p. 664.

constitution of Japan did not emerge as a brand new creation *ex nihilo*. It was borne of a carefully orchestrated delivery process that paid minute attention to maintaining legal continuity with the prewar system.

If the mandate for preserving the imperial past was an integral part of SCAP's directive, it would be further amplified in the process of its reception and implementation by the Japanese side. This of course is most visible in the fact that the new constitution was formally made public via the aforementioned Promulgation Edict of 3 November 1946, which not only conveyed the impression that the emperor is still the sovereign constituent agent, but also adhered closely to the requirements of a prewar regulation on the form and ritual for issuing imperial rescripts.[70] In fact, it was the emperor who ostensibly initiated the whole process of revising the constitution by issuing a series of edicts. On 5 March 1946, as per Article 73, Hirohito granted an imperial rescript (*chokugo*), reported in the newspapers the following day, in which he "commanded" the cabinet to prepare a draft for a new constitution.[71] Then, on 20 June 1946, another imperial rescript (*chokusho*) was sent to the Imperial Diet, along with the draft constitution prepared by the cabinet, in which the emperor urged the lawmakers to revise the constitution on the basis of "the freely expressed will of the people." After the diet passed the "amendments to the Imperial Constitution," the Privy Council, following prewar formalities, recommended to the emperor that he promulgate the new constitution. Seen in this light, the emperor appears as the single most important actor who "superintended" the entire process of constitution-making by closely adhering to the prewar formalities for amendment.

This appearance was in fact the result of a conscious orchestration on the part of the government and the emperor himself. As shown, even after the Allied Powers rejected the Japanese government's suggestion of a "conditional surrender," the eventual surrender announcement by Hirohito on 15 August 1945 included the rather brazen statement that Japan's national polity had been preserved.[72] For the Japanese leaders, acceptance of the Potsdam Declaration

70 The precise form and substance of the Promulgation Edict were dictated by the prewar Regulation on Official Forms (*Kōshikirei*), which was repealed as of 3 May 1947, the very day that the new constitution went into effect.

71 According to Koseki Shōichi, the real reason for attaching the imperial rescript to draft constitution came from SCAP himself who, in order to protect Hirohito from demands of abdication and prosecution, urgently needed to show the world that the emperor was leading the efforts to democratize Japan. Koseki, *Tanjō*, pp. 198–207.

72 In fact, the announcement does not even contain the term "surrender." On its face, it is merely a decision by the emperor to stop fighting because "the war situation has developed not necessarily to Japan's advantage," primarily due to the enemy's deployment of "a new and most cruel bomb."

was – indeed, had to be – compatible with the mandate to "safeguard and maintain the national polity" (*kokutai no goji*). Postwar Japan would not be different from what it had been before and during the war. This theme of continuity is in fact also highlighted in the aforementioned Humanity Declaration of Hirohito, which repudiated emperor worship and militarist imperial ideologies. Although the GHQ had intended it to be a declaration of radical change, the document actually began with a verbatim recitation of the famous "Charter Oath" of the Meiji Emperor, Hirohito's grandfather. Issued in 1868 immediately after the Meiji Restoration, the five-point Oath had signaled the opening of a new era. By prefacing his own renunciation of divinity with this Meiji Oath, the Shōwa Emperor was now intimating that the new democratic Japan to be built from the devastation of defeat would represent a continuation or resuscitation of ideals from Japan's own past. As Dower observes, "[f]or many conservatives, this was the very heart and soul of the New Year's Day proclamation. The Charter Oath would become a touchstone, a talisman, a comforting historical and psychological anchor by which they could claim that the 'new Japan' was firmly grounded in the past."[73]

All in all, the Japanese government did its best to maintain the fiction that, despite the momentous changes being introduced by the new constitution, very little was actually new. Since the preservation of national polity had been its foremost objective since the last days of the war, it was in fact not in a position to acknowledge publicly that a wholly new system of government was being established. No matter how alien the symbol emperor system may seem, the government had to maintain that it was a continuation of the prewar system. It was in a particularly awkward position because the bill for a new constitution had been introduced as the government's own draft. The problem was that, to most readers of the bill for "amending" the Imperial Constitution, it was rather obvious that the position of the emperor would be drastically altered. The old guards in the government as well as in the diet could not help but be concerned that *kokutai* as they knew it was no more.

During diet deliberations, thus, the government was repeatedly challenged to clarify whether the national polity was preserved under the new constitution. In order to appease their fellow conservatives in the diet, the government had no choice but to insist that *kokutai* would not be changed. In order, however, to placate the lawmakers on the left and other liberal groups, as well as the GHQ, the government also had to maintain that sovereignty now lay with the people. They were thus forced to argue the impossible – revolutionary change had taken place, but the most basic features of the national polity

73 Dower, *Embracing Defeat*, p. 313.

remained intact. Their way out of this bind was essentially to redefine the status of emperor and *kokutai* by culling examples from history that might be used to demonstrate that national polity "properly understood" had always meant the symbol emperor system. In a classic case of "invented tradition," they engaged in a selective resuscitation of useable pasts to sustain the fiction that no essential change had been ushered in, at least nominally, while at the same time confirming substantively radical discontinuity. Kanamori Tokujirō, the Yoshida cabinet's Minister of State during diet deliberations in charge of explaining the government draft to the lawmakers, was particularly instrumental in presenting this impossible argument. To the criticism that the new constitution would alter the *kokutai*, he responded that, although sovereignty now belongs to the entire people of Japan, also included among "the people" is the emperor.[74] Kanamori was thereby able to claim that, although the emperor was now a symbol without political powers, he still had a share in sovereignty. Leaders of the Japanese government thus sought to argue that the new constitution did not change the national polity even as it introduced popular sovereignty.[75]

This idea of "the people including the emperor" would be hotly debated throughout diet interpellations. Socialist and communist lawmakers thought it was the height of sophistry and demanded that the government unequivocally affirm that sovereignty now belonged to the people and not the emperor. Most conservatives, by contrast, thought it was an ingenious idea. In fact, the idea may have originated from a conservative lawmaker, Kita Reikichi, on the very first day of deliberations in the House of Representatives.[76] Asserting that Japan has always been characterized by "joint/common rule of king and people" (*kunmin kyōchi/ dōchi*), he argued that this tradition might be reinterpreted as sovereignty residing in the "totality that binds the king and the people."[77] Prime Minister Yoshida Shigeru went even further by invoking yet another pair of terms expressing the mystical unity of the emperor and his subjects. For him, between the imperial family and the people, there was absolutely

74 RM325. House of Representatives: Committee on Revision: second meeting (1 July 1946). RM325.PM.SP4. When asked, however, whether the emperor would be entitled to the right to vote, as one of the "people," Kanamori answered in the negative. RM322. House of Representatives: plenary (28 June 1946). RM322.AMPM.SP10. This was a matter of course because members of the imperial family were not registered in the household registry, which was used as the criterion for granting voting rights. This effectively put him "outside the boundary of the people" (*kokumin no soto*), to use the phrase employed in the very first law on household registry enacted during the Meiji era. For more details, see Chapter 4.

75 Inoue, *MacArthur's Japanese Constitution*, pp. 190–1.

76 Koseki, *Tanjō*, p. 262.

77 In the Japanese original, it reads: *kunmin o sōgōseru zentai*. *Dai 90-kai Teikoku Gikai Shūgiin Giji Sokkiroku*, No. 5 (26 June 1946), p. 70.

no distinction – "king and subjects are as one" (*kunshin ichinyo*) and "king and subjects form one family" (*kunshin ikka*).[78] On this view, harmony and unity between the emperor and the people were the distinctive features of Japanese political tradition. It was hardly an innovation that the emperor was one with his people as the symbol of their unity.

Accordingly, *kokutai* was given a new lease on life. Taking a cue as it probably did from Hirohito's Humanity Declaration, the government argued that *kokutai* did not mean an absolute monarchy based on mythical claims of divine origin and unbroken line of succession. Rather, according to Kanamori, it referred to a spiritual and affective bond between the emperor and his subjects who together constituted "the people." Although the Imperial Constitution may give the impression that *kokutai* consisted in the emperor's political and institutional authority to determine state policy and command absolute obedience, the true essence of the Japanese state had to be discerned in the more intangible and ethereal realm of spirits, attitudes, and attachments.[79] The correct definition of *kokutai* was therefore "the peculiarity of this country, where the people are united by their common feeling of traditional relation with the Emperor that is rooted deep in their innermost minds, and where the Emperor has been and is the focus of what may be termed reverential love of the nation."[80] Rather than the superintendent of sovereignty, the emperor was to be understood as the "center of the people's devotion."[81] Kanamori was convinced that a dispassionate view of history would confirm that his conception was closer to "traditional practices than were the doctrines that prevailed during the 1930s."[82] The wartime militarist ideology had been a deviation from the real meaning of *kokutai*. As long as the people's devotion to the emperor did not change, *kokutai* would remain the same. Indeed, the symbol emperor system represented a restoration of Japan's authentic tradition.[83]

78 Koseki, *Tanjō*, p. 263.

79 Moore and Robinson, *Partners for Democracy*, pp. 197–8.

80 RM325. House of Representatives: Committee on Revision: second meeting (1 July 1946). RM325.PM.SP4.P22.

81 While this expression has been customarily understood to have originated from Kanamori's answers during diet interpellations, it was actually part of a carefully planned strategy laid out by the government. In preparation for the lawmakers' interrogation, the Cabinet Legislation Bureau drew up a list of anticipated questions and tried to provide model answers to be used by government representatives at the diet. The idea is said to have been Satō Tatsuo's. Moore and Robinson, *Partners for Democracy*, pp. 177–80.

82 Moore and Robinson, *Partners for Democracy*, p. 205.

83 The communist diet member Nosaka Sanzo ridiculed this line of reasoning as utter nonsense. See, e.g., RM322. House of Representatives: plenary (28 June 1946). He asked: "Can we find any other country in the world where the monarchy is founded on the sentiment of the people?" For him, *kokutai* "based on the sentiment of the people, this cannot be a constitution, but a novel." RM322.AMPM.SP47.P2.

In sum, there was no rupture or discontinuity. By prefacing the Humanity Declaration with the Meiji Oath, Hirohito himself intimated that the prewar period would be recast as an inspiration for the postwar democracy. The implication was that, while militarism and its ideology of emperor worship had to be rejected, other ideals of the Meiji Restoration could be tapped for the task of reconstruction and democratization. During the deliberation process, the conservative leaders went even further. According to Ashida Hitoshi of the controversial "Ashida Amendment," the Meiji Oath had inaugurated the "era of modern democracy" in Japan.[84] Evidently, he was referring to its directives to establish "deliberative assemblies" and to encourage public debates as well as to abolish class distinctions. For Yoshida, too, the Oath was proof of an earlier, indigenous democratic tradition in Japan. He went so far as to claim that nothing had changed in the political life of postwar Japan: "our political principle has always embodied the democratic way of thinking, both before and after the new Constitution."[85] For many leaders in the government and the diet, the most powerful presence of the past in the birth of Japan's postwar Peace Constitution was the Imperial Constitution itself.

Symbol Emperor and Useable Pasts

The government leaders' desire to see the new constitution, particularly the symbol emperor system, as being rooted in Japan's past was more than just sophistry designed to save face. They were politically compelled to argue the impossible, that is, declaring radical rupture and uninterrupted continuity at the same time. Beyond such political exigency, however, there seems to have been a more genuine desire on the part of the Japanese public to establish some continuity between the new constitution and indigenous traditions. Particularly, a number of influential intellectuals sought historical grounding for the refashioned imperial institution. Even before the government draft was made public, they insisted that "symbol" was actually a more accurate and proper designation for the emperor, at least from the historical and cultural perspective. In an article originally written in January 1946, for instance, the historian Tsuda Sōkichi claimed (to the surprise of many intellectuals who knew his liberal reputation) that the imperial house had been the foundation of Japanese identity throughout history and regarded as a symbol of a "feeling of being one ethnic group." If the position of the emperor was to survive into the postwar period, its significance would lie in its role "as the center of the

84 Moore and Robinson, *Partners for Democracy*, p. 276.
85 Moore and Robinson, *Partners for Democracy*, p. 299.

people's unity, as the living spiritual symbol of the people."[86] On this view, the symbol emperor system was a return to Japan's authentic tradition that predated the wartime militarism and ultra-nationalism.

Even more famously, Watsuji Tetsurō, a leading ethicist at the University of Tokyo, asserted that it was the emperor system under the Imperial Constitution that had been an aberration from the entrenched tradition.[87] For him, the emperor had always expressed the unity of the Japanese people, and the idea of *kokutai* referred to the timeless cultural characteristic of Japan that had nothing to do with the locus of sovereignty. He reminded his readers that there have been plenty of times in Japanese history when the emperor had not been the "superintendent of sovereignty" (*tōchiken no sōransha*). It was a grave misunderstanding to equate, as did Sasaki Sōichi, *kokutai* with imperial sovereignty. What Sasaki mistook for *kokutai* was actually the more mutable "form of government" which might be referred to as *seitai*.[88] On this view, *kokutai* means something like "national cultural essence" rather than any particular institutional arrangement. What was being changed by the new constitution was *seitai*, not *kokutai*.[89] For Watsuji, the symbol emperor system was quite consistent with Japan's cultural tradition, and there was no need to conclude that its adoption in the new constitution resulted in an alteration of *kokutai*. This even allowed him to suggest that the emperor was still the sovereign. Since the people are the sovereign agent according to the new constitution, and since the emperor has always symbolized the unity of the people, he is now the symbol of their sovereignty as well.[90] Presaging Kanamori's position in the diet, Watsuji could maintain that the emperor remained sovereign even after the introduction of popular sovereignty as the basic principle of the new constitution.

Arguably, the most extraordinary argument for continuity between the pre- and postwar *kokutai* was made by Otaka Tomoo, a legal phenomenologist and Miyazawa Toshiyoshi's colleague at the University of Tokyo. In a famous

86 Kenneth J. Ruoff, *The People's Emperor: Democracy and the Japanese Monarchy, 1945–1995* (Cambridge, MA: Harvard University Asia Center, 2001), pp. 46–7.

87 Ruoff, *People's Emperor*, p. 49.

88 Titus, "Symbol Emperor System," p. 543.

89 This in fact was the very argument made by the representatives of the government, such as Kanamori, Shidehara, and Yoshida, during diet deliberations. This distinction between *kokutai* and *seitai* had a long history in Japanese academia. It can be found, for example, in the writings of Hozumi Yatsuka, professor of constitutional law at the University of Tokyo and the main architect of the notorious "family state" ideology during the late Meiji period. See Richard H. Minear, *Japanese Tradition and Western Law: Emperor, State, and Law in the Thought of Hozumi Yatsuka* (Cambridge, MA: Harvard University Press, 1970), pp. 64–71.

90 Titus, "Symbol Emperor System," p. 544.

critique of the August Revolution theory, he argued that *kokutai* should not be understood, as was done by Miyazawa, as a question of the locus of sovereign power in a given polity. Might cannot make right, and sovereignty, if that term is to be retained at all, should be attributed to some kind of everlasting "ideal of law" – or *nomos*. While the lawmaking power may have shifted from the emperor to the people, both were subject to the dictates of *nomos* to the extent that both had the solemn responsibility to make laws in accordance with the ideal of law. This meant, for Otaka, that *nomos* was the true sovereign, both before and after the adoption of the new constitution.[91] Yet, Otaka also recognized that, although *nomos* is a universal ideal, it is realized in different time and place in correspondingly different ways. Insofar as Japan was concerned, *nomos* had been symbolized throughout the millennia by the transcendental "Great Heart of the Emperor" (*ōmigokoro*). As such, it is never erroneous and unfailingly righteous irrespective of who wields actual power on its behalf. In the postwar era, it was now the will of the people that had to embody the same *nomos*. The idea of *nomos* thus ensured that there would be a unity between the emperor's heart and the people's will.[92] According to Otaka's "*Nomos* Sovereignty" theory, in other words, the postwar constitutional order based on the new principle of popular sovereignty was merely another means by which this immutable ideal of law was implemented in Japan. Over and above the ephemeral changes in the institutional arrangements, there remained an enduring ideal that persisted throughout Japanese history ever since its mythic foundations. Seen from the perspective of this *nomos*, no alleged revolution was powerful enough to negate the majestic continuity that undergirded Japan's *kokutai*.[93]

For these influential public intellectuals as well as for the government leaders, Japanese political tradition was reinterpreted and invoked to provide justification for the newly defined imperial institution. In this way, the symbol emperor system made sure that various traditions during different periods of Japanese history would constantly be discussed and made present, even as it sought to refute and reject the past. For Yoshida and Ashida, the Meiji legacy, before its distortion by the wartime militarism, was the major source of

91 Nonaka et al., *Kenpō*, vol. I, pp. 85–8.

92 Titus, "Symbol Emperor System," pp. 538–41.

93 This historic debate between Otaka and Miyazawa is commonly viewed as having ended in the latter's victory. This may have been due to the fact that Miyazawa's theory, with a far subtler emphasis on continuity, responded better to the political demands of the day. Some scholars still express skepticism regarding the logical strength, or "scientific" nature, of the August Revolution theory. For a critical reflection on Miyazawa's theory, see Yasuo Hasebe, "The August Revolution Thesis and the Making of the Constitution of Japan," *Rechtstheorie*, vol. 17 (1997), pp. 338–41.

useable past. For Tsuda and Watsuji (and Kanamori to a large extent), by contrast, the incorrect understanding of *kokutai* was a direct product of the Meiji system itself which had in effect fabricated a new national identity and foisted it upon the people through force and indoctrination. The Meiji idea of *kokutai* was a foreign import and corruption of Japan's authentic imperial tradition.[94] In the long view of history, emperor was and always will be the focal point of people's affective allegiance, forming the basis of the nation's identity. Such time-immemorial tradition and immutable identity of Japan, according to Otaka, still continued to provide the ultimate fount of just law for postwar democracy erected on the new principle of popular sovereignty.

Not everyone who rejected the Meiji legacy, however, wished to return to such putatively primordial models of Japanese culture. Those intellectuals associated with the Constitution Research Association, for example, also shared the view that the recent ideology of emperor worship propagated during wartime had been a willful deviation from earlier currents in Japanese political tradition. Their primary point of reference was, however, a relatively more recent and more democratic trend that had been stifled and preempted by the promulgation of the Imperial Constitution, namely, the Freedom and People's Rights Movement (*Jiyū Minken Undō*) of the late nineteenth century.[95] Suzuki Yasuzō, as the only member of the association who had more than a passing knowledge of constitutional law, was steeped in the ideas of this rare democratic tradition in Japanese history and paid close attention to the private constitutional drafts produced during the movement. For Takano Iwasaburō, the senior leader of the association, that movement represented an unfulfilled vision of republicanism and the people's zeal for democracy, which had been betrayed by the reactionary enshrinement of the sovereignty of a "sacred and inviolable" emperor in the Imperial Constitution. Not satisfied with the association's draft constitution, which retained the imperial institution, albeit for ceremonial purposes only, Takano eventually published his own private draft, which made Japan a republic headed by a popularly elected president.[96] For Takano and Suzuki, the making of a new democratic constitution had to be understood and

94 According to Tsuda, the elevation of the emperor far above the people was originally a Chinese notion alien to Japanese tradition. The idea of direct rule (*shinsei*) by the emperor was also associated with European ideas, which pitted the emperor and the people against one another. Perhaps he did not notice the irony that the alleged return to the symbol emperor system was not exactly a local initiative but rather the result of another foreign influence. Ruoff, *People's Emperor*, pp. 46–7.

95 Koseki, *Tanjō*, pp. 38–44.

96 RM108. Takano Iwasaburo's draft constitution (28 Jan. 1946) POLAD to Secretary of State.

justified as a restoration and rehabilitation of the early Meiji ideals of the Freedom and People's Rights Movement.[97] It was the other side of the Meiji legacy, not the side represented by the conservative Imperial Constitution, that needed to be restored for postwar democracy.[98]

Justifying the symbol emperor system thus required rummaging through the entire span of Japanese history to find some practice or idea that could be held up as a precedent. Building on the Meiji Oath and going back further into the Tokugawa era and even to the pre-Shogunate period, the conservative government was able to argue that the emperor had never ruled directly and always stayed above day-to-day politics. As Kanamori put it, "we have committed error in bringing down the emperor from this ideal, transparent and colorless position and letting him take sides in actual politics."[99] Perhaps the clearest articulation of such view is the following oft-quoted statement by Ashida:

> In short, the first Chapter of the revised Constitution expressly provides that the Emperor of one line, unbroken through the ages, is assured of his position as a Monarch who, on the basis of the sovereign will of the people, unifies them coevally with Heaven and Earth, from eternity to eternity. Thus, it has been possible to confirm the solemn fact that the Emperor, while being in the midst of the people, stands outside the pale of actual politics, and still maintains his authority as the center of the life of the people and as the source of their spiritual guidance.[100]

It was with these words that Ashida concluded the section on the emperor in his report to the plenary session of the House of Representatives.

In summary, practically all of Japan's history, except for the recent, short period of militarism, was marshaled to support the thesis that the emperor had always been a symbol. The inconsistency of invoking the Tokugawa

[97] Koseki, *Tanjō*, p. 71.

[98] For the same purpose, Fujita Shōzō wrote an essay on the occasion of the centennial of the Meiji Restoration. He concluded the essay by asserting that the "Spirit of the Restoration" (*ishin no seishin*) was "institutionally guaranteed by the postwar Constitution of Japan" and the "spiritual inheritor of the Restoration will emerge from the struggle to protect this guarantee." Turning the table on those conservatives who criticized the Peace Constitution in the name of prewar tradition, evidently, this leading liberal intellectual of postwar Japan found the universal norms and values, as embodied in the postwar constitution, to be the "true" spirit of the homespun Meiji Restoration – not mere novel imports as their conservative detractors held. Fujita Shōzō, *Ishin no Seishin* [Spirit of the Restoration] (Tokyo: Misuzu Shobō, 1997), p. 43.

[99] Moore and Robinson, *Partners for Democracy*, p. 202.

[100] RM420. House of Representatives: plenary (24 Aug. 1946). RM420.AM.SP1.P8. Also quoted in Koseki, *Tanjō*, pp. 265–66 and Dower, *Embracing Defeat*, p. 390.

history alongside the Meiji Restoration, which had been a violent rejection thereof, was a minor historical glitch that could be glossed over. The constitutional search for useable pasts is never an exercise in historical scholarship; it was only less so in postwar Japan. The alleged August Revolution might as well have been a "Restoration," or even "Glorious Revolution," that had recovered Japan's "ancient constitution," so to speak, at long last. In this way, the symbol emperor system under the new constitution had the ironic effect of bringing the past into the present and making sure that the Japan's prewar political traditions would have a permanent place in its new postwar constitutional identity.

It was not only at the level of political rhetoric and intellectual discourse, furthermore, that one past or another was creatively tailored to garb the novel institution of symbolic emperor in an outfit of historical continuity. At the level of actual practice, too, the imperial past would continue to influence the interpretation and implementation of the symbol emperor system thus justified in theory. Such a practice was possible, since the new constitution was found to be unclear even with regard to such fundamental questions as whether Japan was a monarchy or republic. Minobe insisted that even after sovereignty had been transferred to the people, Japan remained a monarchy, while his student Miyazawa claimed that Japan had effectively become a republic.[101] In a 1954 article on the emperor's constitutional status, Kuroda Satoru lamented that under the new constitution, it was not clear "if the emperor was a monarch or not, if he was the head of the state or not, or if Japan was a monarchy or a republic," suggesting that this unsettled situation symbolized the very status of the emperor.[102] Interestingly, the upshot of such ambiguity was that, under the new constitution, the emperor came to enjoy powers far beyond those of a mere symbol. The prewar practice of imperial prerogative seems to cast a long shadow into the postwar democracy.

Despite the absence of the word "head of the state," or *genshu*, it is undeniable that the emperor occupies a status, and possesses certain authority, beyond those envisioned by the symbol emperor system. A good example might be the continuation, despite the lack of constitutional authorization, of the prewar practice by which government ministers periodically brief the emperor on political matters of national and international concern. According to Kenneth Ruoff, these ministerial briefings demonstrate that, throughout

[101] Ruoff, *People's Emperor*, pp. 55–6.

[102] Kuroda Satoru, "Tennō no Kenpōjo no Chii" [Constitutional Status of the Emperor], *Kōhō Kenkyū*, vol. 10 (1954), p. 3.

the postwar period, Hirohito never accepted merely being a ceremonial figurehead, even believing in private "that it was his job to nurture and supervise prime ministers."[103] In fact, it quickly became apparent that many of the emperor's public acts did not fall under the category of "acts in the matter of state" specifically enumerated in the new constitution. These constitutionally dubious acts included attending the National Diet to deliver an opening statement. This was an act largely unanticipated, if not positively prohibited, by the constitution, which nevertheless became routine in postwar Japan "out of respect for tradition."[104] Another, perhaps more troubling, example was the emperor communicating with foreign governments on such sensitive policy issues as security alliance with the United States and the extension of American military occupation of Okinawa.[105] Such acts have caused many scholars to debate the constitutional merits of creating and recognizing an additional category of imperial actions called "public acts in his status as symbol."[106] In many a practice, in short, the emperor has continued to act and be received as Japan's "head of the state" despite the clear absence of such an appellation in the constitutional text.

Even those acts sanctioned by the constitution have sometimes been interpreted and carried out in a way that presents the emperor as much more than a symbol. In an instance of what Higuchi Yōichi has called "concealed revisionism," for example, the government continued to draft ambassadors' letters of accreditation in such a way as to convey the impression that they are issued by the emperor, despite the fact that his only constitutional role in this matter is confined to that of mere "attestation."[107] Another, possibly more ominous, example concerns the emperor's authority to dissolve the House of Representatives as provided in Article 7. Such a role was originally sanctioned with the expectation that it would be merely pro forma. Yet, it would prove to be a channel through which prime ministers could circumvent their political accountability – in a way reminiscent of prewar practices.

In fact, when the government draft of 6 March 1946 was first unveiled, Takano Iwasaburō of the Constitution Research Association commented that the prerogatives of the emperor were much broader than those stipulated in his association's draft. In particular, he insisted "on removing ... the right of dissolving the House of Representatives which shall certainly not meet with

103 Ruoff, *People's Emperor*, p. 94.
104 Ruoff, *People's Emperor*, p. 58.
105 Ruoff, *People's Emperor*, p. 96; Bix, *Hirohito and the Making of Modern Japan*, pp. 626–7.
106 Ashibe, *Kenpō*, p. 51; Nonaka et al., *Kenpō*, vol. I, p. 136.
107 Yōichi Higuchi, "The Constitution and the Emperor System: Is Revisionism Alive?," in Luney and Takahashi (eds.), *Japanese Constitutional Law*, p. 63.

approval."[108] During diet deliberations, it was pointed out that the draft constitution did not clearly specify to whom the power to dissolve the lower chamber belonged and under what conditions. Lawmakers asked if the dissolution must be preceded by a vote of non-confidence or whether loss of confidence could be inferred from the failure of a cabinet-sponsored bill to pass the diet. In response, Kanamori clarified in no uncertain terms that, although the conditions for exercising it would be hard to anticipate, the power would belong to the cabinet.[109]

Before long, this became a real-life issue when Yoshida tried to dissolve the House of Representatives right after the formation of his second cabinet. By the end of 1948, Yoshida found himself the leader of a minority cabinet and wished to dissolve the lower chamber to force an early general election. He planned to implement his plan without going through a vote of non-confidence, and, instead, by relying on Article 7, which appeared to make dissolution of the House an imperial prerogative. For GHQ, however, this smacked of "a carryover from the philosophy of the old Emperor system."[110] They blocked Yoshida's plan on grounds that dissolving the House should depend on an explicit vote of non-confidence as provided for in Article 69. Interestingly, however, the article merely states that the cabinet should resign when a non-confidence resolution has been passed "unless the House of Representatives is dissolved within ten days." In other words, it does not specify who has the power of dissolution. Be that as it may, GHQ took the view that using Article 7 as the sole ground for dissolution was tantamount to a return to practices under the Meiji system in which the emperor could unilaterally dissolve the lower chamber.[111] Still under occupation, Yoshida had to relent.

As it turned out, this was the only time that an Article 69 resolution of non-confidence was made a precondition for dissolving the lower chamber. In 1952, after the occupation had ended, Yoshida secured an imperial rescript to dissolve the House without a non-confidence resolution or the rejection of a confidence resolution. This method has remained the practice ever

[108] RM294. Draft revision criticized (8–9 Mar., 4 Apr. 1946) Professors Asai Kiyoshi, Takano Iwasaburō, Sugimori Kōjirō, Hirano Yoshitari, and Suzuki Yasuzō. RM294.TEXT2.2.2.P1.

[109] Moore and Robinson, *Partners for Democracy*, pp. 236–7.

[110] Masumi, *Postwar Politics, 1945–1955*, p. 177.

[111] Kades reports that at the time of drafting, one officer in the Government Section had warned that failure to give the prime minister authority to dissolve the legislature would gravely compromise the workability of the cabinet system. Even so, in the context of postwar Japan, it was inevitable that conferring such power on the prime minister would strike an ominous chord in the minds of most observers wary of the way in which prewar governments had been run under the guise of imperial authorization. Charles L. Kades, "The American Role in Revising Japan's Imperial Constitution," *Political Science Quarterly*, vol. 104, no. 2 (1989) p. 245.

since. Scholarly debate over its constitutionality notwithstanding, it has been reflected in the official imperial rescript announcing dissolution. Since 1952, no reference to Article 69 has been made in the imperial announcements, leaving Article 7 power of the emperor the sole constitutional ground.[112] It appears that Takano's fear has been realized, and the prerogative of the sovereign *genshu* emperor has made a comeback.

The symbol emperor system was introduced as a means of moving away from the imperial ideology of prewar and wartime Japan. In particular, it was integrally related to efforts to introduce and implant popular sovereignty. It has been understood and implemented, however, in ways that constantly bring back various elements of the past in both theory and practice. Now recast as the "center of the people's devotion," the symbol emperorship has been justified in terms of Japan's allegedly authentic cultural and political tradition. Even the close past that it was meant to overcome has been selectively preserved in practice. The old body politic still lies unmastered under the emperor's new clothes.

THE ONCE AND FUTURE REPUBLIC OF KOREA

The past figured prominently in the making of Korea's Founding Constitution. Compared to the Japanese case, the emphasis was more on repudiating the past, particularly the period of colonial occupation. Indeed, constitution-making was widely seen as the culmination of decades-long efforts on the part of a subjugated people to regain sovereign independence. The establishment of an independent state in 1948 symbolized the Korean people's resolve to reject the past and to embark on a brand new era of equality and prosperity. Whereas the Japanese experience of constitutional founding involved efforts to reimagine the past with a view to establishing continuity between the new constitution and the nation's history, the Korean case was weighted more toward highlighting discontinuity. Founding in postcolonial Korea meant liquidating the dark and soiled past and opening a bright new chapter in the nation's history.

To be sure, framers of the Korean constitution also engaged in selective reinterpretation and reimagination of the past. Most significantly, a "Great Revolution" was projected onto the past, whose animating spirit was then invoked to impart legitimacy on the act of founding. It is worth noting, however, that their main objective was not so much to claim inheritance, but

[112] Nonaka et al. (eds.), *Chūshaku Kenpō*, vol. I, pp. 291–3.

rather to emphasize discontinuity and to proclaim that a new state had been established where none existed before. In other words, "useable pasts," and even "counterfactual history," were conjured up to assert a constitutional *tabula rasa*. The theme of rupture and discontinuity looms far larger than that of conservation or continuity. One reason for this tendency was that the past to be exorcised included not only the colonial period but even the pre-colonial dynastic order. For the drafters of the Founding Constitution, rejection of Japanese imperialism could not mean the restoration or resurrection of the monarchy that had preceded the colonial occupation. The desire to make a clean break, to create a new constitutional order from scratch, was that much stronger because the new order had to be something truly unprecedented in Korean history – a democratic republic where "We the People" were in charge of their own destiny.

As it were, a *tabula rasa* had to be effected through a double negation of the past, or by effacing the memory of "double tyranny."[113] Negating Japanese colonialism was not enough; it had to be accompanied by the negation of the pre-colonial dynastic order as well. This call for negating the legacy of the monarchical order is expressed most emphatically in Article 1, which declares: "Republic of Korea shall be a democratic republic." The demand for liquidating the colonial past was also given constitutional recognition in Article 101, which authorized the punishment of those who committed "malicious anti-national acts" during Japanese occupation. Korea's Founding Constitution was bookended with these two mandates that were meant to negate the double tyranny of the past.

The process of implementing these demands for leveling the constitutional ground, however, revealed tensions within the constitution which made the goal of creating a *tabula rasa* ultimately unattainable. For one, the constitution itself mandated, in Article 100, the maintenance of continuity with the colonial legal system. In part a legacy of the U.S. military government, this mandate, along with the accompanying need for the personnel required to maintain legal continuity, inevitably militated against the demand for making a clean break from the colonial past. Further, the

[113] The term was coined by Yun Ch'i-ho (1865–1945), who was one of the first Korean intellectuals to be educated in America and a prominent leader for modernization of Korea until it succumbed to the Japanese takeover. Although he later collaborated with the colonial regime (and died a broken man shortly after liberation), this expression, used in 1905 to describe the Korean state of affairs to an American acquaintance, well captures the aspirations of the Korean patriots of this period who yearned for both national independence and democratic republicanism. "25 October 1905," *Yun Chi-Ho's Diary, 1903–1906*, vol. 6 (Seoul: National History Compilation Committee, 1976), p. 179.

special law enacted to carry out the mandate for lustration highlighted a tension between Article 1 and Article 101. In the political context of immediate postcolonial Korea, swift and uncompromising pursuit of transitional justice called for a concentration of powers in the legislature. All other branches of the government were reputed to be so encumbered with the past that they could not be entrusted with the historic task of national cleansing. By contrast, the mandate to establish a democratic republic meant adherence to the principle of separation of powers, which was especially important for the founding generation as a key feature that distinguished the Republic of Korea from the nascent Stalinist regime in the north dedicated to the principle of proletariat dictatorship. More importantly, perhaps, the particular manner in which the separation of powers was given institutional form in the constitution practically ensured an ongoing tug of war between the legislature and the executive, which in turn would ultimately cripple the constitutional project of lustration. Although based on a thick political consensus in postcolonial Korea, the "hybrid regime" adopted by the constitution turned out to be too unstable and fragile a framework in which to pursue such a high-political project.

The new Republic of Korea was to be founded on a clean slate after rejecting the "double tyranny" in its entirety. Under the political and historical exigencies of the times, however, complete and thoroughgoing repudiation of the past threatened to derail the very process of founding itself. Constitutional founding of Korea, in other words, was faced with the difficulty of pursuing the twin, but often conflicting, goals of transitional justice and state-building. This dilemma was not peculiar to postcolonial Korea; it was only more crippling there.

Leveling the Constitutional Ground

Conveniently, perhaps, for the drafters of the Founding Constitution, the status of Korea had already been declared a *tabula rasa* by the U.S. occupation authorities. According to their own self-understanding, the American troops that landed in the southern part of Korea in September 1945 had marched into a territory where no sovereign authority existed. Writing in his capacity as the legal advisor to the USAMGIK, the German-born jurist Ernst Fraenkel drew up a famous memorandum in 1948 describing the structure and powers of the military government, in which he asserted that the termination of Japan's sovereign rights over Korea had resulted in "neither the revival of the pre-annexation Korean state nor the establishment of a new Korean state." The American occupying forces "took over a country which, from the point of view of international law, was a 'no man's land.'"[114] Korea was in a legal vacuum, in other words, which meant that the postcolonial state to be established at the end of the U.S. military occupation would truly be a "newborn" nation. Hirohito's famous radio broadcast on 15 August 1945, then, had signaled not only the termination of hostilities but also a radical break with the past in Korea. Eliminating the Japanese colonial empire without restoring the "pre-annexation" monarchy, the U.S. occupation authorities had declared Korea to be a legal *tabula rasa*.

This understanding is borne out by the initial policies of the American troops in Korea, whose very first proclamation to the Korean people was that the U.S. occupying authorities shall be the only legitimate government in Korea. As Fraenkel points out, the conventional norms of international law regarding military occupation were of limited applicability in the Korean context because such norms presupposed "that sovereignty rests with the government of the occupied country."[115] The usual assumption, in other words, was that military occupation will be temporary and limited to restoring and ensuring public order and safety. The 1907 Hague Convention on the Laws and Customs of War on Land, for example, provided that the occupying authority shall respect the "laws in force in the country" (Article 43) and that private property shall not be confiscated (Article 46). By contrast, Fraenkel notes, Korea had an "unprecedented international legal status" characterized by the "absence of a sovereign government," which in turn required the Commanding General of the USAFIK to exercise "vicariously" the authority of the Korean government until one was established in the future.[116] On the basis of such self-understanding, USAMGIK proceeded to embark on a massive project of revamping the entire legal system. Since there were no laws that demanded the respect of the occupying authorities, a new legal system had to be created. That is why, unlike the conventional forms of occupation anticipated by the Hague Convention, the structure of USAMGIK included a code drafting bureau and other units geared toward the creation of a whole new state.[117] Such extraordinary legislative activities of USAMGIK are inexplicable

[114] Ernst Fraenkel, "The Structure of United States Army Military Government in Korea" (1948), reprinted in *Journal of Modern Korean Studies*, vol. 2 (Dec. 1985), p. 69.

[115] Fraenkel, "Structure of Military Government," p. 70.

[116] Fraenkel, "Structure of Military Government," p. 70.

[117] For example, it commissioned one of its legal advisors to draft an entirely new civil code. Charles Lobingier drafted a "Proposed Civil Code for Korea" which was published in a Korean legal periodical in 1949. His efforts apparently had no impact on the later drafting process that began after the Korean War. For an analysis on Lobingier's draft, see Yun Tae-sŏng, *Migunjŏng Shidae ŭi Han'guk Minpŏpchŏn P'yŏnch'ansaŏp* [Compilation of Korean Civil Code under United States Military Government] (Seoul: Han'guk Haksul Chŏngbo, 2009).

unless we recognize their underlying legal premise – that Korea was a "no man's land."

Given this premise, on which USAMGIK governed Korea for three years, it is perhaps not surprising that the National Assembly formed in May 1948 at the end of the U.S. military occupation would exhibit a similar outlook. In their self-understanding, the National Assemblymen who adopted the constitution were engaged in the establishment of a brand new state where none existed. The framers of the constitution were thus in agreement with Fraenkel's assessment that the termination of Japan's rule, in and of itself, had brought about neither the revival of the pre-colonial dynasty nor the creation of a new state. This outlook can be seen in the oft-used term *kŏn'guk*, which literally means the "founding of a new state." Clearly presupposed in this mantra of the day is an assumption that no state existed on the Korean Peninsula at the time of liberation. This view was widespread throughout the three-year period of American military government, when various political groups, both left and right, organized themselves for the purpose of laying the groundwork for the eventual *kŏn'guk*. In 1941, even before liberation, the Korean Provisional Government issued a famous constitutional document entitled *Kŏn'guk Kangnyŏng*, which can be rendered, "Essential Points for Founding a New State." Deeply imbued with the aforementioned Principle of Three Equalities, this declaration outlined the general framework of the government and rights regime to be enshrined in the constitution for an independent Korean state. KPG members were clearly working to prepare for the creation of an entirely new political and legal order, and such an epochal consciousness was widely shared in the National Assembly.

Despite the basic agreement that immediate postcolonial Korea was a *tabula rasa*, however, there was one crucial difference between the outlook of the American occupying forces and that of the locals. Whereas Fraenkel assumed that Korea had become a legal "no man's land" by dint of Japan's surrender in August 1945, the Korean drafters of the constitution took the view that Korea had already been a *tabula rasa* since March 1919. For them, a "Great Revolution" had taken place on 1 March 1919 when millions of Koreans rose up in a nationwide peaceful protest against the Japanese colonial rule. On this view, the March First Movement had ushered in a new era and effected a clean break with the past by demonstrating Korean people's unmistakable resolve for national independence as manifested in its famous Declaration of Independence. Even though – or, perhaps, because – the uprising was violently and ruthlessly suppressed by the colonial authorities, the event had "proven" to the world the moral bankruptcy of the Japanese colonial empire.

The so-called Spirit of the March First Revolution became a shorthand for Korean people's will to independence and a new beginning.

Not surprisingly, this spirit figures prominently in the Founding Constitution. Specific reference is made to this watershed event in the Preamble, whose relevant parts read as follows:

> We the People of Korea, proud of a glorious tradition and history from time immemorial, following the great spirit of independence as manifested in the establishment and worldwide proclamation of the Republic of Korea by the March First Movement of 1919, presently engaged in the re-establishment of a democratic independent state, … do hereby ordain and establish this Constitution.

Writing in 1948, the authors of this text made it abundantly clear that their goal was to inherit the revolutionary spirit of the March First Movement and to establish a "democratic independent state." This self-assertion was largely the result of the forceful plea, during the drafting process, by Syngman Rhee, who wished to declare to the outside observers, particularly the United States and the Soviet Union, that the republican form of government adopted by the constitution was not the result of foreign instruction or guidance, but the fulfillment of indigenous ideals and aspirations. He urged the drafters to include a statement "at the very beginning of the document" indicating the fact that the Republic of Korea had already been established at the hands of Koreans themselves in the wake of the "March First Revolution of 1919."[118] The Preamble thus states that "We the People of Korea" are "re-establishing" this democratic republic borne of the revolution in 1919.

To be sure, the democratic republic ostensibly established in 1919 had been in name only, at least from the perspective of international law. There had been a declaration of independence, and a nationwide mass movement in support of it, but the demonstrations had lasted only a few months before they were completely put down by the colonial authorities. The Provisional Government, established immediately after the "Great Revolution," had been neither in effective control over Korea, nor elected by the Korean people themselves. Throughout the period of Japanese rule, moreover, the KPG never succeeded in gaining the recognition of the international community of nations (except for China). By claiming the legacy of the March First Movement, the framers of the constitution were conjuring up, as it were, an "alternative history." Their goal in invoking this largely notional republic was to drive home the point that a clean break in history had been made, rather

[118] *CNA Minutes*, Session 1, No. 22 (1 July 1948), pp. 346–8.

than to claim succession to any real or concrete government. As an exercise in counterfactual imagination, in other words, the validity of their claim to reconstruct this "independent state" was not predicated on historical or legal fact. Lack of international recognition or effective control was irrelevant. For the drafters, "re-establishment" was important because it allowed them to imagine a republican tradition that could be invoked to posit a historic rupture in the year 1919 – a republican ground-zero, as it were.

While the drafters shared a commitment to the revolutionary spirit of the March First Movement, the counterfactual nature of this republican tradition was a cause for certain ambivalence and equivocation in the text of the constitution. Although the preamble states that the constitution was "re-establishing" the state that had been established in 1919, it nevertheless employs a verb that suggests that its authors were, by the same act, seeking to highlight discontinuity with the KPG. According to the text, the National Assembly, acting on behalf of "We the People of Korea," had met in 1948 to "ordain and establish" an entirely new constitution, rather than to revise the existing constitution of the KPG. If the National Assembly had been genuinely committed to maintaining continuity with the republic established in 1919, it could have done so by shoring up the KPG constitution. Yet, it used an active verb *chejŏng*, meaning "to enact," which implies pointedly that its authors were not "revising" (*kaejŏng*) any pre-existing constitution. Rather, they were making a brand new charter for the new independent republic. In doing so, the drafters were making a conscious choice. During the drafting process in the National Assembly, the idea of revising or amending the KPG constitution had in fact been suggested, but was summarily dismissed.[119] What was being succeeded to was only the "spirit" of that government, it was argued, rather than any of its particular institutions or charters. Similarly, when one member of the National Assembly pointed out that "re-establishment" of the republic did not mesh with their activity of drafting a new constitution, other members did not see a contradiction.[120] The fact that the Provisional Government itself is not specifically named in the preamble is also suggestive. The text only refers to the Republic of Korea that had been established in 1919.[121] Even for

119 CNA *Minutes*, Session 1, No. 18 (26 June 1948), p. 229 (statement of Assemblyman Sŏ Sang-il). Prior to the convocation of the National Assembly, more than a few private and semi-official draft constitutions had taken the constitution of the KPG as their base text. Kim Su-Yong, *Kŏn'guk kwa Hŏnpŏp* [Founding and the Constitution] (Seoul: Kyŏngin Munhwasa, 2008), pp. 64, 81.

120 CNA *Minutes*, Session 1, No. 27 (7 July 1948), p. 512.

121 There is of course a political background to this equivocation. On the one hand, many of the prominent godfathers of the Founding Constitution, such as Syngman Rhee and Shin Ik-hee (respectively the chairman and vice-chairman of the National Assembly) had solid KPG backgrounds in one form or another. Given the popular reverence for the KPG, it was

Syngman Rhee, who insisted on using the Republican Calendar (e.g., 1948 was the "thirtieth year of the Republic"), the legacy being sought was the "spirit" of the March First Revolution rather than any earthly history of the Provisional Government.[122]

According to such a self-understanding, it seems natural that it was mostly the name for the brand-new republic that the drafters sought to inherit consciously. According to the Founding Constitution, the new state being formed in 1948 would be called, in Korean, *Taehan Min'guk*, which had been the name used by the Provisional Government in 1919. *Min'guk* meant republic, and *Taehan*, literally, "Great Han." The official name of the new state was thus the "Great Han Republic." Yet, even retaining this name caused controversy during the drafting process. Some argued for *Chosŏn*, the name of the dynasty that had ruled Korea since 1392 until its penultimate king changed the name of his realm to the Empire of Great Han in 1897. Others supported *Koryŏ*, the dynasty which had preceded *Chosŏn*, while still others preferred the more colloquial *Han'guk*. In the eventuality, all these dynastic names were rejected because they were deemed unsuitable for a new republic. Particularly, *Chosŏn* was unacceptable because it was layered with so many objectionable pasts. To begin with, it had been used by the Japanese empire for its Korean colonial territory.[123] Also, the fact that it had been the name used by the pre-colonial dynasty under the Chinese tributary system made it unappealing to them. Similarly, the more recent use of *Chosŏn* by the leftists and eventually by the communist regime across the 38th parallel made it repugnant to the drafters. The fact that Korea under U.S. military occupation had

a useful legacy by which to bolster South Korea's regime legitimacy vis-à-vis the domestic left-wing factions and the communist North Korea. On the other, Kim Ku, who was KPG's most emblematic leader, had boycotted the general election of 10 May 1948, which created the National Assembly that drafted the constitution. Insisting that leaders of both north and south should continue to work toward the creation of a unified Korean government, he chose not to participate in any election that would lead to the establishment of a separate South Korean government. Without Kim Ku on its side, the National Assembly could not claim a complete monopoly on the KPG legacy.

122 As far as Rhee was concerned, in fact, the "Republic" referred not to the united KPG established in Shanghai, but its precursor that had been organized in Seoul immediately after the March uprising in 1919, and which had appointed him "President." Yun Tae-wŏn, "Imshi Chŏngbu Pŏpt'ongnon ŭi Yŏksajŏk Yŏnwŏn kwa Uimi" [Historic Origins of KPG Succession Debate and Its Meaning], in Ko Chŏng-hyu et al., *Taehan Min'guk Imshi Chŏngbu ŭi Hyŏndaesachŏk Sŏngch'al* (Paju: Nanam, 2010), p. 101.

123 During the colonial period, Korea's official name as a territory of the Japanese Empire had been *Chōsen* [*Chosŏn* in Korean pronunciation]. On the day of annexation in 1910, the Japanese government issued an announcement which provided: "Korea shall hereafter be named 'Chōsen.'" "Announcement of the Japanese Foreign Office," *American Journal of International Law*, vol. 4, no. 4, Supplement: Official Documents (Oct. 1910), p. 284.

also been called *Chosŏn*, in continuation of the colonial practice, also did not help its candidacy as a name for the new republic.

To be sure, *Taehan* also had its share of detractors. After all, it had been the name of the short-lived "empire" that was responsible for Korea's loss of national sovereignty. One assemblyman went so far as to call it a "congenital deformity" born of the 1895 Treaty of Shimonoseki.[124] The reference was apparently to Japan's victory in the First Sino-Japanese War, which put Japan in a position to urge Korea to proclaim itself an empire and declare "independence" from China. Japan's move was widely interpreted to have been a mere prelude to its subjugation of Korea as a protectorate in 1905 and eventual annexation in 1910. Against this historical background, *Taehan* was apparently not free of the colonial past and thus inappropriate as the name for an independent republic of Korea. Nevertheless, the National Assembly adopted *Taehan* because, for most of its members, it referred to the first republic declared in 1919 in defiance of Japanese imperialism, not to the defunct empire.[125] The name's association with the revolutionary spirit as manifested in the March First Movement was much more powerful than any connection to the largely sham empire proclaimed on the eve of Korea's colonization.

Along this line, perhaps the most dramatic instance of using counterfactual history was occasioned in December 1948, shortly after the constitution was formally adopted. Having promulgated the constitution in July, the same National Assembly enacted a Nationality Law in pursuance of Article 3 of the Constitution which provided: "The requirements for being a national of the Republic of Korea shall be determined by law." The proposed bill's primary criterion was that a person shall be a Korean national if his or her father is "a national of Republic of Korea at the time of the person's birth." This blanket declaration naturally caused some assemblymen to inquire about the propriety of this requirement. Since the republic had been established only a few months earlier, the problem was by what criterion the father's Korean nationality might be verified. To avoid this difficulty, a revision was proposed to redefine a Korean national as an individual whose father was an "ethnic Korean" (*Hanin*). In response, however, Justice Minister Yi In who explained the bill

[124] CNA *Minutes*, Session 1, No. 20 (29 June 1948), p. 284.

[125] When leaders of independence movement met in Shanghai to set up a provisional government in 1919, a similar debate on the name of the republic took place. The idea of calling it *Taehan* was initially opposed on grounds that it had been the name briefly used by the monarchy before it expired, and therefore not worth reviving. Yet, it is reported that the argument, "[s]ince Korea had collapsed as *Taehan*, it should be resurrected as *Taehan*," carried the day. Despite its association with the defunct monarchy, it was apparently preferable to the name given by the colonial authorities. See Lee Seon-min, *'Taehan Min'guk' Kukho ŭi T'ansaeng* [The Birth of the State Name *Taehan Min'guk*] (Paju: Nanam, 2013), pp. 88–94.

made a revealing statement that highlighted the need to supplement facts with counterfactual imagination in launching a new constitutional order. His interpretation was that, while the government of Korea may have been inaugurated on 15 August 1948, a state called the Republic of Korea had been in continuous existence even prior to that date. For him, it was a postulate of all constitutional systems that its members be thought to have had membership in that system even before the constitutional founding. Both "legally and spiritually," all Koreans now living under the jurisdiction of the republic must be deemed to hold Korean nationality from time immemorial.[126] Governments may come and go, and there may even be times when no government is in place, but the state never ceases to exist.[127] As it were, the name "Republic of Korea" had to be projected back onto the past in order to identify the current members of that state. Uninterrupted existence of an independent state had to be presupposed in order to identify the people as members of the new constitutional order.

In sum, the drafters wished to ensure that the new independent Korean state would be created on a constitutional *tabula rasa*, and they sought to do so by invoking the revolutionary spirit of the March First Movement. Ironically, the attempt to level the constitutional ground and to negate the past entailed bringing back in the past again, or more precisely, conjuring up an alternative history for the purpose of positing a counterfactual revolution. Through a highly selective and imaginative invocation of the past, in other words, the framers of Korea's Founding Constitution intended to effectuate a revolutionary rupture by which they could claim that the past had been repudiated once and for all.

Effacing the "Double Tyranny"

Beyond serving as a source of inspiration for the drafters, the spirit of the March First Revolution had to be given some constitutional expression in the text. Besides the Preamble, Article 1 and Article 101 were meant to embody and institutionalize this revolutionary spirit. Article 1 defines the new state as a democratic republic, whereas Article 101 mandated the punishment of those who collaborated with Japan's colonial rule. These two provisions were both

[126] CNA *Minutes*, Session 1, No. 118 (1 Dec. 1948), pp. 1144–5, 1151–2.

[127] Another assemblyman supported the minister by drawing an analogy to family relations. If the father changes his name, his sons and daughters have to be identified henceforth as the children of the father under the new name, even if they had been born prior to the name change. CNA *Minutes*, Session 1, No. 119 (2 Dec. 1948), p. 1158 (statement by Assemblyman Cho Hŏn-yŏng).

institutional expressions of the desire to repudiate the past and, as it were, to level the constitutional ground. Clearly, the past to be rejected included not just the colonial experience. In addition to negating the Japanese empire, the constitution also expressed the drafters' firm resolve that the pre-colonial empire of Korea shall not be revived. The affirmation of "democratic republic" reflected this desire to reject the dynastic order that had preceded colonial rule. The Republic of Korea was to be built on the ruins of both empires.

This doubly negative outlook on history goes back to the 1919 Declaration of Independence whose very first sentence reads: "We hereby declare that Korea is an independent state and that Koreans are a self-governing people."[128] Taking advantage of the huge throng that had been gathering in Seoul in anticipation of the funeral of Emperor Kojong, scheduled for 3 March, the organizers of the protest decided to read the Declaration and to spark mass demonstrations throughout the land. For a document proclaimed to a funeral crowd, the text was conspicuously silent with regard to the monarchy and utterly lacking in nostalgia or any restorative outlook. Independence was being declared in the name of the "self-governing people" of Korea, not the defunct dynasty. That is why the spirit of the March First Revolution could be deployed as an expression of the ardent desire for not only national independence but also democratic self-rule. The whole project of constitution-making was, in short, bound to be a symbolically charged act aimed at wiping out the memory of subjugation under both foreign and domestic tyrannies. As a result, the Founding Constitution was bookended by two militant mandates against the "double tyranny" that it aspired to overcome.

Article 1, which rejected the monarchic order, was not a new idea that emerged during the drafting process. The fact is that, even during the colonial period, the pre-colonial dynasty inspired neither loyalty nor nostalgia in the hearts of most Koreans.[129] Those few who advocated dynastic restoration soon became a negligible minority. For example, in 1915 after the outbreak of World War I, one group of independence activists conspired to smuggle the former

[128] Peter H. Lee (ed.), *Sourcebook of Korean Civilization*, vol. II (New York: Columbia University Press, 1996), p. 432.

[129] This was due to many factors. Rightly or wrongly, the loss of independence in 1910 was widely blamed on the political and moral bankruptcy of the monarchy, particularly its ruling establishment. During the colonial period, members of the former imperial family of the Empire of Great Han had largely been Japanized. Japan even created a separate category of royal class called *ōkōzoku* to incorporate them into Japanese imperial household, and they were granted similar honor and privileges. Many also served in the Japanese imperial army. For a study of their legal status as affected by annexation and liberation, see Sakamoto Shin'ichi, "Chosŏn Wangshil Chasondŭl kwa kŭ Taehan Min'guk Kukchŏk" [Offspring of Chosŏn Royal Family and Their Korean Nationality], *Sŏul Kukchepŏp Yon'gu*, vol. 6, no. 1 (1999).

Emperor Kojong out of Korea to lead the independence movement in exile. They advocated restoring, or at least using, the former imperial house based on naïve international strategic reasoning. The idea was that Korea must be allied with Germany and China because they were Japan's principal adversaries in East Asia, and that independent Korea should readopt monarchy because both enemies of Japan were empires.[130] Such quixotic efforts, however, would naturally dwindle and all but disappear by the war's end. Indeed, many who took part in this restorationist plot would join the group that adopted the famous "Declaration of Harmonious Unity" (*Taedong Tan'gyŏl ŭi Sŏnŏn*), which was one of the earliest manifestos for popular sovereignty. Written in 1917 to urge cooperation and unity among various independence groups, this historic document declared that the ceding of sovereignty in 1910 by the last emperor of Korea to the Japanese emperor was null and void. For, according to history's "unwritten fundamental law of the state," when a monarch forfeits his sovereignty, it is the people, rather than some foreign prince, who inherits his power and authority. Since the emperor had relinquished his sovereign powers, it was only natural and proper that the people should become the sovereign of Korea. The day that the emperor's power expired was indeed the birthday of the sovereign people.[131] Especially after the March First Movement of 1919, this kind of call for republicanism and popular sovereignty became the mainstream view within the independence movement. Worth noting here is the contrast between this emerging consensus and the "constitution" of the Empire of Great Han issued less than two decades earlier. According to the "National Polity of the Great Han" (*Taehan'guk Kukche*) of 1899, Korea was an eternal "despotic polity" (*chŏnje chŏngch'i*), or absolute monarchy, ruled by an emperor with unlimited powers.[132] Less than a decade after the demise of this unabashedly "despotic polity" in 1910, the call for restoration of the old monarchy had precipitously lost all adherents.

130 Suh Hee-Kyung, *Taehan Min'guk Hŏnpŏp ŭi T'ansaeng* [The Birth of the Constitution of the Republic of Korea] (Seoul: Changbi Publishers, 2012), pp. 66–7.

131 "Taedong Tan'gyŏl ŭi Sŏnŏn" (1917), p. 4, available at http://db.history.go.kr/item/imageViewer.do?levelId=haf_062_1600.

132 Some scholars argue that republicanism had in fact been seriously considered during the last decades of the nineteenth century. For the modernization of the decaying dynasty, the reform groups led by the Independence Club and the king had agreed on the creation of a "people's assembly" and the establishment of a constitutional monarchy. On this view, Kojong's 1897 proclamation which turned Chosŏn into the Empire of Great Han and the 1899 declaration of absolute monarchy were a betrayal of that agreement. Suh, *Hŏnpŏp ŭi T'ansaeng*, pp. 40–8; Shin Woo-Cheol, *Pigyo Hŏnpŏpsa: Taehan Min'guk Iphŏnjuŭi ŭi Yŏnwŏn* [Comparative Constitutional History: The Origins of Korean Constitutionalism] (Seoul: Pŏpmunsa, 2008), pp. 66–78.

These political awakenings culminated in the 1919 Declaration of Independence and were quickly followed by a number of attempts to better organize independence movements, all of which advocated the establishment of a democratic republic without a single exception. On 11 April 1919, a group in Shanghai issued a "Provisional Charter of the Republic of Korea" (*Taehan Min'guk Imshi Hŏnjang*), Article 1 of which declared: "Republic of Korea shall be a democratic republic." This was the first time such a bold assertion appeared in Korean history. Article 3 also stated that the people of the Republic of Korea shall know no distinction based on gender, social class, or property. As such, the charter contained an unmistakable defiance against not only Japanese colonialism but also the pre-colonial, monarchical polity and institutions. The Shanghai provisional government was not the only one proclaimed in the wake of the March First Movement. During the month of April 1919, there appeared numerous provisional governments in various regions, both in and outside Korea. Some were only "paper governments," while others had more substance, but all of them declared themselves to be some kind of republican polity.[133] Of these, the most significant were the ones formed in Seoul and the Russian Far East in addition to the one in Shanghai. By September 1919, these three groups agreed to merge and formed the united "Provisional Government of the Republic of Korea." A "Provisional Constitution" (*Imshi Hŏnpŏp*) issued by the united KPG on 11 September 1919 stated that the sovereignty of the Republic of Korea shall reside in the entire people of Korea and reiterated the principle of political and social equality. Popular sovereignty had thus become an entrenched part of Korea's constitutional tradition.

While the KPG constitution would undergo numerous amendments and even relabeling, no alteration was ever made to the principle that Korea shall be a democratic republic and that it shall be founded upon popular sovereignty. Of particular interest is the aforementioned "Essential Points for Founding a New State" of 1941, for it makes explicit the two pasts, the double tyranny, which the KPG sought to overcome. According to this constitutional document, the March First Movement had been a "Great Revolution" that unequivocally expressed the resolve of the Korean people to throw off the yoke of colonial rule. For its authors, however, it had been a "Great Revolution" in yet another sense. Through the uprising, Koreans sought not only to topple the despotic rule of a foreign government but also to destroy the "five-thousand

[133] Park Chan-Seung, *Taehan Min'guk ŭn Minju Konghwaguk ida* [The Republic of Korea Shall Be a Democratic Republic] (Seoul: Dolbegae, 2013), pp. 127–33.

year-old encrustation of monarchic rule."[134] It was an expression of the desire and determination to sever all ties with the dynastic rule that had preceded the Japanese occupation. Under this interpretation, shared by both the KPG in 1941 and the National Assembly in 1948, the March First Movement had commenced a democratic revolution as well as a war of independence, in a manner similar to the American Declaration of Independence of 1776. This long-held commitment, at least since 1919, to a democratic republic and popular sovereignty was never contested, or even debated, in postcolonial Korea. By the time the Founding Constitution was drafted, there was no doubt that the Republic of Korea would be a democratic republic. This is reflected in the text as Article 1 and Article 2, which read, respectively: "The Republic of Korea shall be a Democratic Republic" and "The sovereignty of the Republic of Korea shall reside in the people and all state authority shall emanate from the people."

In addition to the pre-colonial dynastic past, an even more important target of repudiation was the colonial past, which, strangely enough, hardly makes an appearance in the text. The only explicit reference to the Japanese colonial rule is found in Article 101, which provides: "The National Assembly which enacted the Constitution may establish a special law dealing with the punishment of malicious anti-national acts committed prior to 15 August 1945." Brief, even perfunctory, as it may seem, this provision resonated strongly with the pervasive postcolonial zeal for transitional justice and was thus pivotal for the legitimacy of the new independent republic. Without legal-punitive lustration as mandated by Article 101, the Republic of Korea could not be "re-established" on a clean slate.

Yet, the process by which this provision became part of the constitutional text was by no means uncomplicated. Article 101 in fact was the product of a convoluted process that had begun even before Japan's unconditional surrender on 15 August 1945 and long before the National Assembly met to draft the constitution. The aforementioned "Essential Points for Founding a New State," for example, demanded that those who collaborated with the "enemy" be deprived of the rights to vote and to be elected to public office.[135] Along this line, the urgent need for punishing the "pro-Japanese national traitors" (*ch'inil minjok panyŏkcha*) was taken for granted in postcolonial Korea, and the only

[134] "Taehan Min'guk Kŏn'guk Kangnyŏng," Chapter I, Part 5, in Chong Jong-sup (ed.), *Han'guk Hŏnpŏpsa Mullyu*, pp. 85 and 91. When referring to the struggle for independence against the Japanese, the text also employs a more jingoistic term, "Blood War of the March First" (*Samil Hyŏlchŏn*).

[135] "Taehan Min'guk Kŏn'guk Kangnyŏng," Chapter III, Part 4, in Chong Jong-sup (ed.), *Han'guk Hŏnpŏpsa Mullyu*, pp. 87, 94.

issue was its scope and extent.[136] The most concerted efforts at lustration were made by the Korean Interim Legislative Assembly formed within USAMGIK. KILA's final bill passed on 2 July 1947, "Special Act on National Traitors, Pro-Japanese Collaborators, and Crafty Profiteers," defined the specific categories of anti-national collaborators and stipulated the types of punishment to be meted out, including prison sentences, property confiscation, and restrictions on their political rights. Unfortunately, however, this first effort to legislate a framework for lustration was vetoed by the U.S. military governor. After sitting on the bill for months, Major General Charles Helmick finally informed KILA on 27 November 1947 that he had decided to withhold his "concurrence." By that time, the United States had already passed the issue of Korean independence on to the United Nations, and USAMGIK apparently felt that the punishment of collaborators should be dealt with through the government of Korea soon to be established, rather than by a law made by an interim legislature.

The KILA's failure most likely provided the immediate impetus for the inclusion of Article 101 in the Founding Constitution. As will be seen in Chapter 4, KILA's bill for lustration did have an influence on the election law used to form the National Assembly in May 1948. Certain categories of ex-collaborators as defined by the KILA bill were barred from participating in the general election. Yet, there was still no law for their punishment. Thus, when the National Assembly met to draft the constitution, there was naturally a strong demand across the board for including a constitutional mandate for lustration. The so-called Kwŏn Sŭng-yŏl Draft, one of the two base texts officially adopted by the Drafting Committee, provided for the punishment of "traitorous acts committed prior to the enactment of the constitution" through a law which shall be applied "retroactively to the time of the acts."[137] The committee relied on this article to write the lustration provision, which provoked some controversy during the subsequent plenary session. The committee's draft provision allowed for the retroactive punishment of ex-collaborators by making a constitutional exception to the normal rule of criminal law – enshrined in

136 When, for instance, the U.S.-Soviet Joint Commission invited local political groups to submit ideas on the form of government to be established for independent Korea, the questionnaire included an item on how to purge ex-collaborators. In response, the moderates and rightists tended to call for the establishment of a special tribunal and special investigative committees throughout the country, while cautioning against the possibility of the process being abused to instigate a naked class warfare between the haves and have-nots. Leftists called for a more vindictive measure for the alleged traitors and provided rather detailed and sweeping definitions of the scope of those punishable as well as various forms of punishments. See Kim Su-Yong, *Kŏn'guk kwa Hŏnpŏp*, pp. 127, 136, 143–4.

137 Kim Su-Yong, *Kŏn'guk kwa Hŏnpŏp*, pp. 251, 321.

Article 23 – which precluded punishment for acts that did not constitute a crime at the time of their commission. But the debates on the floor were not concerned with this question of retroactivity. Evidently, abrogating a key constitutional right was a small price to pay for enabling the urgent task of colonial lustration. The issue, instead, mostly involved how extensive the scope of the punishable anti-national acts should be and whether lustration would also target those subversive (read communist) acts committed after liberation. In the end, the draft provision was ratified as Article 101 without any change and became the constitutional ground for the National Assembly to enact a lustration law.

In sum, Article 1 and Article 101 were included in the Founding Constitution as declarations of the framers' firm resolve to negate the double tyranny of the past and to establish a new state on a clean slate. Effacing the memory of colonial occupation required the purging of ex-collaborators, whereas repudiation of the pre-colonial dynastic order mandated the establishment of a democratic republic. The categorical rejection of all forms of subjugation – whether foreign or domestic – demanded the inscription and enshrinement of national independence and popular sovereignty in the constitution.

Judiciary and Legal Continuity

Making a declaration in the constitutional text is of course much easier than implementing it in the real world. This is particularly so for those provisions intended to efface the past because in actuality they can only be implemented in a world that is still haunted by forces of the past, which tend to lurk in rather unexpected places. Regarding the implementation of Article 101, the forces of the past may have been particularly powerful. Evidently, any project of lustration entails some form of judicial proceeding, especially if the project is designed to take the form of a trial and imposition of punishment, as was the case in Korea. It may have been natural, therefore, to turn to the judiciary to implement transitional justice. As it turned out, however, the special law enacted by the National Assembly pursuant to Article 101 accorded the judiciary almost no role in this historic project. A special tribunal was to be formed as an adjunct to the Supreme Court, but it was not composed of professional judges but rather a mixture of judges, lawyers, politicians, and ordinary citizens. Furthermore, the National Assembly had the sole power of determining who would sit on the special tribunal. The reason for this all but complete exclusion of the judiciary, to put it bluntly, was because it was seen as being especially encumbered with the colonial legacy. The courts in postcolonial

Korea, in other words, were often suspected of being part of the past that had to be rejected.

This deep association of the courts with the colonial past was due to two factors. The first was institutional legacy. One of the interesting features of Korea's constitutional founding is that a fully functioning judiciary was already in place well before the adoption of the constitution. The executive branch was formed according to the procedures prescribed in the Founding Constitution after it was promulgated on 17 July 1948. It was preceded by the National Assembly, which opened its doors on 31 May with the understanding that it would not only draft the constitution, but also continue thereafter to sit as the regular legislature.[138] By contrast, a national court system – staffed by Korean judges – had been in continuous operation since shortly after the American occupying forces took control of the southern half of the peninsula in September 1945.[139] Hence, we see a rather anomalous phenomenon during the drafting process in which the Supreme Court was able to convey to the drafters in the National Assembly its own preferences regarding the structure and powers of the judiciary to be established under the Founding Constitution. Even though there was no constitution, in other words, the judiciary was already a "going concern" with distinct institutional interests and outlook. The courts' primary role was of course to interpret and apply the laws in force at the time, a majority of which were those left behind by the Japanese. Their responsibility consisted primarily of continuing to uphold the legal system of the former colonial masters.

As soon as it arrived in Korea, USAMGIK declared that all laws in effect as of 9 August 1945 were to "continue in full force and effect until repealed by express order."[140] Although the policy of maintaining legal continuity may seem inconsistent with Fraenkel's claim (that, legally, Korea is no-man's land), the U.S. authorities saw no contradiction because this fiat created a new ground of legitimacy for the same old colonial laws. Initially, the American occupying forces even preserved the colonial government apparatus along with its entire

[138] On the role and legal nature of the first National Assembly, see Chong Jong-sup, "1948 nyŏn Kukhoe ŭi Pŏpchŏk Sŏngkyŏk e kwanhan Yŏn'gu" [The Legal Nature of the 1948 National Assembly], *Sŏul Taehakkyo Pŏphak*, vol. 45, no. 2 (2004).

[139] This was the result of USAMGIK's early policy of "Koreanizing" the judiciary. Apparently, the Department of Justice, to which the courts were attached, was the first unit within the U.S. military government to complete the process of Koreanization. United States Armed Forces in Korea, "History of United States Armed Forces in Korea" (unpublished manuscript, n.d., on file at Yonsei University Library, Seoul), vol. III, ch. 5, p. 43.

[140] USAMGIK Ordinance No. 21 (2 Nov. 1945). A handful of particularly offensive colonial legislations were abolished by an earlier ordinance. USAMGIK Ordinance No. 11 (9 Oct. 1945).

Japanese staff. Although this policy was quickly reversed at Washington's instruction, it was evident that, unlike their counterpart in Japan, USAMGIK had not come with any missionary zeal to introduce radical changes. Their first priority was the maintenance of law and order, which inevitably meant that they would rely heavily on the legal apparatus left behind by the colonial government.[141] Those laws not "repealed by express order" of the U.S. authorities would remain effective even after the founding of the Republic of Korea. This legal continuity was authorized by virtue of Article 100 of the Founding Constitution, which provided that "[e]xisting laws and ordinances shall be in effect to the extent that they do not conflict with this Constitution." Under such circumstances, the courts could not but be the emblem of continuity with the colonial past.

The second reason had to do with human legacy since most, if not all, members of the bench had become lawyers under the Japanese system. One of the initial problems facing USAMGIK was the utter shortage of qualified Korean personnel who could take over various government positions from the Japanese. This shortage was particularly severe in the case of trained lawyers. With the dismissal and repatriation of Japanese judges, a large number of vacancies had been created on the bench throughout the country. The military government's policy was not to take over the existing court system, but to let the locals run it as it had been prior to the surrender.[142] The problem was that there were an estimated 140 lawyers in all of South Korea at the time, while as of 1943 there had been 246 judges in the colonial court system.[143] Of these Korean lawyers, only a handful had any experience serving as judges in the colonial courts, and even fewer as public prosecutors. In order to prevent the collapse of the court system, USAMGIK thus could not afford to be discriminating when recruiting local lawyers for various court appointments.[144] Along with those who continued to sit on the bench, these

[141] Moon Joon-Young, *Pŏpwŏn kwa Kŏmch'al ŭi T'ansaeng* [The Birth of the Judiciary and the Public Prosecutor's Office] (Seoul: Yŏksabipyŏngsa, 2010), p. 610.

[142] Although a part of USAMGIK's system of Military Occupation Courts, the local courts were largely allowed to operate with minimal interference by occupation authorities. USAMGIK Ordinance No. 21. See also Moon, *Pŏpwŏn kwa Kŏmch'al*, pp. 633–5.

[143] "History of United States Armed Forces in Korea," vol. III, ch. 5, pp. 38, 62.

[144] For example, USAMGIK administered makeshift exams to grant license to Koreans who had been clerks in the colonial courts so as to make them judges. In some cases, at the order of the military governor, American legal officers or Korean individuals with no legal background at all were admitted to the Korean bar. This provoked complaints and criticism from other lawyers. Lee Kuk-woon, "Haebang Konggan esŏ Sabŏpkigu ŭi Chaep'yŏn Kwajŏng e Kwanhan Yŏn'gu" [A Study of the Reorganization of Judicial Institutions Following Liberation], *Pŏp kwa Sahoe*, vol. 29 (2005), p. 149.

newly appointed judges and prosecutors were the frontline bearers of legal continuity in postcolonial Korea.

To be sure, not all Korean jurists were regarded with suspicion or distrust. Some, in fact, had established a reputation for themselves as "nationalist attorneys" during the Japanese occupation by defending *pro bono* fellow Koreans prosecuted for resisting the colonial authorities. Such individuals included Kim Yong-mu, who was appointed Chief Justice of the Supreme Court, Kim Pyŏng-no, who was made Director of the Department of Justice, and Yi In, who became Chief Public Prosecutor. Aside from such exceptional cases, however, the majority of lawyers recruited and hired by USAMGIK were widely regarded as having benefitted, if not actively collaborated, under Japanese rule. Regardless of their colonial reputation, further, it was difficult to deny that these jurists, who had occupied at best a marginal position in the colonial legal system, were suddenly given enormous responsibilities in the legal profession. Repatriation of Japanese judges and attorneys had presented them with an unexpected opportunity to advance in the profession and to reach positions previously unavailable under Japanese rule.[145] Moreover, they finally had a chance to attain genuine judicial independence, which had never been possible during the period of colonial occupation. In this, they were encouraged by the American occupation authorities, who brought with them the idea that judicial independence was an essential ingredient of democracy. In other words, liberation and the influx of American legal values enabled the judiciary to be more assertive, despite the popular perception that they symbolized continuity with the colonial past.

Indicative of the courts' increasingly assertive posture during this period was an extraordinary decision rendered by the Supreme Court in 1947. Later dubbed "Korea's first debate on constitutional adjudication,"[146] the case involved the continuing applicability of a provision in the Japanese Civil Code that limited the legal capacity of married women. Declaring such a provision to be incompatible with the new "national principle" (*kukshi*) of democracy, the Supreme Court held that it could not be used as a basis to dismiss a lawsuit that had been filed by a woman without the consent of her husband.[147] Even though judicial review had never been a part of the inherited legal system of the Japanese empire, and even though there was no constitution against

[145] Lee Kuk-woon, "Sabŏpkigu ŭi Chaep'yŏn," pp. 143–5.

[146] Yang Chang Soo, "Uri Nara Ch'oech'o ŭi Hŏnpŏp Chaep'an Nonŭi" [The First Debate on Constitutional Adjudication in Our Country], *Sŏul Taehakkyo Pŏphak*, vol. 40, no. 2 (1999).

[147] Supreme Court, 1947 Nyŏn Minsang No. 88 (2 Sept. 1947) (S. Kor.). Until the Korean Civil Code was enacted in 1958, rules of the Japanese Civil Code continued to be applied by the courts.

which to adjudge the validity of a legal provision, the Supreme Court asserted that Koreans were about to establish a new state on the foundation of democracy, which required the elimination of sexual inequalities. Ironically, it was the least democratic branch, burdened as it was with the colonial legacy, that proclaimed democracy as the "national principle" even before the formal establishment of a "democratic republic."

This decision immediately provoked a controversy among scholars and practitioners at the time. Many criticized it as an unlawful decision for which the judiciary had no basis or authorization. Among its defenders, some claimed that Korea was a "state in the making," which might not yet have a "constitution in the formal sense," but which nevertheless had a "constitution in the substantive sense," which in turn could be identified with the principle of democracy.[148] Others defended the decision by arguing that the case should not be seen as a constitutional adjudication, but rather as a routine operation of the standard legal principle that allows a court to preclude the application of a legal provision in case of drastic changes in the social status quo.[149] Whether the Supreme Court acted properly in utilizing the principle of democracy as a quasi-constitutional yardstick need not concern us here. To be noted is the fact that the court considered itself to have sufficient authority to intervene even in the absence of a constitutional mandate or authorization from USAMGIK. One commentator actually likened this decision to the famous *Marbury v. Madison* in which the U.S. Supreme Court "invented" the powers of judicial review for itself.[150] More significant is the fact that, even in the absence of manifest authorization, the court was asserting the power to rule on the applicability of inherited Japanese laws. By specifically refusing to apply the discriminatory provision in a colonial law, the court may well have sought to claim for itself the authority, both legal and moral, to oversee the process of exorcising the specter of the colonial past.

Such an extraordinary self-assertion may perhaps be attributed to the fact that the idea of judicial review was quickly gaining currency among Korean lawyers and politicians at the time. Justified in terms of judicial independence and tacitly encouraged by the U.S. occupation authorities, the institution of judicial review was widely thought to be an integral component of new democracy. As such, most draft constitutions put forth by various political groups endowed the Supreme Court with the power to review the constitutionality of

148 Hong Chin-gi, "Sabŏp Chaep'anso ŭi Pŏmnyul Shimsa" [Review of Statute by a Judicial Court], *Pŏpchŏng*, vol. 14 (Nov. 1947), p. 7; Yang, "Hŏnpŏp Chaep'an," p. 136–7.

149 Chang Hu-yŏng, "Minpŏp Cheshipsajo ŭi Unmyŏng" [The Fate of Civil Code Article 14], *Pŏpchŏng*, vol. 18 (Apr. 1948), pp. 6–7; Yang, "Hŏnpŏp Chaep'an," pp. 139–40.

150 Hong, "Sabŏp Chaep'anso ŭi Pŏmnyul Shimsa," p. 5.

legal norms.[151] Needless to say, constitutionalizing judicial review was consistent with the institutional interests of the Korean judiciary. When USAMGIK proposed in early 1947 to make the judiciary more autonomous and independent from its own Department of Justice, members of the courts seized the opportunity to actively promote judicial review. They actually prepared and submitted to the occupation authorities a draft law on court administration, which included judicial review as one of Supreme Court's enumerated powers. In its final form, however, the Court Organization Law of May 1948 did not provide for judicial review.[152] Given that the UN-sponsored general election to form a National Assembly was scheduled to take place within less than a week, the occupation authorities appear to have concluded that such issues should be better left to the constitution-drafting process about to commence.

As it turned out, the Founding Constitution refused to grant the power of judicial review to the courts. Such hostility toward the judiciary was, in fact, evident even before the drafting process officially commenced in the National Assembly. The base draft used by the Constitution Drafting Committee had already been under preparation for several months before the Committee was formed in early June 1948. In June 1947, a Code Drafting Commission had been set up within USAMGIK with the mandate to "consolidate, coordinate, and expedite the work of drafting basic codes" already begun in the Department of Justice.[153] The task of drawing up a draft constitution was commissioned to Yu Chin-o, who began the work in the fall of 1947 and throughout the following winter.[154] He approached the task with four basic principles. The legislature would be bicameral, the government structure would be a parliamentary-cabinet system, farmland reform would be made a constitutional priority, and state ownership or control of major enterprises would be the basic principle of the economic order.[155] In comparison with these four guiding principles, the issue of constitutional adjudication was

[151] Lee Young-lok, "Cheil Konghwaguk Hŏnpŏp Wiwŏnhoe Chedo ŭi Hyŏngsŏng" [Formation of the Constitution Committee System of the First Republic], *Hŏnpŏphak Yŏn'gu*, vol. 11, no. 2 (2005), pp. 309–13.

[152] USAMGIK Ordinance No. 192 (4 May 1948).

[153] "History of United States Armed Forces in Korea," vol. III, ch. 5, p. 60B.

[154] During the Japanese occupation, few Koreans took interest in constitutional law largely because the constitution of the Japanese empire was never in force in the colonies. There were, as a result, only a handful of Korean legal academics at the time of liberation who could claim to have much knowledge in constitutional law. Even Yu Chin-o had been originally trained in criminal law. He confesses that, although he had had eighteen years of experience teaching public law, it was only after liberation that he began studying the subject in earnest and with enthusiasm. Yu, *Hoegorok*, pp. 7–9.

[155] Yu, *Hoegorok*, p. 19.

given relatively low priority, but this did not mean that he was indifferent about the matter.

As a strong advocate of the parliamentary-cabinet system, Yu was rather disinclined toward strict separation of powers, especially between the executive and the legislature.[156] American-style judicial review was not favored because it was premised on absolute judicial independence, even tending toward judicial supremacy. At the same time, a system with no venue for constitutional adjudication was also unacceptable because that implied parliamentary supremacy. For Yu, separation of powers meant that none of the three branches of the government could be allowed to overpower the other two.[157] Yu also held against judicial review because it was a remnant of what he called the "eighteenth century conception of democracy," which had brought about such unsavory outcomes as the Lochner Court in the United States.[158] His prejudice against judicial review was further fueled by the local reality in which the courts and the judicial profession itself were too often associated with the colonial past.[159] Yu was also skeptical of the Korean judge's knowledge and competence regarding issues of constitutional law because, under the Japanese system, courts never had jurisdiction over constitutional matters.[160] In the end, all these theoretical and practical considerations led him to reject American-style judicial review and, instead, design a hybrid system of sorts that could prevail upon all three branches of the government. Drawing on the European constitutional courts and the French Constitutional Council (of the Third Republic), he proposed to endow a special ad hoc "Constitution Committee" with the power of constitutional review.[161]

For all too understandable reasons, however, Yu's innovative scheme was opposed by the judiciary.[162] In early May 1948, shortly before the historic general election was held, Yu began working on yet another draft constitution

[156] Lee Young-lok, "Hŏnpŏp Wiwŏnhoe Chedo," p. 319.
[157] Yu, *Hoegorok*, p. 243,
[158] Yu, *Hoegorok*, p. 42. For the same reason, Yu was against granting life tenure for judges. Lee Young-lok, "Hŏnpŏp Wiwŏnhoe Chedo," p. 319.
[159] Yu, *Hoegorok*, pp. 53–4.
[160] Yu, *Hoegorok*, p. 41.
[161] The Constitution Committee was to be chaired by the president and composed of the speakers of the both Houses and the chief justice as well as three experts whom the president appoints with parliamentary consent. Lee Young-lok, "Hŏnpŏp Wiwŏnhoe Chedo," p. 320.
[162] During the winter of 1947 when Yu was working on the draft, for instance, he received advisory assistance from one Judge Chŏng Yun-hwan, who strongly argued for an American-style system of judicial review. Given Chŏng's senior status, his opinion was interpreted by Yu as the considered view of the entire judiciary. His draft submitted to the Code Drafting Commission, therefore, included a note indicating the existence of alternative views on the matter. Yu, *Hoegorok*, pp. 24, 38.

at the invitation of a semi-private group called Administration Research Association (*Haengjŏng Yŏn'guhoe*). This group had also prepared a draft constitution, but wished to secure Yu's collaboration for political reasons. For, although put together by Shin Ik-hee who had solid KPG credentials, the Association consisted primarily of former Korean officials and judicial bureaucrats who had served in the Japanese colonial government, including some still serving as judges under the U.S. occupation. The group evidently needed Yu's academic reputation to shore up their respectability. The draft produced through this collaboration would become the base text used by the Drafting Committee.[163] While many of Yu's original ideas would be reflected in this collaboration draft, one important alteration had to do with the system of constitutional review. In point of fact, it was the most contentious issue in the process of agreeing to a common draft. At the relentless insistence of the group's members from the court,[164] Yu acquiesced to the American-style judicial review – with the caveat that he could not fully support such a scheme during the process of deliberation in the National Assembly.[165]

Indeed, American-style judicial review would be eventually discarded during the National Assembly deliberations. This outcome is rather remarkable because the other base text, that is, the Kwŏn draft, had also granted the courts the power of judicial review. At one of the meetings of the Constitution Drafting Committee, one assemblyman raised issue with the system of constitutional adjudication proposed in the base drafts. As an expert advisor to the Committee, Yu promptly agreed that such a system was problematic indeed, and the result was the restoration of his brainchild, the Constitution Committee, in the final draft to be submitted to the plenary session.[166] According to Yu's

163 This draft has been commonly known as the "Yu Chin-o Draft." The label, however, is both confusing and inaccurate since this draft is different from the one, mentioned previously, that Yu had prepared, mostly on his own, at the request of the USAMGIK Code Drafting Commission. Some scholars thus prefer to call it the "Collaboration Draft" to make clear that it was the product of a joint effort between Yu and the Administration Research Association. Kim Su-Yong, *Kŏn'guk kwa Hŏnpŏp*, pp. 237–8; Shin Woo-cheol, *Pigyo Hŏnpŏpsa*, p. 499.

164 The popularity of American-style judicial review among judges had been reinforced when the USAMGIK sent a delegation of Korean jurists to the United States in order to have them study the American legal system in the summer of 1947. Lee Young-lok, "Hŏnpŏp Wiwŏnhoe Chedo," p. 315.

165 Yu says that his compromise was due to the time pressure to complete the draft by the end of June 1948. Yu, *Hoegorok*, pp. 43–4.

166 The method of its composition was, however, different from Yu's original idea. This change was made out of the suspicion that the president would have disproportionate influence in the make-up of the Constitution Committee as originally proposed by Yu Chin-o. Article 80 of the final draft of the Drafting Committee provided that chair shall be the vice-president and its membership composed of five members each from the Supreme Court and the National Assembly. Lee Young-lok, "Hŏnpŏp Wiwŏnhoe Chedo," pp. 325–6.

retrospective, this reversal took place without much controversy, since the prevailing consensus on the floor was that "the courts did not have sufficient credibility and authority to be empowered to counteract the legislature" due to their colonial past.[167] When the plenary session of the National Assembly began deliberations on the final draft, the judiciary made one final attempt to gain jurisdiction over constitutional adjudication. The Supreme Court sent an opinion to the National Assembly advocating a return to the system of judicial review as outlined in the original base texts. The Chief Justice's appeal, however, was greeted with surprisingly little response, even silence, from the floor. The Constitution Committee system was passed as such without much discussion and became Article 81 of the Founding Constitution.

The judiciary fought for judicial review until the very end, but its own checkered past could not be overcome. For members of the National Assembly as well as for Yu Chin-o, entrusting such powers to the Korean judiciary, with its perceived connection to the colonial past, was simply not acceptable. Under these circumstances, it was all but inconceivable that the judiciary would be empowered to implement the constitutional mandate of lustration. From the courts' perspective, one might say, the mandate of Article 100 (maintenance of legal continuity) had effectively precluded them from partaking in the project of lustration as mandated by Article 101. The judiciary was a part of the past to be mastered – especially from the legislature's perspective.

Power-Sharing and Transitional Justice

Having effectively bypassed the judiciary for the task of lustration, the Anti-National Activities Punishment Law (hereafter Anti-National Law) granted a practical monopoly to the legislature for the entire project. It not only set up a Special Investigative Committee composed exclusively of members of the National Assembly, but also empowered the same assembly to elect members of both the Special Prosecutor's Office and the Special Tribunal (Articles 9, 19, and 20). Of the sixteen judges in the Special Tribunal, five were to hail from within the National Assembly (Article 19).[168] The law even created a separate, albeit temporary, constabulary force to assist the investigators and the prosecutors. On the surface, these were independent entities not attached to any particular branch of the government, but it was unmistakably clear that the legislature was calling all the shots. This may have been

[167] Yu, *Hoegorok*, p. 53.

[168] The remaining eleven were to be drawn from judges and attorneys (six), and the general public (five).

a matter of course given the widespread perception that many of the potential targets of the Anti-National Law were parts of the judicial and executive branches. Particularly, the national police force created during the U.S. military occupation was considered a stronghold of pro-Japanese collaborators. Implementation of Article 101 of the constitution seemed to call for an extraordinary concentration of powers in the National Assembly.

From the point of view of the constitution that had just gone into force, however, this could not but be problematic. As mentioned, the mandate of Article 1, which stipulated that the Republic of Korea shall be a democratic republic, was understood to require a separation of powers. Especially in the context of the founding period, this had tremendous ideological significance. With the onset of the Cold War in Korea, a distinction had been introduced into the political vocabulary of the day between "democratic republic" and "people's republic." The former was the ideal of those on the right and center of the political spectrum, while the latter became the rallying cry of the left including communists. In institutional terms, a democratic republic was understood to require a government structure based on the liberal principle of separation of powers. By contrast, a people's republic implied the concentration of powers as prescribed by the communist doctrine of proletariat dictatorship. In other words, for the founding generation, separation of powers was what distinguished the newly formed democratic republic in the south from the people's republic in the north.[169] The core mandate of Article 1 was separation of powers.

As such, Article 1 and Article 101 of the constitution seemed to pull in opposition directions. It has been shown that both provisions were included in the text to institutionalize the desire to sever the past and to effectuate a rupture. For this purpose, the way in which the separation of powers and the mandate for lustration were institutionalized needed to be made mutually supportive. Successful pursuit of transitional justice required a constitutional structure with a separation of powers scheme that was both stable and agile enough to handle such an exceedingly sensitive and politically charged issue. As it turned out, however, the power structure prescribed by the Founding Constitution was a highly unstable "hybrid regime" of sorts, which would be an open invitation to an ongoing political tug of war between the president and the National Assembly. The legislature's attempt to monopolize the whole process was immediately greeted with objections, even resistance, from the other branches, especially the executive. The president took issue with the Anti-National Law as enacted by the National Assembly. Syngman Rhee took it as an affront to the presidency, particularly to his powers to appoint members of

[169] Park Chan-Seung, *Taehan Min'guk*, pp. 338–40.

his administration, and challenged the law based on the constitutional principle of separation of powers.[170] In short, once put to the test of reality, these two provisions tended to collide with each other.

The constitution prescribed a hybrid regime, for it essentially mandated an uneasy coexistence between a strong presidential system and elements of the parliamentary-cabinet system. Although both the president and the vice-president were given four-year fixed tenure with a chance to run for another term, both offices were to be elected by the National Assembly (Article 53). In order for the president's policy initiatives to be effectuated, they had to be countersigned by the entire cabinet as well as the prime minister, who was appointed by the president but only with the National Assembly's concurrence (Articles 68 thru 72). As in a parliamentary-cabinet system, further, the legislature was able to audit the executive branch (Article 43), and the cabinet ministers, who were *not* forbidden to retain parliamentary seats, could attend legislative sessions (Article 44). Despite these parliamentary biases, still, the legislature lacked the most crucial power to dismiss the prime minister and hold the cabinet accountable to the legislature, leaving them in effect dependent entirely on the president's discretion. Under such a system, it was perhaps inevitable that there would be confusion as to the proper balance of power within the government. It was a recipe for political volatility. As such, it may have been a foregone conclusion that the attempt to implement the call for lustration would be met with obstacles and complications stemming from the hybrid government structure.

The reason that the Founding Constitution adopted such a confusing and unstable structure is the subject of scholarly debate. According to conventional wisdom, it was the result of arm-twisting on the part of Syngman Rhee, who compelled a last-minute change from a parliamentary-cabinet system to a government structure based on strong presidential powers.[171] Another

170 According to Article 5 of the Anti-National Law, certain categories of individuals who had served in the Japanese colonial government could not be appointed as government officials.

171 The parliamentary-cabinet system as originally proposed by the Yu draft was consistent with the political ambitions of the right-wing Korean Democratic Party, which saw a better chance of protecting its vested interests in a pure parliamentary system with a president only as a ceremonial head of the state. That nominal post, no one doubted at that time, would be occupied by Syngman Rhee, then the speaker of the National Assembly and one of the most prominent leaders in postcolonial Korea. Not a man to be sidelined this way, Rhee threatened to withdraw his support for the entire constitution-making project. Given that Kim Ku and Kimm Kiusic (a.k.a. Kim Kyu-sik) had boycotted the May General Election, this move by the last of the triumvirate in postcolonial Korea would have further undermined the precarious legitimacy of the new republic as well as their conservative hegemony. Rhee's blackmailing thus resulted in a sudden reversal of course in the direction of presidential system, which was grafted hodge-podge onto a parliamentary structure. Yu Chin-o states that he first complained against such unprincipled mixing of government forms, but ultimately had to give his acquiescence. Yu, *Hoegorok*, pp. 74–80.

explanation highlights the fact that a "tradition" of hybrid regimes had already been established with KPG's first constitutional experiment with forms of government.[172] On this view, an unintended consequence of Rhee's intervention was a return to an already existing "thick consensus," or norm, in the Korean constitutional tradition, to which the Yu draft was an exception.[173]

Perhaps more important, the meaning of this constitutionally sanctioned mixture of power was interpreted differently by different political actors at the time, which in turn exacerbated the confusion and instability in the government. President Rhee believed the parliamentary elements to be mere leftovers from the Yu draft that would be cleared out in a future constitutional revision.[174] For instance, the parliamentary confirmation of the president's appointment of prime minister was merely a means by which the appointee's qualification might be double-checked, similar to the hearings in the U.S. Senate. His opponents in the National Assembly, however, interpreted the same provision otherwise, as a kind of parliamentary vote of (non-)confidence by other means. According to this interpretation, elements of presidentialism were merely a façade, a temporary concession to the elderly president, which

172 All constitutional documents of KPG, including the "Essential Points for Founding a New State," had incorporated both presidential and parliamentary elements in their government provisions with varying degrees of emphasis. As a semi-covert organization for armed resistance and independence movement, KPG needed a unified leadership at the helm – hence, the strong presidency in its constitutions. A government only in name and hardly recognized by the international community during the war, KPG was compelled to reinforce its legitimacy by claiming a mandate, legal-fictional though it may be, from the entire Korean people – hence, the constitutional supremacy of the legislative branch. Shin Woo-Cheol, "Taehan Min'guk Hŏnpŏp (1948) ŭi 'Minjujuŭi Chejedo Surip'" ['Establishment of Democratic Institutions' in the 1948 Constitution of Korea], in Han'guk Mirae Hakhoe (ed.), *Chehŏn kwa Kŏn'guk* (Paju: Nanam, 2010), pp. 118–20. KPG's mixed power regime was also the result of a more mundane need to share power across ideological, factional, and partisan lines within KPG, which could not be easily bridged otherwise.

173 While there were some exceptions, a great majority of constitutional drafts produced after liberation also show signs of converging on this institutional "path-dependency" of sorts, according to which a mixed regime with a stronger emphasis on presidential powers may have appeared the natural choice. For instance, the constitution adopted by the KILA provided for a direct election of the president and a relatively clear-cut separation of power in accordance with an ideal-typical presidential system. Yet, a prime minister was put in charge of the cabinet, which was made accountable to both the president (who appoints the cabinet) and the parliament (which may refuse to confirm president's appointments). Sung Ho Kim and Choi Sun, "1948 nyŏn Kŏn'guk Hŏnpŏp e Nat'anan Honhapchŏk Kwŏllyŏkkujo ŭi Kiwŏn" [Origins of the Mixed Power Structure of the Founding Constitution], in Han'guk Mirae Hakhoe (ed.), *Chehŏn kwa Kŏn'guk*, pp. 13–15, 25–9.

174 Lee Young-lok, "Chehŏn Kwajŏng esŏŭi Kwŏllyŏkkujo Nonŭi e Nat'anan Taerip ŭi Chŏn'gae Kwajŏng kwa Kyŏlgwa e kwanhan Yŏn'gu" [A Study on the Clash of Ideas on Power Structure During the Constitution-Drafting Process and Its Outcome], *Hŏnpŏphak Yŏn'gu*, vol. 28 (2003), pp. 198 and 216.

would be removed and a genuine parliamentary-cabinet system restored as soon as he was gone.[175] The only common understanding between them was that, when it came to power-sharing, the constitutional settlement was far from settled. Seen in this light, the constitutional crisis occasioned by the issue of lustration was merely the second round of this constitutional politics that went back to the drafting process. The politics of transitional justice was indeed constitutional politics by other means.

Under this unstable arrangement, the National Assembly attempted to take the initiative on the issue of lustration even before the new government was formed. As early as 5 August, a motion was made to establish a special drafting committee to make the Anti-National Law. The most heated debate was waged around the scope of the punishable anti-national acts, but the issue of the institutional arrangement also provoked much discussion. Some members of the National Assembly recognized the anomaly of arrogating all three – investigative, prosecutorial, and judicial – powers to the legislature itself. They argued that doing police work and indicting suspected collaborators was inconsistent with their role as lawmakers.[176] Others countered by pointing to the need to enact the law before President-elect Rhee filled his cabinet and other posts with ex-collaborators. On their view, such an extraordinary concentration of powers was simply unavoidable because most of the potential targets of the law were lodged in the administrative, constabulary, and judicial bureaucracies, which thus could not be trusted with their own purge.[177]

The untested power structure of the constitution was thereby put under enormous strain. On 19 August, only four days after the new republic was officially inaugurated and even before the Anti-National Law was formally enacted, an overwhelming majority in the National Assembly passed a resolution urging the president to purge ex-collaborators from the government.[178] Perceiving this as a grave challenge to his constitutionally vested power of appointment, Rhee responded the next day by making a public statement that no purge could be carried out before the Anti-National Law was passed and a proper procedure established.[179] On 3 September, while the National Assembly was deliberating on the bill, the president issued another public statement calling for moderation and respect for due process of law. After the Anti-National Law

[175] Lee Young-lok, "Kwŏllyŏkkujo," pp. 198–200, 218.

[176] Suh Hee Kyung, "Yi Sŭng-man ŭi Chŏngch'i Ridŏship Yŏn'gu" [A Study on Syngman Rhee's Political Leadership], *Han'guk Chŏngch'ihak Hoebo*, vol. 45, no. 2 (2011), pp. 57–8.

[177] Heo Jong, *Panmint'ŭkwi ŭi Chojik kwa Hwaltong* [Organization and Activities of the Special Committee on Anti-National Activities] (Seoul: Tosŏch'ulp'an Sŏnin, 2003), p. 133.

[178] *CNA Minutes*, Session 1, No. 44 (19 Aug. 1948), pp. 829–40.

[179] Suh, "Chŏngch'i Ridŏship," pp. 59–60.

was enacted on 22 September, Rhee again stated that, while he intended to respect the law, its implementation should focus on repentance and forgiveness rather than on revenge and punishment.[180] In fact, Rhee and his cabinet members had originally decided to veto the bill. They had even prepared his veto message outlining his reasons for returning the bill to the National Assembly. The message pointed out that the law had constitutional difficulties – it violated the principle of separation of powers and potentially infringed upon the constitutional right to be tried by qualified judges.[181] Although the veto was withdrawn at the last minute (in order to secure the legislature's support for the president's agricultural agenda) and the bill duly signed by the president, the message well summed up the executive branch's legal position, which remained consistent throughout the constitutional-political crisis that followed. At stake, at least on the surface, was the constitutional principle of separation of powers.

In return, the National Assembly criticized the president for obstructing transitional justice and the nation's rebirth. Especially, the hardliners in the National Assembly styled themselves as the only agent with the moral qualifications as well as the people's mandate for this historic task. They charged that Rhee's "politics of public statements" (i.e., his act of bypassing the legislature and directly appealing to the general public) was itself potentially unconstitutional since the president was not directly elected by the people. From their perspective, the president was defying the authority of the only elected representatives of the people in the National Assembly. As one assemblyman put it, the role of the executive was to implement the laws duly made by the legislature, and if the president was unable or unwilling to do so, he might as well quit the job.[182] For the National Assembly, separation of powers meant a parliament-centered system in which the non-elected president was mainly the chief executor of legislative decisions. This kind of extraordinary concentration of power in the legislature was simply unacceptable to Rhee, who understood separation of powers as practiced in a presidential system. On a collision course here were not only different approaches to the process of lustration, but also different interpretations of the hybrid regime as prescribed in the Founding Constitution.

In principle, Rhee also appreciated and recognized the need for transitional justice. His only concern, he argued, was the timing and manner of

[180] Suh, "Chŏngch'i Ridŏship," p. 62.

[181] Heo, *Panmint'ŭkwi*, p. 141.

[182] *CNA Minutes*, Session 1, No. 57 (4 Sept. 1948), pp. 1084–5 (statement of Assemblyman Kim Myŏng-dong).

pursuing this undeniably compelling goal. For him, the issue of lustration required a more prudent and deliberate approach than was being taken by the National Assembly. As such, it was better to await the full establishment of the independent Korean state and functioning government apparatuses.[183] Although the Republic of Korea was formally inaugurated on 15 August 1948, the transfer of government powers from the U.S. military authorities would not be completed until 13 September. Even after that, the new republic had to struggle with mounting threats to its own survival. The inauguration of the republic had been promptly greeted, on 9 September 1948, with the establishment of a rival regime across the 38th parallel. The division of the Korean nation was then followed in quick succession by the beginning of the withdrawal of the U.S. armed forces in the South (15 September), declaration of martial law on Cheju Island (8 October), and the outbreak of military mutiny in the southern regions of Yŏsu and Sunch'ŏn (19 October).[184] This chain of events ultimately contributed to the introduction, on 9 November, of a bill in the National Assembly, which became the notorious National Security Act. Immediately upon inception, in short, the new republic was in a virtual state of war.

Under these dire circumstances, the only apparatus that the Rhee government could count on were the administrative bureaucracies, especially the national police and constabulary forces. Although these agencies were manned largely with ex-collaborators, dismissing them from their positions seemed to threaten the very life of the fledgling republic. From the president's perspective, Korea was suffering from a severe shortage of human capital necessary for state-building. Arguably, he had little choice but to employ the service of whomever was available.[185] As far as Rhee was concerned, there would be no Republic of Korea if the process of lustration effectively got rid of all the well-trained personnel, especially those able to deal with security threats, both internal and external. For Rhee the realist, in short, no new future would be in store if the past was completely repudiated. For his idealist opponents,

[183] Suh, "Chŏngch'i Ridŏship," p. 63.

[184] For a detailed account of the "resistance to the southern system" and the "guerrilla conflict," both before and after the inauguration of the government, see Cumings, *Origins*, vol. II, chs. 7 and 8.

[185] According to one of Rhee's supporters, once the nascent republic excluded all those in North Korea, the leftists and the moderates in South Korea who had boycotted the May 10th General Election, and the pro-Japanese national traitors, it would be left with an extremely limited pool of talents from which to recruit individuals with the requisite skills for establishing a state. Suh, "Chŏngch'i Ridŏship," pp. 56–57 (quoting a statement by Assemblyman Yu Chin-hong).

however, the colonial past had to be thoroughly repudiated in order to usher in a new future. In Korea's "Machiavellian moment,"[186] the mandate for transitional justice collided with exigencies of state-building. Caught between the conflicting demands of past and future, the founding generation would learn firsthand that the past is ultimately unmasterable.

Given this unbridgeable disagreement, then, crisis was all but inevitable. The legislature's Special Committee on Anti-National Activities, the main investigative agency created by the Anti-National Law, made its first arrest on 8 January 1949, and on 15 February, President Rhee once again bypassed the National Assembly and issued another public statement. In a highly inflammatory tone, he condemned the Committee's activities as a manifest violation of the separation of powers and ordered his cabinet's Legislative Bureau to prepare a revision bill.[187] In return, chairman of the Special Committee accused the president of overstepping the limits of his constitutionally vested powers, to which the Chief Justice of the Supreme Court also gave public support by stating that the question of unconstitutionality could only be decided by the Constitution Committee, not the president.[188] This constitutional debate quickly degenerated into a violent political contestation. Open sabotage and covert resistance, especially by the police, became alarmingly abusive and menacing. Mass demonstrations were mobilized by Rhee's supporters to denounce lustration as an act of communist conspiracy. In early June, more than a dozen of the hardliners in the National Assembly, including a member of the Special Prosecutor's Office, were rounded up under charges of espionage under the new National Security Act. Under these hostile circumstances, a revised Anti-National Law, reducing the statute of limitations, was passed in early July, which prompted the resignation en masse of the Special Committee members including its chairman. Coupled with internal feuds in the National Assembly itself, wind had already been taken out of its sail. The Committee unceremoniously closed its doors five days after the new statute of limitations expired on 31 August.[189] Although the Anti-National Law was not officially repealed until February 1951, another revision in October 1949 further emasculated the law by transferring the remaining investigative and

[186] J. G. A. Pocock, *The Machiavellian Moment: Florentine Political Thought and the Atlantic Republican Tradition* (Princeton, NJ: Princeton University Press, 1975).

[187] President Rhee even charged the Committee with using terror and tortures. O Ik-hwan, "Panmint'ŭkwi ŭi Hwaltong kwa Wahae" [Activities and Dissolution of the Special Anti-national Committee], in Song Kŏn-ho et al., *Haebang Chŏnhusa ŭi Inshik*, vol. 1 (Seoul: Han'gilsa, 1991), pp. 145–6.

[188] O Ik-hwan, "Panmint'ŭkwi," pp. 146–8.

[189] O Ik-hwan, "Panmint'ŭkwi," p. 171.

judicial functions to the Ministry of Justice and the Supreme Court, respectively. The legislature's well-intentioned but hasty attempt to cleanse the colonial past thus came to an ominous end.[190]

Effective lustration requires politics at the highest level, which in turn calls for prudential, even visionary, statesmanship and a sturdy government structure. Unfortunately, such resources were in short supply in the nascent Korean republic. Regarding the quality of political leadership, neither the legislature nor the president proved to possess the virtues of patience and cooperation. As for the government structure, the Founding Constitution's hybrid regime was under-designed, to say the least, to manage the potentially conflicting mandates of state-building and transitional justice. In the final analysis, the much-needed lustration of the colonial past, as envisioned by the National Assembly's special law, was a strain too great to be borne by the fragile government structure mandated by the Founding Constitution. Sure, President Rhee should bear the lion's share of responsibility for the fateful decision to indulge the colonial past, which still remains controversial in Korea. But not to be overlooked is the tension between Article 1 and Article 101, which was also responsible for making the colonial past as unmasterable as it turned out to be.

The Founding Constitution established the Republic of Korea by negating the "double tyranny" of Japanese colonialism and pre-colonial monarchy. In this self-understanding, the pivotal year was 1919, when the "March First Revolution" broke out. Invoking this largely counterfactual revolution to level the constitutional ground in 1948, however, was not powerful enough to repudiate the past completely. The colonial past, especially, proved to be recalcitrant to the constitutionally mandated project of lustration since the constitution also authorized legal continuity and a government structure that was far too unsettled and volatile to manage this urgent task. The ghost of empire past could not but be present at the creation of the once and future republic.

REVOLUTIONS AND RESTORATIONS

It is all too understandable that constitutional founding should be accompanied by a fervent desire to sever the past and to erect a new state on a clean slate. All that is associated with the pre-founding era must be condemned as

[190] In the final count, a total of 688 individuals were investigated, among whom 293 were prosecuted and 79 sentenced in the Special Tribunal. A meager ten received actual prison terms in the eventuality. Heo, *Panmint'ŭkwi*, p. 234.

retrograde and reactionary. Any remaining vestiges of the status quo ante must be proactively annihilated and effaced before a new constitutional order can properly be inaugurated. That, at least, is the conventional theory premised on what we have called the *tabula rasa* syndrome. The experiences of postwar Japan and postcolonial Korea show that such a theory cannot fully capture the meaning and practices of constitution-making. Explicit or not, the need to maintain continuity with the pre-founding era is an unavoidable dimension of the founding process. Even an overbearing foreign power intent on replacing emperor worship with popular sovereignty had to recognize this dimension. The symbol emperor system may have been intended to introduce drastic changes in the political life of Japan. And yet, from the beginning, it also acknowledged the supreme importance of the imperial institution – in whatever form – for the Japanese society, and the locals received it, not surprisingly, in ways that allowed for the maintenance of continuity between prewar and postwar Japan. While some saw it as a violent obliteration of *kokutai*, others were able to affirm that *kokutai* had been preserved unaffected and had survived the defeat and even the foreign imposition unscathed. More importantly, the symbol emperor system guaranteed that Japan's prewar traditions would continue to exert a powerful influence on the constitutional identity of postwar Japan. Even the theory of August Revolution, originally proposed to emphasize the magnitude of the constitutional rupture that Japan experienced as a result of surrender, also had the curious effect of affirming respect for prewar formalities.

The desire to posit a revolution, even a counterfactual one, to explain and justify constitutional founding is of course a classic symptom of the *tabula rasa* syndrome.[191] Characterizing the March First Movement as a revolution was obviously a move to level the constitutional ground in Korea. More interesting, however, is the fact that this revolution actually became the vehicle through which the past could be made a part of the constitutional present. The March First Revolution allowed the framers to simultaneously reject and reaffirm the past. Laying claim to the spirit of that revolution was not only a negation of the double tyranny of the pre-founding era, but also an invocation of a tradition of republicanism that preceded the founding. Similarly, adoption of *Taehan* as the official name of the new republic denoted a rejection of

[191] Whether the counterfactual quality of the revolution was greater in Japan or in Korea may be a fascinating exercise in political theology. In Korea, while there may have been nationwide protests and demonstrations in March 1919, they resulted in no change in the government, whereas in Japan, although not a single barricade was raised on the streets in August 1945, rather momentous changes in the constitution did follow.

colonial and dynastic pasts, while also signifying a return to some primordial state of sovereign independence.

Such tension or ambiguity between rupture and continuity, found in various parts of the constitution in both Korea and Japan, does not cohere well with the view that constitutional founding must take place on a *tabula rasa*. Anything less than a total and unequivocal rejection of the past is deemed illegitimate. That is why, for many in Korea, the fact that the project of lustration was compromised continues to be a reason for doubting the efficacy and legitimacy of the republic's founding. Aided in part by the myth that punishment of ex-collaborators was more effectively carried out in North Korea, the unmasterable past continues to haunt the South Korean constitutional identity. Similarly, given the argument that the symbol emperor is the "center of the people's devotion" and a reflection of Japan's more authentic traditions, some question whether the people have actually become the sovereign agent.[192] One scholar has even suggested that the people's deep-seated respect for the imperial institution might be impeding the formation of democratic citizenship in contemporary Japan.[193] Ironically, the symbol emperor system, which was intended to highlight the new doctrine of popular sovereignty, may have contributed to the preservation of an emperor-centered identity for the people.

Yet, of itself, the presence of the past in the founding of a new constitutional order cannot be a reason for skepticism. The more interesting and relevant question has to do with whether or not the past, as represented and reinterpreted in the constitution, contributes to the formation of a narrative that allows the people to feel ownership in the constitutional order. To a certain extent, debates and disagreements regarding the past are integral to a healthy constitutional order. The fact that the emperor system has been the cause of much disunity and conflict among the people, rather than being the symbol of their unity,[194] may be an indication of a vibrant constitutional democracy in postwar Japan. The fact that demands for full lustration continue to be heard in contemporary Korea may be indicative of a mature constitutional order willing to confront its own shortcomings. As such, ongoing discussions of the past and even dissatisfactions regarding the way that the past is dealt with may

[192] Higuchi Yōichi has noted that the presence of the symbol emperor system has tended to generate conformism, as seen in the society-wide "self-restraint" during the prolonged period of Hirohito's illness that preceded his death. Higuchi, "Constitution and the Emperor System," pp. 64–6.

[193] Katsutoshi Takami, "From Divine Legitimacy to the Myth of Consensus: The Emperor System and Popular Sovereignty," in Yoichi Higuchi (ed.), *Five Decades of Constitutionalism*, pp. 22–4.

[194] Nagao, *Shisō toshite no Nihon Kenpōshi*, p. 202.

play positive roles in a dynamic constitutional democracy. Of crucial importance is whether they enable the people to identify with the constitution in a reflexive manner. Whether for or against, the people's engagement with the past via constitutional founding and/or interpretation will be beneficial to the extent that it yields a narrative about their collective identity and common destiny. As a pole of identity and contestation in the ongoing story of democratic peoplehood, presence of the unmastered and unmasterable past is essential to the making of a healthy and enduring constitutional democracy.

4

A Room of One's Own

SHIFTING BOUNDARIES

Constitutional founding involves the making of a people as much as the drafting of a text. This means that "We the People" that comes into being through constitutional founding must be distinct, at least analytically, from any pre-existing group defined in terms of culture, ethnicity, or language. It also means, however, that prior to the founding, it may be difficult, if not impossible, to determine in the abstract which individuals are to be included within the political bounds of constitutional peoplehood. This gives rise to the theoretical paradox of how constitutional founding could ever get off the ground if the relevant boundary of the people cannot be fixed beforehand. Yet, as seen in Chapter 1, this is a problem only if we "freeze" our mental frame and imagine a static and ahistorical people that pre-exists the establishment of a constitutional order. If one conceives of constitution-making, as we do, as an activity of self-constitution in which the people defines its own identity by the act of making a constitution, it makes little sense to imagine a pre-formed people that exists independently of the constitution. We cannot simply presume a pre-defined group with its identity and membership firmly determined which goes about making a constitution. We know from recent historical cases that constitutional founding rarely leaves intact previous understandings of membership and identity. With the founding, the constituent people constructs a new identity as the subject of a new constitutional order, an identity that is defined through the constitution that they jointly bring into being.

To be sure, there are times when the specific contours of the state's territory are at issue. Sometimes, even the continued existence of the state itself may be contested. Japan and Korea in the postwar context are cases in point. Yet, if anything, this is one more reason for not thinking of the making of a constitution as some mystical process by which an unchanging transhistorical people living in "eternal present" somehow breaks into the historical, temporal dimension. When revolutionary changes occur with regard to a state's territory or even its very existence, it probably comports better with not only the historical reality but also the political spirit of such events to say that a new people has been created. At the least, we must say that the boundary and definition of constitutional peoplehood has undergone a major realignment or readjustment.

The important point to bear in mind is that such readjustments never take place in a vacuum. They occur as the result of concrete historical negotiations and political contestations among various actors – both domestic and foreign. Redrawing a state's territorial and human boundary necessarily presupposes an intense process of interaction with other states. Particularly if the readjustment is done involuntarily, as at the end of a war, the active role of "others" is logically all but presupposed. Regardless of the degree of their involvement, external actors, and the process of negotiating with them, constitute an integral part of the process through which the people's boundaries are given shape.

Further, this interaction between local and external actors is always conditioned by the historical context. It necessarily takes place through the medium of laws and institutions inherited from the previous era. As such, these legal and institutional legacies play an important role in readjusting the boundary of the people and giving them a new identity as the subject of a constitutional order. While some laws are invariably rejected in the process of founding, others having to do with categorizing and classifying individuals are taken up and put to new use by relevant actors to arrive at a new definition of the people. In order fully to appreciate the shifting of the people's boundaries that occurs with constitutional founding, we must therefore pay due attention to both of these dimensions – how the inherited past resources are utilized and manipulated, and how the process is characterized by diverse forms of negotiations with external actors. Just as the constitution cannot be created *ex nihilo*, so the people cannot be forged except through interaction with others and the status quo ante.

In the cases of postwar Japan and postcolonial Korea, this calls for examining the varied roles played by the U.S. occupation forces as well as the different attempts by the locals to deal with that external agent in formulating the boundaries of new democratic constituent peoples. It also entails considering the difference brought about by changing geopolitical exigencies that the United States had to contend with, namely, the onslaught of the Cold War in the region. This is why the Korean story of peoplehood tends to become more complicated by the entrance of other external actors not present in the Japanese story, such as the Soviet Union, the emerging North Korean regime, and the United Nations. Regarding the institutional legacy of the past, consideration must be given in both countries to the laws that were inherited from the prewar/colonial era having to do with making people identifiable to the state. This means focusing on those institutions that had allowed the authorities to categorize, label, and document individuals for various purposes. The most important among them was the household registry instituted in both countries by the Japanese imperial and colonial authorities.

Originally a part of Japan's project to build a modern nation-state, the household registry system quickly became the primary instrument through which residents of overseas colonies were turned into imperial subjects. Although it had a built-in mechanism to maintain a distinction between the second-class colonial subjects and the "true" Japanese on the main islands, the logic of the war eventually impelled the dilution of that distinction and the strengthening of the rhetoric of complete integration. On the eve of Japan's unconditional surrender, legal mechanisms for differentiating via household registry had all but disappeared, such that full integration of all who were listed in any of the imperial registries had almost become a reality. This changed overnight, however, with the end of the war. In the postwar context, the household registry would be used in both Japan and Korea as the chief criterion for differentiation and even discrimination. A new democratic constituent people had to be formed in the two countries, and this was to be achieved via the dismemberment of the empire in Japan and the division of the peninsula in Korea. The household registry, in both contexts, would prove to be instrumental in carrying out the job of demarking the new boundaries of the people. Since the road to creating the constituent peoples of Japan and Korea was paved with the legacy of the imperial system of household registration, we begin now by tracing the development of that system during the prewar era.

SEEING LIKE AN EMPIRE

Like other nations influenced by Chinese laws and institutions, both Korea and Japan had a long history of household-based population registration since ancient times. While contemporary knowledge of these premodern institutions still remains sketchy, scholars agree that their purpose was to document and identify the households and their members so that they might be taxed and conscripted for labor. In James Scott's terms, they were devised to make the people "legible" to the state.[1] These would be reformed and modified as the two countries attempted to transform themselves into modern states.

[1] James C. Scott, *Seeing Like a State* (New Haven, CT: Yale University Press, 1998).

More effective means for cataloguing and categorizing persons were needed. Of course, Korea's own attempt to modernize its registration system would become moot with the loss of independence, which resulted in the adoption of the Japanese system. Examining how the Japanese system developed and was later adapted throughout the empire is therefore imperative for understanding the story of the human boundaries of the two states. For it is a story of how the human boundaries were imagined, articulated, merged, and then ultimately broken up via the operation of the household registries.

To be sure, there were other institutions and forces at work during the prewar period that influenced the way the people and the state continually adjusted the criteria for membership. Particularly, the principle underlying the regime of voting rights seems to have been at odds with the way in which the household registries sought to define who belonged and who did not. Toward the end of the war, the shifting scope of military conscription also affected the way in which the empire's human boundary was conceived. Yet, if political rights and military duties had a role in defining membership, that role was always mediated and refracted through the household registration system, which was itself a complex mechanism of simultaneous integration and differentiation. Understanding where this system stood at the end of the war is thus critical for our investigation of the process by which the constituent peoples of Japan and Korea were formed in the postwar period.

The Origins of the Household Registration System

In Tokugawa Japan, individuals were documented on an elaborate system of registries (*Shūmon Ninbetsu-chō*), which had recorded them by households according to social status and occupational categories. Since each household registry was tied to a fixed class and locality, its unyielding implementation made it virtually impossible for people to migrate across geographical as well as social boundaries.[2] Through this system of tight control, the Shogunate was able to maintain discipline and surveillance over the population at large. Yet, the principle of strict categorization, even segregation, of population into classes and localities hindered the development of a common civic-national identity among the people of Japan as a whole. It was indeed not until the end of the Tokugawa era that the household registry system began to be used to integrate and delineate the boundaries of a nascent Japanese nation. With the

[2] For a general survey of premodern forms of population registration in Japan, see, e.g., L. L. Cornell and Akira Hayami, "The *Shūmon Aratame Chō*: Japan's Population Registers," *Journal of Family History*, vol. 11, no. 4 (1986).

conquest of the remote northern territories, the indigenous Ainu tribes had to be assimilated into the people of Japan. By recording them in a newly created household registry under Japanese-style names, they were claimed to be under the authority of the Edo government. At the same time, even as the northern aborigines were being made "Japanese," their registries were clearly marked off as different from those of other areas, making sure that they would be kept separate from, and unequal to, their conquerors.[3] In other words, the household registry proved to be a handy instrument for the central government to make legible the residents of various islands claimed by Japan as its territory while making them clearly distinguishable. From the very beginning, it was a system that differentiated *and* integrated the people of Japan.

As Meiji Japan embarked on its state-led project of modernization, household registration, with this dual function of integration and differentiation, was further refined and given a modern legal dressing. The new government decreed the Household Registration Law (*Kosekihō*) in 1871, only four years into the Meiji Restoration and long before other key legal infrastructures – such as the Imperial Constitution (1889), Civil Code (1898), and Nationality Law (1899) – were put in place. In order to become a modern sovereign state in the Western sense of the term, the new Meiji nation-state required a better framework for increasing the people's legibility.

Compared to its premodern counterpart, the Meiji registration system was distinct in a few significant ways. The traditional four-tiered class system of "samurai-peasants-artisans-merchants" was abolished by having all but the imperial family members recorded under a single social label, "commoners" (*heimin*) and by keeping a uniform national registry based on domicile. For the first time in Japanese history, the vast majority of the Japanese people had come to have an identical and homogeneous status – all were equal subjects *de jure* of the recently restored imperial house.[4] Also recorded as commoners in this nationwide, uniform registry were those who had traditionally been regarded as non-Japanese. These included the inhabitants of the newly acquired territories such as Hokkaido and the Ryukyu islands. Bloodline and racial identities were less important at this stage, and the new registry covered all people in the areas over which Japan claimed jurisdiction. Those who had been excluded from the Tokugawa registry system because of their foreign

3 Hanazaki Kōhei, "Ainu Moshir and Yaponesia: Ainu and Okinawan Identities in Contemporary Japan," in Michael Weiner (ed.), *Race, Ethnicity and Migration in Modern Japan: Imagined and Imaginary Minorities* (New York: Routledge, 2004), p. 216.

4 For a brief overview of the Meiji family registration system, see Fujiko Isono, "The Evolution of Modern Family Law in Japan," *International Journal of Law and the Family*, vol. 2, no. 2 (1988), pp. 183–5.

origin were also listed. For example, the ethnic Koreans in Satsuma, descendants of prisoners taken during the Japanese invasions of Korea in the late sixteenth century, were registered for the first time. Even Westerners residing in the Ogasawara Islands, which had recently become part of Japan, could be included in the new national registry under Japanese-style names, thereby acquiring *de facto* Japanese nationality.[5]

Until March 1899 when the Nationality Law was promulgated, then, the Japanese people legally recognized as such were all natural persons, irrespective of class and race, residing in the realm the Japanese government claimed as its sovereign territory. Arguably, the first modern legal boundary of Japanese peoplehood was drawn according to the principle of *jus soli* or *jus domicile* (i.e., territoriality) in marked contrast to that of *jus sanguinis* (i.e., personality) of the later Nationality Law.[6] Anyone listed in the household registry of any parcel of land over which Japan claimed territorial jurisdiction would be deemed a "Japanese national" even before such a category was adopted.[7] This link between territory and the household registration system provided the powerful means for integrating the disparate populations of various regions of the nascent Meiji nation-state. This was also the reason that the household registry would prove to be such an indispensable tool for the Japanese government in later years when it began to pursue overseas colonial expansion.

Crucial as this integrative function was for the Meiji nation-building project, however, the household registration system was also underwritten by a built-in mechanism of differentiation within, and even discrimination among, Japanese people. Although the feudal distinctions among the four classes were abolished, that hardly meant the elimination of traditional privileges or social stigma. In fact, a new peerage (*kazoku*) was established and given legal recognition in the household registry in 1884, thereby co-opting the former courtiers (*kuge*) and ex-feudal lords (*daimyō*) into the Meiji system. The traditionally

5 David Chapman, "Geographies of Self and Other: Mapping Japan through the *Koseki*," *Asia-Pacific Journal: Japan Focus* (18 July 2011).

6 Haruka Nomura, "Making the Japanese Empire: Nationality and Family Register in Taiwan, 1871–1899," *Japan Studies*, vol. 30, no. 1 (2010), p. 71; Endō Masataka, *Kindai Nihon no Shokuminchi Tōchi ni okeru Kokuseki to Koseki: Manshū, Chōsen, Taiwan* [Nationality and Household Registry in Modern Japan's Colonial Rule: Manchuria, Korea, Taiwan] (Tokyo: Akashi Shoten, 2010), p. 118.

7 In 1874, one of the leading Meiji bureaucrats and foreign minister during the First Sino-Japanese War, Mutsu Munemitsu, would define the Japanese people as all those "residing in the territory … ruled under this imperial government." Quoted in Yoon Keun-Cha, *Nihon Kokuminron: Kindai Nihon no Aidentiti* [On the Japanese People: The Identity of Modern Japan] (Tokyo: Chikuma Shobō, 1997), p. 95.

untouchable class, variously called *eta* or *hinin*, could still be differentiated and discriminated against through markers in the new household registry that referred to these outcasts as "new commoners" (*shinheimin*) or "former *eta*" (*motoeta*). The new uniform registry in fact helped to legally perpetuate the class stratification that had characterized the premodern feudal system.[8] In conjunction with the basic principles of family law enshrined in the Meiji Civil Code (*Minpō*) of 1898, further, the household registry systematically institutionalized the traditional discrimination against women.

In conscious opposition to the Western model of individual-based identification and documentation, the Meiji reformers opted to make the people legible to the state via the lens of what they deemed the "traditional" family (*ie*) system. The Civil Code was enacted to give legal status to this family system, which was also reflected in the household registry. Under this new scheme, all subjects of the emperor were to be identified and documented by being grouped according to their families, which were each headed by a male "master of the house" or "household head" (*koshu*).[9] This master was given the duty of reporting changes in his household, such as birth, death, marriage, divorce, and adoption, without which those actions could not have legal effects. For example, a marriage was legally effectuated only after the house masters of both families, not the couple, reported the status change to the government. Without the consent of the household head, in other words, no marriage could be given legal recognition. In addition, the Civil Code provided that family property be inherited exclusively by the eldest son (or other male heir), thereby enabling the patrilineal continuation of these family units via primogeniture. Women, by contrast, even the legitimate wife of a household head, were largely deemed legally incompetent, and, as a general rule, denied rights to family assets and the status of the household head.[10] This legal arrangement gave the master a sweeping power of supervision over his family members, and the state could oversee individual subjects via these masters of the house. One might say that the Meiji household was less a family in the

8 Yoon Keun-Cha, *Nihon Kokuminron*, pp. 91–4.

9 For a brief outline of the Meiji Civil Code, see Isono, "Family Law in Japan," pp. 189–91. For details, see one of the original drafter's (largely self-congratulatory) explanation in Nobushige Hozumi, *The New Japanese Civil Code, As Material for the Study of Comparative Jurisprudence* (Tokyo: Tokyo Printing Co., 1904).

10 Isono, "Family Law in Japan," p. 189. For the oppressive nature of the family registration system in general, see, e.g., Taimie L. Bryant, "For the Sake of the Country, for the Sake of the Family: The Oppressive Impact of Family Registration on Women and Minorities in Japan," *UCLA Law Review*, vol. 39, no. 1 (1991).

usual private sense of the term than a public unit of administration through which the government could penetrate into people's everyday lives.[11]

Legally grafting the household registry onto notions of the "traditional" Japanese family had important ramifications for understanding the boundaries of modern Japanese peoplehood. First, this meant that those not registered as a member of one of these households under a house master were deemed outside the bounds of Japanese people. Without a household address through which one could be identified and made legible to the state, it was practically impossible for anyone to claim legal status as Japanese. In the feudal past, peasants had been tied to the fiefdom; commoners in Meiji Japan were now chained to their household registry address. As early as 1871, the preface of the decree establishing the household registries declared that

> for each and every person to live a happy and comfortable life, government's protection and supervision are indispensible. Thus those who run away from this registration ... would voluntarily choose to fall "outside the nation" (*kokumin no soto*), wherein lies the reason for creating the people's household registry (*jinmin koseki*).[12]

While it is debatable as to whether at this juncture the term *kokumin* was a legal term meaning "national," it seems clear that the household registration system was to become the foundation on which the wall between Japanese and non-Japanese people would be built. For sure, the so-called traditional family of Japan was a case of an invented tradition. The basic template for the household was what the Meiji reformers imagined to have been the ideal samurai family, which was familiar to only a fraction of the Japanese people at best.[13] To be a member of the modern Japanese state, still, one had to belong to this imagined family.

Second, moreover, this form of family, reinvented in the name of tradition and uniformly implemented through household registries, became the template for reorganizing villages, local communities, and even the state at large. Undergirded by the Confucian principles of parental benevolence and filial duties, as well as male domination and female subjugation, the household was held up as the seedbed of civic-moral virtues required of members of the modern Japan. As a result, the entire Japanese people were reconceived

[11] Yamanaka Einosuke et al. (eds.), *Nihon Gendai Hōshiron: Kindai kara Gendai e* [Discourses on Modern Japanese Legal History: From Early Modern to Contemporary Period] (Kyoto: Hōritsu Bunkasha, 2010), p. 203.

[12] Endō, *Kokuseki to Koseki*, pp. 116–17.

[13] See, e.g., Itō Mikiharu, *Kazoku Kokkakan no Jinruigaku* [Anthropology of the Family State Ideology] (Tokyo: Mineruva Shobō, 1982).

along the image of a family. The emperor was now deemed to be the supreme patriarch for the entire nation, ruling all Japanese people as his extended family. Now the Japanese nation was reimagined as a blood-kin group, and its members owed the emperor the kind of absolute obedience and loyalty that children owed their parents – or "filial piety 'writ large'" according to Hozumi Nobushige, one of the drafters of the Meiji Civil Code.[14] For him, it "is not a metaphor, but a literal truth" that the "Empire is one great family; the family is a little empire."[15] The Civil Code was the institutional basis of the so-called family state (*kazoku kokka*) ideology as much as it was a culmination of the Household Registration Law of 1871.[16]

In sum, the household registration system, undergirded by the family state ideology, was used as the grassroots-level incubator for the "loyal subjects of the imperial realm" (*kōkoku shinmin*) and, which amounted to the same, the boundary-setting device for modern Japanese peoplehood at large.[17] More than a mere technical device to increase people's legibility, it was designed to play a dual function. On the one hand, its goal was to forge a new national people who were internally integrated as equal and homogenous subjects of the emperor. On the other, it simultaneously operated to entrench differentiation of, even discrimination against, a large number of Japanese people, most notably women but ultimately all those who did not fit the legally sanctioned

[14] Nobushige Hozumi, *Ancestor-worship and Japanese Law* (Tokyo: The Maruzen Kabushiki-Kaisha, 1912 (originally 1901): BiblioBazaar ed.), p. 105.

[15] Hozumi, *Ancestor-worship*, p. 104. It was his brother and an influential constitutional scholar in his own right, Hozumi Yatsuka, who plugged this family state ideology into the notorious theory of "national polity" (*kokutai*). See, e.g., Richard H. Minear, *Japanese Tradition and Western Law: Emperor, State, and Law in the Thought of Hozumi Yatsuka* (Cambridge, MA: Harvard University Press, 1970), pp. 73–4. For the rise and fall of the "family state" ideology, see Walter Skya, *Japan's Holy War: The Ideology of Radical Shinto Ultranationalism* (Durham, NC: Duke University Press, 2009).

[16] This is why the family system, as institutionalized in the Civil Code and the household registry system, was deemed an important target of reform by the U.S. occupation authorities. See Kurt Steiner, "The Occupation and the Reform of the Japanese Civil Code," in Robert E. Ward and Sakamoto Yoshikazu (eds.), *Democratizing Japan: The Allied Occupation* (Honolulu: University of Hawaii Press, 1987), p. 189. This is also why the GHQ/SCAP insisted on including in the new constitution a detailed provision (Article 24) for transforming the patriarchal family into one based on "individual dignity and the essential equality of sexes." In the early 1950s when the constitutional revision was pursued in earnest by the conservatives led by later premier Kishi Nobusuke, in fact, this provision was singled out as a primary target of amendment. For these conservatives with deep prewar roots, the family registration system was indeed one of the essential components of Japan's *kokutai*. See Oppler, *Legal Reform in Occupied Japan*, p. 119.

[17] Fujita Shōzō, *Tennōsei-kokka no Shihaigenri* [The Principle of Domination in the Emperor-State] (Tokyo: Misuzu Shobō, 1998), pp. 8–11, 26–7, 91–2.

model of the deeply gendered and patriarchal model of the Japanese family. Those misfits, outcasts, and less than blindly loyal subjects would have to be assimilated, by coercion if necessary, into the family state that was imperial Japan.

Registering Taiwanese as Japanese Subjects

This dual function of the household registration system would become even more pronounced as the Meiji nation-building project entered its next phase – colonial-empire-building. With the acquisition of new overseas territories, beginning with Taiwan after the First Sino-Japanese War in 1895, came the challenge of incorporating the new populace. At each stage, from Taiwan to Korea, the response was to document and identify all subjects of the vast colonial empire according to their domicile under the same conceptual rubric. In the case of Taiwan, this reliance on the household registration system was all the more necessary because, at the time, major legal apparatuses for the empire were still in the process of formation. The Imperial Constitution had gone into force only five years before, the Civil Code was still on the drafting board, and the Nationality Law would not be enacted until four years later in 1899. Indeed, the occupation of Taiwan seems to have complicated the project of consummating the legal framework of the empire by bringing into relief a host of issues relating to the immediate task of administration as well as the more distant goal of assimilation and "civilization" of a population considered more different than those whom Japan had absorbed until then.[18] With neither a seasoned administrative apparatus nor a well thought-out vision for the expansion, Japan proceeded to incorporate the residents of Taiwan into the human boundary of the empire – by means of the household registry.

According to the terms of the Shimonoseki Treaty, by which Taiwan was ceded to Japan, those living in Taiwan were given a probationary period of two years during which they could leave the island. At the end of that period, in 1897, those who chose to remain were considered subjects of the Japanese emperor.[19] Even before the two-year probation ended, however, Japanese

[18] Another concern for the Meiji leaders was to demonstrate to the West that Japan was a "modern" state capable of running an overseas territory. At the same time, they also wanted to show that their policy was different from and more humane than the West's brutal colonial exploitations. For the importance of this "external" dimension for the imperial policy toward Taiwan, see Nomura, "Making the Japanese Empire," pp. 67–79.

[19] When the Nationality Law was passed in 1899, thus, it was immediately deemed applicable to residents of Taiwan, which the governor-general reconfirmed with a special decree in 1906, declaring that all people in Taiwan had become Japanese nationals as of 8 May 1897. Edward I-te Chen, "The Attempt to Integrate the Empire: Legal Perspectives," in Ramon H. Myers and Mark R. Peattie (eds.), *The Japanese Colonial Empire, 1895–1945* (Princeton, NJ: Princeton University Press, 1987), pp. 245–6.

authorities began to implement a household registration system in Taiwan. The colonial government issued the Regulation for Surveying Taiwan Residents' Household Registry (*Taiwan Jūmin Koseki Chōsa Kisoku*) on 1 August 1896, which was followed soon by the Household Regulation (*Kokō Kisoku*) in 1905.[20] This of course was a way of measuring the size of the population now under their control. Household registration was also considered necessary because the locals were expected to report their numbers by the household. If the family head (*jiazhang*) declared that he would remain on the island and become a Japanese subject, all of his household members would also be given status (*bungen*) as Japanese.[21] In order to facilitate the process of incorporation, it was therefore necessary to ascertain who belonged to which family.[22] This was the main reason that the household registry was a natural choice for surveying and documenting the Taiwanese population.

Predictably, though, initial efforts to establish a household registry system for the Taiwanese residents seem to have encountered difficulties since the structure of the local households did not correspond exactly to that of the Japanese family. As a result, during the early stage of implementation, the registry was made much simpler than the Japanese *koseki* and did not show the full extent of the family as a patriarchal unit. Even non-family members were recorded in the same registry if they lived together at the same address. More important, the household head (*koshu*) in Taiwan was still not an inheritable legal status with extensive rights over other family members. The Taiwanese registry therefore could not serve the same function as the Japanese *koseki* did of certifying the legal status and capacity of an individual within the family. Thus, it was difficult to apply the exactly same template as codified in Japan's Household Registration Law to make the Taiwanese population fully legible through the lens of the household. Be that as it may, it cannot be debated that the Taiwanese locals were still accounted for by the colonial authorities primarily through the system of household registration. At least, the registry showed the name, age, and address of all persons residing in the same household. For sure, it was not on account of registration status that the Taiwanese

20 Asano Toyomi, *Teikoku Nihon no Shokuminchi Hōsei: Hōiki Tōgō to Teikoku Chitsujo* [Colonial Legal System of the Japanese Empire: Integration of Legal Domains and the Imperial Order] (Nagoya: University of Nagoya Press, 2008), p. 34; David Chapman, "Tama-chan and Sealing Japanese Identity," *Critical Asian Studies*, vol. 40 (2008), p. 431.

21 The idea of "family head" (*jiazhang*) according to Taiwanese custom was different from the Japanese civil law concept of household head (*koshu*), which would be introduced later with the Household Regulation of 1905. Even after its formal introduction, it took years to take root in Taiwan. See Tay-sheng Wang, *Legal Reform in Taiwan under Japanese Colonial Rule, 1895–1945* (Seattle: University of Washington Press, 2000), pp. 161–4.

22 Asano, *Shokuminchi Hōsei*, pp. 33–5.

subjects were given Japanese nationality under the new Nationality Law of 1899, especially for the purpose of international law.[23] Domestically speaking, though, being listed in the household registry in Taiwan was now enough to certify that the person was a Japanese subject and therefore entitled, in theory, to travel to other parts of the empire – even the Japanese main islands – without a visa. Despite initial difficulties, the Taiwanese registry functioned as the primary legal instrument through which the new colonial subjects were incorporated into the human boundary of imperial Japan.

Needless to say, the fact that the newly absorbed people of Taiwan were listed under the new Japanese-style registry did not mean that they were accorded equal constitutional status in the political, economic, and social hierarchy of the colonial empire. The newly colonized people were to be absorbed into imperial subjecthood, but not without a clearly legible marker for their inferior legal status vis-à-vis the Japanese people proper. As will be shown, the very fact that they were registered under a colonial registry was enough to maintain a hierarchy between what might be called "subnationalities" within the empire.[24] They were incorporated into the fold of the empire through the *koseki* system, but it was unmistakably clear to everyone that it was the *koseki* of "Taiwan," which was kept segregated from that of the main islands.

Interestingly, given that the legal framework of the empire was still under formation when Taiwan was first ceded to Japan, it was not obvious initially that the new colonial subjects would be relegated to the status of second-class citizenship. For the heart of the issue was the extent of the Imperial Constitution's applicability in the new colony.[25] Ume Kenjirō, one of the drafters of the Civil

[23] It also turned out that a system of household registry would not be needed, at least for the purpose of granting Japanese nationality to the locals. This was because the government eventually took the position that, unless a person declared otherwise, all persons on the island would automatically be given *bungen* as Japanese people on the day that the peace treaty with China went into effect. The only system needed was one for recording those individuals unwilling to become Japanese and expelling such undesirable elements from the island. The rest of the population would be regarded as Japanese as a matter of course. See Asano, *Shokuminchi Hōsei*, pp. 39–40.

[24] William Wetherall, "Nationality in Japan," in Sooim Lee, Stephen Murphy-Shigematsu, and Harumi Befu (eds.), *Japan's Diversity Dilemmas: Ethnicity, Citizenship, and Education* (Lincoln, NE: iUniverse, 2006), pp. 27–8.

[25] For an overview of the different positions, see Ebashi Takashi, "Shokuminchi ni okeru Kenpō no Tekiyō: Meiji Rikkentaisei no Ichisokumen" [Application of the Constitution in the Colonies: One Aspect of the Meiji Constitutional System], *Hōgaku Shirin*, vol. 82, nos. 3 & 4 (1985), pp. 21–30. See also Koseki Shōichi, "Teikoku Shinmin kara Gaikokujin e: Ataerare, Ubawarete kita Chōsenjin, Taiwanjin no Sanseiken" [From Imperial Subject to Foreigner: How Political Rights Were Given to Korean and Taiwanese and Then Taken Away], *Sekai*, vol. 809 (Oct. 2010), p. 34.

Code who was also instrumental in efforts to modernize the Korean legal system, argued that, with the incorporation of Taiwan into the empire's territory, the constitution applied to its inhabitants as a matter of course, and the uniform set of rights and duties should be given to the colonial subjects, as well as to Japanese proper, including rights to political participation and the duty of military service.[26] By contrast, Minobe Tatsukichi, a renowned liberal constitutionalist, countered by holding that the application of the constitution to the newly acquired territory should be contingent on its inhabitants' attainment of the requisite level of civility and enlightenment. It was obvious for him that Taiwan had not attained the proper conditions necessary, and therefore its residents could not be granted the same rights.[27] A middle position of sorts was suggested by the conservative scholar Hozumi Yatsuka, who was a leading theorist, along with his brother Hozumi Nobushige, of the "family state" ideology. As a constitutional law specialist, his premise was that the Imperial Constitution applied to all subjects of the emperor, even those residing in the colonies. Yet he also saw no problem in maintaining discrimination in terms of rights. As a matter of constitutional law, he argued, not to be confused with the constitution's rights provisions for the subjects was its function of integrating the empire under the sovereign emperor, and these two different constitutional aspects could be applied to colonial subjects in separation.[28]

Hozumi's position was shared by Yamada Saburō, a young conflict-of-laws specialist, who would be instrumental in the construction and implementation of a system of "states within a state"[29] as the organizing principle of the empire's legal system. He argued that the acquisition of Japanese nationality, or *bungen*, by the Taiwanese through their enrollment in the household registry merely signified a change in their international-legal status. Whether they would be given equal rights under the constitution was wholly at the discretion of domestic legislation.[30] He would later maintain the same position

26 Marie Seong-hak Kim, *Law and Custom in Korea: Comparative Legal History* (Cambridge: Cambridge University Press, 2012), pp. 108–09, 146–7.

27 Minobe is reported to have later modified his views by admitting the applicability of certain parts (e.g., provisions on the emperor's absolute powers) of the constitution to the colonies. Regarding the rights provisions, however, he continued to maintain his earlier position. See Kim Chang Rok, "Ilbon Chegukchuŭi ŭi Hŏnpŏp Sasang kwa Shingminji Chosŏn" [Constitutional Thoughts of Imperial Japan and Colonial Korea], *Pŏpsahak Yŏn'gu*, vol. 14 (1993), pp. 154–70.

28 Oguma Eiji, *'Nihonjin' no Kyōkai: Okinawa, Ainu, Taiwan, Chōsen Shokuminchi Shihai kara Fukki Undō made* [Boundaries of the 'Japanese': From Colonial Control of Okinawa, Ainu, Taiwan, Korea to Reversion Movement] (Tokyo: Shinyōsha, 1998), pp. 126–9.

29 Tessa Morris-Suzuki, "Migrants, Subjects, Citizens: Comparative Perspectives on Nationality in the Prewar Japanese Empire," *Asia-Pacific Journal: Japan Focus* (1 Sept. 2008).

30 Marie Kim, *Law and Custom in Korea*, p. 182.

on the occasion of Korea's annexation by Japan in 1910.[31] For Yamada, the household registry was the key instrument by which colonial subjects could be identified and kept separate from the people of the metropolis. It was for this reason that he advocated the creation of a family registration system in colonial Korea in close conformity to that in Japan, which, however, ought to be kept separately and independently. He warned that, otherwise, there would be no way to stop Koreans from "becoming" Japanese by simply migrating to mainland Japan and setting up a household address there.[32]

While the constitutional issue was never really settled and continued to be debated through the end of the colonial period, the practice of identifying colonial subjects via household registry and denying them equal rights quickly became entrenched. A colonial registry address would ensure that Koreans and the Taiwanese remained subject to differential treatment even when they resided in the metropolis. Just as it had done during the early Meiji era, the household registration system was expected to effectuate an elaborate scheme of entrenched differentiation and exclusion, as well as integration, among the imperial subjects of Japan.

Integration and differentiation, the two poles of the household registration system, had to be constantly negotiated against each other, especially with the further expansion of the Japanese colonial empire. This tension built into the system of marking the boundaries of Japanese imperial peoplehood would become ever more severe as increasingly different sorts of people were incorporated, while the empire rushed along the path of militarism toward forced assimilation of the population. In Taiwan, the families listed in the household registry were gradually transformed with the passage of time, through judicial interpretation and administrative intervention, to conform more closely to the Japanese-style family system. By the 1930s, the courts were proclaiming that the institution of household head was now a fully entrenched "custom" of Taiwan, and the Household Regulation was revised in 1935 to reflect such alleged changes. The government also decreed that the wife shall henceforth use only her husband's surname, instead of following the traditional custom of writing both the husband's and her own maiden name. The final step was taken when the Household Regulation was revised again in 1940 to allow "exemplary" Taiwanese who demonstrated their worth as imperial subjects to adopt Japanese-style names.[33] Now that the Taiwanese were allegedly living

[31] Asano, *Shokuminchi Hōsei*, pp. 41–2, 274–5.

[32] Oguma, *'Nihonjin' no Kyōkai*, p. 160.

[33] Lee Seung-il, "Shingminji Chosŏn kwa Taeman ŭi Ch'angssigaemyŏng Kaesŏngmyŏng Pigyo Yŏn'gu" [A Comparative Study of the Policy of Adopting Japanese-style Names in Korea and Taiwan during the Colonial Period], *Taedong Munhwa Yŏn'gu*, vol. 76 (2011), pp. 421–9.

in Japanese-style families, they could have the honor of using Japanese-style names and become true members of the Japanese "family state." With this transformation, perhaps more importantly, Taiwanese subjects were deemed ready at last to serve the emperor in full capacity – as loyal imperial soldiers (*kōgun*). Implementation of the name-change (*kaiseimei*) would be followed closely by military conscription.

In sum, the institution of household registry became the tool with which the colonial subjects in Taiwan were molded ever more closely in the image of the Japanese people of the metropolis. Going beyond merely identifying and documenting imperial subjects, it performed a deeply transformative function as well. While it was a system that worked toward inscribing difference and discrimination, it also had to provide a means for turning the residents of Japan's first overseas colony into subjects whose loyalty toward the emperor was expected to be on a par with those on the main islands. The push toward assimilation and integration, primarily based on military needs, would increasingly grate against the differentiating aspect of the household registry. This built-in tension would manifest itself even more acutely as Japan acquired more colonies abroad.

Integrating and Differentiating Koreans Within the Empire

Perhaps the greatest challenge to the imperial policy of simultaneously integrating and differentiating colonial subjects came with the formal annexation of Korea in 1910. From the beginning, it was quite evident that ruling Korea would be very different from Japan's previous colonial experiences in Taiwan or Karafuto.[34] Aside from the sheer size of its territory and population, Korea's proximity to the Japanese main islands as well as the complicated historical relations ensured that governing Korea would be an entirely different enterprise. The magnitude of the problem, as well as the relative importance of Korea for the Japanese Empire, can be seen in the fact that many governors-general of Korea, after their tour of duty in Seoul, returned to Tokyo to become the prime minister of the imperial government. Imperial policies had to be formulated

[34] Acquisition of Karafuto (the southern half of the Sakhalin Island acquired after the Russo-Japanese War in 1905) followed the pattern set in the Taiwanese case – granting a right of initial exit followed by forcibly registering the remaining locals in a new household registry modeled after the Japanese one. This was part of an unyielding policy of assimilation via Japanization, which culminated in the official incorporation of the entire colony as one of the local prefectures in 1943 when the Imperial Diet passed a bill making all of its laws automatically applicable to Karafuto. See Chen, "Attempt to Integrate the Empire," p. 256; Tessa Morris-Suzuki, "Northern Lights: The Making and Unmaking of Karafuto Identity," *Journal of Asian Studies*, vol. 60, no. 3 (2001), pp. 645–71.

increasingly with Korea in mind, such that the mounting tension between integration and differentiation would strain the entire imperial edifice. The wartime needs for both material and human resources especially demanded the near-complete integration of Koreans as full-fledged subjects of the emperor. This meant that the differentiating dimension of the household registration system would be constantly questioned, if not actually eroded, under the exigencies of the war. It also meant that, in the postwar period, the "Korean question" would become the central issue for the task of redrawing the boundaries of the Japanese people.

The most important point that needs to be understood in this context is the fact that, despite the official rhetoric of spreading the blessings of the emperor with "impartiality and equality for all" (*isshidōjin*), the legal framework of the empire was actually an assemblage of different legal systems that were applicable to different parts of the empire. Especially with the colonization of Korea, it became clear that the laws for governing Korea had to be different from those for Taiwan and that the laws for both could not be the same as those for the Japanese main islands.[35] Fairly early on, the authorities developed the concept of "region" or "domain" (*chiiki*) to refer to the different territories within the empire where different legal regimes prevailed. Under this scheme, Taiwan and Korea, as well as the Japanese main islands, were all separate "domains with different laws" (*ihōchiiki*) where different rules applied for making and executing laws.[36] Even the Imperial Constitution was differentially applied according to the regions. A law enacted by the Imperial Diet in the metropolis was not automatically applicable in other regions. Instead, in both Taiwan and Korea, the governor-general wielded extensive legislative prerogatives. If an imperial law was considered useful in the colonies, it was made applicable through a special decree issued by the governor-general, which usually came with numerous exceptions and qualifications.[37]

The Civil Code is a case in point. Parts of it were implemented in Korea through a Korea-specific law called the Ordinance on Civil Matters in Korea

35 Asano, *Shokuminchi Hōsei*, p. 310.

36 Marie Kim, *Law and Custom in Korea*, p. 151. For a recent reflection on the different legal domains and their significance for understanding the Japanese empire as a legal entity, see Yamamuro Shin'ichi, "Kokumin-Teikoku Nihon ni okeru Ihōiki no Tōgō to Kakusa" [Integration and Differentiation of Different Legal Domains in the Nation-Empire of Japan], *Jinbun Gakuho*, vol. 101 (2011).

37 For details on the numerous forms of laws utilized throughout the vast colonial empire, see Chen, "Attempt to Integrate the Empire," pp. 254–62. For the legal structure of colonial Korea, see Chulwoo Lee, "Modernity, Legality, and Power in Korea under Japanese Rule," in Gi-wook Shin and Michael Robinson (eds.), *Colonial Modernity in Korea* (Cambridge, MA: Harvard University Asia Center, 1999).

(*Chōsen Minjirei*), first issued in 1912, which also stipulated that local "customary" norms would apply for certain matters like the rules on family and succession relations.[38] Sometimes a law passed by the metropolitan diet was never applied in the colony at all. A good example is the Nationality Law of 1899, which was held to be inapplicable to Koreans even though their nationality had become Japanese after 1910. The government took the position that the statute need not be applied because it was obvious that all subjects of the Empire of Great Han (*Taehan Cheguk*) had become subjects of the Japanese emperor by virtue of the 1910 Annexation Treaty.[39] The governor-general thus had the power not only to pick and choose which laws of the main islands would become applicable to the colony, but also to make new laws for the territory under his control.[40] Reflecting the system of "states within a state," the legal relationship among different domains of the Japanese colonial empire was little different from that between independent sovereign states.

Naturally, the same situation obtained for the system of making the people legible to the empire through household registries. As such, the registries in different parts of the empire were established on different legal grounds. The Household Registration Law enacted by the Imperial Diet in 1871 was only for the Japanese main islands. As mentioned, Taiwan came to have its own Taiwan Household Regulation issued by the colonial government in 1905. Similarly, the Korean registries were established by virtue of the Korean Household Registry Ordinance (*Chōsen Kosekirei*), issued in 1922 by the governor-general of Korea. Indeed, the different registries with different legal bases formed the bedrock of the system of differentiation inherent in the imperial legal framework. Even though all subjects of the emperor were Japanese nationals from

[38] Maintenance and development of a colony's local customary norms was an important means to protect the powers of the colonial government in Seoul vis-à-vis the metropolitan government in Tokyo. On the evolution of the Ordinance on Civil Matters in Korea, see Marie Kim, *Law and Custom in Korea*, pp. 172–9.

[39] Unlike the case of Taiwan or Karafuto, the people of Korea were not given the initial option of exit. Moreover, in order to retain tight control over Koreans wherever they went, the authorities precluded the application of the Nationality Law in Korea because the statute contained a rule allowing imperial subjects to change their nationality. They made sure that Koreans would not avail themselves of the provision, which stated that a Japanese subject would lose her nationality if she acquired the nationality of another country. Instead, relying on a putatively pre-annexation Korean law that seemed to prohibit changes of nationality, they insisted that Koreans were still under Japan's jurisdiction even if they became naturalized as Chinese or Russians. Endō, *Kokuseki to Koseki*, pp. 56–7.

[40] Oguma Eiji uses the term "Government-General Kingdom" to refer to this system of giving undivided, autocratic prerogative powers to the governor-general. Oguma, *'Nihonjin' no Kyōkai*, pp. 111–46.

the international-legal standpoint, their domestic status within the empire differed according to the specific registry through which they were made legible to the government.[41]

Furthermore, it was decided early on that a person could not change the place of her registration. Even if one was permitted to relocate to a different "domain" within the empire, one had to maintain the registration status in one's place of origin.[42] The household registry, in other words, had the effect of binding the people to the place where they were registered – more precisely, to the address of their permanent residence. As a result, the laws applicable to a particular individual were determined by ascertaining the legal domain to which the person was attached. In short, what is commonly described as "personality principle" in international law was the very foundation on which the imperial legal system operated, a "lynchpin" without which it could not be held together.[43] From the perspective of colonial subjects, this meant that the registry was more than a simple means of ascertaining their place of residence. It was a legal certificate of stigma. For it also functioned as a verification of their station in the social and political hierarchy of the empire, which in turn determined the particular set of legal rights and duties granted to them.[44]

This hierarchy was eventually crystallized in the nomenclature employed to refer to the different household registries. As opposed to the household registry of Japanese main islands, which was called "inner land" (*naichi*) registry, those of overseas colonies like Korea and Taiwan were referred to as "outer land" (*gaichi*) registries. To be sure, this terminology was not used from the beginning of the empire. Earlier documents apparently used the term *naichi* to refer to the Japanese main islands without employing the corresponding term *gaichi* as the common label for all the overseas territories of the empire.[45] In a 1918 statute called the Law of Common Affairs (*Kyōtsūhō*) the metropolis was referred to as *naichi*, while the various colonies were enumerated by name. By 1929, however, efforts to bring some coherence into the administration of the colonial empire resulted in the establishment of a new Ministry of Colonial Affairs (*Takumushō*), which was accompanied by attempts to encompass all of

41 Oguma, *'Nihonjin' no Kyōkai*, p. 155.

42 Endō, *Kokuseki to Koseki*, pp. 132–3.

43 Asano, *Shokuminchi Hōsei*, p. 336.

44 Uchida Jun, *Brokers of Empire: Japanese Settler Colonialism in Korea, 1876–1945* (Cambridge, MA: Harvard University Asia Center, 2011), p. 121.

45 Lee Seung-il, "Ilche Shigi Chosŏnin ŭi Ilbon Kukminhwa Yŏn'gu" [A Study of the Transformation of the People of Chosŏn into Japanese *Kokumin* during the Colonial Period], *Han'gukhak Nonjip*, vol. 34 (2000), pp. 75–7.

its colonies under the label *gaichi*.[46] The term *gaichi* was thus adopted in official documents as well as by the general public as the common designation for the overseas territories. Interestingly, this choice was apparently deemed better because it provided a way of avoiding the term "colony," or *shokuminchi*, which was thought to be too blatantly discriminatory and exploitative, as well as being evocative of European imperialism from which Japan wished to distance itself.[47] Be that as it may, every Korean knew that being an "outer lander," or *gaichijin*, meant being relegated to the status of a second-class citizen of the empire. The household registries operated to create and maintain different "subnationalities" among allegedly equal imperial subjects.

Alongside this function of differentiation and discrimination, however, Japan's household registry did have a role in integrating and assimilating Koreans into the empire. Indeed, the differentiating aspect could be felt all the more acutely precisely because the laws of the different legal domains in the empire were essentially based on the same model. The laws in force in Korea were imperfect copies – with severe restrictions and distortions – of those applicable to the people of *naichi*. The Korean Household Registry Ordinance of 1922 was in fact an attempt by the colonial authorities to bring the system one step closer to that of the main islands. It should also be noted that, even before this law was enacted, the household registration system in place since 1910 had already incorporated many features of the *naichi* Household Registration Law in order to "Japanize" the new colonial subjects. The 1922 Ordinance had been preceded by another legislation called Population Registration Law (Kr. *Minjŏkpŏp*; Jp. *Minsekihō*) of 1909. Although putatively a pre-colonial law, this had been passed by the Japanese-controlled government of the Empire of Great Han, which had already become a "protectorate" of Japan since 1905. As its purpose was to prepare for the official annexation, the Population Registration Law had already introduced many concepts and institutions from Japan which were alien to Korean society. Most of them pertained to the family structure, as it was part of a project to bring the Koreans into the fold of the empire by turning them into members of the purportedly traditional Japanese family system.

Given the Japanese role in the design and implementation of the 1909 law, it was natural that it would be retained by the new colonial government. Nevertheless, in administering the system, the colonial authorities soon encountered difficulties similar to those experienced by their counterpart in Taiwan, inducing them to judge the population registry of 1909

[46] Endō, *Kokuseki to Koseki*, p. 129; Marie Kim, *Law and Custom in Korea*, p. 181.
[47] Nomura, "Making the Japanese Empire," p. 69.

incomprehensive and inadequate. As in Taiwan, the main problem had mostly to do with the fact that the local family structure and living arrangements did not fit the "family" embodied in the Japanese registration system. The registry also still retained a few features of the traditional Korean family system, thus not corresponding accurately to the registration system in force in the *naichi*. In order to bring uniformity in the registration system throughout the empire, a new law had to be made. In the end, the Korean Household Registry Ordinance was issued in 1922 by the colonial government. Perhaps most important was the change of the name of the registration system from *minseki* (population registry) to *koseki* (household registry). This was not merely a change in nomenclature since it was part of a deeply transformative project of assimilation. Now, all household registries throughout the empire were called *koseki*. They were all based on the same conceptual scheme, that is, the putatively traditional family system of the samurai class governed by its patriarchal head. This 1922 ordinance would remain in force even after the end of the colonial era and prove to be most instrumental in identifying the constituent people of South Korea.

To Live and Die as the Emperor's Equal Subjects

The fact that every subject of the emperor was now catalogued under the same conceptual scheme, however, did not mean that the walls between the different legal domains were abolished. The household registries still operated on the basis of different laws issued by different authorities. At the same time, due to the fact (or fiction) that all persons in different domains were equally the subjects of the emperor and to the possibility (albeit limited) of mobility within the empire, cases arose that could not be handled by the registration law of one domain alone. A Japanese woman residing in Korea might marry a Korean man. Sometimes a Korean man might be adopted by a Japanese family and even become its heir (i.e., head of the household). In such cases there was a need to coordinate the changes in the family status of the persons involved and to have them reflected properly in the household registries of both Korea and Japan.

The aforementioned Law of Common Affairs of 1918 was enacted as a response to this need. It started out by stating that a "domain" as used in the law refers to *naichi*, Korea, Taiwan, or *Kantōshū* (Kwantung Leased Territory) (Article 1). As a set of conflict-of-laws principles, the law was intended to coordinate the problem of sorting out the applicable laws for issues involving the family status of persons from different domains. It mandated that when a person newly enters the household of one domain according to the laws of that domain, that person shall be removed from the household of other domains (Article 3). If a Japanese woman married a Korean man and became a member of his household according to the laws of Korea, she was now to be stricken from her father's registry in Japan so that she would no longer be regulated by *naichi* laws. Since the laws of each region did not provide for procedures for dealing with interregional marriages, a marriage lawfully consummated in one region might not be recognized by the laws of another region. The Law of Common Affairs was a way of dealing with such issues, by making sure that interregional changes in a person's family status did not create administrative tangles.[48]

This might be taken to imply that individuals had the freedom of moving to a different domain and having one's registry transferred there. In reality, however, such changes in a person's place of registration were allowed only under exceptional circumstances where inconsistent rules among the domains might result in intractable situations. The default rule, as mentioned, was that a person was bound to the region where her household registry was located. This was clearly implied in Article 2 of the Law of Common Affairs, which explicitly drew an analogy between "the law of the domain to which the person is attached" and *lex patriae* in the international-legal context.[49] It provided that the law of that domain shall be deemed the person's *honkokuhō*, or "the law of one's own country," in case of conflict of laws within the empire. In short, the basic premise of this law was that all persons within the empire were legally fixed to a particular domain. Cases that the law was expected to deal with were the exception that proved the rule. Moreover, those exceptions were to be allowed only when the preservation of the family system was at stake.[50] If the transfer of the wife's registry from the *naichi* to Korea was not permitted, for example, that would have created an intolerable situation where the husband and the wife were listed under different household registries in different domains. Clearly, that was not acceptable to a regime dedicated to maintaining the integrity of the "family" embodied in the registry system as the ideological foundation of the empire.[51]

The Law of Common Affairs was an attempt to integrate the empire while maintaining the differentiation based on different household registries. It may have worked at the time. As time went on, however, demand for further integration was bound to grow. One scholar reports of a petition filed

48 For the Law of Common Affairs in general, see Asano, *Shokuminchi Hōsei*, pp. 347–64.

49 Asano, *Shokuminchi Hōsei*, pp. 229, 332.

50 Endō, *Kokuseki to Koseki*, pp. 133–4.

51 For more intolerable administrative entanglements that necessitated the enactment of the Law of Common Affairs, see Marie Kim, *Law and Custom in Korea*, pp. 183–5.

in 1936 by one Chi Yŏng-gu, a Korean attorney from the city of Kwangju, in which he requested the implementation of the *naichi* Household Registration Law in Korea so as to allow colonial subjects to become true "inner landers" (*naichijin*) and to remove the discrimination among the subjects of the emperor.[52] The petition was summarily rejected by the Ministry of Colonial Affairs. A year later, however, with the outbreak of the Second Sino-Japanese War, calls for further integration would begin to be voiced from within the government itself. In order to meet the exigencies of the war, the government intensified its campaign to transform colonial subjects into loyal "subjects of the emperor's land" (*kōkoku shinmin*). Ultimately, this transformation, or *kōminka*, meant preparing colonial subjects – mostly Koreans – to take up arms and die for the glory of the emperor.[53]

Previously and throughout most of the imperial period, colonial subjects had not been subject to military duty. Indeed, they had been prohibited from serving because their loyalty toward the emperor was deemed suspect. The Military Service Law of 1927 had provided that all male imperial subjects had the duty to serve in the military, but in order to prevent colonial subjects from joining the military, the law stipulated that only "those subject to the Household Registration Law" were to be recruited. As the war escalated in China, however, the Japanese government decided at last to recruit from the colonies.[54] At first, they began with "volunteers." In 1938, Koreans were "allowed" to join the imperial army, and in 1943, the imperial navy opened its doors to both Koreans and Taiwanese. Finally, in 1944, as the war of attrition intensified in the Pacific theatre, mandatory military service was introduced for all colonial subjects. While many in the government were apprehensive of arming Koreans, for obvious reasons, they had no choice but to tap the human resources in the largest colony of the empire. All subjects of the emperor had to become truly equal in serving the empire, and that required almost complete integration.

This new circumstance naturally necessitated changes in the law. One solution would have been to expand the application of the *naichi* Household Registration Law to all of the *gaichi* territories. This could have been done by a simple decree from the colonial governments, without any formal changes to the Military Service Law itself. This route, however, was rejected and the Military Service Law was amended in 1943 to require military service of "those subject to the Household Registration Law or the rules on

52 Endō, *Kokuseki to Koseki*, p. 169.
53 Uchida, *Brokers of Empire*, pp. 378–80.
54 Endō, *Kokuseki to Koseki*, pp. 170–1.

household registry in the Ordinance on Civil Affairs in Korea."[55] In 1944, the Military Service Law was revised again so as to conscript all colonial male subjects of eligible age. Interestingly, this was done by eliminating the provision specifying who shall be required to serve. On the surface, it may appear as if the distinction according to household registry had finally been eliminated. With universal mandatory service, there was no longer a need to enumerate which of the emperor's subjects were to be conscripted. Yet, as Endō Masataka notes, the law was changed this way in order to avoid expanding the application of the Household Registration Law to *gaichi* territories. The imperial government could thereby safeguard the fundamental principle that the Household Registration Law applied only to *naichi* subjects.[56] Apparently, integration into the imperial military had to proceed while maintaining the *naichi/gaichi* distinction.

These changes in the military conscription law only intensified the tension already inherent in the system, and the imperial government had to confront a series of deeper and more practical challenges that followed. As compulsory education had never been implemented in the colonies, this meant that most Korean conscripts would be illiterate. More importantly, they would not even speak Japanese.[57] This is why the *kōminka* campaigns during wartime included reform of the colonial education system, and other efforts to change the colonial subjects' "habits of the heart" so that they would speak, think, and behave like true Japanese. Simultaneously with the recruitment of "volunteers" from Korea, the colonial authorities stepped up their efforts to force the use of "national language" in schools and homes. The illiterate recruits had to be given cram courses in Japanese language and culture before being sent off to the frontlines. Of course, the government realized that transforming the whole identity of Koreans would take several generations,[58] but that was a luxury the war did not allow them to indulge in. Yet, if they could not change the way Koreans thought and felt, they could at least change the way they were classified and categorized. If they were going to conscript colonial subjects into the imperial military, it was deemed unacceptable to have persons with non-Japanese names, such as Kim or Park, among the ranks.

55 Oguma, *'Nihonjin' no Kyōkai*, p. 441.

56 Endō, *Kokuseki to Koseki*, pp. 188–9.

57 As of late 1942, only 20% of the Koreans spoke Japanese. The percentage was even lower among the rural population, from which would come the majority of colonial conscripts. Miyata Setsuko, *Chōsen Minshū to 'Kōminka' Seisaku* [Korean Masses and the Policy of Turning People into Imperial Subjects] (Tokyo: Miraisha, 1985), pp. 114–15.

58 Miyata, *'Kōminka' Seisaku*, p. 104. For Japan's long preparation for the conscription of Korean soldiers and the reasons for its delay, see, e.g., Brandon Palmer, "Imperial Japan's Preparations to Conscript Koreans as Soldiers, 1942–1945," *Korean Studies*, vol. 31 (2007).

In order to become fully Japanese by having the opportunity to fight for the emperor, one at least had to bear a Japanese name. Thus, in preparation for the recruitment of Koreans as volunteers, the decision was made in 1939 to force all Koreans to adopt Japanese-style names.[59] Unlike in Taiwan, where the Japanese names were granted as a privilege, in Korea all persons were required to create Japanese names and have them registered in the household registry. At least on paper, there would be no distinction between imperial subjects from the *naichi* and those from Korea.

Yet, beyond making the conscripts' colonial identity unidentifiable, this policy of "creating family names and changing given names" (*sōshikaimei*) also had the effect of consummating the transplantation into Korea of the abstract and standardized Japanese family. The family name in Korea had been an indicator of a person's patriarchal ancestry and considered almost sacred, such that changing one's family name was inconceivable even if one underwent a change of status, including marriage. Because a wife retained her maiden surname, it was natural that a Korean household would have members with different family names. The family name of the household head would be different from those of his wife and his mother.[60] In Japan, by contrast, the family was considered a homogeneous legal unit, whose name had to be held in common by all of its members the moment they entered it – be it through birth, marriage, or adoption. This was reflected in the household registration system by the requirement that all persons enrolled in the same household registry be identified by a common family name. The Japanese considered this form of household and the naming practice to be the core of their traditional, and therefore ideal, family system.[61] Thus, requiring the Korean colonial subjects to create Japanese-style family names meant more than a coerced change of identity at the individual level. It was an imposition of a new definition of the

[59] For historical background, see Mizuno Naoki, *Sōshikaimei: Nihon no Chōsen Shihai no naka de* [Adoption of Japanese Names: Within the Context of Japan's Rule over Korea] (Tokyo: Iwanami Shoten, 2008), pp. 21–55.

[60] Since the family name never changed, adoption in Korea was only possible within the same patriarchal group, i.e., from among those with the same surname (and only from the same generation as the son of the household head). It was inconceivable that a person born with a different family name could be adopted and become a member, let alone heir, of the family. See Lee Seung-il, "Ch'angssigaemyŏng," pp. 433–5; Mizuno, *Sōshikaimei*, pp. 45–6.

[61] Historically, however, this system of requiring every family member to hold the same family name seems to have been an invented tradition. In 1876, the Meiji government issued a decree that women, upon marriage, shall retain their maiden family name. This was later reversed during the drafting of the Civil Code on grounds that in the more advanced nations of Europe married women adopted their husbands' names. See Yamanaka et al., *Nihon Gendai Hōshiron*, p. 203.

family,[62] as well as a more effective system by which the state could use the family as a means for controlling the populace.

This in turn required changing the Ordinance on Civil Matters in Korea (*Chōsen Minjirei*) as well as modifying the household registration forms in Korea to better conform to those used in the *naichi*.[63] In fact, implementing the name-change policy revealed that, even after almost thirty years of colonial rule, the Korean household registries were utterly unreliable. Nearly twenty percent of the households were unaccounted for, and changes in individuals' status were not properly reflected in the registries. This sorry situation prompted the colonial government to embark on a massive effort to update the registries. As Oguma Eiji notes, the name-change policy provided the occasion for verifying the registry records in preparation for the conscription of colonial subjects.[64] In order for colonial residents to be identified as "equal" loyal subjects ready to die for the emperor, their registries not only had to be put in order but also transformed to fully mimic the *naichi* registries.[65]

The final push toward full integration was made literally months before the empire capitulated to the Allied Powers. Up to that point, integration had only meant equal treatment in terms of the "privilege" of defending the emperor's sacred realm. It was only by risking a violent death for the emperor's *Götterdämmerung* (physical decimation) under an alien name (symbolic obliteration) that the colonial Koreans and Taiwanese were permitted to live as equal subjects of the Japanese empire. They could be treated as fully Japanese only in the emperor's "Valhalla" – that is, the Yasukuni Shrine. It was therefore all but inevitable that imposing the duty of military service on colonial subjects would give rise to increasing calls for more rights, particularly voting rights.

Indeed, when Korean subjects were first recruited as volunteers, the government tried to preempt such calls by declaring that this did not imply granting

62 This involved a complex process by which the different terms signifying "family name" or "surname" were reinterpreted to fit the policy demands of the empire. At first the colonial government took the position that the terms *sŏng* (Jp. *sei*) and *ssi* (Jp. *shi*) both meant the same thing, i.e., the family name. Later, however, *ssi* was held up as the "real" family name, i.e., the Japanese-style name attending the Japanese family structure, and therefore lacking in the Korean context. The argument was that while Koreans may have a name indicating their individual paternal ancestry (*sŏng*), they did not have a name for their "family" (*ssi*). Hence, the need for "creating family names" (*sōshi*). See Lee Seung-il, "Ch'angssigaemyŏng," pp. 437–43; Mizuno, *Sōshikaimei*, p. 48.

63 Endō, *Kokuseki to Koseki*, pp. 172–5.

64 Oguma, *'Nihonjin' no Kyōkai*, pp. 441–2.

65 For the changes in registry forms in 1944, see Endō, *Kokuseki to Koseki*, pp. 180–4.

more political rights.[66] The authorities stressed that serving in the imperial military itself was a privilege and an opportunity to enjoy true equality with *naichi* subjects.[67] Perhaps realizing the futility and absurdity of the argument, the leadership in the military soon began pushing for the recognition of colonial subjects' right to take part in the political affairs of the empire. In order to conscript them into military service, at least some gesture was needed in the direction of improving their status.

On 1 April 1945, the very day American troops landed on the shores of Okinawa, the emperor issued the "Imperial Rescript on the Participation of Residents of Korea and Taiwan in National Politics." In this rescript, he expressed satisfaction at the progress of assimilation as well as the contribution of colonial subjects in the war efforts and announced his decision to grant them political rights. That same day also saw the promulgation of amendments to the Election Law for the House of Representatives, establishing electoral districts in Korea and Taiwan.[68] The revised law allotted twenty-three representatives from Korea and five from Taiwan to be elected to the Imperial Diet. The distinction based on different household registries seemed to be finally becoming irrelevant. Constitutional rights enjoyed by *naichi* residents could now be enjoyed by all subjects of the emperor. To be sure, the colonial subjects still had to meet certain property requirements,[69] something that had been abolished in 1925 for the *naichi* subjects, but all members of the empire were now given a chance to participate in government affairs – at least in theory. This even suggested that laws passed by the Imperial Diet might be directly applicable to colonial subjects, which in turn implied a severe diminution of the autonomous lawmaking powers of the governors-general.[70] Now that both military duty and political rights were granted to every Japanese "national" residing in the territory of the empire, it made less sense to retain the system of "subnationality," most vividly represented in the legal ban on transferring one's household registration to a different domain.

66 Endō, *Kokuseki to Koseki*, p. 170.

67 Miyata, *'Kōminka' Seisaku*, pp. 107–08.

68 Endō, *Kokuseki to Koseki*, p. 191.

69 According to the new scheme, unlike in Japan proper, colonial subjects in Korea and Taiwan had to have paid at least fifteen yen in annual direct tax to be eligible to vote. Asano, *Shokuminchi Hōsei*, p. 551. This meant that only 2.3% of the population of Korea would be allowed vote, of which 29% would have been Japanese residents in Korea. Lee Seung-il, *Chosŏn Ch'ongdokpu Pŏpche Chŏngch'aek* [Legal-Administrative Policies of the Government-General in Korea] (Seoul: Yŏksa Pip'yŏngsa, 2008), p. 356.

70 Oguma, *'Nihonjin' no Kyōkai*, pp. 450–5.

Before colonial subjects of Korea and Taiwan ever had a chance to exercise their newly given rights, however, the war came to an end. More importantly for the story of peoplehood, the ban on transferring one's registry address was maintained until the very end.[71] The registry-based "personality" principle of differentiation was thus never abandoned even under pressure toward integration as embodied in the "territoriality" principle underlying the electoral system. The end of the war actually occasioned a swift reversal of these integration policies, and the household registry was picked up once again in the postwar era as the major criterion for differentiating those with rights and those without – in both Japan and Korea.

DISMEMBERING THE JAPANESE EMPIRE

World War II in China and the Pacific came to an abrupt end on 15 August 1945 following Japan's acceptance of the Potsdam Declaration, which was legally consummated on 2 September with the signing of the Instrument of Surrender on the USS Missouri. But closing a war takes more than a ceremony on the victor's battleship, for "embracing defeat" required a literal re-constitution of the vanquished nation. The Japanese state and society had to be reorganized along democratic principles, and the Japanese people, remade to live on those principles. This is why the significance of Japan's postwar constitutional founding cannot be fully appreciated by merely focusing on the drafting of a document. It was a project that demanded a radical alteration of the nation's culture and deep psychology as well as its political and economic institutions. Remaking the people therefore required a program of re-education and re-socialization. Yet, it also entailed something more fundamental. Re-constituting the country required a new answer to the question of who is included in the ambit of "We, the Japanese People."

For one thing, this was a corollary of Japan's acceptance of the Allies' terms for ending the hostilities. The blueprint for postwar Japan charted out in the various Allied proclamations clearly indicated that territorial reduction would be mandatory. As early as 1941, the Atlantic Charter stated, in Article 3, that the United Kingdom and the United States "wish to see sovereign rights and self government restored to those who have been forcibly deprived of them." The Cairo Declaration of November 1943 made it clear that Japan's postwar territory would not include any land that had been seized "by violence and greed" and that Manchuria, Taiwan, and Korea

[71] Endō, *Kokuseki to Koseki*, pp. 184–7.

would all be seceded from Japan.[72] This principle of territorial reduction was given a more definitive statement in the Potsdam Declaration, which specified in Article 8 that "Japanese sovereignty shall be limited to the islands of Honshu, Hokkaido, Kyushu, Shikoku and such minor islands as we determine." So, for the U.S. occupation forces that landed in Japan in late August 1945, the overall mandate was relatively clear. As part of their mission to dismantle the imperial establishment as thoroughly as possible, they were to carry out the dismemberment of Japan in its territory and population. The boundary of the Japanese people had to be readjusted.

This in effect set a backward-looking or aversive tone for the postwar constitutional founding of Japan. It was aimed at bringing the war that had just ended to a full closure by making sure that Japan would be reduced to a position where it would not pose a threat to world peace ever again. As discussed in Chapter 2, Article 9 is a case in point, since this peace provision was created mainly to put to rest international apprehensions about the resurgence of Japan's militarist past. This obviously cohered well with the goal of dismembering the empire. In order to seal the defeat, Japan had to be turned from a sprawling, multiethnic, and militaristic empire into a small-scale, de-industrialized, and democratic island-nation.

The readjustment of the boundaries of Japan's peoplehood was thus a result of externally given circumstances. The U.S. occupation forces were implementing the Allies' mandate, which had been determined during wartime, before the onslaught of another global war. That does not mean, however, that the Japanese were passive receivers of a new definition of their peoplehood imposed by outsiders. The new boundary of the Japanese people was delineated through a complex process of negotiation in which the locals were very much the active agent. Nor was this the first time that Japan went through a reshuffling of its human boundary; ever since the beginning of the Meiji era, as seen, the modern nation-state and colonial empire of Japan had undergone redefinitions of its boundary, both human and territorial. To that extent, the postwar instance of redefining its peoplehood may be seen as but the latest in a long series of legal and political maneuvers to determine whom to

[72] The relevant parts of the Cairo Declaration are as follows:

> It is their purpose that Japan shall be stripped of all the islands in the Pacific which she has seized or occupied since the beginning of the first World War in 1914, and that all the territories Japan has stolen from the Chinese, such as Manchuria, Formosa, and The Pescadores, shall be restored to the Republic of China.
>
> Japan will also be expelled from all other territories which she has taken by violence and greed. The aforesaid three great powers, mindful of the enslavement of the people of Korea, are determined that in due course Korea shall become free and independent.

include in the Japanese peoplehood. This is particularly so given the crucial role played by the institution of household registry. Even before the process of constitution-drafting began in earnest, the household registry would be employed to predetermine the boundaries of "We, the Japanese People." The logic of integration and differentiation built into that system of identifying Japanese people would be put to innovative use in coming up with a new definition of the human boundaries of the new democratic Japan. In sum, the new answer to the persistent question of who belongs to the people of Japan would be given through the postwar constitutional founding, which took place at the interface of parameters set by external forces and institutional tools inherited from the past.

Predetermining the Human Boundary through Election Law

Implementing the Allied mandate of reducing Japan's territorial boundary to its prewar status necessarily entailed a massive population movement across different parts of the former imperial expanse, creating an administrative nightmare for the under-prepared occupation forces. Within a relatively short span of time, millions of Japanese soldiers and civilians in the former colonies had to be shipped back to the main islands. Perhaps more intractable was the problem of sorting out ex-colonial subjects long resident in the Japanese main islands and repatriating them to their newly liberated homelands.[73] The largest group in this latter category was the Korean population, numbering over two million at the time of defeat. Their vast majority had been forcibly brought to Japan as "slave labor" during wartime. Only too eager to return, a total of 1.3 million Koreans had already left Japan even before the official registration system for repatriation was set up in April 1946. Quite a few, however, had voluntarily come to Japan looking for opportunities that were not available back in colonial Korea, and they were more ambivalent about going back since their livelihood had deeper roots in Japan than in Korea. GHQ/SCAP's policy of capping the amount of assets that could be taken back at a meager 1,000 yen per person did not exactly encourage their early repatriation. Besides, the division of the Korean Peninsula and the subsequent establishment of two rival governments made it difficult for some to choose a homeland to go back to. By 1949, as many as 600,000 Koreans opted to stay despite the authorities' basic policy of repatriation.[74]

[73] On this two-way repatriation process after the war, see Lori Watt, *When Empire Comes Home: Repatriation and Reintegration in Postwar Japan* (Cambridge, MA: Harvard University Asia Center, 2009).

[74] Mark E. Caprio, "Resident Aliens: Forging the Political Status of Koreans in Occupied Japan," in Mark E. Caprio and Yoneyuki Sugita (eds.), *Democracy in Occupied Japan: The U.S. Occupation and Japanese Politics and Society* (New York: Routledge, 2007), p.186.

The occupation authorities' ground for this policy was the Cairo and Potsdam Declarations, which categorized resident Koreans as foreign nationals in postwar Japan. Further, they were recognized as victims of Japanese imperialism, and, as a result, Koreans, along with 40,000 Taiwanese, were officially designated as "liberated peoples" by Washington.[75] The method of liberation was to sort out Koreans and send them back to the peninsula. If liberation was the goal of repatriation, then it naturally followed that those who wished to stay should also be given the freedom to do so on the assumption that Japanese nationality would be retained. This was why repatriation was encouraged, even insisted upon, but never forcibly imposed by the occupation authorities. GHQ/SCAP policy was, in short, to repatriate as many Koreans as possible and to assimilate those who opted to remain.[76]

Implementing this policy, however, was not so simple as it seemed. From the very beginning, the same directive from Washington also stipulated that resident Koreans could be treated as "enemy nationals," should military security require it. This apparent contradiction is understandable in view of the fact that some of these former colonial subjects had been collaborators in Japan's war effort, even enemies on the battlefields, until a few months earlier.[77] The occupation's equivocation was also motivated by the perceived reality that, during the social and economic chaos that engulfed defeated Japan, resident Koreans were often suspected as communist-sympathizers and black-market profiteers, and these charges (mostly by the Japanese authorities) were not entirely groundless. Under the circumstances, GHQ/SCAP was compelled to find a way to repatriate Koreans, while keeping those who chose to stay under the policing power of the Japanese government on which they relied for domestic security. The solution was an ad hoc approach to the issue, according to which Koreans were treated as *de jure* foreigners for the purpose of repatriation and *de facto* Japanese in other matters (e.g., food rationing).[78]

75 "Basic Initial Post-Surrender Directive to Supreme Commander for the Allied Powers for the Occupation and Control of Japan" (JCS 1380/15) 3 Nov. 1945, paragraph 8 (d), in *PRJ*, p. 432.

76 Erin A. Chung, *Immigration and Citizenship in Japan* (Cambridge: Cambridge University Press, 2010), p. 75.

77 In fact, as many as 42 Koreans and Taiwanese were later sentenced to death and 270 imprisoned for war crimes. See Caprio, "Resident Aliens," p. 183.

78 For example, a 17 February 1946 memorandum of GHQ/SCAP ordered all Koreans, Chinese, Taiwanese, and even Okinawans to register with the Japanese government, thus confirming the view that these populations were non-Japanese nationals. By contrast, another GHQ/SCAP document dated 21 May 1946 stipulated that all resident Koreans (and Taiwanese) be treated as "presumptively" having Japanese nationality for purposes of domestic security. See Takemae Eiji, *The Allied Occupation of Japan* (London and New York: Continuum, 2002), pp. 447–51.

This dualistic approach was also adopted by the Japanese government but apparently with greater consistency. On the assumption that former colonial subjects were no longer Japanese nationals, the government's preferred course of action seems to have been "mass deportation" of such persons.[79] This view was also reflected in the derisive label used to refer to resident Koreans and Taiwanese – "third country nationals" (*daisankokujin*), that is, neither Allied nor Japanese nationals. In conformity with the GHQ/SCAP policies, however, Korean and Taiwanese residents were still presumed to retain Japanese nationality on certain issues. The major motivation behind this stance was again to keep these former colonial subjects under the taxing, policing, and judicial authority of the Japanese government.[80] When it came to duties and obligations, in other words, they continued to be treated as Japanese. When it came to rights and benefits, however, they were not deemed fully Japanese. The Japanese government thus insisted that these former colonial subjects were not entitled to government pensions or compensations for wartime services. As non-Japanese, more importantly, they were no longer entitled to the full enjoyment of political and civil rights provided for in the prewar constitution.

This consistent policy of terminating rights while continuing to impose duties was put on full view as early as December 1945, in the process of revising the House of Representatives Election Law. Without prompting from the occupation authorities, the Japanese government took the initiative of reforming its election law in October, in preparation for the first postwar general election expected to be held the following year. In the name of democratization, women were given suffrage rights, and the voting age was lowered. Against the new zeitgeist, however, the revised law also mandated the disenfranchisement of former colonial subjects residing in Japan. Its Supplementary Rule Number 2 stipulated that the voting rights of resident Koreans and Taiwanese would be suspended "for the time being."[81] The disenfranchisement of the

79 This expression is attributed to Shirasu Jirō, Yoshida's close advisor and the cabinet liaison to GHQ. See Chung, *Immigration and Citizenship in Japan*, p. 74.

80 Chikako Kashiwazaki, *Nationality and Citizenship in Japan: Stability and Change in Comparative Perspective* (Ph.D. dissertation, Brown University, 1998), p. 162.

81 The same rule also disenfranchised those from the Ryukyu Islands even before these lands were formally handed over to the U.S. administration. Almost identical provisions disenfranchising former colonial subjects and Okinawans would find their way into the House of Councilors (upper house) Election Law and Local Election Law, both of 1947. For a general survey of the legislative process by which the disenfranchisement was done, see Mizuno Naoki, "Zainichi Chōsenjin Taiwanjin Sanseiken 'Teishi' Jōkō no Seiritsu" [The Making of the Provision that 'Suspended' the Suffrage Rights of the Koreans and Taiwanese in Japan], *Sekai Jinken Mondai Kenkyu Senta, Kenkyū Kiyō*, no. 1 (March 1996).

former colonial subjects may seem a matter of course, since they were now considered "liberated people" to be repatriated. The debates during the revision process, however, reveal that this was far from a foregone conclusion.

In fact, the initial draft of the revised election law prepared by the Interior Ministry and endorsed by the newly formed Shidehara cabinet on 13 October 1945 had *not* disenfranchised Koreans and Taiwanese.[82] The cabinet specifically dealt with this question in its "Outline for Revision of Electoral System for the House of Representatives" and concluded that Koreans and Taiwanese would retain their rights to vote and to run for office. Given that colonial subjects residing in *naichi* Japan had participated in elections at least since the 1920s, stripping them of their rights would have seemed inconsistent with the overall mandate of the reform bill, which was to democratize the electoral process by extending the franchise. This was probably all the more so, since even colonial subjects residing in the *gaichi* had been given suffrage rights – limited, to be sure, and too late to be implemented – only six months earlier. Undoing this decision and going in the reverse direction would not have been agreeable to the inert bureaucracy of the ministry.[83] More importantly, for the officials in the cabinet, there were ample legal grounds for maintaining the ex-colonial subjects' right to vote. It was but a logical corollary of the government's official position that the issue of their nationality would be determined by the peace treaty to be concluded in the future with the Allied Powers. Until then, the status quo would be maintained, which meant that former colonial subjects residing in Japan would retain Japanese nationality. As Japanese nationals, it was only natural that they would continue to have suffrage rights.

This position, however, was immediately greeted with extensive criticism from members of the Imperial Diet, particularly Representative Kiyose Ichirō, who was regarded as an expert on matters of voting and election. This reputedly liberal lawyer, who later represented Tōjō Hideki during the Tokyo Tribunal, circulated a memorandum in both the diet and the cabinet, in which he argued that the signing of the Instrument of Surrender had already terminated the Japanese nationality of the Koreans and Taiwanese in Japan, and, by extension, their suffrage rights as well. Quite palpable in the Kiyose memo is the apprehension that, if their rights were retained, Japan would have to deal with two million voters of Korean and Taiwanese extract, and in the next election, the cry for the abolition of emperor system would probably come from candidates who had Japanese nationality and *naichi*

82 Mizuno, "Sanseiken 'Teishi'," pp. 45–6.
83 Koseki, "Teikoku Shinmin," p. 38.

addresses.[84] Kiyose's call for disenfranchisement, in other words, derived from the political need to protect the emperor and other domestic security reasons. Legally, though, his argument was built on the same ground as the Interior Ministry's position, namely, that voting rights are predicated on nationality status. The only difference was that, for Kiyose, the ex-colonial subjects' nationality had already been terminated by the act of surrender, whereas, for the cabinet, such a definitive change had not taken place yet.[85]

This bureaucratic impasse was breached by the intervention of the elite Cabinet Legislation Bureau. Satō Tatsuo, its Deputy Chief who would play a pivotal role during the constitution drafting process a few months later, seems to have come up with a compromise solution, which became official with the cabinet endorsement on 13 November. The result was that Koreans and other minority groups of colonial origin would formally retain Japanese nationality and thus have voting rights (as the Interior Ministry had assumed), but, since their status change would be all but inevitable after the conclusion of a future peace treaty, their rights would be suspended for now so as to prevent them in reality from participating in the upcoming election (as Kiyose had argued).[86] The government thereby preserved the legal formality of retaining jurisdiction over former colonial subjects, while making sure to bar them from participating in the upcoming general election.

The final text of the provision in the new election law's supplementary rule thus stated: "The rights to vote and to run for office of those who are not subject to the Household Registration Law shall be suspended for the time being."[87] Notice that the law does not explicitly refer to Koreans or Taiwanese. Instead, it invokes the yardstick of whether or not a person is subject to the Household Registration Law, the legal basis for household registries in the *naichi* which was not in force in *gaichi* colonies during the prewar period. Not being subject to that law meant that one was not listed in a *naichi* registry. So, according to the revised law, if one was not listed in a *naichi* registry, one could not vote or run for office, even if one lived in the *naichi*. It will be recalled that under the prewar household registration system, while colonial subjects were allowed to relocate and reside in the *naichi* legally, they were

84 Mizuno, "Sanseiken 'Teishi'," pp. 48–9; Gotō Mitsuo, "Nihonkoku Kenpō Seiteishi ni okeru 'Nihonkokumin' to 'Gaikokujin'" ['Japanese National' and 'Foreigner' in the Making of the Japanese Constitution], *Hikaku Hōgaku*, vol. 45, no. 3 (2012), p. 15.

85 Matsuda Toshihiko, *Senzenki no Zainichi Chōsenjin to Sanseiken* [Resident Koreans and Voting Rights in Prewar Japan] (Tokyo: Akashi Shoten, 1995), pp. 120–4.

86 Mizuno, "Sanseiken 'Teishi'," pp. 50–5.

87 This supplemental rule was carried over and inscribed in the 1950 Public Officials Election Law, which is still in force today. Koseki, "Teikoku Shinmin," p. 41.

still listed under their *gaichi* registries created and maintained according to separate colonial ordinances. By relying on this *naichi/gaichi* differentiation inherent in the colonial household registration system, the postwar Japanese government was able to ensure that ex-colonial subjects would not be allowed to vote or run for public office. In doing so, they appeared to be merely preserving and extending one of the fundamental principles of the prewar system of delineating the human boundaries of Japan. The only irony may have been that the same system that undergirded the emperor system and the "family state" ideology was now being called upon to prepare for the first "democratic" election of the postwar era.

As consistent and natural as it may seem, however, this use of the household registry was quite innovative and abrupt, concealing a legal transformation far more profound than meets the eye. For it brought about a fundamental change in the organizational principles that had underwritten the electoral system up to that point. In brief, the election laws of Japan during the prewar period had *not* been based on the household registration system. Rather, they were predicated on a kind of territoriality principle whereby suffrage rights were given to imperial subjects residing in a territory where the election law was in effect. Not a question of voting rights, strictly speaking, the only legal ground for Korean colonial subjects' ineligibility to vote was simply the fact that the House of Representatives Election Law was not in effect in the *gaichi* territories.[88] This can be clearly seen by the fact that if one resided in an overseas territory, it did not matter whether one was registered under the *naichi* or *gaichi* household registry – no one residing in the colonies, not even Japanese colonial settlers, could vote. Conversely, if one resided in the *naichi*, where the Election Law was in force, all subjects of the emperor – including those listed under *gaichi* registry – were allowed to vote. This was so even before 1925, when universal male suffrage was first introduced with the removal of property qualification proviso.[89]

In 1920, the Interior Ministry issued an official notice to its regional offices which clarified that imperial subjects from Korea residing in the *naichi* had the right to vote. This was a correction of its earlier position, which had mistakenly

[88] Oguma, *'Nihonjin' no Kyōkai*, p. 369.

[89] The 1925 election law was no doubt a historic development, which resulted in the enfranchisement of nearly 12,000 colonial subjects from Korea for the general election of 1928. See Edward G. Griffin, "The Universal Suffrage Issue in Japanese Politics, 1918–25," *The Journal of Asian Studies*, vol. 31, no. 2 (1972). It is important to note, however, that the new election law simply provided that "male imperial subjects over twenty-five years of age shall have the right to vote," without any mention of subjects of colonial extract. The sudden increase in Korean participation was not because the law suddenly recognized colonial subjects' right to vote, but because it removed the property requirement, which most Koreans had been unable to meet.

linked the right to vote to the duty of compulsory military service.[90] It thereby made plain that conscription and suffrage were two distinct issues governed by different principles under Japanese imperial law. Conscription was a matter of personality principle, which meant that those listed in the *naichi* registry were subject to compulsory military service even if they resided in a *gaichi* territory. Their place of residence was irrelevant. By contrast, suffrage was governed by territoriality, which meant that all imperial subjects physically residing in the *naichi* were allowed to vote, whereas no imperial subjects living in the *gaichi* were. Their registry, or "subnationality," was irrelevant; "registration law has nothing to do with the election law" according to the Cabinet Legislation Bureau in 1921.[91] This was the reason behind the Interior Ministry's revised instruction that the suffrage rights of Korean subjects in the *naichi* were independent of their personal standing vis-à-vis conscription. As long as they could meet the strict property qualification, they should be allowed to vote. Indeed, in the general election of 1920, Koreans were reported to have voted albeit in extremely small numbers. That number would surge in the 1928 general election under the revised Election Law of 1925, which eliminated property qualifications.[92]

In sum, under the prewar legal system, the Household Registration Law was essentially irrelevant to the question of suffrage rights. It is against this prewar grain of thought that the postwar revision of the election law, and especially the abrupt manner in which it was done in late 1945, comes across as deeply transformative, even revolutionary. For, by using the household registration system to disenfranchise former colonial subjects, it was introducing a kind of personality principle hitherto unknown in election laws. It was, in effect, subverting the organizational principle, or the conceptual architectonics, on which the Japanese electoral system up until that time had been built.[93] This

90 Matsuda, *Senzenki no zainichi*, pp. 19–22.

91 Matsuda, *Senzenki no zainichi*, pp. 22–3.

92 The surge would have been even greater had it not been for the requirement contained in the new law that a voter should have been residing at his current address for at least one year. This residency requirement was introduced specifically to exclude the Korean laborers who did not have stable residential addresses. The lawmakers apparently felt that the original draft bill, which had required continued residence for a six-month period, would not be effective in excluding the Koreans and thus raised it to one year. This explains why, compared to the Japanese population of whom 20% had voting rights, only 9% of Koreans were able to participate in the general election of 1928, the first one held under the revised election law. Matsuda, *Senzenki no zainichi*, pp. 39–40.

93 It is thus ironic that, in the postwar context, differentiation along the *naichi/gaichi* fault line, which had been eliminated (at least on the surface) even from the conscription law would be invited back in to transform the election law, which during the prewar era had actually been premised on a more inclusive principle.

may have been yet another reason why the Interior Ministry had initially advocated not disenfranchising former colonial subjects.

In all, suspending the suffrage rights of former colonial subjects through this innovative use of the household registry system had the effect of excising them from the boundary of the new Japanese constituent peoplehood. For the revision of the Election Law in 1945 had been done in preparation for the April 1946 election for the last Imperial Diet, which was expected to draft and ratify a new constitution. This background explains the haste with which the Japanese government decided to revise the election law before any prompting or intervention from GHQ/SCAP, as well as the near unanimity with which the Imperial Diet endorsed the disenfranchisement of the resident Koreans and Taiwanese. The revision of the election law was, in effect, intended to predetermine who was and was not to be included in the new "sovereign" peoplehood of Japan, in whose name the postwar constitution would be drafted and promulgated.

Negotiating the People and Its Boundary through the Constitution

When the GHQ's draft constitution was first translated by the Foreign Ministry into Japanese for the cabinet's review in February 1946, the term "people" in the English original had been rendered *jinmin*. The holder of sovereignty, as well as the bearer of various rights guaranteed by the new constitution, was uniformly referred to as *jinmin* throughout the translation. Interestingly, this word had a relatively more progressive connotation in the postwar Japanese lexicon, because it was the term heavily and favorably used by the socialists and communists of the time. That is not to say that the translators at the Foreign Ministry were leftists. Rather, they probably chose that word because it seemed more appropriate to convey the ideals of democracy being espoused by the Americans.[94] According to Miyazawa Toshiyoshi, the association of *jinmin* with Marxism or socialism was more a postwar phenomenon; during the prewar era, the word had been more commonly used in contradistinction to "official" or "bureaucrat" to mean "civilian."[95] The choice may thus have better cohered with their sense of the need to reduce the power of the imperial government by drafting a new democratic constitution based on the principle of popular sovereignty. In the final Japanese version of the constitution, however, all references to "people" were changed from *jinmin* to the more state-centric term, *kokumin*.

94 Inoue, *MacArthur's Japanese Constitution*, p. 189.
95 Miyazawa Toshiyoshi, *Kenpō Kōwa*, p. 108.

Evidently, this term was much more agreeable to the conservative leaders of the Japanese government and the diet, who were apprehensive about the considerable surge of leftist and/or anti-emperor groups in postwar Japan. For them, *jinmin* conveyed a sense of the people resisting authority, whereas *kokumin* had a less adversarial connotation of the people being harmoniously merged with the state. With the "people" thus rendered as *kokumin*, the new idea of popular sovereignty as the foundation of the new constitution could be tamed and introduced as something less than revolutionary. It did not mean stripping powers from the emperor, because the "people," or *kokumin*, according to Minister Kanamori, was a flexible term which could even encompass the emperor as well. In fact, this was the word chosen by Emperor Hirohito himself in his "Humanity Declaration" of 1 January 1946, which declared that the bond between his "people" (*kokumin*) and himself was not grounded in any false conception that the emperor was divine. Conspicuously missing from that document was any mention of the term "subject," or *shinmin*, which had been the official label for the Japanese people until the end of the war.[96] Only eight months earlier, for example, when voting rights were granted to the residents of Korea and Taiwan, they had been referred to as *shinmin* in the imperial rescript of 1 April 1945. More recently, in the famous rescript announcing the "termination of war," too, the emperor had commanded his *shinmin* to endure the unendurable and to follow him in building a peaceful state. By using a new term only four months later to address his subjects, the emperor seemed to be signaling that his people would henceforth be called *kokumin*. Before the "sovereign people" could have a chance to pick a designation for themselves, the emperor was apparently exercising for one last time his patriarchal prerogative of naming the members of his extended family.

Perhaps cognizant of this imperial choice of words, Satō Tatsuo of the Cabinet Legislation Bureau, who was the single most important legal expert on the Japanese side during the actual drafting process, insisted that the term for "people" in the Japanese version of the constitution be changed to *kokumin*.[97] All references to *jinmin* were struck from the new constitution. Similarly, all mention of the term "subject," or *shinmin*, were deleted. The article on nationality in the Imperial Constitution had stated: "The conditions necessary for being a Japanese *shinmin* shall be determined by law." The new constitution contained an almost identical provision (Article 10), except that the term

96 Interestingly, all the ministers who countersigned the Humanity Declaration continued to refer to themselves as *daijin*, which literally means "great subject." The term is still in use today as the official name for the various cabinet ministers.

97 Koseki, *Tanjō*, p. 184.

shinmin was now replaced with *kokumin*. Instead of being the subjects of the emperor, the members of the new Japan would simply be called Japanese "people." In that regard, this article might be understood to signal an intention to move away from the imperial past. At the same time, the word *kokumin* itself was not entirely new either; it too had an imperial past. Particularly sinister was the fact that the term had been used by the fanatic militarists during the last years of the war to mobilize the entire nation to sacrifice themselves for the emperor. Indeed, conservatives who had been inured to the more imperial connotations of the word had trouble grasping the idea of *kokumin* as a constituent agent.[98] For them, it probably smacked of a contradiction to say that those whose defining feature was merely to sacrifice and die for the emperor were now claiming to actively establish the state by ordaining a new constitution. In the end, choosing *kokumin*, with all its checkered history, to refer to the members of the new Japan proved to be an ingenious move, for it provided the flexibility and ambiguity needed to accept the new way of relating to one another politically while preserving a sense of continuity.[99]

Using *kokumin* as the translation for the "people" would also have far-reaching ramifications for the way in which boundaries of membership were redrawn, as well as for the members' mode of relating to non-members. This was largely due to a certain ambiguity and inconsistency that was introduced in the new constitution. Coupled with the urgent task imposed on the Japanese government of dismembering the empire, this opened the way for understanding the new constitution in a very exclusivist and even discriminatory manner. That the holder of sovereignty is referred to in Japanese as *kokumin* seems innocuous enough. Yet, with the substitution of *jinmin* with *kokumin* for all reference to the "people," even universal rights ascribable to humanity in general were now provided for in the constitution as belonging only to members of the Japanese state. For example, the title of the entire chapter on rights and duties indicates that the constitution's rights provisions apply only to *kokumin*. The article proclaiming the principle of non-derogation of "fundamental human rights" also describes those rights as belonging to Japanese *kokumin*.[100] This is more than a bit ironic for a constitution whose defining characteristic is often portrayed to be its protection of universal human rights.[101] Article 97 actually

98 For example, Matsumoto Jōji is reported to have expressed displeasure with the very concept of "the Japanese people." Koseki, *Tanjō*, p. 187.

99 Inoue, *MacArthur's Japanese Constitution*, p. 189.

100 Article 11: "The people [*kokumin*] shall not be prevented from enjoying any of the fundamental human rights."

101 John Maki, for example, cites pacifism, popular sovereignty, and fundamental human rights as the three foundations of Japan's postwar constitution. Maki, "The Constitution of Japan," p. 39.

states that these fundamental human rights "are fruits of the age-old struggle of man to be free" and its Preamble also declares that the principle of popular sovereignty is "a universal principle of mankind."[102] The individual articles on specific human rights, however, proclaim Japanese *kokumin* to be their bearer and beneficiary. When read literally, therefore, the constitution seemed to sanction the exclusion of non-Japanese from rights protection.

To be sure, there is broad consensus today that, despite their wording, rights provisions that have *kokumin* as their subject should also apply to foreigners to the extent possible. Both case law and constitutional scholarly opinion support this view.[103] Further, there are some provisions in the constitution that specifically refer to "all persons" (*nanbito mo*), rather than *kokumin*. It might be inferred from this that the drafters intended to make a distinction between rights provisions applicable to all humankind and those intended for Japanese nationals only. Nevertheless, the text of the constitution does not bear this out. The distinction between articles for rights held by "all persons" and those held by *kokumin* does not seem to correspond to the distinction between universal human rights and the rights of Japanese nationals.[104]

More important than this textual inconsistency is the fact that, at the time of its drafting, there seems to have been a not-so-hidden contest between the members of the GHQ Government Section and the Japanese government regarding the scope of rights protection. In other words, even though later interpreters have attempted to construe the constitution in a more inclusive manner, Japanese participants in the drafting process appear to have made a concerted, if understated, effort to make sure that the protection afforded by the new constitution did not extend to non-Japanese.[105] This can be seen most clearly in the way that the provision on equal protection of the law was negotiated between the Americans and the Japanese. Especially, who would be entitled to the equal protection of law appears to have been a deeply contested issue.

[102] In Japanese "man" and "mankind" are both rendered *jinrui*, a term that refers to the entirety of humankind.

[103] See, e.g., Higuchi, *Kenpō*, pp. 184–6.

[104] For example, Article 22 on the freedom to choose and change one's residence and to choose one's occupation is written as belonging to "all persons," but it is universally recognized that foreigners are subject to much heavier restriction than Japanese nationals are. Similarly, the freedom to move to a foreign country and to divest one's nationality, provided in the same article, is obviously intended only for Japanese nationals. By contrast, Article 30 on the duty to pay taxes refers to *kokumin*, but this has never been taken to mean that foreigners in Japan are exempt from the duty to pay taxes.

[105] Hamano, "Japanese Constitution and Human Rights," pp. 435–8.

The final version of Article 14, Section 1 of the new constitution, proclaiming the equal protection of law, reads in full: "All of the people are equal under the law and there shall be no discrimination in political, economic or social relations because of race, creed, sex, social status or family origin." In the original GHQ draft, the article on equal protection stated, "All *natural persons* are equal before the law," and made it clear that there shall be no discrimination on account of "caste or national origin."[106] It even had a separate article proclaiming that "[a]liens shall be entitled to the equal protection of law."[107] During the process of initial translation, the Japanese government had the first sentence changed to "All of the *people* are equal under the law" and dropped "caste or national origin" as impermissible bases of discrimination, replacing them with "family origin." Needless to say, the Japanese term for "people" here was *kokumin*. The separate article guaranteeing equal protection to aliens was changed to: "Foreign national shall possess the right of equal protection under the law."

During the negotiation at the famous all-night marathon conference on 4–5 March 1946, this separate article on foreign nationals' right to equal protection was struck out for reasons of redundancy. It was argued by the Japanese side, more specifically Satō Tatsuo, that foreigners are included in "all of the people" who are guaranteed equal rights, and therefore a separate provision was unnecessary. This was accepted by the Americans. Yet, for the main article on equal protection, the Government Section insisted that the original language, "all natural persons" and "caste or national origin," both be put back in. In fact, the article was made even stronger and clearer by inserting that all natural persons, "whether Japanese citizen or not," shall be entitled to equal protection.[108] Evidently, this was to compensate for the deletion of the separate article on foreigners. This was agreed to by the Japanese side. Thus, the Japanese government draft, as it stood on the eve of its first public unveiling, contained an unmistakable pronouncement that nationality or citizenship was irrelevant for purposes of equal protection.

Even after this agreement, however, the Japanese government did not relent and made another, last minute effort to change it before presenting the draft constitution to the Imperial Diet on 6 March. The Japanese proposal, apparently initiated by Satō and conveyed through a nighttime telephone call by Shirasu Jirō, was to have the article on equal protection start with "[a]ll of

[106] Article 13 of GHQ draft (emphasis added).

[107] Article 16 of GHQ draft. In this regard, the GHQ draft was innovative and progressive. Except for Portugal (1933), Czechoslovakia (1922), and Italy (1848), virtually all constitutions in Europe up to this time reserved the equal protection of law to citizens or subjects.

[108] Koseki, *Tanjō*, p. 182.

the people" and to replace "caste or national origin" with "family origin."[109] For reasons not fully explained, this was quickly accepted by GHQ, and the final draft no longer spoke of "[a]ll natural persons whether Japanese citizen or not." Similarly, it included no mention of "caste or national origin," but instead spoke only of "family origin." According to Satō's retrospective, "the idea of treating foreigners as equal was bad enough in itself, but having to include Article 16 in the Japanese draft was particularly objectionable."[110] In all, the final result of his successful objection and GHQ's inexplicable capitulation was a return to the Japanese government's initial translation in which equal protection was provided to the *kokumin* only with no ban on discrimination based on "national origin." Moreover, as the separate article on aliens' equal rights was never restored, all traces of the original expansive notion of equal protection had been expunged from the final draft.[111]

Subsequently, this provision of pointedly reduced scope was ratified by the diet without any debate as to whether aliens were entitled to equal protection. The issue, instead, that attracted the most attention in relation to the equality provision was whether the article also applied to the emperor. After all, the government had insisted all along that the emperor was included in the term "people." As many diet members pointed out, however, the constitution itself was treating the emperor differently by making him the symbol of the state and of the people's unity. The government was already conceding that certain provisions such as the right to vote and to hold public office did not apply to the emperor and the imperial family members. Some lawmakers queried whether the equality clause mandated the revision of the Imperial Household Law so as to make female descendants eligible for the throne.[112] In marked contrast, the issue that sparked one of the most concerted efforts at modification on the Japanese side during the behind-the-scenes negotiation was not even entertained by the diet members, and the question of whether non-nationals were covered by the article on equal protection was not addressed at all throughout the entire deliberation. Perhaps this was because most assumed that "all of the people" in Article 14 included foreigners, as Satō had argued during the all-night conference in March. It is more likely, however, that everyone took it for granted that the equal protection clause, as well as the entire chapter on

[109] Koseki, *Tanjō*, p. 196.
[110] Takemae, *Allied Occupation*, p. 437.
[111] Koseki, *Tanjō*, p. 182; RM227. Discussion of equal protection clause (6 Mar. 1946) Satō Tatsuo.
[112] In response, Prime Minister Yoshida stated that the government did not consider the equality provision to be applicable to matters of imperial succession and was "not considering the question of a female sovereign." RM370. House of Representatives: plenary (23 July 1946). RM370. ANSWER.P4.1.

rights and duties, applied only to people with Japanese nationality – that is, *kokumin*.

This was due to the fact that the same word, *kokumin*, was used to translate both "people" and "national" in different parts of the constitution. During the marathon negotiation in March, members of the Government Section of GHQ had questioned the propriety of using *kokumin* to translate "people" in the context of rights provisions. The Japanese delegation repeatedly assured them that the Japanese word had exactly the same meaning as the English term. When Article 10 on nationality requirements was later inserted during diet deliberations, however, the American monitors had no reason to suspect that what was being translated into English as "national" would be the same word translated as "people" in the article on equal rights.[113] The result was that all the constitutional provisions designed to protect the rights of the "people" (*kokumin*) could plausibly be interpreted in Japanese as applying only to Japanese "nationals" (*kokumin*). The constitutional prohibition against discrimination was only applicable to holders of Japanese nationality, for example, because according to the language of Article 14, "all of the *kokumin*" were equal under the law. That is why the diet interpellations focused on groups like the emperor, peerage, or even the untouchables (*burakumin*), for whom there was no dispute on their Japanese nationality. The only concern was that they had traditionally been the subjects of special treatment and/or discrimination. In other words, it could be argued that non-Japanese were not the intended beneficiaries of equal rights protection.

It is unclear whether this was an intentional terminological legerdemain by the Japanese drafters of the new constitution.[114] The last minute concession on the part of the Americans is certainly quite inexplicable. Well-informed about the discriminatory practices against minority groups in prewar Japan, the Civil Rights Subcommittee members of the Government Section had originally been very insistent on guaranteeing the equal rights of foreigners in Japan.[115] What prompted them that night to agree to the shrinking of the scope of equal protection remains a mystery.[116] More understandable is the Japanese government's insistence on excluding foreigners from the purview of equal rights protection. Unlike the Americans, who

[113] Koseki, *Tanjō*, p. 278.

[114] John Dower holds that it was clearly a "linguistic subterfuge" on the Japanese side. Dower, *Embracing Defeat*, p. 394.

[115] Takemae, *Allied Occupation*, pp. 435–7.

[116] One contemporary record by a Japanese participant actually indicates that the "change was made by our side without obtaining the understanding of the Americans." RM278. Fourth Conference on March 6 Draft (15 Apr. 1946) CLO: Katō's notes.

were probably concerned about the status of foreigners like themselves once the occupation came to an end, the Japanese were more worried about a different group of "foreigners," that is, former colonial subjects.[117] When it came to the rights of non-nationals, that is to say, the two sides may have had quite different referents in mind. The Americans, as victors, would have been easily persuaded that their rights would not be disrespected even in the absence of an express provision in the constitution. This probably explains their acceptance of the late night proposal from the Japanese side. By contrast, for the Japanese, there was an urgent need to excise the former colonial subjects from their peoplehood, making sure that they did not become a domestic political pestilence in the postwar era. For the conservative leaders of the Japanese government, it was inconceivable that Koreans and Taiwanese would be included in the *kokumin* to whom Hirohito had addressed his Humanity Declaration. Further, if these undesirable "third country nationals" were to be the primary reference group for "foreigners," it certainly would not do to grant them a constitutional status equal to the *kokumin*. Once coerced to become members of the emperor's *shinmin*, they would now be legally and abruptly expelled from within the boundary of the new democratic Japan's *kokumin*.

Post-Constitutional Settlement of the Human Boundary

The new constitution seemed to deny equal protection rights for non-nationals, but it still remained unclear who exactly was inside and who outside the human boundary of the Japanese people. Through the revision of election laws, the former colonial subjects had *de facto* been cut out from the boundary of the constituent people and had not been allowed to participate in the general election that formed the Imperial Diet, which in turn adopted the new constitution. Yet, this had been done by "suspending" their voting rights "for the time being." Still lacking was a permanent and definitive answer to the question of who belonged to the people of Japan. Officially, the position of the government was that such an answer would be given by the peace treaty to be signed with the Allied Powers. In reality, however, the government would not wait. It took unilateral measures which ensured that all former colonial subjects, including those residing in the *naichi*, would be permanently excised from the human boundary of the new Japan.

[117] "Sato almost certainly had in mind Koreans and Formosan residents, whose legal status had become ambiguous since the liberation of their homelands from Japanese rule." Takemae, *Allied Occupation*, p. 437.

The first of such measures came with the Ordinance on Alien Registration of 2 May 1947. This immigration control regulation, which required all aliens in Japan to register with the authorities, included a provision stipulating that former colonial subjects shall be "regarded as aliens for the time being." For this purpose, the law actually created a new registry for "third country nationals" (i.e., Koreans and Taiwanese). They had to be so treated because they were neither Allied nor Japanese nationals. It further provided that violation of this ordinance would be punishable by forced deportation, even for holders of *de jure* Japanese nationality. In other words, all former colonial subjects were now deprived of their rights as Japanese nationals, not just in relation to elections but across the board. To be noted here is the timing of this ordinance. As the very last "imperial ordinance" issued under the prewar system, it was promulgated on 2 May 1947, the day before the new constitution went into effect.[118] This had the effect of ensuring that the constituent "We, the Japanese People," in whose name the new constitution was adopted, did not include any resident Koreans or Taiwanese, even though, technically, their nationality remained Japanese.

Also noteworthy in this context is the legal device by which this task of exclusion was done. Perhaps to be expected, the ordinance relied on the familiar logic of differentiation embedded in the household registration system.[119] Similar to the new election law, it redrew the boundary of Japanese peoplehood by declaring that "those not subject to the Household Registration Law" shall be regarded as aliens. Anyone not listed in the *naichi* registry would henceforth be regarded as a foreigner. Put differently, those with *gaichi* registry status, or colonial subnationality, would fall "outside the nation" (*kokumin no soto*) as the 1871 Meiji decree establishing the household registry had it. The last of the prewar ordinances issued in the emperor's name would invoke the yardstick of household registry one last time to make a proclamation that *gaichi* registries, which had been transformed to replicate those of the *naichi*, were not really Japanese registries, and those listed therein were not his subjects. Needless to say, this was a sharp turnaround from the final days of the empire when the entire policy and rhetoric of government had been geared toward obliterating the *naichi/gaichi* distinction. A few wartime leaders had even gone on record as promoting intermarriage among *naichi* subjects of the emperor and those from the colonies. Also advocated by some was the elimination of the ban on inter-domain movement of household registration.[120]

[118] Takemae, *Allied Occupation*, p. 450; Koseki, *Tanjō*, p. 196.
[119] Chung, *Immigration and Citizenship in Japan*, p. 76.
[120] Oguma, *'Nihonjin' no Kyōkai*, pp. 445–6.

This would have allowed for not only genuine freedom of movement, but also the possibility of colonial subjects truly "becoming" a *naichijin* at least in theory. Overnight, as it were, these people went from being the target of coercive assimilation to being the object of unilateral expulsion and excision from peoplehood.

The issuance of this ordinance one day prior to the new constitution's effectuation may suggest that the terminological legerdemain involved in using *kokumin* for both "national" and "people" may not have been wholly fortuitous or innocuous. This suggestion is supported by the fact that Article 10 on nationality requirements was originally not in the draft that was so painfully negotiated over by both sides in early March. It was introduced later in July 1946, as an amendment to the bill for the new constitution during diet deliberations. Officially, it was jointly presented by three conservative parties and agreed to by the Socialist Party without much debate. The real author of the amendment, however, appears to have been the Cabinet Legislation Bureau, which had been instrumental in removing the equal protection clause for foreigners.[121] Recall that it was the same agency that had suggested, apparently under Satō's leadership, the solution of "suspending" the voting rights of former colonial subjects in the course of preemptively revising the election law in late 1945.

To be sure, the proposition that this was all a carefully orchestrated plan on the part of the Japanese government may seem rather farfetched. It is, however, quite consistent with the overall approach of denying nationality status in relation to rights and privileges, while recognizing it for matters relating to duties and security issues. More important is the fact that, in tandem with the constitutional provisions that excluded non-nationals from equal rights protection, the Ordinance on Alien Registration had the effect of making sure that former colonial subjects would continue to be consigned to the status of *de facto* second-class citizenship even in the new democratic Japan. In the postwar period, pervasive discrimination would be justified against longtime Korean residents of Japan through the operation of precisely these legal technicalities.

It should be noted, however, that this ordinance was still premised on the position that the final solution to ex-colonial subjects' nationality should await the conclusion of the peace treaty. It therefore provided that those not listed in the *naichi* registry would be treated as aliens "for the time being." It was technically a temporary measure, although, for all practical intents and purposes, it meant that these people would be forever shut out from the purview

[121] Koseki, *Tanjō*, pp. 277–9.

of Japan's new constitution. When the government proceeded to revise the Nationality Law in 1950 to carry out the mandate of the constitution to define the "requirements of being a Japanese *kokumin*" (Article 10), it did not even bother to deal with the former colonial subjects. Since the new constitution was already understood to be a constitution of, by, and for the people of the *naichi*, it was perhaps a matter of course that its implementation would exclusively focus on the nationality issues of *naichijin*.[122] It was plain to everyone that those registered as aliens were not Japanese nationals – even if their nationality was still legally Japanese. As such, the new Nationality Law did not introduce much new standards for acquiring or losing Japanese nationality. Although acquisition and relinquishment of nationality were made to be more a matter of individual choice than a "family" affair, in its fundamentals, it merely reconfirmed the prewar system of granting Japanese nationality on the basis of *jus sanguinis* principle.[123]

In the event, the Japanese government did not await the signing of the peace treaty with the Allied Powers to reach a permanent resolution. The new and definitive answer to the question of who belongs to the Japanese people would be given unilaterally in a directive issued by the government to regulate the administration of household registries once the peace treaty was concluded. The Justice Ministry's Circular No. 438 ("Concerning Nationality and Family Registration of Koreans, Taiwanese and Other Alien Residents after the Peace Treaty") issued to its regional offices announced the uniform and permanent loss of Japanese nationality for Koreans and Taiwanese, even if they resided in the *naichi* more or less permanently. Just as the Ordinance on Alien Registration had been issued on the eve of the new constitution's effectuation, this circular came out on 19 April 1952 – just before Japan became a sovereign state again, a mere nine days prior to the effectuation of the San Francisco Peace Treaty.[124] If the ordinance had been a tentative clarification of Japan's human boundary for purposes of launching a new constitution, the

[122] Besides, the prewar Nationality Law had never applied to colonial subjects of Korean extract in the first place. In contrast to Taiwan, where the colonial authorities pronounced the implementation of the Nationality Law as soon as it was enacted, the government-general in colonial Korea deliberately chose not to make it applicable to Koreans. See Endō, *Kokuseki to Koseki*, pp. 55–8. Given that the primary source of concern in the postwar context was the Koreans in *naichi* Japan, it may have seemed inconsistent with previous practices to insert provisions about such persons in the new Nationality Law.

[123] Kashiwazaki, *Nationality and Citizenship in Japan*, pp. 168–70. For the basic architectonic and the historical development of Japan's Nationality Law, see Hosokawa Kiyoshi, "Japanese Nationality in International Perspective," in Swan Sik Ko (ed.), *Nationality and International Law in Asian Perspective* (Dordrecht: Martinus Nijhoff Publishers, 1990).

[124] Takemae, *Allied Occupation*, p. 511.

circular was its permanent settlement for purposes of rejoining the international community. As has been noted by many, the irony was that just before the peace treaty with the Allied Powers went into effect, Japan acted against the expectation of the international community by unilaterally revoking the nationality of its former colonial subjects. It even made sure that they would not qualify for the special procedure for naturalization available for persons who had once held Japanese nationality (Circular No. 438, Article 1, Item 5).

Initially, the Japanese government seemed to have shared with the occupation authorities the view that when the time came former colonial subjects would be given the option of choosing whether or not to remain as Japanese nationals. After all, this had been the recommendation of GHQ/SCAP, as well as the emerging norm in the international community. In late 1945, during deliberations on the revised election law, one member of the diet asked about the exact meaning of "suspension" of voting rights. Interior Minister Horikiri Zenjirō answered that, after a peace treaty, "suffrage right could be restored to resident Koreans and Taiwanese in Japan once they choose to adopt Japanese nationality."[125] This assumption that some form of choice would be given continued to be taken for granted right until the negotiations for the San Francisco Peace Treaty began in earnest. During the negotiations, however, the Japanese government quickly learned that the United States did not have much interest or stake in how the nationality issue of former colonial subjects should be resolved. Besides, the Americans seemed to consider matters of nationality inappropriate for inclusion in an international peace treaty. The Japanese government thereupon seized the opportunity and issued a separate regulation that unilaterally and summarily stripped the former colonial subjects of their Japanese nationality.[126] The so-called temporary suspension of rights and the temporary treatment as aliens had become permanent. They were now *de jure* foreigners as well, subject to the authority of the newly created immigration control system and with unclear rights to equal protection of the law. For Koreans, this also meant that they were *de facto* stateless people because the two governments recently established in the Korean Peninsula at the time were engaged in an internecine war, both too busy to claim them as their nationals.

Relying on the household registration system in this process was certainly an innovative use of the past. As an institution that had integrated the people of the empire while simultaneously differentiating them, it now marked the outer boundaries of the Japanese people in the new era by excluding those it

125 Gotō, "'Nihonkokumin' to 'Gaikokujin'," p. 13.

126 Kashiwazaki, *Nationality and Citizenship in Japan*, pp. 174–5.

had attempted to assimilate and by confirming that only those in the *naichi* registries shall become "We, the Japanese People." Incidentally, using the household registry as the basis of the identity of the people of new Japan meant that not a few Japanese, mostly women, who were registered in Korean or Taiwanese registries due to marriage would also lose their nationality.[127] Moreover, since the imperial family had never been subject to the registration law, this also meant that they would not be eligible to vote or hold electoral office. Despite Kanamori's insistence that the "people" of the new constitution included both the emperor and his subjects, the emperor evidently still stands apart from his people.

Koseki Shōichi describes the process of elimination of equal protection for foreigners as one of the key examples of how the Japanese government succeeded in "Japanizing" the draft constitution originally formulated by the GHQ.[128] Indeed, the whole process of excising the former colonial subjects, particularly the resident Koreans, appears to have taken place at the initiative of the Japanese and without much involvement by the occupation authorities. The "suspension" of their voting rights was part of the electoral reform that was carried out entirely without GHQ/SCAP guidance. The exclusion of equal rights protection for foreigners and the insertion of the article on nationality seem to have taken place behind the Americans' back by evasion and even outright deception. Similarly, the stripping of nationality through the Circular No. 438 apparently was done outside Washington's scope of interest. In that sense, these developments suggest Japan's active role, or agency, in determining the boundaries of its own peoplehood. Yet, ironically, in light of the larger Allied mandate to dismember the Japanese empire and to repatriate its former colonial subjects, these steps to exclude and eject them may be seen more as faithful implementation by Japan of the directive given by external forces. For they were done in strict conformity to the Allied Powers' wartime decisions and the subsequent occupation policy of dismembering the empire. After all was said and done, it was part of "embracing defeat."

DIVIDING THE KOREAN PENINSULA

In terms of international law, immediate postcolonial Korea may have been a "no man's land."[129] Historically, though, the initial problem was that Korea was

[127] Circular No. 438, Article 1, Items 2 and 3. By the same logic, if a person from Korea or Taiwan had for some reason been entered into a *naichi* registry, that person was now fully a Japanese national. Despite the principle of *jus sanguinis* for determining nationality, blood seems to have been less than determinative in this instance.

[128] Koseki, *Tanjō*, pp. 195–6. Chapter 7 of the book is titled "Struggles toward Japanization."

[129] Fraenkel, "The Structure of United States Army Military Government in Korea," p. 69.

too many peoples' land. Up to a million Japanese civilians and soldiers were on the Korean soil; two million overseas Koreans of varied sorts were crowding back into the peninsula. Further complicating the situation was the division of Korea along the 38th parallel by the U.S. and Soviet occupying forces. These unanticipated turns of event triggered a massive migration of refugees fleeing the emerging communist regime in the north. Sorting out people in postcolonial Korea was a formidable task.

Compared to Japan's postwar experience with people-making, the question in Korea was not only that of bringing a war that had just ended to a full closure. Korea's experience was perhaps more analogous to that of Germany, where territorial dismemberment (as imposed on Japan) was accompanied by a division (which did not happen in Japan). Closing the war in Europe also entailed a territorial reduction of Germany, including the historic East Prussia and Pomerania, and massive migration of more than 20 million ethnic Germans. But the subsequent division between East and West Germany was not part of a similarly backward-looking process of closing the war; it belonged more properly to the initial phase of a new global conflict that became the Cold War. In Korea, too, within a short span of time from Japan's unconditional surrender in 1945 to South Korea's constitution-making in 1948, the U.S. and the Soviet Union were ratcheting up for another war as well as clearing out the debris of the war that had just ended. The latter task involved separating Korea from Japan, both in territory and population,[130] whereas the former culminated in consolidating what initially began as an ad hoc arrangement into a semi-permanent division between North and South Korea.

The story of peoplehood in postcolonial South Korea, then, may be described as a progressive contraction of its human boundary. The dismemberment of the Japanese Empire meant that the "union of one hundred-million hearts" (*ichioku isshin*), as the Japanese wartime propaganda had it, was to be broken up, and the former imperial subjects of Korean descent, numbering thirty million out of those one hundred million, were to be separated and given independent peoplehood. Further, the subsequent consolidation of the division in effect mandated that, eventually, those Koreans residing in the southern part of the peninsula would form their own constituent peoplehood for the establishment of a separate South Korean state. Until August 1945, Koreans were *de jure* subjects of a political unit whose human boundary had been coterminous

[130] As stated in the "Basic Initial Directive" transmitted to MacArthur on 17 October 1945, the official aim of the U.S. administration of civil affairs in Korea was, among other things, "[t]o effect a complete political and administrative separation of Korea from Japan and to free Korea from Japanese social, economic and financial control." SWNCC 176/8 in *FRUS* 1945, vol. VI (1969), p. 1074.

with that of the Japanese imperial expanse. By August 1948, with the establishment of the Republic of Korea, they would become citizens of a political unit whose *de facto* human boundary corresponded to the southern half of the Korean Peninsula.

This story of progressive contraction is noteworthy for a number of reasons. Local resistance and negotiations notwithstanding, the new boundary was imposed on the Korean people externally. It was largely a product of the tumultuous geopolitics of the day, which was refracted onto the Korean soil through the often inchoate occupation policies of an emerging superpower. For sure, such an externally induced partition of territory and population is not uncommon. Postcolonial Southeast Asia and Middle East were subjected to similar treatments, where religious and ethnic rifts ran deep. But nowhere was it as unilaterally imposed and ideologically charged as in comparatively homogeneous Korea. Also to be noted is that, overriding as it was, the United States' implementation of the boundary-setting could not be completely free from the local context. When it came to defining the South Korean peoplehood, especially, a complicated negotiation was bound to take place, in which locally embedded institutional practices and legal infrastructure could not be done away with. In fact, the U.S. occupation authorities relied heavily on those legal inheritances in separating Japanese from Koreans during the early stage of occupation, and, later, in marking a legible boundary for the South Korean people. For both tasks, the household registration system of imperial Japan would prove to be most critical.

It was this conflation of the new Cold War exigencies and the Japanese colonial past that would shape the South Korean peoplehood in the course of its constitutional founding. The consequence has been the inscription of an indelible fault line into the constitutional identity of the South Korean people which persists to this day. For the *de facto* contraction of its human boundary was not given *de jure* recognition in the constitutional text itself, which refused to accept the fact of division as such. This critical disjuncture between fact and norm, or reality and aspiration, would set the tone for the later constitutional development of South Korea. But, for now, we turn to its origin to see how the seed was first sown between 1945 and 1948.

Separating Peoples by Vesting Properties

Japan's unconditional surrender had duly set off a population movement of ten million lives across different parts of the vast imperial territory. No small part of this story, the exodus of the Korean residents from the Japanese main islands, and the way it was implemented by both the GHQ/SCAP and the

Japanese government, have already been explained. The postwar migration could not be unidirectional, naturally, and equally massive was the voluntary and forced evacuation (*hikiage*) of the former Japanese colonial settlers, most notably, from China, Manchuria, and Korea.

Legally speaking, though, the Japanese repatriation was not a matter of course. The Japanese government's initial policy was to withdraw troops and government officials pursuant to the Allied policy, but not all civilians, especially the long-term colonial settlers, were to be brought back home at once. The reason for this policy was twofold. The settlers were expected to safeguard the Japanese industrial and other economic interests in the former colonies. This remarkable disregard for its own subjects' safety was based on the government's quixotic expectation that the colonial gains may be retained by "peaceful" means even after defeat. The policy was also driven by the apprehension that a sudden influx of six to seven million overseas Japanese, about ten percent of the total population, would further strain the war-torn economy and social stability of mainland Japan. Thus, for example, the Foreign Ministry even planned to instruct settlers in China to adopt local nationality in order to stave them off Japan proper on the questionable assumption that they might somehow be able to hold onto Japanese economic interests in the ex-colonies.[131]

This kind of wishful thinking was also shared by some colonial settlers, since many of them had deeper social, economic, and even cultural roots in the colonies than in mainland Japan. Especially in the southern part of Korea, where the history of Japanese settlement in some cases went back to the 1890s, long-term settlers did not want to take the defeat to mean leaving the only home that many of them had known for generations.[132] The French settlers in postcolonial Algeria, for instance, were given an option to stay. No such option would be given in Korea, however, due to strong local resentment against Japanese settlers and, more important, to the Allied occupation policies.[133] At the time of defeat, in Korea, there were nearly one million Japanese soldiers, officials, civilians, and refugees (from the invading Red Army in Manchuria). By the end of 1945, the number would shrink to less than thirty thousand.

[131] For the Foreign Ministry's policies, see Yi Yŏn-sik, *Chosŏn ŭl Ttŏnamyŏ: 1945 nyŏn P'aejŏn ŭl majŭn Ilbonindŭl ŭi Ch'oehu* [Leaving Chosŏn: The Last of the Japanese after Defeat in 1945] (Seoul: Yŏksa Pip'yŏngsa, 2012), p. 55. For the essentially same instruction (the notorious "stay put" directive) given by the Interior Ministry, see Watt, *When Empire Comes Home*, pp. 63–4.

[132] Watt, *When Empire Comes Home*, p. 42.

[133] For instance, "[o]n March 8, 1946, the Military Government in Korea indicated that all Japanese … must leave Korea as soon as possible, and on April 1, added that people who remained would be punished." Watt, *When Empire Comes Home*, p. 43.

Arguably, the Japanese indulgence over postcolonial Korea was not entirely without legal grounds as the U.S. State Department seems to have entertained similar ideas. A secret legal memorandum, dated 31 August 1945 and titled "Transfer of Title to Korea," stated that the U.S. military occupation of Korea had not automatically terminated Japan's sovereign rights over Korea. Its legal effectuation would have to await an official peace treaty in the future. In the meantime, the report recommended to have the Japanese government, or even the emperor himself, make a special proclamation to that effect. In case the Japanese side did not comply, it went on to recommend, a joint communiqué among the United States, United Kingdom, Soviet Union, and China should declare trusteeship over Korea in order to make an alternative international-legal claim as per the UN Charter.[134] Apparently, this second option was adopted at the Moscow Conference of December 1945, thereby bringing an end to the legal limbo in Korea. One might say that this legal uncertainty was reflective of the difficulty of separating Korea from Japan and even perhaps contributed to the haste with which USAMGIK pursued repatriation.[135]

Indeed, these legal inconveniences did not at all deter the occupation authorities in Korea from swiftly implementing the Allied wartime policy of reverting Japan's territory and population to those preceding the First Sino-Japanese War of 1895. This reversion was part of a larger plan in which postwar Japan was to be reduced, geopolitically speaking, to a small peace-loving democracy with limited industrial power and no military potentiality. The other side of this vision of "weak Japan" was the U.S. strategy that regarded Nationalist China as the pivotal ally in the regional governance of the postwar Far East and beyond. Certainly, the initial occupation policy of restoring status quo ante was the first step in such a direction, but it also involved more than just a banal postbellum meddling with the territory and population of a defeated nation.

Underwriting the imposed mass migration was the U.S. plan to utilize Japan's prewar industrial infrastructures in Manchuria to boost postwar China's

[134] "Transfer of Title to Korea," Discussion 2, 31 August 1945, Records of the Office of Assistant Secretary and Under Secretary of State, Dean Acheson, 1941–48, 50, RG59, Box 12, National Archives and Records Administration. For more on this document and Washington's understanding on this legal issue in general, see Nagasawa Yuko, "Ilbon P'aejŏnhu ŭi Hanbando Chanyŏjukwŏn kwa Hanil 'Pulli'" [Residual Sovereignty over the Korean Peninsula and the 'Separation' of Korea and Japan after Japan's Defeat], *Asea Yŏn'gu*, vol. 55, no. 4 (2012), pp. 60–4.

[135] Put in this context, the famous Fraenkel memo, cited previously, may have been drafted for the purpose of legally separating Korea from Japan. That is to say, his provocative claim that immediate postcolonial Korea was a "no-man's land" may have been intended to emphasize the termination of Japanese sovereignty over Korea.

economic growth and military build-up. In Korea, too, the Japanese properties were to be used to jumpstart its postcolonial economic development. In fact, the United States expected Japan's former colonies to become more prosperous than their former master.[136] Going even further than the GHQ/SCAP's initial policy of dissolving large conglomerates (*zaibatsu*), thus, Truman's Pauley Mission of November 1945 was recommending a large-scale extraction of industrial plants and other *zaibatsu* facilities within Japan proper to former colonies for war indemnities and reparations.[137] Owen Lattimore, the intellectual mastermind behind the Pauley Report, would cite Japan's long history of physical and economic abuse toward its Asian neighbors to justify such a drastic measure that went beyond mere reparations. Edwin Pauley himself stated to MacArthur that this method would propel all "Eastern Asia [toward] political stability and peaceful progress [in which Japan will] no longer [be in] a place of leadership and control."[138]

Under these draconic circumstances, retaining Japanese economic interests in the former colonies was simply out of question, and they were duly confiscated without compensation. In fact, it was for the same goal that the homebound Japanese diaspora were prohibited from taking beyond the nominal amount of 1,000 yen per person, the same amount allowed to Korean returnees from Japan.[139] The goal was that the people should be repatriated, but their movement had to be tightly insulated from that of economic goods across new borderlines. For at stake was the U.S. plan to replace Japan's "Greater East Asian Co-Prosperity Sphere" with a more horizontal constellation of power and economy under its own hegemony in the region.[140]

Against this larger background, the U.S. occupying forces were bound to reverse their initial policy of protecting private property rights of the Japanese repatriates. The very first decree issued by General MacArthur to the people of Korea on 7 September 1945, one day before the arrival of American troops on South Korean soil, had declared that "property rights shall be respected"[141] and confirmed that Japanese residents in Korea were included in that protection.

136 Michael Schaller, *The American Occupation of Japan: The Origins of the Cold War in Asia* (New York: Oxford University Press, 1987), p. 23.
137 Schaller, *American Occupation of Japan*, p. 33.
138 Schaller, *American Occupation of Japan*, p. 35.
139 Watt, *When Empire Comes Home*, p. 92.
140 John K. Emmerson, a junior diplomat dispatched to Tokyo, recalls a brief encounter with a Japanese corporate executive in October 1945, who remarked to him in front of a wartime Japanese wall map depicting the Co-Prosperity Sphere: "There it is.... We tried. See what you can do with it." At that moment, the vast scope of the occupation was first brought home to him. See Schaller, *American Occupation of Japan*, p. 22.
141 Proclamation No. 1 by General of the Army Douglas MacArthur (7 Sept. 1945), Article IV.

Even in the Ordinance No. 2 (25 September) of the USAMGIK on the prohibition of the transfer of titles, those involving Japanese-owned properties were recognized as valid if such transfers were reported to and granted permission by the occupation authorities (Section 3). All these initial policies were pursuant to the U.S. Army field manuals for military occupations and the Hague Convention of 1907. The complete reversal of this early policy came, however, with the controversial Ordinance No. 33 of 6 December 1945 ("Vesting Title to Japanese Property Within Korea"). It provided for a summary confiscation of all properties in South Korea owned or controlled "directly or indirectly, in whole or part" by the "Government of Japan, or any agency thereof, or by any of its nationals, corporations, societies, associations, or any other organization" (Section II), vesting the title to all those properties in the USAMGIK. This was followed by the administrative order of 19 December, which confiscated all agricultural lands owned by Japanese private citizens as well as government.[142] The message was clear – Japanese people had to go back, but their properties had to be left behind. The crucial question that followed was how to identify Japanese people and their properties.

In part, this task was carried out by undoing the colonial laws. Koreans who had been forced to adopt Japanese-style names were allowed to revert back to their original names. An ordinance was issued which specifically commanded the "restoration of Korean names."[143] This was especially important for Koreans who wished to avoid confiscation of their properties or being deported to Japan. In the end, however, differentiating Japanese from Koreans was done mostly by preserving a key legal infrastructure from the colonial past – that is, the household registration system. The Korean Household Registry Ordinance of 1922 was still in force under USAMGIK, and the differentiating function of the system would be picked up and carried to its extreme to completely sever Koreans from the Japanese. As explained, the prewar registration system was also used in postwar Japan for the same purpose. This time, however, it was the Japanese people who were being marked out for disadvantage and exclusion. Thus, the USAMGIK Department of Justice repeatedly made it clear in its legal opinions that "[q]uestions of nationality in the meaning of the Ordinance 33 are decided *exclusively* on the basis of the family register."[144] For those on the margins, such

142 USAMGIK Custody Order No. 3 (19 Dec. 1945).

143 USAMGIK Ordinance No. 122 (23 Oct. 1946).

144 Opinion No. 1055 in *Migunjŏnggi Chŏngbojaryojip: Sapŏppu Pŏphaesŏk Pogosŏ, 1946. 3–1948. 8* [Intelligence Materials during the U.S. Military Occupation: Legal Opinions of the Department of Justice, March 1946–August 1948] (Ch'unch'ŏn: Institute of Asian Culture Studies, Hallym University, 1997), p. 338 (emphasis added).

as intermarried couples, the household registration played the decisive role, too. For instance, a Korean wife of a deceased Japanese man was still deemed to have Japanese nationality as long as she remained in her husband's *naichi* household registry;[145] by the same token, a Japanese woman legally married to a Korean husband was deemed Korean.[146] As a result, the former's property was confiscated despite her indisputable Korean descent, whereas the latter's was not even though she was Korean only in this narrow legal sense.

The vested property issue provided the first occasion for legally articulating the human boundary between the people of Japan and Korea in the postcolonial context. The yardstick was the household registry compiled and maintained by the Japanese colonial bureaucracy. All those *not* determined to be Japanese by this legal test were residually deemed Korean. Charles Pergler, the highest-ranking legal advisor to the USAMGIK, claimed that

> pursuant to higher directives, property of Japanese nationals, located in Korea, was vested by Ordinance 33 in the Military Government. Naturally, property of Korean nationals was not so vested. That called for establishing a test of Korean nationality, and this, for the time being, has been done by adopting the rule that those are Korean nationals who are registered in a Korean family register (Hojuk).... The test devised in connection with vested and non-vested property has worked on the whole satisfacterily [*sic*].[147]

During the early phase of the occupation, all in all, it was a matter of course that USAMGIK would be in a position of overriding power and influence. Also, the overall goal of occupation policies was relatively clear, namely, the swift dismemberment of Japan's imperial territory. Insofar as Korea was concerned, this meant a complete severance from Japan in territory, population, and even properties. It was in the course of implementing this occupation policy in postcolonial Korea that the first legal attempt was made to clarify the human boundary of the Korean people. The irony was that the Japanese settlers were driven out, sometimes against their will, and their properties completely confiscated in accordance with the legal yardstick that they had implanted in Korea. Later, this entrenched role of the household registration system would again prove to be useful and critical in determining *South* Korean peoplehood during the constitutional politics. But, this time, it would involve a dynamic that was far more complicated and convoluted.

[145] Opinion No. 245 in *Migunjŏnggi Chŏngbojaryojip*, p. 77.
[146] Opinions No. 332 and 582 in *Migunjŏnggi Chŏngbojaryojip*, pp. 103, 180.
[147] Opinion No. 1269 in *Migunjŏnggi Chŏngbojaryojip*, p. 405.

Draft Constitutions and the Division at the 38th Parallel

The Moscow Agreement of December 1945 marked the beginning of Korea's constitutional politics, since it was not until then that the political arrangement, as well as interim legal status, for postcolonial Korea was agreed on by the Allied powers. The decision was, in essence, three-fold: a four-power trusteeship (under the United States, the United Kingdom, China, and the Soviet Union) of "up to five years" would be put in place instead of an immediate grant of independence; a "provisional Korean democratic government" would be set up during this period to prepare for full independence; and a U.S.-Soviet Joint Commission would be established to facilitate the formation of the provisional government, in consultation with local "democratic parties and social organizations." The issues of trusteeship and how to form a unified provisional government under divided occupation would set the basic template for local politics in which the ideological rift between the left and the right would only become wider until the entire scheme was finally abandoned in 1947.

As far as the boundary of the people was concerned, the trusteeship issue proved to be the most divisive one. Having lived through thirty-five years of Japanese domination, most Koreans found the prospect of living under another foreign rule all but unbearable. This is why a nationwide protest erupted when the contents of the Moscow Agreement were reported in late December 1945. When the communists and the far-left abruptly withdrew their initial opposition, towing the Soviet line, and declared their support for the trusteeship plan, this provided a perfect excuse for their right-wing opponents to brand them as "traitors" on a par with those who had collaborated with the Japanese colonial rule.[148] As one scholar notes, this resulted in the leftists losing their nationalist credentials and allowed their opponents to argue for their exclusion from the bounds of the "people" who deserved to participate in the construction of an independent Korean state.[149] The human boundary of the new Korean state, yet to be established, was deeply contested as the Cold War arrived in the peninsula.

With the benefit of hindsight, one might say that the Moscow process was doomed to failure from the very beginning. For it was hinged on the

[148] Choi Sang-Yong, "Trusteeship Debate and the Korean Cold War," in Bonnie B. C. Oh (ed.), *Korea Under the American Military Government, 1945–1948* (London: Praeger, 2002), pp. 14–27. Although the U.S. military government in Korea was also a party to the trusteeship plan, it silently stood by as Koreans vented their anger at the leftists and the Russians.

[149] Park Chan-Pyo, *Han'guk ŭi Kukka Hyŏngsŏng kwa Minjujuŭi* [Korean State-Formation and Democracy] (Seoul: Humanitas, 2007), pp. 168–9.

continuation of the wartime partnership between the United States and the Soviet Union, which quickly proved to be unsustainable with the onslaught of the Cold War. Be that as it may, the project of constitutional founding and people-making in Korea had to proceed in this environment of disintegrating trust and increasing animosity between the two superpowers. The brief interbellum period between World War II and the Cold War, in other words, turned out to be a time of constitutive constitutional politics for Korea. It was during this period that major constitutional drafts were produced and debated, based on different assumptions about the boundary of the Korean constituent people. In the southern zone under the U.S. occupation alone, hundreds of different draft constitutions were published by Korean political groups across a wide spectrum of ideological outlooks.[150] Evidently, Koreans were all too eager to create a new state and many of them regarded a constitution to be the "birth certificate"[151] that would verify its independence and legitimacy.

As regards the issue of the people's boundary, of special interest are the draft constitutions produced by the Korean Interim Legislative Assembly, because of the way they dealt with the externally imposed division at the 38th parallel. These drafts are also noteworthy because it was not until KILA was formed that constitutional debate could be conducted in an open forum that claimed some kind of electoral legitimacy from the general populace.[152] As the Korean legislative arm of the USAMGIK, KILA was originally established in late 1946 as a body representing the south with which the U.S.-Soviet Joint Commission might consult if and when negotiations resumed for creating the "Provisional Korean Democratic Government" as mandated in the Moscow Agreement.[153] Not surprisingly, the most contentious issue during the first Joint Commission meeting in March 1946 turned out to be which local political groups would be represented in the future provisional government. Russians held fast to the position that any group that opposed the trusteeship, mostly right-wing

[150] According to one account, there were 397 drafts submitted in response to solicitation by the U.S.-Soviet Joint Commission. Chong Sang-Woo, *Migunjŏnggi Chungganp'a ŭi Hŏnjŏnggusang e kwanhan Yŏn'gu* [A Study of the Constitutional Designs of the Centrist Group Under U.S. Military Occupation] (Ph.D dissertation, Seoul National University, 2007), p. 203.

[151] Jacobsohn, *Constitutional Identity*, p. 117.

[152] Of the draft constitutions that preceded the KILA drafts, those produced by such organizations as the so-called Korean Representative Democratic Council of South Korea (*Nam Chosŏn Taehan Kukmin Taep'yo Minju Uiwŏn*) and the Administration Research Association are considered historically significant. Yet, these bodies were not formed with any kind of electoral mandate since the former was essentially a self-appointed "council" and the latter was a private study group.

[153] USAMGIK Ordinance No. 118 "Establishment of Korean Interim Legislative Assembly" (24 Aug. 1946), Sec. II.

nationalists, should be excluded, and the Americans could not comply for obvious reasons.[154] During the same meeting, it also quickly became clear that the south under U.S. occupation was not so politically organized and unified as the north was, which would put the U.S. negotiation for a unified provisional government at a considerable disadvantage. In order to strengthen its position in future negotiations with the Soviet Union, the United States needed to broaden Korean participation in the administration of the zone under its occupation and to show that its position had local popular support.[155] For the same purpose, the representative body would be so constructed as to enable the participation of not just the rightists but a wide spectrum of political viewpoints.[156] For all these external reasons, KILA was convened in December 1946, comprising ninety members, half of whom were elected and the other half appointed by the USAMGIK. Limited as KILA's authority was, it was the only representative institution that could claim some kind of popular legitimacy in South Korea until the Constituent National Assembly was elected in May 1948.

Having been born under these political circumstances, KILA was not expected to prepare a constitutional draft. After all, as the name indicates, it was to be an "interim" institution for the southern half of the peninsula only. Besides, all of its legislation had to receive the U.S. military governor's sanction in order to become effective. Once established, nevertheless, its members proceeded to draft a constitution; one of their very first actions was to set up a Committee for Drafting the Provisional Constitution. As critically noted by Joseph E. Jacobs, the political adviser to the U.S. military governor, KILA was effectively "arrogat[ing] unto itself the powers of a constitutional convention."[157] With or without legal authorization, however, KILA was convinced that its first order of business must be the drafting of a constitution.

In fact, KILA produced not one but three draft constitutions for different purposes and with different outlooks on the division of the peninsula and, by extension, on the boundary of the Korean people. One of them was labeled the "Transitional Charter for South Korea" (*Nam Chosŏn Kwado Yakhŏn*), which was drawn up to prepare for the transition from U.S. military rule to

[154] Choi, "Trusteeship Debate," pp. 27–34.

[155] Cumings, *Origins*, vol. I, pp. 252–4.

[156] Cumings, *Origins*, vol. I, pp. 259–60. This is reflected in the fact that when the elections for choosing the elected half of the first KILA members returned a predominantly rightist group, the other appointed half was filled by USAMGIK with mostly centrists and left-of-center liberals.

[157] Joseph E. Jacobs, "Letter to the Secretary of State" (3 Sept. 1947), in *Migungmusŏng Han'guk Kwan'gye Munsŏ* [U.S. State Department Documents Related to Korea], vol. 10 (Seoul: Arŭm Ch'ulp'ansa, 1995), p. 147.

a civilian government by Koreans themselves. Prepared in February 1947 by the conservative clique within KILA, it was designed to be a full-scale constitution, albeit a temporary one, to govern the southern half of Korea. Its first article explicitly states that "Korea south of thirty-eight degrees north latitude" shall be governed by the people according to democratic principles. While the bill also contained the proviso that it shall be in effect until a unified provisional government of north and south is established, the ulterior intention of its sponsors appears to have been to create something close to a separate government for the south. Although it was denied that they were aiming for the creation of a separate state, they nevertheless argued for a full transfer of all government authority to Koreans so that a representative civilian government might engage in diplomatic negotiations with various countries to speed up the establishment of a united government of south and north.[158] Such a gesture naturally invited suspicion from the occupation authorities, for diplomacy was clearly beyond the scope of KILA's competence.[159] Letting it go unchecked might even imply the "abdication of United States authority, which is beyond the powers of the Military Governor."[160]

Another draft constitution was billed the "Temporary Charter for Democratic Korea" (*Chosŏn Minju Imshi Yakhŏn*) and submitted to KILA in late March 1947. Although the full text is no longer extant, this was actually the product of KILA's official constitution committee. In contrast to the conservative "Transitional Charter for South Korea," this one was intended for implementation in all of Korea, rather than just the southern half. This was obviously beyond the competence of KILA, but its local political context must be mentioned to understand such usurpation of powers. Apparently, it was an attempt by those KILA members who were opposed to the right-wing group's suspected plan to create a separate government in the south.[161] Commonly referred to as the centrist group, these relatively liberal elements within KILA still adhered to the ideal, or hope, of establishing a united government for all of Korea. In their view, making a constitution for the southern part only was dangerously close to making permanent the division at the 38th parallel.

This political tension between the right and the center continued even after a compromise was reached by agreeing to merge the two draft constitutions. The deliberation process over this third, combined draft only reconfirmed the

158 "*Nam Chosŏn Kwado Yakhŏn Chean Sŏlmyŏngsŏ*" [Explanations for Presenting the Bill for Transitional Charter for South Korea], in Chong Jong-sup (ed.), *Han'guk Hŏnpŏpsa Mullyu*, pp. 137–8.

159 Suh, *Hŏnpŏp-ŭi T'ansaeng*, p. 177.

160 Jacobs, "Letter to the Secretary of State," p. 147.

161 Kim Su-Yong, *Kŏn'guk kwa Hŏnpŏp*, pp. 112–13.

sharp difference of opinions within (and without) KILA on how to reach the goal of establishing an independent Korean state. A case in point was the small yet highly symbolic controversy over whether the draft should be labeled a constitution for "South Korea" (*Nam Chosŏn*). At issue was how to characterize a constitution made by representatives of the southern half, which was designed to apply only to the south but also expected to become the basis of a constitution for unified Korea. No one dared expressly to take the position that the draft should be seen as the constitution for a separate state in the south. Everyone professed the view, at least officially, that it was just a stepping stone toward the creation of a final constitution encompassing the entire peninsula.[162] Under such circumstances, inclusion of the word "South" in the title could be read as a desire to highlight the bill's tentative character. It could, however, also be seen as an expression of a hidden intention to establish a separate "South Korea" and to solidify the division along the 38th parallel. By contrast, not inserting the word might be preferable if the bill was meant to become applicable, someday, to the northern part. Yet, that raised the issue of whether KILA, as a body representing the southern half, had proper authority to make a constitution for residents of the north. In the end, with no clarification of the issue, the bill was passed in August 1947, and the title of the bill was simply the "Temporary Constitution of Korea" (*Chosŏn Imshi Yakhŏn*).

The KILA constitution, however, never went into effect because USAMGIK withheld its approval. In September 1947, Joseph E. Jacobs expressed numerous reasons as to why the bill should not be endorsed:

> The drafting of a national constitution, temporary in name but permanent in character, by an improvised body provisionally representing only a part of the country and its population would seem to be unpractical under any circumstances. In view of the realities of the situation, chiefly the fact that the constitution cannot possibly be exercised in the foreseeable future, it might even seem ridiculous. It ignores existing American authority; it ignores the provisional government to be established by the four-powers; and it ignores the firm hold on the northern half of the country by the North Korean Government, with a constitution of an entirely different kind.[163]

This inside opinion was finally made public when acting Military Governor Charles G. Helmick sent an official letter to KILA on 20 November 1947. He stated that, as half the KILA membership was appointed by the occupation authorities (and the other half chosen through indirect elections), KILA could not be seen as representing the Korean people properly, and that making a

[162] Kim Su-Yong, *Kŏn'guk kwa Hŏnpŏp*, pp. 148–63.
[163] Jacobs, "Letter to the Secretary of State," p. 146.

constitution only for the southern half would create an unnecessary obstacle for the later task of drafting one for the unified Korea.[164] Despite the absence of "South" in the title, evidently, the military governor understood the bill to be intended for the southern part only.

In fact, the prospect for unified Korea was growing dimmer by the day. In August 1947, Washington had already decided to refer the Korean question to the United Nations and abandon the Moscow process.[165] As it was, the U.S.-Soviet Joint Commission was grinding to a halt for one last time. Indeed, Washington had long been considering the idea of taking the Korean question to the United Nations as a way of exiting the scene gracefully.[166] At last, this alternative approach became official when U.S. Secretary of State George C. Marshall formally placed the Korean issue before the United Nations on 17 September 1947. As the United States was clearly aware, this move involved the risk of giving up on creating a unified Korean state, which essentially meant the establishment of a separate government in the south. In other words, by the time Helmick vetoed the KILA constitution, the UN General Assembly had already voted to create a UN Temporary Commission on Korea (UNTCOK) for the purpose of preparing for a general election in Korea.[167] For USAMGIK, more important than making a constitution was the

[164] Suh, *Hŏnpŏp ŭi T'ansaeng*, pp. 179–80.

[165] The specifics of the plan were laid out in August in SWNCC 176/30. In Seoul, Jacobs would also write to his superiors in the State Department, in apparent exasperation: "After more than 2 years of effort to reunite Korea and set up a government therein, I feel that it is high time to get away from the 'provisional' concept of the govt to be established. If possible a govt of permanent character should be established with permanent constitution." "The Political Adviser in Korea (Jacobs) to the Secretary of State" (21 Aug. 1947), in *FRUS* 1947, vol. VI (1972), p. 761.

[166] Bruce Cumings holds that such an option was being considered in Washington as early as March 1946. See Cumings, *Origins*, vol. II, p. 65.

[167] In the north, the Russians had actually all but completed their plans to create a separate government under their influence and were not about to let some putatively international approach ruin that. In February 1946, they had set up an Interim People's Committee for North Korea, and the next month, even before the first meeting of the U.S.-Soviet Joint Commission, they completed their program of land redistribution. By November 1946, an election was held to choose the members of the Interim People's Committee, from whose name "Interim" would be dropped in February 1947, to make it a permanent organization. The Soviets therefore criticized the plan to hold general elections in Korea under United Nations auspices as an American ploy to create its puppet state in the south. The UNTCOK would not be allowed to enter the northern part of Korea. For a recent thorough analysis of the establishment of the North Korean regime, see Kim Hakjoon, *Pukhan ŭi Yŏksa, Che 2 kwŏn: Miso Naengjŏn kwa Soryŏn Kunjŏng aresŏŭi Chosŏn Minjujuŭi Inmin Konghwaguk Kŏn'guk, 1946 nyŏn 1 wŏl – 1948 nyŏn 9 wŏl* [A History of North Korea, vol. 2: The Establishment of the Democratic People's Republic of Korea under the U.S.-Soviet Cold War and the Soviet Military Rule, January 1946–September 1948] (Seoul: Seoul National University Press, 2008), esp. ch. 27. For a different account of the early state-formation in North Korea, see Charles K. Armstrong, *The North Korean Revolution, 1945–1950* (Ithaca, NY: Cornell University Press, 2003).

task of preparing a framework for the upcoming election, which the UN recommended be held "not later than 31 March 1948."[168] As the brief interbellum period was nearing its end, KILA quickly became obsolete, and so did its draft constitution.

United Nations and Election Laws

USAMGIK's rationale for rejecting the KILA constitution contained an element of truth when they questioned its legitimacy. In addition to the fact that half the seats were appointed, the other half were filled through a highly distorted, indirect electoral system.[169] Instead of drafting an entirely new election law for KILA, apparently, the American authorities relied on an old Japanese system that had been designed for severely limited local elections during the colonial era.[170] It was, indeed, for this reason that USAMGIK had been pushing for electoral reform through KILA. Now that the upcoming general election would be closely monitored by the United Nations, there was an added urgency for such a reform. Working under this new external constraint, even the USAMGIK could not have a completely free hand insofar as the election law was concerned. Unlike the household registration system, this legal legacy from the colonial past had to be scrapped altogether.

In an interesting contrast to the GHQ/SCAP in Japan, USAMGIK was less interested in constitution-making and more concerned with enacting an election law, which in Japan had been done by the locals without American intervention. To be sure, the occupation authorities in Korea were not completely indifferent to constitution-making either. Emery Woodall, Director of the USAMGIK Department of Justice, actually prepared a draft constitution fairly early on, even before the first U.S.-Soviet Joint Commission met in May 1946. Nevertheless, there is no evidence that this was presented to KILA for deliberation or that the Americans wished to make it the basis of the constitution of an independent Korean state.[171] Although Yu Chin-o mentions the Woodall

[168] UNGA Res. 112 (II), 14 Nov. 1947.

[169] Donald S. MacDonald, "The 1946 Elections and Legislative Assembly in South Korea: America's Bumbling Tutelage," *Journal of Northeast Asian Studies*, vol.1, no. 3 (1982), pp. 56–9.

[170] See Cumings, *Origins*, vol. I, pp. 260–2; E. Grant Meade, *American Military Government in Korea* (New York: King's Crown Press, 1951), p. 187.

[171] In his 1954 report, John W. Connelly, Jr., who served as Director of the Department of Justice after Woodall, recalls that "an American lawyer in the Department of Justice of Military Government did some work on the skeleton outline of a Constitution for Korea which might be used in future discussion." He then goes on to state that he neither examined the outline nor was given any instruction on the subject, and that he has no recollection of "what became of the skeleton draft." Connelly, "Report on Economic Provisions," p. 16.

draft as one of his reference sources when preparing his draft constitution, it is unclear if the occupation authorities ever intended it to influence his work.[172]

By contrast, USAMGIK would show a singular and lasting interest in drafting an election law. Initially, this interest stemmed from the fact that KILA itself was originally slated to become a fully elected body in order to further strengthen the American position in the U.S.-Soviet Joint Commission.[173] From the very beginning, thus, KILA was urged to enact a general franchise law that would regulate the next round of elections for itself. On numerous occasions throughout early 1947, the military governor, Major General Archer L. Lerch, sent letters to the Chairman of KILA, Kimm Kiusic, urging the assembly to give top priority to enacting election laws. He even conveyed a draft bill prepared by members of the military government for the assembly's reference. Lerch expressed hope that the KILA would act early enough to enable the opening of a new, fully-elected legislative body by 30 June 1947. He also ordered the USAMGIK Department of Justice, then under the direction of Kim Pyŏng-no, to draw up an ordinance for a general election in case KILA failed to act on schedule.[174]

USAMGIK's fidgeting was understandable since KILA was bogged down with the thorny issue of lustration from the beginning. From the American point of view, passing judgment on Korean collaborators during the colonial era was a matter of lesser importance that could await the opening of a more fully representative legislative body. For many centrist KILA members, however, the issue was more urgent because it related to the scope of the "people" who would be allowed to take part in the electoral process. Before holding any election, measures had to be taken to ensure that collaborators were barred from running for public office and even from voting. In other words, lustration and enfranchisement were closely interconnected agendas for the centrist members.[175] Given the politically charged nature of the issue, it is not surprising that KILA was not making much progress. Despite USAMGIK's insistence on separating these two issues, in the eventuality, the lustration law and election law would be passed almost simultaneously. More to the point, the latter would disenfranchise colonial collaborators in strict accordance with the definitions

[172] Until recently, the existence of this document had been known only by its name. Its contents as well as its whereabouts were a mystery until Yu Chin-o's papers were made public in 2009. For a discussion of the Woodall draft, see Suh, *Hŏnpŏp-ŭi T'ansaeng*, pp. 162–2.

[173] Section II of USAMGIK Ordinance No. 118 stated: "Eventually all [KILA members] will be elected."

[174] Park, *Hanguk ŭi Kukka Hyŏngsŏng*, p. 327.

[175] Park, *Hanguk ŭi Kukka Hyŏngsŏng*, p. 328.

and categories as provided in the former.[176] Like the KILA constitution, however, these two interconnected initiatives by KILA would ultimately be rejected by USAMGIK. It refused to endorse the lustration law altogether. As for the election law, it would initially be endorsed and promulgated by USAMGIK, but was later superseded before the general election actually took place on 10 May 1948. Nevertheless, it is worth reviewing the convoluted negotiations over this ill-fated election law, as the same issues would be rehearsed when UNTCOK became involved to prepare a new law for the election.

First, USAMGIK opposed the plan of KILA's right-wing members to set the voting age at twenty-five and the right to stand for election at thirty years of age. That was deemed too restrictive not just on principle, but also in view of the fact that it would effectively disenfranchise the younger population who were deemed more left-leaning or centrist. In the end, KILA capitulated, and the final bill lowered the age to twenty-three for voting and twenty-five for being elected.[177] Second, Americans also tried to oppose the system whereby voters were required to register by writing their own names on registration forms; voting would also be done by writing the names of the candidate on the ballot sheet. That would have effectively imposed a literacy requirement and disenfranchised nearly 80 percent of the electorate. On this issue, KILA refused to give in.[178]

Third, of particular interest in relation to the issue of membership in the Korean state was the scheme of creating a separate electoral district for those who had fled the emerging communist regime in the north and were now residing in the south.[179] In the final version of the KILA law, this unique system

[176] Section II of the KILA election law enumerated the category of individuals who are "not eligible to vote or to be elected," which incorporated the definition of traitors, collaborators, and profiteers as provided for in the lustration law.

[177] Park Chan-Pyo, "Chehŏn Kukhoe Sŏn'gŏpŏp kwa Han'guk ŭi Kukka Hyŏngsŏng" [Constituent National Assembly Election Law and State-formation in Korea], *Han'guk Chŏngch'ihak Hoebo*, vol. 29, no. 3 (1995), pp. 76–8.

[178] Park, "Chehŏn Kukhoe Sŏn'gŏpŏp," p. 79.

[179] The number of North Korean refugees has been a contentious issue. The right-wing factions during the constitutional politics suggested 4.6 million, comprising almost 25% of the total population in the South. It seems all but certain that this number was highly inflated for political purposes. The Department of State reported in 1948 that, during the period of occupation, the recorded entries of the refugees from the North amounted to about 600,000, although it also noted that, between 1945 and 1946 alone, the number of unrecorded entries was estimated at 1 million. U.S. Department of State, *Korea 1945 to 1948*, p. 26. On the southward stream of refugees from the north during early period following liberation, see Cumings, *Origins*, vol. I, pp. 425–6.

was meant to establish a single, nationwide district in which only those "who have their family register … in North Korea and residence in South Korea" could vote, if they so wish, to elect their own representatives from among the refugees (Section 43). The rationale was that, since they are relatively unknown in the communities of their current residence, they would in effect be denied representation if no allowance was made for their special situation.[180] The political motivation behind this right-wing initiative was to ensure that this fiercely anti-communist bloc of the population would be given full, even over, representation, in the legislative assembly.[181] On this initiative, too, KILA managed to prevail over USAMGIK, which sought to oppose it on grounds of administrative difficulty. The decision to retain the scheme was nearly unanimous on the floor.[182]

Despite these disagreements, USAMGIK endorsed the KILA draft and promulgated it on 3 September 1947 as the "Law for the Election of Members of the Korean Interim Legislative Assembly."[183] By this time, however, the reason for its endorsement seemed to have changed from that behind USAMGIK's initial push for the election law in early 1947. As a part of the last minute effort to salvage the Moscow framework, the United States suggested to the Soviet Union on 26 August 1947 that a unified provisional government be established (as provided in the Moscow Agreement) through two respective elections in the north and south according to rules of its own and under the United Nations monitoring (which was a departure from the agreement).[184] Evidently, the KILA election law that USAMGIK approved on 3 September was to prepare for this interim election. Immediately upon Moscow's expected rejection of this proposal, the United States took unilateral action by officially referring the Korean question to the United Nations on 17 September. To be sure, the stated objective of the UN General Assembly's resolution was to hold a nationwide general election throughout all of Korea. When the Soviet authorities, however, blocked the UNTCOK's entry into the territory under their control, the United States made sure that the United Nations passed another resolution (by the Interim Committee of the General Assembly) authorizing

180 John Weckerling to General Hodge, memorandum, 18 Mar. 1948, in *Taehan Min'guksa Charyojip: UN Han'guk Imshi Wiwŏndan Kwan'gye Munsŏ* [Documents and Materials on History of the Republic of Korea: UNTCOK Documents], vol. 5 (Kwach'ŏn: Kuksa P'yŏnch'an Wiwŏnhoe, 1987–90), p. 14.

181 Park, "Chehŏn Kukhoe Sŏn'gŏpŏp," p. 79.

182 *KILA Minutes*, No. 132 (12 Aug. 1947), pp. 5–6 [Reprint vol. 3, pp. 277–8].

183 KILA Public Act No. 5 (3 Sept. 1947).

184 "United States Proposals Regarding Korea" (enclosure in a letter from Acting Secretary of State Robert A. Lovett to the U.S. Embassy in the Soviet Union, to be sent to the Soviet Foreign Minister), 26 Aug. 1947, in *FRUS* 1947, vol. VI (1972), pp. 773–4.

elections for the southern part alone.[185] The general election would eventually be held on 10 May 1948 under UN supervision.

In this new context, the previous negotiation between KILA and USAMGIK over the election law quickly became irrelevant. For one thing, the advent of the UNTCOK onto the scene meant the addition of another layer of external dimension in the process of defining Korean peoplehood. USAMGIK had to satisfy the demands of the UNTCOK, whose members were not always so willing to go along with the Americans' designs.[186] In General Hodge's proclamation announcing the general election, he stated that the election would be held in accordance with the KILA Election Law, but he also announced that the law would have to be modified to meet the requirements of UNTCOK.[187] Also, it was becoming clearer that the election law would now be used for organizing an assembly which would enact the constitution for *de facto* South Korea. In light of this, the United States had an added interest in making sure that the election was held through a democratic process, at least nominally. It was for this reason, for instance, that the USAMGIK would promulgate a comprehensive Bill of Rights, the first of its kind in Korean history, just before the election.[188] In the same vein, broadening the popular basis of the assembly was seen as critical, since strong electoral legitimacy would be crucial for the authority and sustainability of the separate regime to be established by that assembly. Perhaps more important for the United States' diplomatic interests was the need to deflect the expected criticism from the Soviet Union and the communist bloc, as well as sustain the fragile support of its allies in the United Nations. The new legislative body would have to be representative of the entire people at least of South Korea.

[185] The resolution was to implement the general election "in such parts of Korea as are accessible to the Committee." "UNTCOK Press Release No. 32: Interim Committee Resolution, 27 February 1948," in *Taehan Min'guksa Charyojip*, vol. 2, pp. 118–21. For an account of the process leading up to the Interim Committee's decision, see Leon Gordenker, "The United Nations, the United States Occupation and the 1948 Election in Korea," *Political Science Quarterly*, vol. 73, no. 3 (1958), pp. 431–5.

[186] For the uneasy relationship between USAMGIK and UNTCOK, see Cumings, *Origins*, vol. II, pp. 70–8.

[187] The proclamation stated that the announced election will be "held under the terms and provisions of Public Act Number 5, dated 3 September 1947, Law for the Election of Members of the Korean Interim Legislative Assembly, with such changes, additions, and emendations as, after consultation with the United Nations Temporary Commission on Korea, may be deemed necessary." Proclamation of Election of Representatives of the Korean People (1 Mar. 1948), Article 2.

[188] Proclamation on the Rights of the Korean People (5 Apr. 1948), in *Taehan Min'guksa Charyojip*, vol. 2, pp. 263–4.

With the advent of an additional external constraint, therefore, the election law had to undergo yet another round of alteration. The most important mandate of UNTCOK was to observe and ensure that a "national assembly" would be formed via a "fair election law." As the U.S. military government prepared for their arrival in Seoul, it made sure that the UN commission would be informed of the election law passed by KILA as well as the law's objectionable features that KILA had insisted on retaining. Subsequent discussion between UNTCOK members and the occupation authorities resulted in the removal of the literacy requirement and lowering of the voting age to twenty-one.[189] The popular basis had to be further broadened to secure democratic legitimacy for the nascent regime in the south.

Also eliminated, as USAMGIK had advocated all along, was Chapter VII of the KILA Election Law on the special electoral district. According to a USAMGIK report, this chapter was struck out in its entirety thanks to the agreement between the USAMGIK and UNTCOK over opposition from the Korean consultants.[190] The ground was that this system would likely count North Korean refugees twice – once for determining the number of assembly seats to be allocated to the special electoral district and a second time for allocating regular district seats. This scheme would result in giving North Korean refugees "dual representation" and a "disproportionate representation of the population of South Korea."[191] The administrative difficulty complained of by the U.S. authorities was a vexing, but not insurmountable, problem. The more serious consideration seems to have been the apprehension that "the special electoral district might organize a Northern bloc within the National Assembly and *then claim to be the duly elected representatives of North Korea*."[192] From the perspectives of USAMGIK and UNTCOK, in other words, the National Assembly to be formed through this election law was not meant to represent the northern half of the peninsula. It was to be as representative as possible of the people in the south *and south only*. North Korean refugees' voting rights would be respected, but only as part of the people of South Korea.

[189] Gordenker, "1948 Election in Korea," p. 439; Park, "Chehŏn Kukhoe Sŏn'gŏpŏp," pp. 84–5.
[190] Park, "Chehŏn Kukhoe Sŏn'gŏpŏp," p. 85.
[191] U.S. Liaison Officer with United Nations Temporary Commission on Korea, "Observation of Election in South Korea of Korean Representatives Which Shall Constitute a National Assembly and Establish a Government of Korea Under Resolutions Adopted by UN General Assembly of 14 November 1947 and Participation of United States Army Forces in Korea Therein," in *Taehan Min'guksa Charyojip*, vol. 1, pp. 98–9 (hereafter "Observations of Election in South Korea").
[192] "Observation of Election in South Korea," p. 99 (emphasis added).

With the UN-mandated deadline for the election fast approaching, USAMGIK could not risk the delay that would be caused by having KILA amend the original election law. In the end, KILA was bypassed and its election law was abandoned in its entirety. A new law was decreed by USAMGIK itself on 17 March 1948 as an ordinance called "Law for the Election of Representatives of the Korean People."[193] More democratic electoral basis but further consolidation of the division was the result of the dual imposition by USAMGIK and UNTCOK.

The Birth of the Constituent People and the Household Registration System

Naturally, the final elimination of the special electoral district elicited criticism from the right-wing factions on grounds that North Korean refugees would be disenfranchised as a unit of their own.[194] Politically motivated as it surely was, the conservative detraction was not without reason because, legally speaking, the new election law mandated in effect that all who wished to take part in the founding election were to do so qua residents of the southern half. North Korean districts were nonexistent insofar as the Election Law was concerned, and the North Korean refugees were no longer to be seen as representing the views of that part of the country. Rather, they now were, or should be, absorbed into the general populace of the south as individual citizens, voting as members of the electorate in whichever district they happened to be in residence. In short, North Korean refugees had to be transformed into South Korean citizens before they could cast a vote for the National Assembly.

According to the UNTCOK/USAMGIK framework, instead, North Korean representation was to be recognized in the National Assembly by allotting one hundred separate seats for the region north of the 38th parallel. Upon the opening of the National Assembly, General Hodge issued a congratulatory note to the elected representatives in which he suggested that the assembly immediately pass a resolution calling on North Koreans to send their representatives to fill those vacant seats.[195] Indeed, the National Assembly adopted

[193] USAMGIK Ordinance No. 175 (hereafter Election Law).

[194] Even after the law was enacted, various groups claiming to represent refugees from the north submitted petitions to both USAMGIK and UNTCOK calling for the institution of a special electoral district, but to no avail. See, e.g., "Northwest Young Men's Society et al. to Lt. Gen. John R. Hodge," 18 Mar. 1948, and "Yi Yun Yung, Chairman, General Assembly of Koreans from North Korea to Lt. Gen. John R. Hodge," 20 Mar. 1948, in *Taehan Min'guksa Charyojip*, vol. 5, pp. 11–13 and 40–1.

[195] CNA *Minutes*, Session 1, No. 2 (1 June 1948), pp. 12–13. Immediately after the Interim Committee of the UN General Assembly gave authorization to proceed with the election in the south, chairman of UNTCOK, Dr. K. P. S. Menon, expressed the idea that, even

such a resolution on 12 June 1948 and urged their "northern brethren" to hold a general election according to the UN resolution to elect the "true representatives of the people."[196] In its self-understanding, the National Assembly formed by the 10 May General Election was truly representative of the entire Korean people. But, at the same time, this resolution itself was a confirmation that the assembly did not (yet) represent the North Korean populace. The members of the National Assembly could probably point to the fact that it had been established and given legitimacy by virtue of the United Nations mandate to create an assembly for the whole of Korea. True, the seats for the northern part still had to be filled, but the National Assembly itself was a "national" institution. If one focused, however, on the fact that the National Assembly owed its very existence to the concrete historical act of general election in the south only, it was hard to make the claim that it had authority over residents of the north, too. Such authority could come only from a desired and imagined future, that is, a unified Korean representation under its fold. In other words, this resolution foreshadowed a lasting fault line between fact (division) and norm (unification) in the constitutional identity of South Korea.

Against this background, arguably, the discarded system of special electoral districts might have worked as one way of bridging this gap. From a constitutional standpoint, the idea of treating North Korean refugees separately by creating a special electoral district may be understood as an attempt to maintain the basic premise that all Koreans residing in the entire peninsula ought to be represented in the constituent assembly. The special electoral district might have been a way of recognizing the reality of the division, while holding on to the presumption, or the demand, that it should not dictate the boundary of the Korean people. Giving legal recognition to a special North Korean electoral district, fictive as it surely was, could have made a stronger case for the claim that the National Assembly represented the entire Korean people and territory. In February 1949, for instance, the government of the Republic of Korea, which was then only six months into its existence, proceeded to appoint the (largely ceremonial) governors and administrative staffs for each of the five provinces located north of the 38th parallel. It was an attempt to give some semblance of substance to its claim over the territory and population of the north. By the same token, instituting special electoral districts for the northern part could have played a similarly symbolic role for the electoral legitimacy

if the residents of North Korea are unable to participate in the general election, "the seats will still be kept open for them." Broadcast made by Dr. K. P. S. Menon (India), Chairman, UN Temporary Commission on Korea (Saturday, 28 February [1948]), in *Taehan Min'guksa Charyojip*, vol. 4, p. 337.

196 *CNA Minutes*, Session 1, No. 9 (12 June 1948), pp. 119–25.

of the National Assembly. That was, indeed, precisely what North Korea did when its turn came to make a separate constitution. Allegedly, its "constituent assembly" was filled with (fictive) representatives from electoral districts in the south as well as the north.[197] Once this option of special representation was foreclosed by the external intervention in the south, however, refugees from the north had to be disaggregated and incorporated individually into a new constituent people of South Korea. The question now was how to find a legal method of implementing and effectuating this complete absorption in time for the general election, newly slated to take place on 10 May 1948.

In legally delineating the state membership of South Korea, the most important milestone should have been the "Temporary Provisions Concerning the Law of Nationality,"[198] which was enacted by KILA at the strong urging of USAMGIK. Logically, a legal definition of the scope of the people eligible to take part in politics (e.g., criteria for nationality) should be set and made known prior to making the rules for holding any elections. Yet, in the case of the general election on 10 May 1948, the Election Law (17 March 1948) was proclaimed before the South Korean state-membership was codified in the Temporary Nationality Provisions (11 May 1948). In other words, the rule for determining nationality did not even come out until after the vote was cast. This irony, even anomaly, may be taken to illustrate the haste and ill-preparedness with which the general election was conducted. It is also to be noted, however, that the situation was little different from that of Japan. As we

[197] North Korea's official propaganda still has it that a secret ballot was held in the south, and the regional representatives thereby elected, numbering 1,080, clandestinely crossed the 38th parallel to form the South Korean Representatives Conference. From this conference, 360 delegates representing the southern districts were elected on 25 August 1948 to form the Supreme People's Assembly, together with 212 representatives from the north, which then proceeded to promulgate the North Korean constitution on 9 September 1948. In point of fact, however, the North's effort at constitution-making had already begun in earnest and openly in November 1947, when the North Korean People's Council officially set up a constitution-drafting committee. United Nations, General Assembly, *First Part of the Report of the United Nations Temporary Commission on Korea*, Official Records: Third Session, Supplement No. 9 (1948), UN Document A/575, p. 21. For this constitution to be at least nominally representative of the entire Korean people, the People's Council, whose jurisdiction was confined to the north of the 38th parallel, had to be transformed into the Supreme People's Assembly. Hence, this legal fiction of secret ballot and alleged representation of the south. This was indeed the ground on which the Soviet Union solicited in vain the UN recognition of the North Korean regime in December 1948 as a government established "by an overwhelming majority of the population of both North and South Korea." *Yearbook of the United Nations 1948–1949* (Lake Success, NY: United Nations Department of Public Information, 1950), p. 289. For a general overview on the constitution-making process in North Korea, see Kim Hakjoon, *Pukhan ŭi Yŏksa*, vol. 2, chs. 38–39 and Suh, *Hŏnpŏp ŭi T'ansaeng*, ch. 7.

[198] KILA Public Act No. 11 (11 May 1948) (hereafter Temporary Nationality Provisions).

have seen already, the summary disenfranchisement of former colonial subjects via the reformed election law of 1945 preceded the official delineation of the postwar Japanese peoplehood in the Nationality Law which was enacted in 1950. In postcolonial South Korea, too, it was the election law that determined the boundary of nationality, and not the other way around. The only difference was that the election law was imposed on South Korea whereas it was not in Japan.

As such, KILA's Temporary Nationality Provisions defined Koreans simply as "any person whose father is Korean" (Section II, Item 1). This definition is frustrating in and of itself because it does not determine how and when the father himself became a "Korean."[199] This had to be inferred from other parts of the law. Section V, for instance, provided that foreign nationals or those listed in the Japanese *naichi* household registry who had abandoned their former nationality or extricated themselves from the Japanese household registry shall be "deemed to be restored to Korean nationality as of, and prior to, 9 August 1945." Unspoken in this provision, but lost on no one at the time, was the assumption that extrication from a Japanese registry meant reentry into the Korean counterpart, and, to that extent, (re)gaining nationality was in effect equated with being listed in the colonial household registry in Korea. According to the Temporary Nationality Provisions, then, Koreans consisted legally of two kinds as of May 1948: 1) those listed in the Korean household registry as maintained by the former colonial bureaucracy, and 2) those who reentered it after abandoning foreign nationalities or Japanese registry status. In other words, the Temporary Nationality Provisions simply reiterated the colonial definition of Koreans, that is, all those listed in the Korean household registry. Since this colonial definition had been made and used prior to the division of the peninsula, it obviously included residents of North Korea, too. It is, then, in manifest tension with the fact that the provisions themselves could be enforced in the southern half only.

More importantly, it did not sit well with the *de facto* definition of peoplehood that emerged from the operation of laws and regulations passed for defining eligibility to vote in the general election. Excepting those barred from voting and election for enumerated charges of colonial collaboration,

199 This alleged deficiency remained unaddressed, as we have seen, even during the legislative debates over the first Nationality Law in December 1948. Even now, this issue continues to be a source of controversy among legal scholars in Korea. See, e.g., Chung In Seop, "Kukmin ŭi T'ansaeng kwa Pŏpchŏk Kyŏnggye" [The Birth of People and Its Legal Boundary], in Han'guk Mirae Hakhoe (ed.), *Chehŏn kwa Kŏn'guk* and Loh Yeong-Don, "Urinara Kukchŏkpŏp ŭi Myŏtkaji Munje e Kwanhan Koch'al" [A Study of Some Problems in the Nationality Law of Korea], *Kukchepŏp Hakhoe Nonch'ong*, vol. 41, no. 2 (1996).

as explained, the Election Law adopted a universal franchise by which voting rights were granted to all Korean "citizens" (*kukmin*), male or female over twenty-one years of age, with eligibility for elected offices set at twenty-five (Section 1). The Election Law itself did not define a Korean citizen as such, though, despite the absence of any nationality law. Such definition appears in the by-law issued on 22 March 1948 by USAMGIK for the purpose of implementing the Election Law.[200] Section 2 of the Election By-law stipulated that a "citizen" within the meaning of Section 1 of the Election Law refers to: "1) any person who is registered in a Korean HOJUK (family register); 2) any person born of Korean parents; 3) any person born of a Korean father and not possessing a foreign citizenship." Given that parentage was legally verifiable only via household registration, this provision in effect equated Korean citizens with those listed in the Korean household registry. This was consistent with the way in which the Temporary Nationality Provisions defined Korean citizenship – except for one subtle but significant difference.

Understanding this difference depends on clarifying the meaning of "any person who is registered in a Korean HOJUK (family register)" in the Election By-law. Its precise meaning can be inferred from yet another USAMGIK ordinance issued at roughly the same time, namely, "Provisions for Temporary Family Registers."[201] The purpose of this law was to provide, until the time of reunification of South and North Korea, "measures for temporary family registers" for those who had their permanent legal address in the territory north of the 38th parallel but were currently residing in the south (Section I). It was a means for controlling such persons as well as enfranchising them for the upcoming election. For these goals, it mandated that the North Korean refugees could reestablish their permanent legal address, or "permanent domicile," at the address of their current residence in South Korea (Section II, Para. a). In order to do so, the refugees had to submit "a copy or extract of material facts from the family registration book and the matters set forth in Section 11 of Government-General Order Number 154, dated December, 1922" (Section II, Para. b). The reference here is to none other than the Korean Household Registry Ordinance, or *Chōsen Kosekirei*, which had been the basis for the colonial registry of Korea. In short, North Korean refugees were given new legal status as members of the constituent people of South Korea by showing proof of their former status as colonial subjects according to the criteria set down by the Japanese colonial authorities. It may be noted in this connection

[200] Regulation for Implementing the Law for the Election of Representatives of the Korean People (22 Mar. 1948) (hereafter Election By-law).

[201] USAMGIK Ordinance No. 179 "Provisions for Temporary Family Registers" (1 Apr. 1948).

that the legal status of original South Korean residents themselves (and other post-liberation returnees from overseas) was also verified by virtue of their being listed in the colonial household registry of the southern part of the peninsula. The "temporary" household registry was a means to transform the North Korean refugees into South Korean citizens, that is, persons listed in South Korean household registries. The definition of "citizen" eligible to vote according to the Election Law therefore had to be read to mean "any person registered in a *South* Korean registry."

In sum, at the time of the general election on 10 May, the constituent people of South Korea were to be identified in the following way. Korean citizens (*kukmin*) eligible to participate in the constitutional founding were those listed in the South Korean household registry *and* those who had set up a temporary household registry at an address south of the 38th parallel by demonstrating their original northern registry status through legal criteria established by the colonial regime. Although neither the Election Law nor the Election By-law required that a voter be registered at an address in South Korea, this was made abundantly clear by the Provisions for Temporary Family Registers which required the establishment of temporary registries for refugees from North Korea.[202]

If this was the case as a matter of law, then, we recognize two features that are noteworthy. First, the "personality" principle of classifying and categorizing persons encoded in the colonial household registration system persisted to frame postcolonial Korean peoplehood. Second, however, this continuity in the system of marking the human boundary of Korea was modified by the introduction of a new "territorial" dimension. By rejecting even a nominal representation of the northern half, which the special electoral district system would have made possible, USAMGIK and UNTCOK made sure that, from now on, the relevant household registries were those located in the southern half of the peninsula. In other words, Korean citizens qua constituent people of the Republic of Korea were *not* everyone who could prove legal status via the colonial Korean household registry (as suggested by the subsequent Temporary Nationality Provisions), but only those who were registered at an address south of the 38th parallel. Ironically enough, the household registration system from the past was recast by external actors to perform a new function of differentiation in a new context. Rather than marking the line between

202 Sung Ho Kim and Myungho Choi, "1948 nyŏn Kŏn'guk Hŏnpŏp Chŏnmun e Nat'anan 'Uridŭl Taehan Kukmin' ŭi Chŏngch'esŏng kwa Chŏngdangsŏng" [The Identity and Legitimacy of 'We the People of Korea' in the Preamble of the Founding Constitution of 1948], *Han'guk Chŏngch'ihak Hoebo*, vol. 42, no. 4 (2008), pp. 101–02.

naichi and *gaichi* during the colonial period, it was now called upon to distinguish between those who belonged to the South Korean state and those who did not.

On this view, the identity of South Korean constituent people was in reality defined on the basis of colonial legal legacy *and* a new territorial dimension introduced by the externally imposed division of the peninsula. This interpretation is patently at odds with the people's self-identity contained in the Founding Constitution. In particular, its territory provision embodies the view that no reduction took place in either territorial or human boundaries of the Korean state.[203] It comports better, however, with the view taken by the United Nations after the election, which was premised on the understanding that its goal of creating an independent Korean state remained only partially fulfilled. Unwelcome as it was, the fact of externally imposed division resulted in the creation of two distinct peoples on the peninsula, which remains difficult to square with the norm embodied in the constitution. This disjunction between fact and norm, and between domestic and international perspectives, has created a built-in "disharmonic" feature in the constitutional identity of the Korean people.

In December 1948, the new independent government of the Republic of Korea was given legal recognition by the United Nations through a General Assembly resolution. During the Cold War era, this would become the main grounds for the South Korean government's claim to represent the people of the entire peninsula. The resolution itself, however, was not so straightforward as to sustain such a claim. For sure, it does clearly recognize the establishment of a "lawful government ... over that part of Korea where the Temporary Commission was able to observe and consult."[204] Nowhere, however, was it as clearly indicated in the text that this "lawful government" represents the *entire* Korean people. This studied ambiguity was indeed reflective of a deep discord even among the UN member states that had supported the U.S. initiative in Korea. Both before and after the inauguration of the government, UNTCOK members consistently expressed discomfort even at the use of the adjective "national" in the formal title of the National Assembly and the new administration.[205] It is against this background that the territory provision in

[203] Article 4 proclaims: "The territory of Korea shall consist of the Korean Peninsula, and its accessory islands."

[204] UNGA Res. 195(III), 12 Dec. 1948.

[205] UNTCOK Main Committee, "Summary Record of the Fifteenth Meeting," Duk Soo Palace, Seoul, 19 July 1948, A/AC.19/SC.4/SR.15, in *Taehan Min'guksa Charyojip*, vol. 3, pp. 130–1. Similar skepticism was entertained by at least one officer of the American military government even before the general election took place. Referring to Menon's idea of reserving seats for North Korean representatives, Brig. Gen. John Weckerling, USAMGIK's liaison

the Founding Constitution needs to be understood. For it was a self-conscious assertion on the part of the National Assembly to be the representative body of the entire Korean people. Writing this constitutional provision (and others), one might say, was the primary avenue through which external impact was negotiated, and the tool by which the National Assembly "bootstrapped" itself into the position of a "national government" in the absence of indisputable authorization either from above (United Nations) or from below (nationwide election including North Korea).

It was through a similar process of bootstrapping that the human, as well as territorial, boundary of the Republic of Korea was given its final legal shape. At about the same time that the UN resolution came out in December 1948, the National Assembly enacted, pursuant to Article 3 of the Founding Constitution, the Nationality Law of the newly established state. Like the territory provision of the constitution, this law gave no recognition to the fact of division. This was actually consistent with KILA's Temporary Nationality Provisions, which it was meant to supersede. As mentioned, the Temporary Nationality Provisions had relied on the household registry as the criteria for verifying nationality regardless of the division at 38th parallel. As a result, in defining the human boundary of Koreans, the new Nationality Law also envisioned all residents of the peninsula as nationals of the Republic of Korea. This is obviously at odds with the boundary of the Korean people as defined in the USAMGIK election ordinances that created the legislature which made this law. It was another case of bootstrapping in that the National Assembly, created by an election in which only the *South* Korean people participated, was now broadening the scope of the people by fiat to include those in North Korea.

Thus was sown a deep tension into the constitutional identity of the Korean people. Ever since the founding, the Republic of Korea has maintained the view that the *de jure* boundary of the people is all those residing in the peninsula. This obviously does not sit well with the *de facto* division that has created two competing regimes on the peninsula as a result of external imposition. At the same time, this tension was a result of a complex process of negotiation with the legacy of the colonial past, some of which were rejected while others preserved and utilized by the U.S. occupation authorities as well as by the Korean people themselves.

officer to UNTCOK, pointed out that it would be "incongruous" to form a "National Korean Government" based on an ordinance issued by the authorities in the south. John Weckerling to General Hodge, memorandum, 2 Mar. 1948, in *Taehan Min'guksa Charyojip*, vol. 4, pp. 354–5.

IMPOSITIONS, LEGACIES, AND "WE THE PEOPLE"

In December 1945, the Japanese government took the initiative of revising its election law for the House of Representatives, the lower house of the Imperial Diet, which was to revise the Imperial Constitution for the purpose of making it more democratic. In order to make the legislature more representative of the people, franchise was given to women for the first time in Japanese history. The same law, however, disenfranchised the former colonial subjects by invoking the household registry as the criterion for the rights to vote and to run for public offices. The boundary of the people to be represented in the process of making a new constitution would be drastically contracted to only those listed under the household registry of Japan's main islands.

This contraction was further given constitutional expression when the government made sure, through subtle negotiations with GHQ/SCAP, that the text of the new constitution referred only to Japanese nationals as the bearer of fundamental rights guaranteed by the constitution. As a result, it became possible to conclude, from a plain reading of the constitution, that foreigners were excluded from rights protection. More importantly, this provided grounds for the view that former colonial subjects were also not entitled to rights protection, as they were on their way to becoming foreigners.

Just before the constitution went into effect, the government issued the Alien Registration Ordinance, which effectively treated Koreans and the Taiwanese remaining on the Japanese main islands as foreigners, even though their nationality remained Japanese. The final act of the contraction, or the full implementation of this constitutional excision of the former colonial subjects, came with the famous Circular No. 438 of the Justice Department, a fiat which officially declared all persons listed under Korean or Taiwanese household registries to be aliens. This was done unilaterally by the Japanese government literally days before Japan regained sovereign independence with the effectuation of the San Francisco Peace Treaty. The exclusion of former colonial subjects, including the sizeable population of Koreans still residing in Japan, was pursued quite consistently by the Japanese government from the very beginning.

The role of the U.S. occupation authorities may seem to have been rather marginal in the whole process. Step by step, the locals appear to have achieved the goal of excising the ex-colonial subjects from the boundary of the new people of Japan without much resistance or input from external actors. From another viewpoint, however, what the locals achieved may actually be described as the full and faithful implementation of the overarching mandate of the Allied Powers regarding Japan. It was imperative for the Allies that, in the postwar period, the Great Empire of Japan should be dismembered and turned into to a peaceful, democratic island nation-state. It was a case in which both the locals and the external actors agreed on the goal of reducing both the territorial and human boundaries of the state in the process of a new constitutional founding.

In the Korean case, the relationship between the locals and the external actors was comparatively more confrontational. The story of redefining the human boundary of Korea began with the repatriation of Japanese colonial settlers in Korea at the time of liberation. As most Japanese returned voluntarily, not much difficulty was encountered. When the U.S. occupation authorities decided to confiscate private property owned by the Japanese, a difficult and tedious task of distinguishing the Japanese from the Koreans presented itself. In both repatriation and confiscation contexts, the relevant criterion relied on by the American military government was the household registry, a legacy from the colonial past. If a person was listed under the registry in Japan, she was Japanese; if listed under the Korean registry, the person was deemed Korean regardless of ethnicity or place of residence. The locals also accepted this differential use of the household registry. When it came to the issue of drafting an election law or a constitution for the new Korean state, however, the goal of the external actors was more at odds with that of the locals.

Regarding the division of the peninsula at 38th parallel, some Koreans in the American zone sought in vain to resist the logic of differentiation in the face of overbearing outsiders. An example was the attempt by the Korean Interim Legislative Assembly to create a special electoral district for those who had fled North Korea. By enabling persons still listed under household registries in the north to participate in the election for establishing a "national" assembly, this scheme might be seen as a way of coping with the reality of the division while refusing to recognize its permanency. In the end, however, both the U.S. authorities and the UN commission sent to oversee the general election rejected the Koreans' proposal. As a result, the 10 May 1948 election that formed the National Assembly represented the people of *South* Korea only. No one would be allowed to participate unless one became a resident of South Korea by establishing a temporary household registry at an address in the south. For external actors, the household registry was, in effect, a means by which to distinguish the South Koreans from North Koreans and, then, to transform the latter residing in the south into the former. Interestingly, however, when the National Assembly was formed by the general election, the locals quickly proceeded to deny the reality of the division. The Founding Constitution drafted by the assembly declared the entire peninsula to be the territory of the Republic of Korea, while the Nationality Law enacted by the same assembly also defined Korean nationals as essentially those listed under the colonial-era household registry. As compared to postwar Japan, the postcolonial Koreans were less successful in negotiating with external others, but they were as resilient, if not more so, in resisting the imposition by other means. Herein lies the seed of unresolved tension in the constitutional identity of South Korea, which persists to this day.

All in all, the cases of postwar Japan and postcolonial Korea hardly conform to the dogma that a constituent people with clear and predetermined boundaries engages in founding and creates a new constitutional universe *ex nihilo*. Rather, they demonstrate that it is in the course of intense constitutional politics that such a people is constituted. This does not mean, however, that the people is passively sitting on the receiving end of the boundary imposition. Even as the constituent people's agency is curtailed by the external interferences, its role can never be underestimated in negotiating its own boundaries. Also, legal legacies from the past, whether welcome by the people or not, surface as the crucial bedrock on which such negotiations unfold. People-formation and constitution-making constitute the two sides of democratic constitutional founding.

Conclusion

In an oft-quoted passage about the nature of the public realm, Hannah Arendt draws an analogy to a table – a human artifact that connects the people seated around it while keeping them apart from one another. The public realm "gathers us together and yet prevents our falling over each other, so to speak."[1] Jeremy Waldron takes this imagery and applies it to the constitution itself. Like a table, a well-designed constitution in the liberal democratic sense "relates and separates men at the same time." It allows people to engage with one another as equal partners in a common venture while preserving the distance and space that are critical for individual freedom and diversity of viewpoints.[2] The table imagery is no doubt useful in highlighting the function of a constitution as an "in-between," to use an Arendtian idiom, but it nevertheless leaves unanswered a crucial question. Unaddressed, that is, in the analogy is the question of the identity of those who are sitting around the table. Who is entitled to a seat at the table in the first place? A good conventional democratic answer might begin with the story of how the table was made. There was an already existing group of people who recognized the common need for a table and together participated in the process of its making. Since they created it, it is a matter of course that they are entitled to seats at the table. In other words, willful agency of the sovereign constituent people is posited as the ground and source of the action of democratic constitution-making.

In modern political and legal theories, such pre-constitutional agency has been variously attributed to the primordial ethnic or cultural nation, the *Volk*

[1] Hannah Arendt, *The Human Condition* (Chicago: The University of Chicago Press, 1958), p. 52.

[2] Jeremy Waldron, "Arendt's Constitutional Politics," in Dana Villa (ed.), *Cambridge Companion to Hannah Arendt* (Cambridge: Cambridge University Press, 2001), pp. 203–05.

as a political unity, or an "eternal people" in the state of nature. Whatever the label, the defining feature of these entities is an almost divine ability to create a new constitutional universe out of nothing in splendid isolation from all others. Even a cursory glance, however, is enough to show that postulating a constituent people with such miraculous powers is a questionable presupposition. This is so not merely because it is not borne out by philosophical inquiries on action and agency or by historical investigations about real-life constitution-making. It is problematic also because such charismatic agency can scarcely be squared with the universal norms and principles that any constitution worth its salt is supposed to embody. Envisioning this sort of a powerful agent will inevitably make it difficult to give due recognition to the claims of moral reasoning, which are likely to be seen as undue constraints on the autonomous will of the people. That is why, in some versions of this latter-day political theology, the sovereign people's constituent will is claimed to be beyond good and evil. Similarly, an ethnic nation's ultimate decision about its political existence is held to be an absolute good that cannot be subjected to moral scrutiny.

In order to avoid this normatively unattractive conclusion, some legal positivists such as Hans Kelsen sought to replace the constituent will with pure norm. Rather than positing a pre-constitutional agent with supreme agency, famously, it was declared that, in the beginning, there was a norm – the *Grundnorm*. Since all constitutions derive their authority from this basic norm, reconciling them with universal norms and principles was not a problem. This approach, however, creates a whole new set of difficulties for making sense of democratic constitutional founding, for positing a norm as the fount of constitutional legitimacy ultimately has the effect of rendering superfluous the human activity of constitution-making. It is hardly possible, on this view, to conceive of the people as having any kind of agency at all. The role of the people as active participants in the process of establishing a constitutional order has little theoretical significance, and can even be dispensed with. It should be obvious that, for purposes of theorizing democratic constitutional founding, the agency of the people is of central importance. Any approach that brackets the *demos* out of democracy cannot but be deeply troubling for theorizing democratic constitutional founding.

We have suggested that this theoretical oscillation between attribution of excessive agency and denial of any agency is the result of an "artificial freezing" of our mental frame. It is due to our habit of thinking that the constitution is an inanimate object created by a single, pre-existing, and readily identifiable agent. What is not given due consideration is the other side of the founding process, namely, the constitution of the people through constitution-making.

Founding creates not only an enduring constitutional structure; also formed by the same process is the people, the body politic itself. The establishment of a structure and the formation of a people are two sides of the same coin. This means that both sides are informed by the same set of procedural rules and normative principles. Shared commitment to the rules of mutual engagement not only endows legitimacy on the constitutional structure, but also enables the identification of a constituent people. Adherence to those normative principles, in other words, is not an external constraint on the constituent people, as they are constitutive of their identity. It is not an exercise in some kind of collective self-constraint either, as there is no prior "self" that could constrain itself by accepting those normative principles. The constituent people, it turns out, are sovereign and constrained at the same time.

Constitutional founding entails a deeply transformative politics whereby self-government and self-constitution are simultaneously enacted. To return to Arendt's analogy, the table is not the outcome of a decision on the part of a pre-existing group to create a legged board around which they can just sit together. Not to be overlooked is the fact that the identity of those who have seats at the table gets defined through their joint project. It is in the process of agreeing on the size of the board and the height of the legs, as well as on the proper spacing between the seats – in accordance with morally acceptable principles – that an identifiable people emerges who are entitled to sit at the table. They may have existed, prior to the joint creation of the table, as a group of individuals with shared cultural, linguistic, or religious heritage. Yet, their identity as rightful seat-holders at the table, defined in terms of their mutual distance and different vantage points, only arises and becomes crystallized as they engage in the table-making process. The constitution and the people are mutually constitutive.

Our suggestion has been that this perspective is suitable even for analyzing and assessing historical cases of constitutional founding, as in Japan and Korea, where people have existed as an identifiable political unit for centuries, if not millennia. Despite their long histories as independent nations, the politics of constitutional founding in both Japan and Korea were constitutive in the sense that it engendered a new identity for the residents. They would henceforth be identified as "We the People" of the constitution. All parties concerned were keenly aware that one of the primary goals of the project lay in transforming the way in which they viewed themselves and one another. They would no longer be defined as subjects of a sovereign and divine emperor, and their loftiest goal in life would no longer consist in serving and dying for his glory. Likewise, Koreans would no longer be viewed as colonial residents subject to oppression and discrimination, or as targets of forced assimilation.

Instead, they would be members of the sovereign people who are entitled to equal rights and duties as specified in the constitution. Both Koreans and Japanese would, in other words, assume a new identity as free and active citizens of a constitutional democracy. In short, even in these two cases where beliefs in national identities were deeply entrenched, drafters of the constitution were aware of the "people-making" dimension of the project.

It is our belief that appreciating the mutually constitutive relationship between the constitution and the people contributes to a more nuanced and sympathetic understanding of actual historical instances of constitutional founding. That is, conventional theories based on what we called the common creed of democratic constitutionalism tend to be inaccurate as a matter of description as well as inappropriate as a matter of normative standard. For rather than trying to create a new political universe *ex nihilo*, those who participate in actual constitution-making processes often invoke and build on the past while recasting it in a different light. Rather than trying to obey some putatively unadulterated will of the local people, they necessarily engage in extensive negotiations with external agents. In other words, very few, if any, real-life attempts to establish a new constitutional order will satisfy the stringent requirements of the common creed. This is because those requirements are not only unrealistic but also ultimately misguided when it comes to assessing the success or sustainability of constitutional founding. We have tried to show that this was so at least in the cases of postwar Japan and postcolonial Korea.

Unfortunately, the common creed still exerts considerable power as a normative yardstick for evaluating historical efforts at constitutional founding. For example, the charge is often heard that the constitutions of Korea and Japan have not been particularly successful in opening a truly new chapter in the political life of the respective nations. Not only was the Japanese imperial system left intact, but the entire conservative establishment that had been in power throughout the prewar years remained largely unaffected. As for Korea, the Japanese colonial regime was replaced by a government run by locals, but the criticism still lingers that the founding was not predicated on a thorough cleansing of the nation's body and soul through an effective lustration of colonial collaborators. In a sense, this is natural given the circumstances under which the two constitutions were made, since it is an understatement to say that they were drafted in haste. In Japan, the original draft in English was drawn up in a week's time by members of the GHQ/SCAP, whereas in Korea the National Assembly's drafting committee took about three weeks to come up with a base draft. While the respective legislatures in both countries were allowed a bit more time to deliberate on the suggested drafts, there is no doubt that the various agents of constituent power were under considerable time pressure. It was seen that MacArthur and his staff wished to seize the short window of opportunity in early February 1946 so as to preempt the activities of the Far Eastern Commission. Similarly, it was decided early on in Korea that the National Assembly, which was convened for its first meeting on 31 May 1948, would need to finish the task of making a constitution and forming a new government in two and a half months so that the new republic could be launched on 15 August, the third anniversary of liberation from Japanese colonial rule. The idea of allowing for extended deliberation by going through "interim" constitutions, as has happened in more recent cases of constitutional founding, was a luxury neither country could afford to indulge in. Given such haste, it is perhaps not surprising that they could not effectuate a radical break with the pre-constitutional past.

If one holds on to the conventional creed, one can scarcely avoid the conclusion that the two constitutions are fundamentally flawed. Not only was there no rupture; in neither case was the constitution an autochthonous document based solely on the supreme will of the local people. Moreover, both were written under conditions that made it difficult to discern the human boundary, if not the existence itself, of a sovereign constituent people. Yet, it may be that such negative assessments miss the point. From our perspective, the more meaningful yardstick for evaluation is one that does not focus exclusively on some putative "constituent moment." To be sure, a constitution drafted under conditions that violate universal moral principles can hardly be called legitimate. As important, however, in evaluating the legitimacy of a constitutional order are the conditions that obtain after the drafting. As mentioned, to freeze our mental frame yields a distorted view of the whole project. We have already suggested that the identity of the constituent people cannot properly be understood without assuming a dynamic, or temporally extended, perspective. The same may be true for appraising the legitimacy of the constitutional structure that emerges from the founding.

For instance, constitutional founding may more appropriately be assessed according to whether the process successfully inaugurated a durable structure that allows for self-government, on the one hand, and an ongoing framework for the continuous self-constitution of the people, on the other. The former aspect would deal with the more familiar issues of protection of individual rights, prevention of autocracy, and a workable relationship among government branches. The latter would ask questions regarding the terms with which the citizens define themselves as a people and through which they contest and adjudicate different visions of their constitutional identity. The important point to note is that, in order to perform either task, one cannot assume a static viewpoint that remains fixated on a particular slice of time. One must have an appreciation for the way in which the structure and terms of the constitution were first negotiated during the founding stage and then subsequently appropriated and/or contested in its aftermath. Obviously, elaborating a fully developed theory of such dynamic constitutional legitimacy has not been our goal in this book. We did note, however, that the founding stage itself must be conceived as temporally extended so as to bring into view the complex negotiations that take place both before and after the actual drafting process. We have also highlighted perhaps the two most important dimensions of that complex negotiation – external impacts and past legacies. We believe that these two dimensions continue to be important in the post-founding phase.

In this connection, our accounts of the Japanese and Korean negotiations with external forces and past legacies were intended not so much to show that the two constitutions were flawed from the beginning. Rather, they were meant to highlight the fact that the various agents who exercised constituent power were often compelled by the realization that the new constitutional order could not be established except through negotiations with overbearing external others and unmasterable pasts. Those knowledgeable about the two countries' current political and constitutional discourse will also recognize that the way in which those early negotiations were conducted is still reverberating in the present. The terms and dynamics that were set seven decades ago tend to inform, if not structure, the way that the people of Japan and Korea are debating their constitutional identities today.

To begin with, external interventions were "present at the creation" in both instances. For Japan and Korea, the setting in which constitutional founding took place was essentially bestowed on them by outside agents. Unconditional defeat was forced on Japan, while liberation came as an unexpected gift to Korea from the Allied Powers. More to the point, the drafters, whether consciously or not, had to engage in extended negotiations with external forces, specifically the United States. Article 9 of Japan's constitution was, from its inception, intended for the international audience as it embodied a promise to become a peaceful and responsible member of the community of civilized nations. Although it was initially accepted with the utmost reluctance, few within the Japanese government had any illusions about the possibility of rejecting the provision, especially in light of the overriding priority given to the preservation of both the office and person of the emperor. Both the foreign lawgiver and domestic leaders were in full agreement that permanent unarmed pacifism must be constitutionalized in order to save Hirohito. Moreover, even when the external authorities changed their minds about the peace provision, the locals successfully negotiated its preservation and further entrenched it as the cornerstone of their postwar constitutional identity. Korea's prime external other was also the United States in the sense that it had not only defeated Japan, but also occupied and directly ruled the southern half of the peninsula which it divided with the Soviet Union at the 38th parallel. The "socialistic" economic regime of the new South Korean republic was inevitably colored by the rules and regulations inherited from the U.S. military government, which had no choice but to exercise tight control over the postcolonial economy on the brink of collapse. The Economy Chapter was also crafted under the shadow of the competing regime being established in the Soviet-occupied zone, because the drafters were keenly aware of the lure of communist propaganda to the poverty-stricken populace in the south. Such a progressive economic system, however, was not to survive as the Cold War intensified after the Korean War. With the further incorporation of South Korea into the American-dominated East Asian economic and security order defined by free enterprise and regional integration, the constitution's economic provisions were drastically modified in the direction of eliminating state ownership or control over major economic resources and enterprises.

To this day, both Japan and Korea still carry the birthmarks left on their respective constitutional orders by external agents. For one thing, both reveal an interesting disjunction between the ideal that was first embodied in the constitution under external influence and the later adaptations that were necessitated by altered external realities. Japan's *de jure* pacifism has been stretched and challenged by the existence of a *de facto* military with a mandate that is increasingly being read expansively and proactively. The constitutional discourse of postwar Japan has, to a considerable extent, revolved around this gap between the constitutional norm encoded in Article 9 and the undeniable social fact of the Self-Defense Forces. In Korea, the fundamental principle of an equitable economy, which had been preserved in 1954, would be further watered down in the subsequent amendments, guiding the constitutional shift toward a more market-oriented regime. Yet, debates still continue as to whether the Founding Constitution's socialistic economic principle has been "betrayed" or "rectified" by subsequent amendments and/or government practices. The terms through which current Japanese and Korean citizens understand and debate their constitutional orders are refracted through the birthmarks created at founding.

We have also seen that, in both countries, the status quo ante could not be simply brushed aside. Despite MacArthur's firm belief that a brand new constitution was necessary to inject popular sovereignty into Japan's body politic, he was also convinced of the need to maintain complete legal continuity with the Imperial Constitution. Thus began the perennial puzzle among Japanese scholars of how logically to square the rupture in legitimacy with the procedural continuity, to which one of the best-known answers is the so-called August Revolution theory. The decision to maintain continuity also spurred debates on whether or not Japan's *kokutai* has been preserved in the symbol emperor system, which both retained and drastically transformed the imperial institution. Symbol emperor has become an emblem of not only the democratic transformations of the postwar era, but also the extraordinary staying power of "a very present past," as Carol Gluck put it. For drafters of the Korean constitution, the desire to extinguish the pre-existing order was relatively stronger, as can be seen in the call for negating the "double tyranny" of the past. Yet, even in Korea, a new order could not be conjured up from out of nothing. Alternative pasts – a revolution and a republican tradition – had to be posited which could function as the springboard for the project of launching a new future. Indeed, the imagined legacy of the republican past was partly responsible for the ambiguous and unstable manner in which the constitution adopted the principle of separation of powers. In addition, legal continuity with the pre-constitutional past was specifically mandated in the document itself. Invocation and preservation of the past obviously created tensions with the other pressing mandate of the day, namely, the punishment of colonial collaborators, which many saw as the *sine qua non* for the successful establishment of an independent Korean republic. Evidently, the idealistic need for a radical break with the past and the practical requirement for maintaining continuity both loomed large in the minds of the drafters.

As mentioned, contemporary political discourse in both Japan and Korea often tends to be preoccupied with questions of "settling" or "overcoming" the past. In Japan, liberals and progressives complain that the militarist past was never fully liquidated, while conservatives protest that too much of the nation's tradition has been lost or rejected. By contrast, in the Korean context, most of the discontent seems to stem from the alleged fact that the colonial past has never been decisively repudiated, with very few taking the view that too much has been eradicated. To that extent, Koreans may exhibit a more severe case of the *tabula rasa* syndrome. Yet, our suggestion has been that it is futile and unproductive to assess constitutional founding by asking whether the past has been successfully extinguished. The more relevant indicator is probably whether the different attitudes toward the past encoded in the constitution are being creatively appropriated to form an effective and enduring story of democratic agency. In this connection, the emergence of an "emperor-centered" postwar identity of the people, if true, does not bode well for the Japan's constitutional democracy. To the extent that the symbol emperor system is contributing to Japan's reluctance to squarely face up to its wartime responsibility, it may actually be disempowering the people. By contrast, the freedom under the present constitution to criticize even the emperor may provide the basis for a more promising story of people's agency and empowerment. Similarly, the story of having established a republic in the face of double tyranny may have redemptive powers today for the democratic agency of the Korean people. The claim, by contrast, that the legacy of the colonial legal system (e.g., the household head system) has been responsible for the persistence of undue social hierarchies and discriminations, if true, will no doubt cast doubts on the formation of an active democratic people. Effacement and re-inscription, two attitudes toward the past encoded at founding in the constitutions of both countries, continue to frame the manner in which the story of peoplehood is narrated.

In a sense, the various agents that exercised constituent power in Japan and Korea may have realized, however dimly, the deeply constitutive nature of the project they were engaged in. Rather than assuming a people whose boundaries are firm, natural, and self-evident, all parties involved recognized that the constitution-making process itself will set the boundaries of a new "We the People." The contours of the sovereign people were determined as they engaged in the complex politics of founding. Since the people would be defined as those individuals who were represented in the assembly that drafted and/or ratified the constitution, issues of suffrage rights and electoral districts were of critical importance to the constituent agents. At stake was the issue of membership in the constituent people, something of prior import than the technical issue of nationality, which would in fact be settled after the adoption of the constitution. Recognition of this importance led the Japanese government to effectuate a swift excision of former colonial subjects so as to ensure that the new constitution would be proclaimed in the name of a newly defined Japanese people "proper." Similarly, in Korea, the issue of a special electoral district for refugees from North Korea was contested precisely because it was recognized that the proper boundary of the constituent people was unsettled. In both Japan and Korea, the people were being formed by the process by which the constitution was being authored by the people.

This mutually constitutive nature of the relationship between the people and the constitution is by no means unique to postwar Japan and postcolonial Korea. It is in fact almost ubiquitous in most historical cases of founding, especially since the mid-twentieth century, when inhabitants of so many regions of the world were regrouped to form new political units and became independent states. Constitution-making is often accompanied by artificial and politically motivated redrawing of the boundaries that separate one putative constituent people from another. In some cases, an entirely new people is formed where none had existed before by drawing arbitrary lines on the map to create new territorial borders. Examples include many countries in Africa and Southeast Asia that gained independence after World War II. In other cases, an already existing political unit may undergo a revolutionary transformation that is accompanied by the adoption of new criteria for membership in the constituent people. This may result in the contraction or expansion of the human boundaries of the people. Post-apartheid South Africa might be a case that saw a massive influx of individuals into the bounds of the sovereign people. Places like China and Vietnam, following the communist revolution, saw the expulsion of former landlords and capitalists from the bounds of politically relevant peoplehood through their categorization as "enemies of the people." In all of these cases, constitutions are not the creation of an already existing "We the People." Rather, who belongs to the sovereign people becomes clear only after (or during) the complex political process that establishes a new constitutional order.

This does not, of course, mean that the people are merely an ideational construct of the constitution. The people must be, and cannot but be, postulated as the active agents of a democratic constitutional order. That agency of the people, however, cannot be regarded as a pre-constitutional power exercised by some primordial entity. Especially, given that the contours of the people are clarified by the process of constitution-making, which necessarily takes place in conversations with external forces, it would be odd, if not positively absurd, to take a nativist approach that pits "We the People" against external others. For example, while the contemporary rise of populist and nationalist political parties in many European countries is understandable given the social strife and economic hardship faced by their citizens, it must be pointed out that their basic premise of an insular and primordial nation rests on shaky grounds. Similarly, while it may be right to be wary of the shift of public decision-making authority away from the traditional bounds of nation-states, it would be both disingenuous and vacuous to advocate a narrow and exclusivist attitude that portrays globalization or regional integration as a major threat to the people's agency. It would be disingenuous because the people themselves are, to an important extent, the product of earlier negotiations with outside forces, and it would be vacuous because the people are not uniformly affected by decisions of supranational authorities. Even vis-à-vis the external others, the people that the populists allegedly speak for do not speak in unison.

Indeed, the most important practical implication of our point on the mutually constitutive relationship between the people and their constitution consists in highlighting the impossibility of assuming a monolithic people with uniform views and interests. Any individual or political group claiming to speak on behalf of the entire people must always be viewed with suspicion.

Any putative unity of the people must be regarded with a grain of salt, because even a successful process of constitution-making that produces a coherent identity for the people must recognize and leave room for the inescapable and insurmountable plurality inherent in the constituent people. "We the People," it turns out, cannot be referred to in the singular. Constitutional founding does not seek to fuse, as Hobbes did, the multitude into "one artificial person," or a Leviathan. Like Arendt's table, rather, it seeks to constitute a framework by which disparate individuals can be identified as partners in an ongoing conversation for adjudicating their different views and interests while continually reconstituting themselves as the sovereign people. A successful founding is one that establishes a framework within which conversation continues to take place among the people. By enabling the ongoing conversation, that is, the constitutional structure set up at founding allows the people to engage in the endless activity of self-constitution.

In that sense, self-constitution of the people is not confined to a "constituent moment," as it were. Even after founding, it often takes place through contestations over the constitution itself, in which the shape and size of the table, and the way in which it was made, feature as the central focus of post-founding constitutional conversations. The original table-making action by which the people constituted themselves as a people continues to influence the manner and substance of their subsequent debates. Through constitutional interpretations and amendments, that is, the identity of the people is continually being adjusted and redefined. Important court decisions regarding the negotiations and choices made at founding will also have an effect on our sense of who we are as a people. To that extent, the founding continues to be present and relevant in the post-founding context rather than fading into the remote and disconnected past. It may be that continuing self-constitution of the people is possible only if the founding is preserved in the present by the people as their constant reference point and sounding board.

Appreciating this mutually constitutive relationship will contribute to a vibrant constitutional democracy insofar as it prompts us ordinary citizens to shed our usual apathy and cynicism toward politics. Since we constitute our own selves by making and remaking our constitution, this recognition should provide us with renewed motivation for spirited participation in constitutional politics of our day. Such a heightened sense of ownership over democratic constitutional politics, furthermore, will encourage each and every one of us to turn inward and reflexively examine the very nature of the common enterprise that we are engaged in. In other words, active civic participation should be tempered by sobriety, inner distance, and self-reflexivity. Democratic constitutional politics is hinged equally on Socratic *vita contemplativa* and Machiavellian *vita activa*. For, at stake in our mutual engagement is much more than the banal issues of rights-protection and power-allocation. It is the very soul and identity of "We the People."

We need to make our own constitution, because it makes us who we are – the sovereign constituent people. We hark back to the founding not out of some blind reverence for an eternal *patria* or the original intent of the founders. Rather, we do so in order to inform ourselves of what Alexander Hamilton called "reflection and choice" as well as the "accident and force" that forged our own identity as a constituent people and to eagerly engage in that ongoing reflexive conversation with the foundational decisions and negotiations. We fashion ourselves into the sovereign people via constitutional founding and refounding, and we will do so with a sense of care and justice for others to the extent that we are mindful of the self-constitutive nature of our democratic engagement. Herein lies, perhaps, the meaning of popular sovereignty free at last of political theology.

Note on Romanization and Sources

Korean terms have been romanized according to the McCune-Reischauer system, except for a few commonly known names (e.g., Seoul). The modified Hepburn system has been used for Japanese terms, with exceptions made for words with conventional English spelling (e.g., Tokyo). In case of Korean authors' names, their own romanization, where known, has been respected. For most East Asian personal names, following traditional practice, the family name has been placed before the given name (with Syngman Rhee being an exception). When an author has chosen to invert the name order for publication in English, the format in the original text has been followed.

For primary materials on Japan, we have relied mainly on the vast CD-ROM database compiled and edited by Ray A. Moore and Donald L. Robinson, *The Japanese Constitution: A Documentary History of its Framing and Adoption, 1945–1947* (Princeton, NJ: Princeton University Press, 1998). Footnote entries that begin with "RMxxx" refer to the document number within that database. When referring to longer documents, we have followed the CD-ROM's instructions by including more detailed information at the end of the footnote entry so as to enable readers to pinpoint the exact paragraph within the document. For a few documents not found in the CD-ROM, we have consulted *Political Reorientation of Japan, September 1945 to September 1948* (Washington, DC: U.S. Government Printing Office), compiled by the Government Section of the General Headquarters of the Supreme Commander for the Allied Powers. Similarly, for certain entries in the minutes of the Imperial Diet not found in the CD-ROM, we referred to the original pages of the *Teikoku Gikai Sokkiroku* available online at http://teikokugikai-i.ndl.go.jp. U.S. diplomatic documents regarding both Japan and Korea are generally drawn from the multivolume *Foreign Relations of the United States (FRUS), 1945–1957* (Washington, DC: U.S. Government Printing Office, 1969–1993).

For materials on Korea, we have relied on a number of different sources. For the minutes of the First (Constituent) National Assembly, we used the *Chehŏn Kukhoe Sokkirok*, reprinted by Yŏgang Ch'ulp'ansa in 1987. When citing the minutes of the Second National Assembly, we referred to the original pages of the *Che 2-dae Kukhoe Sokkirok* available online at http://likms.assembly.go.kr/record/index.html. References to the minutes of the Korean Interim Legislative Assembly are to the multivolume *Nam Chosŏn Kwado Ippŏp Uiwŏn Sokkirok* reprinted by Sŏnin Munhwasa in 1984. For proclamations, ordinances, and other laws of the United States Army Military Government in Korea, we relied on the original gazette included in *Migunjŏng Pŏmnyŏng Ch'ongnam: Yŏngmunp'an*, compiled by Han'guk Pŏpche Yŏn'guhoe in 1971. For materials related to the United Nations Temporary Commission on Korea, we have consulted the multivolume *Taehan Min'guksa Charyojip: UN Han'guk Imshi Wiwŏndan Kwan'gye Munsŏ*, published by Kuksa P'yŏnch'an Wiwŏnhoe from 1987 to 1990. All references to constitutional documents, including the various drafts, are to the text as printed in *Han'guk Hŏnpŏpsa Mullyu*, edited by Chong Jong-sup (Seoul: Pakyŏngsa, 2002).

Bibliography

Agné, Hans. 2012. "Democratic Founding: We the People and the Others." *I•CON: International Journal of Constitutional Law*, vol. 10, no. 3.

Arato, Andrew. 2009. *Constitution Making under Occupation*. New York: Columbia University Press.

1994. "Dilemmas Arising From the Power to Create Constitutions in Eastern Europe." In *Constitutionalism, Identity, Difference, and Legitimacy: Theoretical Perspectives*. Edited by Michel Rosenfeld. Durham, NC: Duke University Press.

Arendt, Hannah. 1977. *Between Past and Future: Eight Exercises in Political Thought*. New York: Penguin Books.

1965. *On Revolution*. New York: Viking Press.

1958. *The Human Condition*. Chicago: University of Chicago Press.

Arjomand, Said Amir. 2007. "Constitutional Development and Political Reconstruction from Nation-Building to New Constitutionalism." In *Constitutionalism and Political Reconstruction*. Edited by Said Amir Arjomand. Leiden: E. J. Brill.

Armstrong, Charles K. 2003. *The North Korean Revolution, 1945–1950*. Ithaca, NY: Cornell University Press.

Asano, Toyomi. 2008. *Teikoku Nihon no Shokuminchi Hōsei: Hōiki Tōgō to Teikoku Chitsujo* [Colonial Legal System of the Japanese Empire: Integration of Legal Domains and the Imperial Order]. Nagoya: University of Nagoya Press.

Ashibe, Nobuyoshi. 2011. *Kenpō* [Constitutional Law] 5th ed. Revised by Takahashi Kazuyuki. Tokyo: Iwanami Shoten.

Beer, Lawrence W., and John M. Maki. 2002. *From Imperial Myth to Democracy: Japan's Two Constitutions, 1889–2002*. Boulder: University of Colorado Press.

Beiner, Ronald. 2003. *Liberalism, Nationalism, Citizenship: Essays on the Problems of Political Community*. Vancouver: University of British Columbia Press.

Berger, Thomas U. 1993. "From Sword to Chrysanthemum: Japan's Culture of Anti-Militarism." *International Security*, vol. 17, no. 4.

Berlin, Isaiah. 1969. "Two Concepts of Liberty." In *Four Essays on Liberty*. Oxford: Oxford University Press.

Bix, Herbert P. 2001. *Hirohito and the Making of Modern Japan*. New York: Harper Collins.

Bodin, Jean. 1992. *On Sovereignty*. Edited and translated by Julian H. Franklin. Cambridge: Cambridge University Press.

Brazinsky, Gregg. 2007. *Nation Building in South Korea: Koreans, Americans, and the Making of a Democracy*. Chapel Hill: University of North Carolina Press.

Bryant, Taimie L. 1991. "For the Sake of the Country, for the Sake of the Family: The Oppressive Impact of Family Registration on Women and Minorities in Japan." *UCLA Law Review*, vol. 39, no. 1.

Caldwell, Peter C. 1997. *Popular Sovereignty and the Crisis of German Constitutional Law: The Theory and Practice of Weimar Constitutionalism*. Durham, NC: Duke University Press.

Caprio, Mark E. 2007. "Resident Aliens: Forging the Political Status of Koreans in Occupied Japan." In *Democracy in Occupied Japan: The U.S. Occupation and Japanese Politics and Society*. Edited by Mark E. Caprio and Yoneyuki Sugita. New York: Routledge.

Chang, Hu-yŏng. 1948. "Minpŏp Cheshipsajo ŭi Unmyŏng [The Fate of Civil Code Article 14]." *Pŏpchŏng*, vol. 18 (April).

Chapman, David. 2011. "Geographies of Self and Other: Mapping Japan through the Koseki." *Asia-Pacific Journal: Japan Focus* (18 July).

2008. "Tama-chan and Sealing Japanese Identity." *Critical Asian Studies*, vol. 40.

Chen, Edward I-te. 1987. "The Attempt to Integrate the Empire: Legal Perspectives." In *The Japanese Colonial Empire, 1895–1945*. Edited by Ramon H. Myers and Mark R. Peattie. Princeton, NJ: Princeton University Press.

Cheon, Kwang-seok. 2010. "Kŏnkuk Hŏnpŏp ŭi Sahoe-Kyŏngje Chilsŏ Kusang [Visions of Socio-Economic Order Embodied in the Founding Constitution]." In *Chehŏn kwa Kŏn'guk*. Edited by Han'guk Mirae Hakhoe. Paju: Nanam.

Chesterman, Simon. 2005. "Imposed Constitution, Imposed Constitutionalism, and Ownership." *Connecticut Law Review*, vol. 37.

Chinen, Mark. "Article 9 of the Constitution of Japan and the Use of the Procedural and Substantive Heuristics for Consensus," *Michigan Journal of International Law*, vol. 26 (2005).

Choi, Sang-Yong. 2002. "Trusteeship Debate and the Korean Cold War." In *Korea Under the American Military Government, 1945–1948*. Edited by Bonnie B. C. Oh. London: Praeger.

Chong, Jong-Sup. 2004. "1948 nyŏn Kukhoe ŭi Pŏpchŏk Sŏngkyŏk e kwanhan Yŏn'gu [The Legal Nature of the 1948 National Assembly]." *Sŏul Taehakkyo Pŏphak*, vol. 45, no. 2.

Chong, Sang-Woo. 2007. "Migunjŏnggi Chungganp'a ŭi Hŏnjŏnggusang e kwanhan Yŏn'gu [A Study of the Constitutional Designs of the Centrist Group Under U.S. Military Occupation]." Ph.D. dissertation, Seoul National University.

Choudhry, Sujit. 2005. "Old Imperial Dilemmas and the New Nation-Building: Constitutive Constitutional Politics in Multinational Polities." *Connecticut Law Review*, vol. 37.

Chung, Erin A. 2010. *Immigration and Citizenship in Japan*. Cambridge: Cambridge University Press.

Chung, In Seop. 2010. "Kukmin ŭi T'ansaeng kwa Pŏpchŏk Kyŏnggye [The Birth of People and Its Legal Boundary]." In *Chehŏn kwa Kŏn'guk*. Edited by Han'guk Mirae Hakhoe. Paju: Nanam.

Colegrove, Kenneth W. 1936. *Militarism in Japan*. Boston, MA: World Peace Foundation.

Conrad, Sebastian. 2014. "The Dialectics of Remembrance: Memories of Empire in Cold War Japan." *Comparative Studies in Society and History*, vol. 56, no. 1.
Connelly, John W., Jr. 1954. "Memorandum: Report on Economic Provisions of the Constitution of the Republic of Korea (24 March 1954)." Records of the U.S. Foreign Assistance Agencies 1948–61. Record Group 469, Entry 422, Box 20. U.S. National Archives and Records Administration (NARA) at College Park, MD.
Cornell, L. L., and Akira Hayami. 1986. "The Shūmon Aratame Chō: Japan's Population Registers." *Journal of Family History*, vol. 11, no. 4.
Cumings, Bruce. 1993. "Japan's Position in the World System." In *Postwar Japan as History*. Edited by Andrew Gordon. Berkeley: University of California Press.
1981/1992. *The Origins of the Korean War*, vols. I & II. Princeton, NJ: Princeton University Press.
Dann, Philipp, and Zaid Al-Ali. 2006. "The Internationalized 'Pouvoir Constituant': Constitution-Making Under External Influence in Iraq, Sudan and East Timor." *Max Planck Yearbook of United Nations Law*, vol. 10.
Derrida, Jacques. 1986. "Declarations of Independence." *New Political Science*, vol. 15.
Dore, Ronald P. 1959. *Land Reform in Japan*. Oxford: Oxford University Press.
Dower, John W. 1999. *Embracing Defeat: Japan in the Wake of World War II*. New York: W.W. Norton & Co.
1993. "Peace and Democracy in Two Systems: External Policy and Internal Conflict." In *Postwar Japan as History*. Edited by Andrew Gordon. Berkeley: University of California Press.
1979. *Empire and Aftermath: Yoshida Shigeru and the Japanese Experience, 1878–1954*. Cambridge, MA: Council on East Asian Studies, Harvard University Press.
Dull, Paul S. 1948. "South Korean Constitution." *Far Eastern Survey*, vol. 17, no. 7.
Dyzenhaus, David. 1999. *Legality and Legitimacy: Carl Schmitt, Hans Kelsen, and Herman Heller in Weimar*. Oxford: Oxford University Press.
Ebashi, Takashi. 1985. "Shokuminchi ni okeru Kenpō no Tekiyō: Meiji Rikkentaisei no Ichisokumen [Application of the Constitution in the Colonies: One Aspect of the Meiji Constitutional System]." *Hōgaku Shirin*, vol. 82, nos. 3 & 4.
Ekbladh, David. 2010. *The Great American Mission: Modernization and the Construction of an American World Order*. Princeton, NJ: Princeton University Press.
Elkins, Zachary, Tom Ginsburg, and James Melton. 2008. "Baghdad, Tokyo, Kabul...: Constitution Making in Occupied States." *William and Mary Law Review*, vol. 49.
Elshtain, Jean Bethke. 2008. *Sovereignty: God, State, and Self*. New York: Basic Books.
Elster, Jon. 2004. *Closing the Books: Transitional Justice in Historical Perspective*. Cambridge: Cambridge University Press.
1994. "Constitutional Bootstrapping in Philadelphia and Paris." In *Constitutionalism, Identity, Difference, and Legitimacy: Theoretical Perspectives*. Edited by Michel Rosenfeld. Durham, NC: Duke University Press.
1993. "Constitution-Making in Eastern Europe: Rebuilding the Boat in the Open Sea." *Public Administration*, vol. 11, nos. 1/2.
Endō, Masataka. 2010. *Kindai Nihon no Shokuminchi Tōchi ni okeru Kokuseki to Koseki: Manshū, Chōsen, Taiwan* [Nationality and Household Registry in Modern Japan's Colonial Rule: Manchuria, Korea, Taiwan]. Tokyo: Akashi Shoten.
Feldman, Noah. 2005. "Imposed Constitutionalism." *Connecticut Law Review*, vol. 37.

Fraenkel, Ernst. 1985. "The Structure of United States Army Military Government in Korea (1948)." Reprinted in *Journal of Modern Korean Studies*, vol. 2.

Frank, Jason. 2010. *Constituent Moments: Enacting the People in Postrevolutionary America*. Durham, NC: Duke University Press.

Frank, Richard B. 1999. *Downfall: The End of the Japanese Empire*. New York: Penguin.

Fujita, Shōzō. 1998. *Tennōsei-kokka no Shihaigenri* [The Principle of Domination in the Emperor-State]. Tokyo: Misuzu Shobō.

1997. *Ishin no Seishin* [The Spirit of the Restoration]. Tokyo: Misuzu Shobō.

Fujitani, Takashi. 1998. *Splendid Monarchy: Power and Pageantry in Modern Japan*. Berkeley: University of California Press.

Gluck, Carol. 1990. "The Idea of Showa." In *Showa: The Japan of Hirohito*. Edited by Stephen R. Graubard. New York: W.W. Norton & Co.

1985. *Japan's Modern Myths: Ideology in the Late Meiji Period*. Princeton, NJ: Princeton University Press.

Gordenker, Leon. 1958. "The United Nations, the United States Occupation and the 1948 Election in Korea." *Political Science Quarterly*, vol. 73, no. 3.

Gotō, Mitsuo. 2012. "Nihonkoku Kenpō Seiteishi ni okeru 'Nihonkokumin' to 'Gaikokujin' ['Japanese National' and 'Foreigner' in the Making of the Japanese Constitution]." *Hikaku Hōgaku*, vol. 45, no. 3.

Greenberg, Udi. 2014. *The Weimar Century: German Émigrés and the Ideological Foundations of the Cold War*. Princeton, NJ: Princeton University Press.

Griffin, Edward G. 1972. "The Universal Suffrage Issue in Japanese Politics, 1918–25." *Journal of Asian Studies*, vol. 31, issue 2.

Grimm, Dieter. 1995. "Does Europe Need a Constitution?" *European Law Journal*, vol. 1, no. 3.

Guthrie-Shimizu, Sayuri. 2010. "Japan, the United States, and the Cold War, 1945–1960." In *The Cambridge History of the Cold War, Vol. 1: Origins*. Edited by Melvin P. Leffler and Odd Arne Westad. Cambridge: Cambridge University Press.

Habermas, Jürgen. 1996. *Between Facts and Norms: A Contribution to a Discourse Theory of Law and Democracy*. Translated by William Rehg. Cambridge, MA: MIT Press.

1995. "Comments on Dieter Grimm's 'Does Europe Need a Constitution?'" *European Law Journal*, vol. 1, no. 3.

Hamano, Sylvia B. 1998–1999. "Incomplete Revolution and Not So Alien Transplants: The Japanese Constitution and Human Rights." *University of Pennsylvania Journal of Constitutional Law*, vol. 1.

Han, Hong-gu. 2009. *T'ŭkkang* [Special Lectures]. Seoul: Hangyoreh Ch'ulp'an.

Hanazaki, Kōhei. 2004. "Ainu Moshir and Yaponesia: Ainu and Okinawan Identities in Contemporary Japan." In *Race, Ethnicity and Migration in Modern Japan: Imagined and Imaginary Minorities*. Edited by Michael Weiner. New York: Routledge.

Handō, Kazutoshi. 2009. *Shōwashi: Sengohen 1945–1989* [A History of the Showa Period: Postwar 1945–1989]. Tokyo: Heibonsha.

Hara, Hideshige. 2004. *Nihonkoku Kenpō Seitei no Keifu: Sensō Shūketsu made* [Genealogy of the Making of Japan's Constitution: Through the End of the War], vol. 1. Tokyo: Nihon Hyōronsha.

Hasebe, Yasuo. 1997. "The August Revolution Thesis and the Making of the Constitution of Japan." *Rechtstheorie*, vol. 17.

Hellegers, Dale M. 2001. *We, the Japanese People: World War II and the Origins of the Japanese Constitution*, vols. 1 & 2. Stanford, CA: Stanford University Press.

Heo, Jong. 2003. *Panmint'ŭkwi ŭi Chojik kwa Hwaltong* [Organization and Activities of the Special Committee on Anti-National Activities]. Seoul: Tosŏch'ulp'an Sŏnin.

Higuchi, Yōichi. 2010. *Kenpō* [Constitutional Law] 3rd ed. Tokyo: Sōbunsha.

1993. "The Constitution and the Emperor System: Is Revisionism Alive?" In *Japanese Constitutional Law*. Edited by Percy R. Luney, Jr. and Kazuyuki Takahashi. Tokyo: University of Tokyo Press.

Hirschl, Ran. 2004. *Towards Juristocracy: The Origins and Consequences of the New Constitutionalism*. Cambridge, MA: Harvard University Press.

Hobbes, Thomas. 1991. *Leviathan*. Edited by Richard Tuck. Cambridge: Cambridge University Press.

Holmes, Stephen. 1988. "Precommitment and the Paradox of Democracy." In *Constitutionalism and Democracy*. Edited by Jon Elster and Rune Slagstad. Cambridge: Cambridge University Press.

Hong, Chin-gi. 1947. "Sabŏp Chaep'anso ŭi Pŏmnyul Shimsa [Review of Statute by a Judicial Court]." *Pŏpchŏng*, vol. 14.

Hong, Sŏng-ch'an. 2001. "Nongji Kaehyŏk Chŏnhu ŭi Taejiju Tonghyang [The Situation of Big Landlords before and after the Land Reform]." In *Nongji Kaehyŏk Yŏn'gu*. Edited by Hong Sŏng-ch'an. Seoul: Yonsei University Press.

Honig, Bonnie. 2001. *Democracy and the Foreigner*. Princeton, NJ: Princeton University Press.

Hosokawa, Kiyoshi. 1990. "Japanese Nationality in International Perspective." In *Nationality and International Law in Asian Perspective*. Edited by Swan Sik Ko. Dordrecht: Martinus Nijhoff Publishers.

Hozumi, Nobushige. 1912. *Ancestor-worship and Japanese Law*. Tokyo: The Maruzen Kabushiki-Kaisha (originally published in 1901).

1904. *The New Japanese Civil Code, as Material for the Study of Comparative Jurisprudence*. Tokyo: Tokyo Printing Co.

Hwang, Sŭng-hŭm. 2004. "Chehŏn Hŏnpŏp Cheyukjang Kyŏngjepyŏn ŭi Hyŏngsŏng Kwajŏng kwa Kŭ Ŭimi [The Formation Process of the Founding Constitution's Chapter VI on Economy and Its Meaning]." *Pŏpsahak Yŏn'gu*, vol. 30.

2002. "Chehŏn Hŏnpŏp sang ŭi Kŭlloja ŭi Iik Kyunjŏmkwŏn ŭi Hŏnpŏphwa Kwajŏng e kwanhan Yŏn'gu [A Study on the Constitutionalization of Workers' Right to Share Profit in the Founding Constitution]." *Kongpŏp Yŏn'gu*, vol. 31, no. 2.

Inoue, Kyoko. 1991. *MacArthur's Japanese Constitution: A Linguistic and Cultural Study of its Making*. Chicago: University of Chicago Press.

Institute of Asian Culture Studies, ed. 1997. *Migunjŏnggi Chŏngbojaryojip: Sapŏppu Pŏphaesŏk Pogosŏ, 1946. 3 – 1948. 8* [Intelligence Materials during the U.S. Military Occupation: Legal Opinions of the Department of Justice, March 1946 – August 1948]. Ch'unch'ŏn: Institute of Asian Culture Studies, Hallym University.

1990. *HQ, USAFIK G-2 Weekly Summary (1948. 1. 31 – 1948. 11. 26)*. Ch'unch'ŏn: Institute of Asian Culture Studies, Hallym University.

Iokibe, Makoto. 2013. "Conclusion: What was Postwar Japanese Diplomacy?" In *The Diplomatic History of Postwar Japan*. Edited by Makoto Iokibe. Translated by Robert D. Eldridge. New York: Routledge.

2013. "Diplomacy in Occupied Japan: Japanese Diplomacy in the 1940s." In *The Diplomatic History of Postwar Japan*. Edited by Makoto Iokibe. Translated by Robert D. Eldridge. New York: Routledge.

Isono, Fujiko. 1988. "The Evolution of Modern Family Law in Japan." *International Journal of Law and the Family*, vol. 2, no. 2.

Itō, Mikiharu. 1982. *Kazoku Kokkakan no Jinruigaku* [Anthropology of the Family State Ideology]. Tokyo: Mineruva Shobō.

Itō, Narihiko. 2001. *Monogatari Nihonkoku Kenpō Daikyūjō: Sensō to Guntai no nai Sekai e* [A Story of Article 9 of the Japanese Constitution: Toward a World without War and Military]. Tokyo: Kage Shobō.

Jackson, Vicki C. 2008. "What's in a Name?: Reflections on Timing, Naming, and Constitution-making." *William and Mary Law Review*, vol. 49.

Jacobs, Joseph E. 1995. "Letter to the Secretary of State (3 September 1947)." In *Migungmusŏng Han'guk Kwan'gye Munsŏ* [U.S. State Department Documents Related to Korea], vol. 10. Seoul: Arŭm Ch'ulp'ansa.

Jacobsohn, Gary J. 2010. *Constitutional Identity*. Cambridge, MA: Harvard University Press.

Jang, Sang-Hwan. 2005. "Land Reform and Capitalist Development in Korea." Paper presented at International Conference on Korean Economy: Marxist Perspectives, Gyeongsang National University, Chinju, Korea (20 May).

Jeon, Yoong-Deok and Young-Yong Kim. 2000. "Land Reform, Income Redistribution, and Agricultural Production in Korea." *Economic Development and Cultural Change*, vol. 48, no. 2.

Johnson, James. 2001. "Inventing Constitutional Traditions: The Poverty of Fatalism." In *Constitutional Culture and Democratic Rule*. Edited by John Ferejohn, Jack N. Rakove, and Jonathan Riley. Cambridge: Cambridge University Press.

Jun, Sang-in. 2001. *Kogae Sugin Sujŏngjuŭi: Han'guk Hyŏndaesa ŭi Yŏksasahoehak* [Revisionism in Decline: Historical Sociology of Modern Korean History]. Seoul: Chŏnt'ong kwa Hyŏndae.

Kades, Charles L. 1989. "The American Role in Revising Japan's Imperial Constitution." *Political Science Quarterly*, vol. 104, no. 2.

Kalyvas, Andreas. 2008. *Democracy and the Politics of the Extraordinary: Max Weber, Carl Schmitt and Hannah Arendt*. Cambridge: Cambridge University Press.

Kashiwazaki, Chikako. 1998. "Nationality and Citizenship in Japan: Stability and Change in Comparative Perspective." Ph.D. dissertation, Brown University.

Kaufman, Erich. 2000. "On the Problem of the People's Will." In *Weimar: A Jurisprudence of Crisis*. Edited by Arthur J. Jacobson and Bernhard Schlink. Berkeley: University of California Press.

Kay, Richard. 1998. "American Constitutionalism." In *Constitutionalism: Philosophical Foundations*. Edited by Larry Alexander. Cambridge: Cambridge University Press.

Kelsen, Hans. 2000. "On the Essence and Value of Democracy." In *Weimar: Jurisprudence of Crisis*. Edited by Arthur J. Jacobson and Bernhard Schlink. Berkeley: University of California Press.

1967. *The Pure Theory of Law*. Translated by Max Knight. Berkeley: University of California Press.

1945. *General Theory of Law and State*. Translated by Anders Wedberg. New York: Russell & Russell.

Kim, Chang Rok. 1993. "Ilbon Chegukchuŭi ŭi Hŏnpŏp Sasang kwa Shingminji Chosŏn [Constitutional Thoughts of Imperial Japan and Colonial Korea]." *Pŏpsahak Yŏn'gu*, vol. 14.

Kim, Hakjoon. 2008. *Pukhan ŭi Yŏksa, Che 2 kwŏn: Miso Naengjŏn kwa Soryŏn Kunjŏng aresŏŭi Chosŏn Minjujuŭi Inmin Konghwaguk Kŏn'guk, 1946 nyŏn 1 wŏl – 1948 nyŏn 9 wŏl* [A History of North Korea, vol. 2: The Establishment of the Democratic People's Republic of Korea under the U.S.-Soviet Cold War and the Soviet Military Rule, January 1946 – September 1948]. Seoul: Seoul National University Press.

Kim, Il-Young. 2004. *Kŏn'guk kwa Puguk* [State-Building and Wealth-Building]. Seoul: Saenggak ŭi Namu.

Kim, Marie Seong-hak. 2012. *Law and Custom in Korea: Comparative Legal History*. Cambridge: Cambridge University Press.

Kim, Sŏng-bo. 2001. "Ippŏp kwa Silhaenggwajŏng ŭl t'onghae bon Namhan Nongji Kaehyŏk ŭi Sŏngkyŏk [The Characteristics of Land Reform in South Korea as reflected in the Legislative Process]." In *Nongji Kaehyŏk Yŏn'gu*. Edited by Hong Sŏng-ch'an. Seoul: Yonsei University Press.

Kim, Sŏng-ho. 2001. "Nambukhan ŭi Nongji Kaehyŏk Yŏn'gu [Land Reform in North and South Korea]." In *Nongji Kaehyŏk Yŏn'gu*. Edited by Hong Sŏng-ch'an. Seoul: Yonsei University Press.

Kim, Sung Ho. 2007. *Max Weber's Politics of Civil Society*. Cambridge: Cambridge University Press.

2007. "A Constitutional Politics of the Extraordinary: Carl Schmitt, Hans Kelsen, and the 1932 Crisis of the Weimar Constitutional Order." *Korean Political Science Review*, vol. 41, no. 2.

Kim, Sung Ho, and Myungho Choi. 2008. "1948 nyŏn Kŏn'guk Hŏnpŏp Chŏnmun e Nat'anan 'Uridŭl Taehan Kukmin' ŭi Chŏngch'esŏng kwa Chŏngdangsŏng [The Identity and Legitimacy of 'We the People of Korea' in the Preamble of the Founding Constitution of 1948]." *Han'guk Chŏngch'ihak Hoebo*, vol. 42, no. 4.

Kim, Sung Ho, and Sun Choi. 2010. "1948 nyŏn Kŏn'guk Hŏnpŏp e Nat'anan Honhapchŏk Kwŏllyŏkkujo ŭi Kiwŏn [Origins of the Mixed Power Structure of the Founding Constitution]." In *Chehŏn kwa Kŏn'guk*. Edited by Han'guk Mirae Hakhoe. Paju: Nanam.

Kim, Su-Yong. 2008. *Kŏn'guk kwa Hŏnpŏp* [Founding and the Constitution]. Seoul: Kyŏngin Munhwasa.

Klug, Heinz. 2000. *Constituting Democracy: Law, Globalism, and South Africa's Political Reconstruction*. Cambridge: Cambridge University Press.

Kobayashi, Naoki. 1982. *Kenpō Daikyūjō* [Constitution Article 9]. Tokyo: Iwanami Shinsho.

Komamura, Keigo. 2010. "Legitimacy of the Constitution of Japan Redux: Is an Imposed Constitution Legitimate?" An occasional paper presented at the Constitutional Revision Research Project, Reischauer Institute of Japanese Studies, Harvard University (11 February).

Korsgaard, Christine M. 2009. *Self-Constitution: Agency, Identity, and Integrity*. Oxford: Oxford University Press.

Koseki, Shōichi. 2010. "Teikoku Shinmin kara Gaikokujin e: Ataerare, Ubawarete kita Chōsenjin, Taiwanjin no Sanseiken [From Imperial Subject to Foreigner: How Political Rights Were Given to Korean and Taiwanese and Then Taken Away]." *Sekai*, vol. 809 (October).

2009. *Nihonkoku Kenpō no Tanjō* [The Birth of Japan's Constitution]. Tokyo: Iwanami Shoten.

2006. *Kenpō Kyūjō wa Naze Seitei saretaka* [Why Was Article 9 of the Constitution Made?]. Tokyo: Iwanami Shoten.

Kramer, Larry D. 2004. *The People Themselves: Popular Constitutionalism and Judicial Review*. Oxford: Oxford University Press.

Kuroda, Satoru. 1954. "Tennō no Kenpōjo no Chii [Constitutional Status of the Emperor]." *Kōhō Kenkyū*, vol. 10.

Lee, Chulwoo. 1999. "Modernity, Legality, and Power in Korea under Japanese Rule." In *Colonial Modernity in Korea*. Edited by Gi-wook Shin and Michael Robinson. Cambridge, MA: Harvard University Asia Center.

Lee, Jong Won. 1996. *Higashi Ajia Reisen to Kan-Bei-Nichi Kankei* [Cold War in East Asia and the Korea-U.S.-Japan Relations]. Tokyo: University of Tokyo Press.

Lee, Kuk-woon. 2005. "Haebang Konggan esŏ Sabŏpkigu ŭi Chaep'yŏn Kwajŏng e Kwanhan Yŏn'gu [A Study of the Reorganization of Judicial Institutions Following Liberation]." *Pŏp kwa Sahoe*, vol. 29.

Lee, Peter H., ed. 1996. *Sourcebook of Korean Civilization*, vol. II. New York: Columbia University Press.

Lee, Seon-min. 2013. *'Taehan Min'guk' Kukho ŭi T'ansaeng* [The Birth of the State Name Taehan Min'guk]. Paju: Nanam.

Lee, Seung-il. 2011. "Shingminji Chosŏn kwa Taeman ŭi Ch'angssigaemyŏng Kaesŏngmyŏng Pigyo Yŏn'gu [A Comparative Study of the Policy of Adopting Japanese-style Names in Korea and Taiwan during the Colonial Period]." *Taedong Munhwa Yŏn'gu*, vol. 76.

2008. *Chosŏn Ch'ongdokpu Pŏpche Chŏngch'aek* [Legal-Administrative Policies of the Government-General in Korea]. Seoul: Yŏksa Pip'yŏngsa.

2000. "Ilche Shigi Chosŏnin ŭi Ilbon Kukminhwa Yŏn'gu [A Study of the Transformation of the People of Chosŏn into Japanese Kokumin during the Colonial Period]." *Han'gukhak Nonjip*, vol. 34.

Lee, Wan-bom. 2007. *Han'guk Haebang Samnyŏnsa, 1945–1948* [Post-liberation History of Korea, 1945–1948]. Paju: T'aehaksa.

Lee, Young-lok. 2006. *Yu Chin-o Hŏnpŏp Sasang ŭi Hyŏngsŏng kwa Chŏn'gae* [Formation and Development of Yu Chin-o's Constitutional Thought]. Paju: Han'guk Haksul Chŏngbo.

2005. "Cheil Konghwaguk Hŏnpŏp Wiwŏnhoe Chedo ŭi Hyŏngsŏng [Formation of the Constitution Committee System of the First Republic]." *Hŏnpŏphak Yŏn'gu*, vol. 11, no. 2.

2003. "Chehŏn Kwajŏng esŏŭi Kwŏllyŏkkujo Nonŭi e Nat'anan Taerip ŭi Chŏn'gae Kwajŏng kwa Kyŏlgwa e kwanhan Yŏn'gu [A Study on the Clash of Ideas on Power Structure During the Constitution-Drafting Process and Its Outcome]." *Hŏnpŏphak Yŏn'gu*, vol. 28.

Lew, Young Ick. 2013. *Kŏn'guk Taet'ongnyŏng Yi Sŭngman: Saengae, Sasang, Opchŏk ŭi Saeroun Chomyŏng* [Founding President Syngman Rhee: A New Look at His Life, Thoughts, and Achievements]. Seoul: Ilchogak.

Lindahl, Hans. 2007. "Constituent Power and Reflexive Identity." In *The Paradox of Constitutionalism: Constituent Power and Constitutional Form*. Edited by Martin Loughlin and Neil Walker. Oxford: Oxford University Press.

2001. "Sovereignty and the Institutionalization of Normative Order." *Oxford Journal of Legal Studies*, vol. 21, no. 1.

Loh, Yeong-Don. 1996. "Urinara Kukchŏkpŏp ŭi Myŏtkaji Munje e Kwanhan Koch'al [A Study of Some Problems in the Nationality Law of Korea]." *Kukchepŏp Hakhoe Nonch'ong*, vol. 41, no. 2.

MacDonald, Donald S. 1982. "The 1946 Elections and Legislative Assembly in South Korea: America's Bumbling Tutelage." *Journal of Northeast Asian Studies*, vol. 1, no. 3.

Machiavelli, Niccolo. 1996. *Discourses on Livy*. Translated by Harvey Mansfield and Nathan Tarcov. Chicago: University of Chicago Press.

Maier, Charles. 1997. *The Unmasterable Past: History, Holocaust, and the German National Identity*. Cambridge, MA: Harvard University Press.

Maki, John M. 1993. "The Constitution of Japan: Pacifism, Popular Sovereignty, and Fundamental Human Rights." In *Japanese Constitutional Law*. Edited by Percy R. Luney, Jr., and Kazuyuki Takahashi. Tokyo: University of Tokyo Press.

1968. "The Documents of Japan's Commission on the Constitution." In *The Constitution of Japan: Its First Twenty Years, 1947–1967*. Edited by Dan Fenno Henderson. Seattle: University of Washington Press.

1968. "The Japanese Constitutional Style." In *The Constitution of Japan: Its First Twenty Years, 1947–1967*. Edited by Dan Fenno Henderson. Seattle: University of Washington Press.

Margalit, Avishai, and Joseph Raz. 1990. "National Self-Determination." *Journal of Philosophy*, vol. 87, no. 9.

Markell, Patchen. 2000. "Making Affect Safe for Democracy? On 'Constitutional Patriotism'." *Political Theory*, vol. 28, no. 1.

Marks, Frederick W., III. 1973. *Independence on Trial: Foreign Affairs and the Making of the Constitution*. Baton Rouge: Louisiana State University Press.

Martin, Craig. 2008. "Binding the Dogs of War: Japan and the Constitutionalizing of JUS AD BELLUM." *University of Pennsylvania Journal of International Law*, vol. 30, no. 1.

Masumi, Junnosuke. 1985. *Postwar Politics in Japan, 1945–1955*. Translated by Lonny E. Carlile. Berkeley: University of California Press.

Matsuda, Toshihiko. 1995. *Senzenki no Zainichi Chōsenjin to Sanseiken* [Resident Koreans and Voting Rights in Prewar Japan]. Tokyo: Akashi Shoten.

Matsui, Shigenori. 2011. *The Constitution of Japan: A Contextual Analysis*. Oxford: Hart Publishing.

McCormack, Gavan. 2007. *Client State: Japan in the American Embrace*. London and New York: Verso.

McCune, Shannon. 1948. "Land Redistribution in Korea." *Far Eastern Survey*, vol. 17, no. 2.

McIlwain, Charles H. 1947. *Constitutionalism: Ancient and Modern*. Ithaca, NY: Cornell University Press.
McNelly, Theodore. 2000. *The Origins of Japan's Democratic Constitution*. Lanham, MD: University Press of America.
Meade, E. Grant. 1951. *American Military Government in Korea*. New York: King's Crown Press.
Michelman, Frank I. 1998. "Constitutional Authorship." In *Constitutionalism: Philosophical Foundations*. Edited by Larry Alexander. Cambridge: Cambridge University Press.
Michizuki, Mike M. 1992. "US-Japan Security Relations in a New Era." In *The United States and Japan: Changing Relations*. Edited by Chae-Jin Lee. Claremont, CA: Keck Center for International and Strategic Studies.
Milhaupt, Curtis J., J. Mark Ramseyer, and Mark D. West. 2006. *The Japanese Legal System: Cases, Codes, and Commentary*. New York: Foundation Press.
Miller, David. 2009. "Democracy's Domain." *Philosophy and Public Affairs*, vol. 37, no. 3.
Miller, Frank O. 1965. *Minobe Tatsukichi: Interpreter of Constitutionalism in Japan*. Berkeley: University of California Press.
Minear, Richard H. 1970. *Japanese Tradition and Western Law: Emperor, State, and Law in the Thought of Hozumi Yatsuka*. Cambridge, MA: Harvard University Press.
Ministry of Foreign Affairs of Japan. 1910. "Announcement of the Japanese Foreign Office." *American Journal of International Law*, vol. 4, no. 4, Supplement: Official Documents.
Mitchell, C. Clyde. 1949. "Land Reform in South Korea." *Pacific Affairs*, vol. 22, no. 2.
Miyata, Setsuko. 1985. *Chōsen Minshū to 'Kōminka' Seisaku* [Korean Masses and the Policy of Turning People into Imperial Subjects]. Tokyo: Miraisha.
Miyazawa, Kiichi. 2007. *Secret Talks between Tokyo and Washington: The Memoirs of Miyazawa Kiichi, 1949–1954*. Translated by Robert D. Eldridge. New York: Lexington Books.
Miyazawa, Toshiyoshi. 1967. *Kenpō Kōwa* [Lectures on Constitutional Law]. Tokyo: Iwanami Shoten.
1967. "Nihonkoku Kenpō Seitan no Hōri [Legal Theory of the Birth of Japan's Constitution]." In *Kenpō no Genri*. Tokyo: Iwanami Shoten (originally published in 1955).
Mizuno, Naoki. 2008. *Sōshikaimei: Nihon no Chōsen Shihai no naka de* [Adoption of Japanese Names: Within the Context of Japan's Rule Over Korea]. Tokyo: Iwanami Shoten.
1996. "Zainichi Chōsenjin Taiwanjin Sanseiken 'Teishi' Jōkō no Seiritsu [The Making of the Provision that 'Suspended' the Suffrage Rights of the Koreans and Taiwanese in Japan]." *Sekai Jinken Mondai Kenkyu Senta, Kenkyū Kiyō* no. 1.
Moon, Joon-Young. 2010. *Pŏpwŏn kwa Kŏmch'al ŭi T'ansaeng* [The Birth of the Judiciary and the Public Prosecutor's Office]. Seoul: Yŏksabipyŏngsa.
Moore, Ray A., and Donald L. Robinson. 2004. *Partners for Democracy: Crafting the New Japanese State Under MacArthur*. Oxford: Oxford University Press.

Morgan, Edmund S. 1988. *Inventing the People: The Rise of Popular Sovereignty in England and America*. New York: W.W. Norton & Co.

Morris-Suzuki, Tessa. 2008. "Migrants, Subjects, Citizens: Comparative Perspectives on Nationality in the Prewar Japanese Empire." *Asia-Pacific Journal: Japan Focus* (1 September).

2001. "Northern Lights: The Making and Unmaking of Karafuto Identity." *Journal of Asian Studies*, vol. 60, no. 3.

Nagao, Ryūichi. 1997. *Shisō toshite no Nihon Kenpōshi* [Japanese Constitutional History as Theory]. Tokyo: Shinzansha.

Nagasawa, Yuko. 2012. "Ilbon P'aejŏnhu ŭi Hanbando Chanyŏjukwŏn kwa Hanil 'Pulli' [Residual Sovereignty over the Korean Peninsula and the 'Separation' of Korea and Japan after Japan's Defeat]." *Asea Yŏn'gu*, vol. 55, no. 4.

Nakamura, Masanori. 1992. *The Japanese Monarchy: Ambassador Joseph Grew and the Making of the 'Symbol Emperor System,' 1931–1991*. Translated by Herbert B. Bix, Jonathan Baker-Bates, and Derek Bowen. Armonk, NY: M.E. Sharpe.

Nomura, Haruka. 2010. "Making the Japanese Empire: Nationality and Family Register in Taiwan, 1871–1899." *Japan Studies*, vol. 30, no. 1.

Nonaka, Toshihiko et al. 2006. *Kenpō* [Constitutional Law], vol. I, 4th ed. Tokyo: Yūhikaku.

Nonaka, Toshihiko et al., eds. 2000. *Chūshaku Kenpō* [Annotated Constitutional Law], vol. I. Tokyo: Yūhikaku.

O, Ik-hwan. 1991. "Panmint'ŭkwi ŭi Hwaltong kwa Wahae [Activities and Dissolution of the Special Anti-national Committee]." In Song Kŏn-ho et al. *Haebang Chŏnhusa ŭi Inshik*, vol. 1. Seoul: Han'gilsa.

Ochoa Espejo, Paulina. 2014. "People, Territory, and Legitimacy in Democratic States." *American Journal of Political Science*, vol. 58, no.2.

Oguma, Eiji. 2002. *A Genealogy of 'Japanese' Self-Images*. Translated by David Askew. Melbourne: Trans Pacific Press.

1998. *'Nihonjin' no Kyōkai: Okinawa, Ainu, Taiwan, Chōsen Shokuminchi Shihai kara Fukki Undō made* [Boundaries of the 'Japanese': From Colonial Control of Okinawa, Ainu, Taiwan, Korea to Reversion Movement]. Tokyo: Shinyōsha.

Oklopcic, Zoran. 2012. "Constitutional (Re)Vision: Sovereign Peoples, New Constituent Powers, and the Formation of Constitutional Orders in the Balkans." *Constellations*, vol. 19, no. 1.

Oliver, Peter C. 2005. *The Constitution of Independence: The Development of Constitutional Theory in Australia, Canada, and New Zealand*. Oxford: Oxford University Press.

Oppler, Alfred C. 1976. *Legal Reform in Occupied Japan: A Participant Looks Back*. Princeton, NJ: Princeton University Press.

Otake, Hideo. 2001. "Two Contrasting Constitutions in the Postwar World: The Making of the Japanese and the West German Constitutions." In *Five Decades of Constitutionalism in Japanese Society*. Edited by Yoichi Higuchi. Tokyo: University of Tokyo Press.

Palmer, Brandon. 2007. "Imperial Japan's Preparations to Conscript Koreans as Soldiers, 1942–1945." *Korean Studies*, vol. 31.

Park, Chan-Pyo. 2007. *Han'guk ŭi Kukka Hyŏngsŏng kwa Minjujuŭi* [Korean State-Formation and Democracy]. Seoul: Humanitas.

1995. "Chehŏn Kukhoe Sŏn'gŏpŏp kwa Han'guk ŭi Kukka Hyŏngsŏng [Constituent National Assembly Election Law and State-formation in Korea]." *Han'guk Chŏngch'ihak Hoebo*, vol. 29, no. 3.

Park, Chan-Seung. 2013. *Taehan Min'guk ŭn Minju Konghwaguk ida* [The Republic of Korea Shall Be a Democratic Republic]. Seoul: Dolbegae.

Park, Myung-lim. 2011. "Constitution, National Agenda, and Presidential Leadership: Focusing on a Comparison between the Articles on Economy in the 'National Founding Constitution' and the 'Post-Korean War Constitution'." *Korean Social Science Review*, vol. 1, no. 1.

2005. *The Requiem for Peace: A Critical-Constructive Reflection on the Korean War*. Paju: Nanam.

Park, Tae-Gyun. 2000. "U.S. Policy Change toward South Korea in the 1940s and the 1950s." *Journal of International and Area Studies*, vol. 7, no. 2.

Pettit, Philip. 2010. "A Republican Law of Peoples." *European Journal of Political Theory*, vol. 9, no. 1.

1997. *Republicanism: A Theory of Freedom and Government*. Oxford: Oxford University Press.

Philpott, Daniel. 1995. "In Defense of Self Determination." *Ethics*, vol. 105, no. 2.

Pocock, J. G. A. 1975. *The Machiavellian Moment: Florentine Political Thought and the Atlantic Republican Tradition*. Princeton, NJ: Princeton University Press.

Port, Kenneth L. 2010. *Transcending Law: The Unintended Life of Article 9 of the Japanese Constitution*. Durham, NC: Carolina Academic Press.

Preuss, Ulrich K. 2007. "The Exercise of Constituent Power in Central and Eastern Europe." In *The Paradox of Constitutionalism: Constituent Power and Constitutional Form*. Edited by Martin Loughlin and Neil Walker. Oxford: Oxford University Press.

2006–2007. "Perspectives on Post-Conflict Constitutionalism: Reflections on Regime Change through External Constitutionalization." *New York Law School Law Review*, vol. 51.

1995. *Constitutional Revolution: The Link between Constitutionalism and Progress*. Translated by Deborah L. Schneider. Atlantic Highlands, NJ: Humanities Press.

Pyle, Kenneth B. 2007. *Japan Rising: The Resurgence of Japanese Power and Purpose*. New York: The Century Foundation.

Rawls, John. 1993. *Political Liberalism*. New York: Columbia University Press.

Rosenfeld, Michel. 2010. *The Identity of the Constitutional Subject: Selfhood, Citizenship, Culture, and Community*. New York: Routledge.

1995. "The Identity of the Constitutional Subject." *Cardozo Law Review*, vol. 16.

Rousseau, Jean-Jacques. 1997. *The Social Contract and Other Later Political Writings*. Edited and translated by Victor Gourevitch. Cambridge: Cambridge University Press.

Rudolph, Lloyd. 1948. "Japanese Constitutionalism and Theory: The Problem of a Democratic Japan." Honors Thesis, Harvard University.

Ruoff, Kenneth J. 2001. *The People's Emperor: Democracy and the Japanese Monarchy, 1945–1995*. Cambridge, MA: Harvard University Asia Center.

Sakamoto, Kazuya. 2013. "Conditions of an Independent State: Japanese Diplomacy in the 1950s." In *The Diplomatic History of Postwar Japan*. Edited by Makoto Iokibe. Translated by Robert D. Eldridge. New York: Routledge.

Sakamoto, Shin'ichi. 1999. "Chosŏn Wangshil Chasondŭl kwa kŭ Taehan Min'guk Kukchŏk [Offspring of Chosŏn Royal Family and Their Korean Nationality]." *Sŏul Kukchepŏp Yon'gu*, vol. 6, no. 1.

Sandel, Michael J. 1984. "The Procedural Republic and the Unencumbered Self." *Political Theory*, vol. 12, no. 1.

1982. *Liberalism and the Limits of Justice*. Cambridge: Cambridge University Press.

Satō, Tatsuo. 1962/1964/1994. *Nihonkoku Kenpō Seiritsushi* [The Legislative History of the Constitution of Japan], vols. I/II/III. Tokyo: Yūhikaku.

Schaller, Michael. 1987. *The American Occupation of Japan: The Origins of the Cold War in Asia*. Oxford: Oxford University Press.

Schauer, Frederick. 2005. "On the Migration of Constitutional Ideas." *Connecticut Law Review*, vol. 37.

Scheppele, Kim Lane. 2008. "A Constitution Between Past and Future." *William and Mary Law Review*, vol. 49.

2003. "Aspirational and Aversive Constitutionalism: The Case for Studying Cross-Constitutional Influence through Negative Models." *I•CON: International Journal of Constitutional Law*, vol. 1, no. 2.

Schmitt, Carl. 2008. *Constitutional Theory*. Translated by Jeffrey Seitzer. Durham, NC: Duke University Press.

1985. *Political Theology: Four Chapters on the Concept of Sovereignty*. Translated by George Schwab. Cambridge, MA: MIT Press.

Schumpeter, Joseph. 1950. *Capitalism, Socialism, and Democracy*. New York: Harper & Bros.

Scott, James C. 1998. *Seeing Like a State*. New Haven, CT: Yale University Press.

Shin, Gi-Wook. 1998. "Agrarian Conflict and the Origins of Korean Capitalism." *American Journal of Sociology*, vol. 103, no. 5.

Shin, Woo-Cheol. 2010. "Taehan Min'guk Hŏnpŏp (1948) ŭi 'Minjujuŭi Chejedo Surip' ['Establishment of Democratic Institutions' in the 1948 Constitution of Korea]." In *Chehŏn kwa Kŏn'guk*. Edited by Han'guk Mirae Hakhoe. Paju: Nanam,

2008. *Pigyo Hŏnpŏpsa: Taehan Min'guk Iphŏnjuŭi ŭi Yŏnwŏn* [Comparative Constitutional History: The Origins of Korean Constitutionalism]. Paju: Pŏpmunsa.

Shin, Yong-Oak. 2009. "Chehŏn Hŏnpŏp ŭi Sahoe-Kyŏngje Chilsŏ Kusŏng Inyŏm [The Founding Constitution's Ideology for Structuring the Socio-Economic Order]." *Han'guksa Yŏn'gu*, vol. 144.

2008. "Chehŏn Hŏnpŏp mit 2 ch'a Kaejŏng Hŏnpŏp ŭi Kyŏngjejilsŏ e taehan Insik kwa kŭ Chihyang [Perceptions of the Economic Order of the Founding Constitution and Its Amendment]." *Sahak Yŏn'gu*, vol. 89.

Sieyès, Emmanuel Joseph. 1963. *What Is the Third Estate?* Translated by M. Blondel. New York: Praeger.

Skordas, Achilles. 2007. "Self-determination of Peoples and Transnational Regimes: a Foundational Principle of Global Governance." In *Transnational Constitution alism: International and European Perspectives*. Edited by Nicholas Tsagourias. Cambridge: Cambridge University Press.

Skya, Walter. 2009. *Japan's Holy War: The Ideology of Radical Shinto Ultranationalism*. Durham, NC: Duke University Press.

Song, Sarah. 2012. "The Boundary Problem in Democratic Theory: Why the Demos Should Be Bounded by the State." *International Theory*, vol. 4, issue 1.
Spector, Ronald H. 2007. *In the Ruins of Empire: The Japanese Surrender and the Battle for Postwar Asia*. New York: Random House.
Steiner, Kurt. 1987. "The Occupation and the Reform of the Japanese Civil Code." in *Democratizing Japan: The Allied Occupation*. Edited by Robert E. Ward and Sakamoto Yoshikazu. Honolulu: University of Hawaii Press.
Stueck, William. 1997. *The Korean War: An International History*. Princeton, NJ: Princeton University Press.
Suh, Hee-Kyung. 2012. *Taehan Min'guk Hŏnpŏp ŭi T'ansaeng* [The Birth of the Constitution of the Republic of Korea]. Seoul: Changbi Publishers.
2011. "Yi Sŭng-man ŭi Chŏngch'i Ridŏship Yŏn'gu [A Study on Syngman Rhee's Political Leadership]." *Han'guk Chŏngch'ihak Hoebo*, vol. 45, no. 2.
Sung, Nak-in. 2013. "Taehan Min'guk Kyŏngje Hŏnpŏpsa Sogo [Reflections on the History of Korea's Economic Constitution]." *Sŏul Taehakkyo Pŏphak*, vol. 54, no. 3.
Sunstein, Cass. 2001. *Designing Democracy: What Constitutions Do*. Oxford: Oxford University Press.
Takahashi, Kazuyuki. 2013. *Rikkenshugi to Nihonkoku Kenpō* [Constitutionalism and the Constitution of Japan] 3rd ed. Tokyo: Yūhikaku.
Takami, Katsutoshi. 2001. "From Divine Legitimacy to the Myth of Consensus: The Emperor System and Popular Sovereignty." In *Five Decades of Constitutionalism in Japanese Society*. Edited by Yoichi Higuchi. Tokyo: University of Tokyo Press.
Takemae, Eiji. 2002. *The Allied Occupation of Japan*. New York: Continuum.
Takii, Kazuhiro. 2007. *The Meiji Constitution: The Japanese Experience of the West and the Shaping of the Modern State*. Translated by David Noble. Tokyo: International House of Japan.
Taylor, Charles. 1985. "Atomism." In *Philosophy and the Human Sciences: Philosophical Papers 2*. Cambridge: Cambridge University Press.
1985. "What's Wrong with Negative Liberty?" In *Philosophy and the Human Sciences: Philosophical Papers 2*. Cambridge: Cambridge University Press.
Teitel, Ruti. 2000. *Transitional Justice*. Oxford: Oxford University Press.
Titus, David A. 1980. "The Making of the 'Symbol Emperor System' in Postwar Japan." *Modern Asian Studies*, vol. 14, no. 4.
Tushnet, Mark V. 2000. *Taking the Constitution Away from the Court*. Princeton, NJ: Princeton University Press.
Uchida, Jun. 2011. *Brokers of Empire: Japanese Settler Colonialism in Korea, 1876–1945*. Cambridge, MA: Harvard University Asia Center.
United Nations. 1950. *Yearbook of the United Nations 1948–1949*. Lake Success, NY: United Nations Department of Public Information.
United States Armed Forces in Korea. n.d. *History of the United States Armed Forces in Korea*. Unpublished manuscript. Yonsei University Library, Seoul, Korea.
United States Department of State. 1948. *Korea 1945 to 1948: A Report on Political Developments and Economic Resources with Selected Documents*. Department of State Publication 3305, Far Eastern Series 28. Washington, DC: U.S. Government Printing Office.

1945. "Transfer of Title to Korea." Discussion 2, August 31, 1945. Records of the Office of Assistant Secretary and Under Secretary of State, Dean Acheson, 1941–48, 50. Record Group 59, Box 12, U.S. National Archives and Records Administration (NARA) at College Park, MD.

Waldron, Jeremy. 2001. "Arendt's Constitutional Politics." In *Cambridge Companion to Hannah Arendt*. Edited by Dana Villa. Cambridge: Cambridge University Press.

2001. "Precommitment and Disagreement." In *Constitutionalism: Philosophical Foundations*. Edited by Larry Alexander. Cambridge: Cambridge University Press.

Walzer, Michael. 1990. "The Communitarian Critique of Liberalism." *Political Theory*, vol. 18, no. 1.

Wang, Tay-sheng. 2000. *Legal Reform in Taiwan under Japanese Colonial Rule, 1895–1945*. Seattle: University of Washington Press.

Watt, Lori. 2009. *When Empire Comes Home: Repatriation and Reintegration in Postwar Japan*. Cambridge, MA: Harvard University Asia Center.

Weiler, J. H. H. 1999. *The Constitution of Europe: 'Do the New Clothes Have an Emperor?' and Other Essays on European Integration*. Cambridge: Cambridge University Press.

1995. "Does Europe Need a Constitution? Demos, Telos and the German Maastricht Decision." *European Law Journal*, vol. 1.

Wetherall, William. 2006. "Nationality in Japan." In *Japan's Diversity Dilemmas: Ethnicity, Citizenship, and Education*. Edited by Sooim Lee, Stephen Murphy-Shigematsu, and Harumi Befu. Lincoln, NE: iUniverse.

Wheare, Kenneth C. 1960. *The Constitutional Structure of the Commonwealth*. Oxford: Oxford University Press.

Whelan, Frederick. 1983. "Prologue: Democratic Theory and the Boundary Problem." In *Nomos XXV: Liberal Democracy*. Edited by J. Roland Pennock and John W. Chapman. New York: New York University Press.

Williams, Justin, Sr. 1979. *Japan's Political Revolution under MacArthur: A Participant's Account*. Athens: University of Georgia Press.

Wolin, Sheldon S. 1989. *The Presence of the Past: Essays on the State and the Constitution*. Baltimore: Johns Hopkins University Press.

Woo, Jung-En. 1991. *Race to the Swift: State and Finance in Korean Industrialization*. New York: Columbia University Press.

Woodall, Emery. 2009. "The Constitution of Korea." In *Hyŏnmin Yu Chin-o Chehŏn Hŏnpŏp Kwan'gye Charyojip* [Constitutional Documents of Yu Chin-o]. Edited by Korea University Museum. Seoul: Korea University Press.

Yack, Bernard. 2012. *Nationalism and the Moral Psychology of Community*. Chicago: University of Chicago Press.

2001. "Popular Sovereignty and Nationalism." *Political Theory*, vol. 29, no. 4.

Yamamoto, Mari. 2004. *Grassroots Pacifism in Postwar Japan: The Rebirth of a Nation*. New York: Routledge.

Yamamuro, Shin'ichi. 2011. "Kokumin-Teikoku Nihon ni okeru Ihōiki no Tōgō to Kakusa [Integration and Differentiation of Different Legal Domains in the Nation-Empire of Japan]." *Jinbun Gakuho*, vol. 101.

2007. *Kenpō Kyūjō no Shisō Suimyaku* [Philosophical Sources of Article 9 of the Constitution]. Tokyo: Asahi Shimbun Publications.

Yamanaka, Einosuke et al., eds. 2010. *Nihon Gendai Hōshiron: Kindai kara Gendai e* [Discourses on Modern Japanese Legal History: From Early Modern to Contemporary Period]. Kyoto: Hōritsu Bunkasha.

Yang, Chang Soo. 1999. "Uri Nara Ch'oech'o ŭi Hŏnpŏp Chaep'an Nonŭi [The First Debate on Constitutional Adjudication in Our Country]." *Sŏul Taehakkyo Pŏphak*, vol. 40, no. 2.

Yi, Tae-gŭn. 2002. *Haebanghu-1950 Nyŏndae ŭi Kyŏngje* [The Economy of Post-liberation Era and the 1950s]. Seoul: Samsung Kyŏngje Yŏn'guso.

Yi, Yŏn-sik. 2012. *Chosŏn ŭl Ttŏnamyŏ: 1945 nyŏn P'aejŏn ŭl majŭn Ilbonindŭl ŭi Ch'oehu* [Leaving Chosŏn: The Last of the Japanese after Defeat in 1945]. Seoul: Yŏksa Pip'yŏngsa.

Yoon, Dae-Kyu. 1990. *Law and Political Authority in South Korea*. Boulder, CO: Westview Press.

Yoon, Keun-Cha. 1997. *Nihon Kokumin ron: Kindai Nihon no Aidentiti* [On the Japanese People: The Identity of Modern Japan]. Tokyo: Chikuma Shobō.

Yu, Chin-o. 1980. *Hŏnpŏp Kich'o Hoegorok* [Recollections on the Drafting of the Constitution]. Seoul: Ilchogak.

1959. *Shin'go Hŏnpŏp Haeŭi* [Constitutional Law Explained, Revised Edition]. Seoul: Ilchogak.

Yun, Chi-Ho, 1976. *Yun Chi-Ho's Diary, 1903–1906*, vol. 6. Seoul: National History Compilation Committee.

Yun, Tae-sŏng. 2009. *Migunjŏng Shidae ŭi Han'guk Minpŏpchŏn P'yŏnch'ansaŏp* [Compilation of Korean Civil Code under United States Military Government]. Seoul: Han'guk Haksul Chŏngbo.

Yun, Tae-wŏn. 2010. "Imshi Chŏngbu Pŏpt'ongnon ŭi Yŏksajŏk Yŏnwŏn kwa Uimi [Historic Origins of KPG Succession Debate and Its Meaning]." In Ko Chŏng-hyu et al., *Taehan Min'guk Imshi Chŏngbu ŭi Hyŏndaesachŏk Sŏngch'al*. Paju: Nanam.

Glossary

anmoku no itchi 暗黙の一致
Anpo Tōsō 安保闘争

bungen 分限

chejŏng 制定
chiiki 地域
ch'inil minjok panyŏkcha 親日民族反逆者
chŏksan 敵産
chokugo 勅語
chokusho 勅書
chŏnje chŏngch'i 專制政治
Chōsen Kosekirei 朝鮮戸籍令
Chōsen Minjirei 朝鮮民事令
Chosŏn (Kr)/Chōsen (Jp) 朝鮮
Chosŏn Imshi Yakhŏn 朝鮮臨時約憲
Chosŏn Minju Imshi Yakhŏn 朝鮮民主臨時約憲
Chosŏn Nodong Chohap Chŏn'guk P'yŏngŭihoe 朝鮮勞動組合全國評議會

daijin 大臣
daimyō 大名
daisankokujin 第三国人
dōi 同意

gaichi 外地
gaichijin 外地人
gassaku 合作
genshu 元首

gunkoku 軍国

Haengjŏng Yŏn'guhoe 行政研究會
Han'guk 韓國
Hanin 韓人
heimin 平民
higaisha ishiki 被害者意識
hikiage 引揚
hiraishin 避雷針
hohitsu 輔弼
honkokuhō 本国法
hosa 補佐

ichioku isshin 一億一心
ie 家
ihōchiiki 異法地域
iik kyunjŏmkwŏn 利益均霑權
Imshi Hŏnpŏp 臨時憲法
ishin no seishin 維新の精神
isshidōjin 一視同仁

jiazhang 家長
jinmin 人民
jinmin koseki 人民戸籍
jinrui 人類
Jiyū Minken Undō 自由民権運動
jogen 助言
jōyu 上諭

kaejŏng 改正
kaiseimei 改姓名
kaishaku kaiken 解釈改憲
kazoku 華族

kazoku kokka 家族国家
Kenpō Chōsakai 憲法調査会
Kenpō Kaiseian 憲法改正案
Kenpō Kaisei Yōkō 憲法改正要綱
Kenpō Kenkyūkai 憲法研究会
kizokuin 貴族院
Kokō Kisoku 戸口規則
kōgun 皇軍
Kokkai 国会
kōkoku 皇国
kōkoku shinmin 皇国臣民
kokuji ni kansuru kōi
国事に関する行為
kokumin 国民
kokumin no soto 国民の外
kokumin shikō no sōi
国民至高の総意
kokusei ni kansuru kennō
国政に関する権能
kokutai 国体
kokutai no goji 国体の護持
kōminka 皇民化
kŏn'guk 建國
Kŏn'guk Kangnyŏng 建國綱領
Koryŏ 高麗
Kosekihō 戸籍法
Kōshikirei 公式令
Kōshitsu Tenpan 皇室典範
koshu 戸主
kukka sahoejuŭi 國家社會主義
kukmin 國民
kukshi 國是
kuni no genshu 国の元首
kunmin kyōchi/dōchi
君民共治/同治
kunmin o sōgōseru zentai
君民ヲ綜合セル全體
kunshin ichinyo 君臣一如
kunshin ikka 君臣一家
kuge 公家
kyōsan 協賛
Kyōtsūhō 共通法

min'i 民意
Minjŏkpŏp (Kr)/Minsekihō (Jp)
民籍法
Minjujuŭi Minjok Chŏnsŏn
民主主義民族戰線
Minpō 民法
motoeta 元穢多
musang molsu, musang punbae
無償沒收 無償分配

naichi 内地
naichijin 内地人
Nam Chosŏn Taehan Kukmin Taep'yo Minju Uiwŏn
南朝鮮大韓國民代表民主議院
Nam Chosŏn Kwado Yakhŏn
南朝鮮過度約憲
nanbito mo 何人も
Ningen Sengen 人間宣言

ōkōzoku 王公族
ōmigokoro 大御心

saikōi no chii 最高位の地位
Samgyunjuŭi 三均主義
Samil Hyŏlchŏn 三一血戰
saenghwal kyundŭngkwŏn
生活均等權
sandō 賛同
seidan 聖断
seitai 政体
shi (Jp)/ssi (Kr) 氏
shimaguniron 島国論
shinchoku shuken 神勅主権
shinheimin 新平民
shinmin 臣民
shinsei 親政
shokuminchi 植民地
shōnin 承認
shuken 主権
Shūmon Ninbetsu-chō
宗門人別帳
sŏng (Kr)/sei (Jp) 姓
sōshikaimei 創氏改名

Taedong Tan'gyŏl ŭi Sŏnŏn
大同團結의 宣言
Taehan Cheguk 大韓帝國
Taehan Min'guk 大韓民國

Taehan Min'guk Imshi Hŏnjang 大韓民國臨時憲章
Taehan'guk Kukche 大韓國國制
Taehan Tongnip Ch'oksŏng Kukminhoe 大韓獨立促成國民會
Taehan Tongnip Ch'oksŏng Nodong Ch'ongyŏnmaeng 大韓獨立促成勞動總聯盟
Taiwan Jūmin Koseki Chōsa Kisoku 台湾住民戸籍調查規則
Takumushō 拓務省
Teikoku Gikai 帝国議会
tennō o fukumu kokumin kyōdōtai 天皇を含む国民協同体
tennōseido 天皇制度
tensonkōrin 天孫降臨
tōbu 頭部
tōchiken 統治権
tōchiken no sōransha 統治権の総覧者

Index